Islam Undressed

The World's Most Dangerous Religion and Prelude to World War III.

Vernon Richards

All rights reserved. No part of this publication may be
reproduced, without the prior permission of the copyright owner.

© Copyright 2024 by Vernon Richards

Published by Snowball Publishing

www.snowballpublishing.com

info@snowballpublishing.com

For information regarding special discounts for bulk purchases, please contact **Snowball Publishing** at

sale@snowballpublishing.com

A Critical Analysis of 'Real Islam'. Its People, Culture, Philosophy, and Practices Yesterday and Today.

Introduction

Foreword
    The View from Outside

Chapter 1

    The Issue at Hand: Survival
    The Emperors Raiment
    The Enemy at the Gates

Chapter 2
    'Real Islam' from the Religious Texts
    The Doctrine of Abrogation
    Chronology and Abrogation in the QUR'AN
    'JIHAD', the Real Meaning

Chapter 3
    The Qur'an and Jihad
    The Diary of Muhammad

Chapter 4
    Muhammad's Actions, Speaking Louder than Words

Chapter 5
    Actions of the four "Rightly Guided" Caliphs

Chapter 6
    Early History of Peaceful Islam
    Chronology of early Islam
    Non-Muslim Christian Violence

Chapter 7
    The Qur'an on Relations with Non-Muslims
    Muslims who Leave Islam
    Islamic Dissent
    Suspected Collaborators

Chapter 8
    Islamic Honesty and Honor

Chapter 9
    The Battle of Badr

Chapter 10
    The American Muslim

Chapter 11
    Worldwide Islam Today, by Country

Chapter 12
    Todays News from Peaceful Islam

Chapter 13
    Real Islam; a Case Study

Chapter 14
    Islamic Psychology 101

Chapter 15
    Islamic Politics 101
    Islamic Economics 101
    The Women of Islam

Chapter 16
    The Infidel POW

Chapter 17
    Beslan, Russia & Islam

Chapter 18

    Persia-Egypt and Islam

Chapter 19
    Islamic Aid (Jizya)

Chapter 20
    Spin …The Art of Ignoring the Obvious

Chapter 21
    The Gathering Storm

Chapter 22
    Seeds of Armageddon

Chapter 23
    Roots of Today's Campaign

Chapter 24
    Liberty Threatened

Chapter 25
    Hard Options in Israel

Chapter 26
    Islamic Contradictions and Hypocrisies

Chapter 27
    Never-Ending Islamic Conspiracies

Chapter 28
    The Final Analysis on Real Islam
    Islamic Culpability

Chapter 29
    The Path Ahead

Epilog
    Dark Premonitions

References

About the Author

Introduction

"A valuable sourcebook to the destructive activities of radical Muslims, and the Islamic texts they use to justify their actions and gain recruits in the Islamic world." --

Robert Spencer, Director of Jihad Watch
and author of "Onward Muslim Soldiers" (Regnery) and "Islam Unveiled" (Encounter).

Foreword
The View from Outside

There are always many different ways to view any event, any individual life, or any movement in history. Though various perspectives may yield very different conclusions, all can be correct from the vantage point of different observers. For example, the world looks very stark and hostile from the viewpoint of a rabbit in the pot just placed over the fire, but hungry children looking at the simmering stew are likely to see a brighter day ahead. Both viewpoints are perfectly reasonable and sound.

Viewing Muhammad from 'inside' the benefits and social structures of Islam yields a very appealing magnanimous character whose company his friends sought and relished. On the other hand, the viewpoint of those looking in from 'outside' Islam has always been very different. Muhammad had two faces that he showed to others, with the difference between the countenances, to put it mildly, quite profound. Which face Muhammad revealed to you depended on whether you were a believer ...or not.

It must first be noted that this work will concentrate on the life and personality of Muhammad from the *outside-looking-in* perspective, essentially from someone who does not believe that the man was a representative of God. As such, this view of the man is bound to be unpalatable to 'insiders' who justify his every word and act as infallible, divine, and unimpeachable. For any Muslim reading this, consider that this study is made strictly from facts extracted from Islamic texts, but without the usual Islamic excuse-making or divine-justifications. This evaluation will make an attempt to be complete, logical, fair, with any judgment compared only to universal standards of human civil behavior now considered acceptable to modern societies. Essentially what will be done is to hold up a looking-glass to Islam, so that it can see the face that has (and is) being shown to Westerners. The vast majority of data evaluated herein is sourced from inside sacred Islamic works and well-known irrefutable historical facts, in an attempt present an image that is both accurate and undistorted. Of course it would be patently unfair to blame the holder of the mirror for the clear reflected image. If Islam is concerned about this objectification, and the growing number of other works documenting the face which Islam shows infidels, then this particular mirror-holder suggests that Islam work to change that projection, instead of issuing ever more fatwas, which only serve to deepen the distrust of outsiders.

There is an abundance of work generated from 'within' Islam that characterizes who Muhammad was and his relationship with fellow Muslims, which will not be repeated in great detail here. That being said, we will do a quick review of Muhammad from the 'inside' Muslim perspective, for the sole purpose of illustrating the dramatic difference in viewpoints between insiders and outsiders.

The following favorable summary of the chief character traits of Muhammad comes from 'THE LIFE OF MAHOMET', by WILLIAM MUIR Vol. II. p.28. [Smith, Elder, & Co., London, 1861]

Personal appearance

Though advancing age may have somewhat relaxed the outlines of his countenance and affected the vigor of his carriage, yet his form, although little above the ordinary height, was stately and commanding. The depth of feeling in his dark black eye, and the winning expression of a face otherwise attractive, gained the confidence and love even of a stranger. His features often unbended into a smile full of grace and condescension. "He was," says an admiring follower, "the handsomest and bravest, the brightest-faced and most generous of men. It was as though the sun-light beamed in his countenance." Yet when anger kindled in his piercing glance, the object of his displeasure might well quail before it: his stern frown was the certain augury of death to many a trembling captive.

Simplicity of his life

A patriarchal simplicity pervaded his life. Custom was to do every thing for himself. If he gave alms he would place it with his own hand in that of the petitioner. He aided his wives in their household duties; he mended his own clothes; he tied up the goats; he even cobbled his sandals. His ordinary dress consisted of plain white cotton stuff; but on high and festive occasions, he wore garments of fine linen, striped or dyed in red. Mahomet, with his wives, lived in a row of low and homely cottages built of unbaked bricks ... The Prophet must be addressed in subdued accents and in a reverential style. His word was absolute. His bidding was law.

Urbanity and kindness of disposition

A remarkable feature was the urbanity and consideration with which Mahomet treated even the most insignificant of his followers. Modesty and kindness, patience, self-denial, and generosity, pervaded his conduct, and riveted the affections of all around him. He disliked to say No; if unable to reply to a petitioner in the affirmative, he preferred to remain silent. "He was more bashful," says Ayesha, "than a veiled virgin; and if anything displeased him, it was rather from his face, than by his words, that we discovered it; he never smote any one but in the service of the Lord, not even a woman or a servant." ... He possessed the rare faculty of making each individual in a company think that he was the most favored guest. When he met any one rejoicing he would seize him eagerly and cordially by the hand. With the bereaved and afflicted he sympathized tenderly. Gentle and unbending towards little children ... He shared his food, even in times of scarcity, with others; and was sedulously solicitous for the personal comfort of every one about him. A kindly and benevolent disposition pervades all these illustrations of his character. Mahomet was also a faithful friend. ...his affections were in no instance misplaced; they were ever reciprocated by a warm and self-sacrificing love.

Moderation and magnanimity

In the exercise at home of a power absolutely dictatorial, Mahomet was just and temperate. Nor was he wanting in moderation towards his enemies, when once they had cheerfully submitted to his claims...

Earnestness and honesty of Mahomet at Mecca

As he was himself the subject of convictions so deep and powerful, it will readily be conceived that the exhortations of Mahomet were distinguished by a corresponding strength and urgency. Being also a master in eloquence, his language was cast in the purest and most persuasive style of Arabian oratory. His fine poetical genius exhausted the imagery of nature in the illustration of spiritual truths; and a vivid imagination enabled him to bring before his auditory the Resurrection and the Day of Judgment, the joys of believers in Paradise, and the agonies of lost spirits in hell, as close and impending realities. In ordinary address, his speech was slow, distinct, and emphatic; but when he preached, "his eye would redden, his voice rise high and loud, and his whole frame become agitated with passion, even as if he were warning the people of an enemy about to fall on them the next morning or that very night." In this thorough earnestness lay the secret of his success. ... His inspiration was essentially oracular. His mind and his lips were no more than a passive organ which received and transmitted the heavenly message.

Benefits of Mahometanism

And what have been the effects of the system which, established by such instrumentality, Mahomet has left behind him? We may freely concede that it banished for ever many of the darker elements of superstition which had for ages shrouded the Peninsula. Idolatry vanished before the battle-cry of Islam; the doctrine of the unity and infinite perfections of God, and of a special all-pervading Providence, became a living principle in the hearts and lives of the followers of Mahomet, even as it had in his own. An absolute surrender and submission to the divine will (the very name of Islam) was demanded as the first requirement of the religion. Nor are social virtues wanting. Brotherly love is inculcated within the circle of the faith; orphans are to be protected, and slaves treated with consideration; intoxicating drinks are prohibited, and Mahometanism may boast of a degree of temperance unknown to any other creed. *(also: Alms are collected and distributed to the needy).*

This picture and representation of the man, beloved and worshiped by Muslims worldwide, sounds like the kind of person anyone would want as a friend or neighbor. Unfortunately this is the side reserved for believers only, and would ***not*** be offered to anyone who did not accept his claim of prophethood. But keep this image in mind, as the contrast between this pleasant personality, and the face he offered non-believers, will be the focus of the remainder of this work.

Chapter 1
The Issue at Hand: Survival

The war we are engaged in, we are told, is a war against 'terror'. But terror is an emotion, and terrorism deployed against a people is a tactic, like blockade, blitzkrieg, ambush, or siege. As such, terrorism is not an enemy per se, but simply a tactical method deployed by unsavory characters. The term 'terror' does *not* describe the philosophical, social, or political motivations of a people adopting terrorist methods, and is an entirely inadequate term to describe the current worldwide conflict. Though such vague nomenclature may be reassuring to our society obsessed with political correctness, it is unnecessarily nebulous. Such poor precision is deception because it prevents rational evaluation of the true threat behind the terrorist weapon deployed against us. Those who limit their thinking to the constraints of the politically-correct *'thought police'* seem content to believe that we are not really fighting individuals or nations, but rather some kind of abstraction, ... as if somewhere there are soldiers with "Republic of Terror" embroidered on their uniforms marching lock-step to attack us. Terrorist acts are simply the weapon of choice deployed by actual enemies of flesh and blood to accomplish some objective. As will be shown, the terrible agenda behind such methods are even broader and more insidious than the individual terror acts they employ.

In reality, we are no more in a war against 'terrorism' than we were ever engaged fighting the scourge of Machine guns in WWI, the plague of Zeros or German Tanks in WWII, or the threat of Nuclear weapons in the Cold War. In wartime, it is not machine guns, kamikaze zeros, tanks, bombs, and bullets which by themselves are responsible for killing people; ... it is actual real people, acting on some nationalistic, political, or religious ideology which pull the trigger and are responsible for all causalities. In fact, all potentially lethal weapons are just inanimate objects, perfectly content to remain safely in storage, until some ideologist chooses to pick it up and use it to advance some personal, nationalistic, or religious cause. Ultimately it is not only the foot soldiers, but the leadership, and in particular the ideology itself, which is responsible for all acts of war committed in its name, by *whatever* weapon. Contrary to popular nomenclature, ours is not a war against "evildoers," a creaky tag that conjures faceless entities lurking in the dark. Terrorism may be the method employed, but Jihad in support of Islam is the ideology all these militant movements share. That simple fact remains difficult to express because of the inferences that naturally follow. It remains unacceptable to draw any conclusions implying that; to effectively ward off Jihadist aggression, we may need to also combat an ideology born of a religion. In the formerly Judeo-Christian (currently relativist-hedonist) West, such a thought triggers near panic: How can religious worship inspire anything but goodwill among men, aren't terrorist tactics opposed by all but a statistically invisible Islamic fringe? Instead of identifying the real enemy, and discrediting the dangerous ideology inciting them, we courageously fight *'terrorism'*, and determinedly target *'evildoers'*. Like the well-intentioned and noble Don Quixote, we slash at windmills. All the while, actual real terrorists with steely determination and considerable support, plot their next massacre.

Most Americans have a benignly positive attitude toward religion, but this partiality allied with political correctness is blinding us, keeping us from asking reasonable questions upon which the survival of our civilization may well depend. Does our culture, obsessed with tolerance, render us incapable of drawing reasonable conclusions about Islam's core values and designs? The general reluctance to criticize any non-Christian religion, and the almost universal public ignorance about Islam, make for a dangerous and potentially lethal mix. The gentle reader should be forewarned that this work delves much deeper into the cultural, spiritual, and religious roots of the current conflict than others dare to go. This is not for the faint hearted, but is presented for the benefit and enlightenment of all lovers of truth, knowledge, and freedom. Unfortunately there are large numbers of Americans leaning one direction or the other on the issue of the 'war' based solely on popular opinion, because they lack either specific knowledge, or the deep moral convictions and strong values that our society has traditionally depended on for its strength and prosperity. Those lacking knowledge or with no convictions are dangerous because, with no moral compass of their own, they can be easily manipulated through misinformation and spin. Stalin referred to these as "the convenient masses".

There are two very practical pieces of advice upon which one can base fair judgment of other people, religions, and governments. In fact those who fail to embrace this advice completely are destined to remain forever as lost as 'old' Europe is today. I believe my source is a good one. The first litmus test to use in judgment is ... "Only through a mans works is his true nature exposed". The other is "By this we can know if man has truly repented ... he will confess and forsake the bad behavior". By these two pieces of advice, one can fairly judge the value of individual and groups actions, and also gauge the progression if and when they realize their actions lead to bad fruit, and make claim to be reformed. Until then, it would be stupid to call the kettle anything other than 'black', even when speaking from a pot that is less than white.

It seems inevitable that this work is likely to be tagged by some as Islamophobic or racist. It may appear (and some will undoubtedly charge) that the facts and views presented herein are extreme. But the data is in fact genuine, accurate, as is the context in which it is presented. It seems inevitable these days that perspectives based on traditional values are quickly tagged as politically 'incorrect', and often judged as coming from the extreme far right. The author admits only to ascribing to a political and social philosophy centered much more on personal responsibility and social/cultural accountability than is currently interpreted as 'politically correct' by the far-left. There is Far-Left, Left, Middle, Right, and Far-Right. Be careful not to limit and ascribe correct thinking and judgment to any one political philosophy. Within all these leanings are valuable perspectives, truth, and sometimes even wisdom. The trick is sorting through the mountains of propaganda necessary to get to any information of true value. Whatever our political affiliation, continued prosperity, as well as our very survival, now dictates that this people put aside their differences and concentrate on the values we share, and the threat common to all of us.

This work will explain exactly why the West waits in vain for Islam to take full responsibility for the vile acts being produced in her name by a myriad of groups. Hopes will remain unfulfilled that majority peaceful Islam, out of a sense of principal and humanity, will actually doing something to reform itself, without having to be pressured by others. Until such a day we must be realistic and realize that what we can expect is more of the same ...a little 'hand wringing' is probably all we will ever see from their regional and world leaders, along with more finger pointing at Israel and the West. The reasons for such pessimism will become clear later. In the mean time, until we see effective action and hear convincingly from this supposed vast silent majority of peace-loving Muslims, it is expedient for the rest of the world to take off the blinders and begin to live with both eyes wide open. From knowledge comes wisdom, from wisdom comes power, and from power comes safety. The only thing that springs from ignorance is error, weakness, and sometimes ...mortal peril. This is one of those times.

The Emperors Raiment

Once upon a time, there was a grand Emperor who enjoyed elaborate clothing and fine robes as ornate and decorated as any great leader of vast kingdoms. Seeking to be the greatest of all he sought ever finer raiment so that others might see outwardly the greatness and power of his office and influence. He had the finest clothes and trappings commensurate with his desires, but a great tailor and wizard from another land came and whispered in his ear that he could create an adornment so beautiful, grand, and powerful that all who saw it would naturally worship the wearer as the greatest of all leaders. He claimed the material to be used possessed the unique quality of being visible only to the truly enlightened and intelligent, but would be invisible to stupid infidels. Work commenced and soon the great one was on proud display with his new robe for the entire world to see. 'The Emperor's New Clothes' by *Hans Christian Andersen* should be studied carefully as it seems more applicable today than any other time in history. Today many view plainly the works of Islam yet continue to issue the usual politically correct euphemisms of how beautiful and perfect the new robes appear (i.e. how peaceful the great religion is). The simple innocence and honesty of an unafraid, unsophisticated child is called for to give the rest of us the courage to state the obvious. Who are the modern-day weavers of the emperor's new clothes today? Islamic apologists, the myopic liberal media, academic elitists, as well as an unusual conflagration of fascists, communists, European socialists, anarchists, and many other far-left and far-right organizations throughout the world. But then even President Bush regularly defends and praises the "great, peaceful world religion", giving it blanket legitimacy irrespective of the inaction and failure of the worlds 'best' religion to put a lid on terrorist acts committed in its name. You can call me stupid, I just don't see it. The reader is hereby promised that if you study without bias the facts herein in their entirety, the robes will also become invisible to you. The spectacle of 'Islam Undressed' is neither benign nor pleasing, and is likely to invoke embarrassment or horror from the on-looker, but should also result in a healthy dose of apprehension and accompanying survivalist thinking. Survival is the first order of the day, once secure, we can return to debating the niceties of various political and cultural differences and resurrect more sensitive approaches to handling differences in religion and culture. Difficult social issues relating to our hyper delicate racial, sexual, and gender sensibilities can be debated again later. For now, the sight of this self-described great emperor needs to be dealt with, particularly his intentions with respect to the sword of Jihad in his right hand already dripping in blood.

The Enemy at the Gates

On September 11, 2001, self-described devout Muslims carried out an act of brutal terrorism and murdered some 3000 people in America and caused over 100 billion in property damage. They hijacked 4 planes, slit the throats of stewardesses, and destroyed the World Trade Center and part of the Pentagon. Remaining Americans were impacted by the trillion dollars in capital and millions of jobs lost. The victims of the World Trade Center, the Pentagon, and the crashing airliners were not armed and did not fall in pitched battle. Of the three thousand dead, none expected their fate, but were nonetheless combat casualties of self-described religious warriors. On March 11, 2004 hundreds in Madrid, Spain experienced the same fate, at the same hands, for the same reasons, with thousands left wounded and maimed. The Israelis know intimately the nature and intents of Islam, while the children of Beslan had their up-close and personal introduction to 'real Islam' Sept 2004. Londoners received their bitter taste of reality on 7/7/05. Today, many not directly affected by these attacks seek to forget those terrible days, to push it out of relevance, but the orphans of those causalities, and children of orphans not yet born, can never forget.

America and other nations responded and went after culpable Muslim terrorist groups in Afghanistan, with a follow-on campaign against a major sponsor of terror in Iraq. Elsewhere in the world, some governments arrested men associated with Islamic extremist groups. Those arrested were members of organizations participating in terrorism, but whether convicted or not, they always claimed to be good devout Muslims badly treated and misunderstood. As it turns out, various terrorist cells, networks, and organizations stretch far and wide. The enemy we pursue has proved to be adept at using false identities and cloaks of privacy to hide. To conceal themselves, their efforts, and their plans, they also make use of our own freedoms of speech, movement, and religion, along with the seemingly always available grass-root support from fellow Muslims.

Following September 11th, many Muslims living in the West defended Islam, stating that it is a religion of peace. At the same time there were many other Muslims in Islamic lands, and even some in America (living in predominately Muslim communities as well as Muslim students on American campuses) who openly celebrated the deaths and destruction. Many throughout the Islamic world were observed rejoicing and calling for the continuing destruction of America chanting "*Death to America*", and "*America is the Great Satan*". Huge numbers openly or quietly rejoiced, with the absence of sincere and coherent outrage palpable. In the West, Muslim spokesmen were much more muted; some proclaimed that "the Muslim terrorists have hijacked our faith" and that real Islam is a kind, tolerant religion not associated with terrorist individuals or events. A claim oft repeated in defense of Islam was that "Islam' is a word which literally means 'Peace'". In response it was pointed out that the Arabic word for peace is *salaam*, and that ***Islam*** is Arabic for *surrender* or *submission*, quite a different concept than peace, and that even ***Muslim*** means *one who submits*. Now the official line from Islam is that "Islam' means Peace through submission to Allah's will", but the opposite camp points out that the newly created definition is illusory in that it does not mention what 'Allah's will' is with respect to Jihad and its role in the advancement of Islam. The two camps often seem to completely contradict each other. Obviously, they both cannot be correct. Those in the West are left to divine, what's the bottom line according to real Islam? Out of an overabundance of prudence, it would be wise to first fortify ourselves with knowledge. If we fail to thoroughly investigate what Islam is truly all about, there is a danger we might inadvertently invite even more horrific sequels to the disasters that have already been perpetrated upon us.

Since that dastardly attack the topic of Islam seems always in the news, and there has been much more discussion about terms like "Jihad". One question commonly asked is "why are so many associated with this religion so violent?" Giving the benefit of the doubt to a poorly understood religion, and to secure the support of the Islamic world, the American political machine has gone out of its way to stress that America and her allies are not fighting Islam, but rather, they are fighting terrorists who have perverted the true teachings of Islam. On the other hand, other voices have raised concerns that indeed there is a violent component within the religion, and that Islam itself is part of the problem. Thus far those expressing concerns about fundamental Islam have been largely muted, out of an excess of political correctness. But this overwhelming desire to view the Islamic world through rose-colored glasses has resulted in significant resistance to critical analysis of Islamic writings, practice, and history.

In addition, there is the problem that most Americans are generally a busy people caught up in various pursuits, who have little time nor inclination to dive into a foreign religious philosophy filled with strange new words. Most of us are too lazy or distracted to learn even our own religious heritage in any depth, let alone one that is as different as Islam. Indeed, almost half of Americans have no interest in religion at all, if not an aversion to studying or understanding any religious culture or philosophy. Of the rest who consider themselves religious, few study with the intent of understanding the details and nuances of a doctrine. Most are content to read their sacred texts occasionally, learn a few key concepts, listen to their appointed leaders, and then go home after church to catch the football/basketball game. The average American needs to understand quickly is that the benefits for non-believers to understand Islam in some detail are tremendous, especially if there are Muslims making Jihad headed your way. Unfortunately many might not be able to appreciate that warning, because many of us have a convoluted perception of what Jihad means.

For us to *truly* understand "Jihad" and Islamic violence in today's time frame, we must start by examining the revered Islamic texts in some detail. A sixty-second sound byte from some "expert" (be they Muslim, Christian, Hindu, or otherwise) is not sufficient. To gain a knowledge base sufficient for fair judgment one must more deeply investigate the three sources of religious philosophy related to Islam in their holy texts ... the Qur'an, Hadith, and Sira. These texts form the foundation of Islamic beliefs and philosophy. But quoting verse is not enough, we will also have to acquaint ourselves with other sources of history surrounding the period to understand the context, background, scope, and applicability of the various passages related to Jihad and violence in Islam. Otherwise, one would be left with many passages that seemingly contradict each other, and be no closer to truly understanding "Jihad", and the application of Islamic violence today. A complete picture must be drawn. A mere phrase such as "Islam means peace", or "Jihad is an internal struggle against internal, sinful desires" or, "Islam is violent", has little support if one does not know the actual teachings of Islam.

Since the death of thousands of Americans has occurred at the hands of self-proclaimed devout Muslims, and since scores of similarly disposed Muslims have vowed to continue to murder Americans, be they men, women, or children, it is incumbent upon us to examine the fundamental teachings of Muhammad, found in the afore mentioned texts, to see how they are being applied or misapplied today. This investigation and study has become all the more urgent because of what is at stake. It is not just American lives (and way of life), which may be at risk, but the lives of anyone living in free, democratic societies, all non-Muslim peoples are at issue. Therefore, readers should understand that when "America", or "American" is referenced, we are also including Britons, Mexicans, French, Germans, Japanese, Brazilians, Russians, Poles, Chinese, Australians, Canadians, and so forth.

For a start, the sometimes-elusive Islamic concept of Jihad must be clearly understood. In particular, we need to determine exactly how it is understood, accepted and supported by a majority (or a large minority) of Muslims today. If it is accepted as it is practiced by the many militants, then by western standards it would really be incorrect to call Islam a religion at all; rather it would represent more a military, political and cultural threat. These hard questions need to be asked to know if the actions of the many devoted murderous Muslims in various organizations and lands today can be identified as truly Islamic and if their violent acts are done in the spirit of real Islam, or if they (and their active and passive supporters) represent a fringe minority. Many prefer to believe that the threat to America comes not from Islam itself, but from an extremist form of the religion espoused by a few terrorists and their small but vocal band of supporters. If they are a tiny insignificant minority, they may be manageable by typical diplomatic, military, and law enforcement methods designed to marginalize, isolate, discredit, and destroy. But a majority (or even a large minority) from a population of about 2 billion is still a huge number of people virtually impossible to manage by those methods, because if millions or billions intend to kill and destroy a particular people or nation, there is very little that society can do to protect itself short of extreme protective self-defensive and even offensive measures. Now, by observation of various Muslim and Western scholars, up to 50% of all Muslims worldwide sympathize with the Jihadist message, …if this is accurate were talking many hundreds of millions of people, a number much too large to monitor and impossible to police.

The task of critically analyzing Islam is not a particularly difficult task, as the writings and history of the 1400 year Islamic movement are quite extensive and prolific. The difficulty arises when anyone identifies any possible fault or point of critics whatsoever. You see Muslims are what you would call hyper-sensitive to any criticism or observation that does not glorify and honor their 'best' religion and in particular their prophet, 'Muhammad'. Whereas all other religions seem to be able to survive all sorts of arguments and disparaging comments, Islam tolerates no such dissent or discussion of any kind. In Islamic lands the punishment for insulting the prophet is the same as it has always been …death. This sort of intimidation has proven to be very effective in lands which are fully Islamic. Muslims yesterday and today are terrified of the response by Islamic fanatics should they accidentally disrespect the Qur'an or say something negative about the prophet or accepted teachings. You can criticize leaders and lay alike only by saying they are not Islamic enough, but suggest that the theology is flawed or needs reforming, and be prepared to be dispatched to hell very quickly. Non-Muslims have also suffered at the hands of 'believers' by making 'insensitive' comments about the religion or their prophet. The first documented violent acts of the religion were when Muhammad attacked and killed several of his critics, which seems to provide Muslims today all the justification they need to continue that practice. Though potentially dangerous, we are keenly interested in cutting through all fog and spin to ascertain what is genuine, authentic, and indisputable. It is much more dangerous to continue to give the religion and its fanatic followers cover through our fear and silence. This book will be completely frank, with no deference given to any group's delicate sensibilities. For the future of our families and country, we need clear understanding and honest answers to the following three questions: **#1** - What are the correct scriptural teachings of Islam with respect to the application of violence to further its cause both yesterday and today? **#2** - Is real Islam behind and does it condone the Sept 11th attack (and others claimed in its name), or were those terrorists doing something outside Muhammad's religion? And… **#3** - What does the future hold for Islam and America (and all other non-Islamic countries)?

Chapter 2
'Real Islam' from the Religious Texts

"Real Islam" is the way of living the 'Messenger of Allah' (Muhammad) practiced and taught, as it is understood by the majority of Muslims today. To understand how Muslims think and what they really believe today, we need to look carefully at the material they have been taught from. One can also look at the history of the different sects within Islam, but all real Islamic philosophy is fully contained in its recognized scripture. By Muslim belief and understanding, no prophet can or will follow Muhammad, and so no further scripture will ever be offered to challenge or replace the existing works. Within several centuries of Muhammad's death, Muslim theologians and jurists, Sunni (including all four main schools of jurisprudence), Shiite, and Sufi (both Sunni and Shiite), constructed from Qur'anic verses, the hadith collections, and the sacred biographies of Muhammad (the Sira). These foundational texts of Islam contain Muhammad's words and deeds over a 23-year period, the Qur'an being dominant in Islamic theology. But even the Qur'anic suras are not given equal weight. As will be shown, the most applicable part of Islamic theology is based more heavily upon Muhammad's final teachings and deeds than earlier writings. This work endeavors to uncover these most important final teachings, exactly as recorded in the Qur'an, using chronology and context identified by the Hadith (the traditions and sayings of Muhammad), and the biographical material in the Sira.

In studying the scripts, it needs to be remembered that many of his words are understood to apply only to a specific people for a specific time or event. It appears that as Muhammad's circumstances changed, his words, teachings, commands, and attitudes also sometimes changed. Thus, as situations changed over time, Muhammad's words and teachings morphed to accommodate them, and so real Islam also changed over time. In the end, at Muhammad's death, the philosophy and conduct of Islam and its followers solidified to a more stable and recognizable form. Therefore, to determine what real Islam teaches regarding Jihad and violence, we must examine these text's chronology, context, scope, and applicability. It is either mistaken or dishonest to take one passage out of context and apply it to a set of circumstances for which it was not meant.

What we are going to do is examine a number of Qur'anic passages related to Jihad and violence. Citations obtained from related Islamic texts (the Hadith and Sira) are also presented to provide background, context, and chronology. Additionally, various references and commentary from early Islamic scholars' (*tafsir*) will be presented. When appropriate, quotations will be presented by other historians, scholars or experts on Islam, be they Muslim, Christian, or secular.

After this, we are going to go a step further. We are also going to examine Muhammad's actions. Actions ever speak louder than words; therefore, let us lend an ear to hear what it is that his deeds speak about the man. A wise sage said, "A man is defined by what he does." Thus, Muhammad's works must be thoroughly scrutinized, for surely they truly portray his heart and show us who he was, and what he truly believed. This is all the more important in our study because Muslims relationship with the God they worship is by and through the words and example of their beloved prophet. The absolute truth accepted by all Muslims is that Muhammad was the 'seal' of the prophets, or the last and final representative of God. Essentially, they believe that God completed his delivery of all revelation and instruction to men by the words and example of His final 'Messenger', and that new revelations or prophets are no longer possible. So the works mentioned, which contain the teachings and example of Muhammad, is all there is for Muslims to follow and pattern their lies after.

We will also briefly review what Muhammad's closest "companions" understood to be his final wishes, which direction they believed were the commands of God to His messenger or apostle. We will refer to the four "rightly guided" Caliphs: Abu Bakr, Umar, Uthman, and Ali. These four hold a special place in Islamic theology and history. If anyone knew what Muhammad truly wanted, they did. Following Muhammad's death, they continued to fulfill and obey his commands, as they understood his final clear directions and wishes. They loved Muhammad, obeyed his commands, and put their lives on the line for him time and again. Hence, we can safely assume that their actions accurately depict their understanding of how Muhammad wanted them to carry on Islam (i.e. *real* Islam).

Now then, if Muhammad's calls to violence found within the texts were only for a specific period, against a specific people, for an understandable cause such as self-defense, or to alleviate the persecution of an oppressed people, then the critics of Islam could not honestly say that Islam is a religion that condones aggressive violence and terrorism. On the other hand, if it can be shown that Muhammad's final intentions for Islam were to attack, conquer, and rule all other peoples, and that the use of violence in various forms, including terrorism, are justified to install Islam as the dominant power, and that philosophy is being extended today by a significant number of believers, then it would be deliberate deception to call Islam a religion of Peace.

In light of the long, often-violent history of Islam's expansion, and the many more recent terrorist attacks in the world, it would be foolish to rely on carefully crafted statements, in English, from prominent Muslims regarding the true nature of Islam. Westerners are inclined to believe religious leaders are normally honest and pious, and we want desperately to believe that all Muslim clerics and imams are similarly disposed, but that is an assumption fraught with peril. Unfortunately, as will be shown, practicing dishonesty and deception towards non-believers is also a part of accepted Islamic doctrine, and success at such deliveries in the advance of Islam is celebrated and rewarded.

So, let us start our study of official Islamic doctrine.

The Doctrine of Abrogation

Statements from Islamic theologians profess that the Qur'an is the immutable and unalterable word of Allah, but such statements should not be taken literally, as what is really meant (and understood by Muslims) is; "*passages that have not been abrogated in the Qur'an* are the immutable and unalterable word of Allah". Understanding the application of Abrogation as it is used in interpreting the Qur'an is critical to this study. This unusual application is an important principal and facet of Islamic studies. We must start with the Qur'an because it is one of the foundations of Islam. Islam is built upon the Qur'an and "Sunnah", or lifestyle of Muhammad. Many Western readers will probably be inclined to apply traditional methods of logic and study of Biblical scriptures to their study of the Qur'an. They will be tempted to take various Qur'anic verses at face value, mistakenly thinking that all the verses in the Qur'an have equal weight and are equally applicable today. They may reason that since the Qur'an in one place says, "there is no compulsion in religion"; it must mean that Muslims are not to force people into Islam. This approach, however, is erroneous. One of the odd facets of the Qur'an is that some verses "abrogate" other verses, or in other words, they cancel them, rendering them null and void and no longer applicable.

"Abrogation" means the canceling or replacement of one Qur'anic passage by another. It seems that as circumstances changed during the 23-year period that Muhammad dictated the Qur'an, the directions and precepts found therein sometimes changed to accommodate new and changing political and military realities, sometimes quite dramatically. Thus, the Qur'an abrogates or cancels itself in various passages and presents seemingly conflicting statements. Muslims do not view this sort of abrogation as a contradiction, but rather, as improvements to better suit varying circumstances or needs, or to fit Muhammad's religious concepts. For example, many Islamic scholars consider that the verse reference above "there is no compulsion in religion", found in 2:256, has been abrogated by the passage found in 9:5, (more on this later). This is widely understood because the more tolerant verse in chapter 2 was spoken about 7 - 8 years earlier than the one spoken in Chapter 9.

The "Dictionary of Qur'anic Terms and Concepts", pages 5 and 6 [1] state: "Qur'anic injunctions themselves may be abrogated, as has happened in a few cases. An example of this abrogation is 24:2 which abrogates the punishment of adultery, (q.v.) stated in 4:15-16. A study of the Qur'an shows first, that only a limited number of Qur'anic verses have been abrogated, and second, that the abrogation pertains to legal and practical matters only, and not to matters of doctrine and belief."

In "Islam: Muhammad and His Religion", page 66,[2] the great Islamic scholar Arthur Jeffery wrote: "The Qur'an is unique among sacred scriptures in teaching a doctrine of abrogation according to which later pronouncements of the Prophet abrogate, i.e.: declare null and void, his earlier pronouncements. The importance of knowing which verses abrogate others has given rise to the Qur'anic science known as "Nasikh wa Mansukh", i.e.: "the Abrogators and the Abrogated"."

The Encyclopedia of Islam, [3], states on abrogation:

> Rather than attempting to explain away the inconsistencies in passages giving regulations for the Muslim community, Kuran scholars and jurists came to acknowledge the differences, while arguing that the latest verse on any subject "abrogated" all earlier verses that contradicted it. A classic example involves the Kuranic teaching or regulation on drinking wine, where V, 90, which has a strong statement against the practice, came to be interpreted as a prohibition, abrogating II, 219, and IV, 43, which appear to allow it.

Therefore, because of the changing circumstances in Muhammad's time, various Qur'anic passages are recognized as having been abrogated, and it is normal that some Islamic doctrine changes over time. As such, rules that were once correctly applied to one set of circumstances, may not necessarily apply to a different reality at a later date. This concept is unusual by Western religious standards in its scope, and there are even minor disagreements within Islam regarding which teaching or doctrine abrogates another. In general, Muslims recognize more recent passages and writings as the most applicable, abrogating earlier references on the same subject matter. Therefore, when discussing Islam and Jihad, what must be considered most applicable are Muhammad's *final* teachings and commands, especially what his last wishes and instructions were regarding Jihad and violence. From the viewpoint of the non-Muslim world, we *must* know which Qur'anic passages are still in force today for the Muslim community, and which are not. Earlier statements related to peace may or may not have been abrogated by later statements related to violence, or visa versa. We must carefully examine the context of the texts to know which Jihadic directions are acceptable and in force today.

The revered work "al-Nasikh wal-Mansukh" (The Abrogator and the Abrogated) deals in great detail with many subject matters addressed in the Qur'an wherein there appears to be some conflict or contradiction. The book goes through every sura (chapter), pointing out in full detail every verse which has been canceled, and the verse(s) which replace it. The author notes that out of 114 suras, there are only 43 which were not affected by this concept. As an example of the scope of abrogation in the Qur'an: there are 125 versus that call for tolerance and patience which have been canceled and replaced by sura 9:5: *"Fight and slay the Pagans wherever ye find them, and seize them, beleaguer them, and lie in wait for them in every stratagem (of war)....."* and sura 5:33: *"For those who do not submit to Allah their punishment is . . . execution or crucifixion, or the cutting off of hands and feet, from the opposite sides, or exile from the land".*

[See: Ibn Hazm al-Andalusi, An-Nasikh wal- Mansukh, Dar al-Kotob al-'Elmeyah, birute, 1986 p.27]

Muslim activists universally fail to reveal to Westerners this major doctrine, hiding the fact that earlier conciliatory passages have been rendered null and void for over 1300 years. When Westerners discover it on their own they complain we misinterpret such writings or misapply their impact. Muslim promoters prefer to polish Islam's image by quoting the earlier abrogated Meccan passages that call for patience and forbearance. Spokespersons hide or omit Medinan passages that clearly call for killing and maiming. When hearing people explain Islam claiming the earlier more peaceful verses are dominant in Islamic philosophy, one must judge between two options; Either the presenter is completely ignorant of genuine Islamic doctrine, or he is practicing officially sanctioned Islamic deceit.

Because opinions with regard to proper conduct between believers and non-believers varies widely, the question of which Qur'anic verses are 'alive' and being applied today, is critical to understanding 'Real Islam', and potentially to our own survival. Ibn Warraq summarizes the Muslim concept of abrogation as follows:

> "Contradictions do abound in the Koran, and the early Muslims were perfectly well aware of them; indeed they devised the science of abrogation to deal with them. It is a very convenient doctrine that, as one Christian unkindly put it, 'fell in with that law of expediency which appears to be the salient feature in Muhammad's prophetic career'. According to this doctrine, certain passages of the Koran are abrogated by verses revealed afterward, with a different or contrary meaning. This was supposedly taught by Muhammad himself, at Sura 2, verse 105: 'Whatever verses we cancel or cause you to forget, we bring a better or its like.' ...Now we can see how useful and convenient the doctrine of abrogation is in bailing scholars out of difficulties- though, of course, it does pose problems for apologists of Islam, since all the passages preaching tolerance are found in Meccan (i.e., early suras), and all the passages recommending killing, decapitating and maiming, the so-called Sword Verses are Medinan (i.e., later); 'tolerance' has been abrogated by 'intolerance'. For, the famous Sword verse,

Sura 9, verse 5, 'Slay the idolaters wherever you find them,' is claimed to have canceled 124 verses that promote tolerance and patience." [4]

Chronology and Abrogation in the QUR'AN

We will next review the general chronology of the Qur'anic listings, with respect to their violent Jihadic passages. As stated earlier, we must explore both the context and chronology of the Qur'anic passages. This is challenging because the Qur'an is not arranged chronologically and in fact, no one knows for certain its complete chronology. There is no standard chronological agreement among scholars, be they Muslim, Christian, or secular, as to when chapters or even portions of chapters were revealed during Muhammad's life. Some of Muhammad's words, spoken as the Qur'an near the end of his life, were folded into passages he spoke near the beginning of his declared prophet-hood. Therefore, the Qur'an is a jumbled chronological hodgepodge. In and of itself, the Qur'an is practically worthless when it comes to determining its chronology. The only corroborating references that are able to provide us a guide as to when certain passages were spoken are the Sira and Hadith. Sometimes they provide chronological details behind the Qur'an's verses. However, as a whole, scholars are unable to completely determine the Qur'an's chronology. Consequently, they only offer their best, educated, opinions. In our study, we are most interested in the opinions accepted by the majority of Muslims today.

A Qur'anic chronology is very important because what Muhammad said earlier in his life did not necessarily apply to later events (due to "abrogation" mentioned previously). By any standard of evaluation, it appears he was always prepared to change his mind, vows, and rules. (See the selection of Hadiths from Sahih Muslim,[5] book 15, #s 4044 – 4062). If we are to understand true Islamic Jihad as it is understood and taught today, then we need to establish his final position with respect to Jihad and aggression. Hence, the last few chronological passages of the Qur'an are of great importance, as are the subsequent actions of his closest companions as they followed that direction.

Note that the majority of various Qur'anic passages relative to "Jihad" or violence come from chapter nine. Most scholars agree that chapter nine is from a very late period - near the end of Muhammad's life. The great Muslim historian Tabari, in volume 8, (who wrote a 39 volume Islamic history and an extensive commentary on the Qur'an)[6], shows that the conquest of Mecca occurred in 630. Ibn Ishaq documented, in a work which is the most authentic biographical material available today, "Sirat Rasulallah", page 617[7], that the main Jihad section of chapter 9 was revealed in AH 9 (i.e. 631). Muhammad died in 632. Therefore, chapter 9 was revealed during Muhammad's last two years, if not in the last year. Chapter 5 is usually thought to be the last chronological chapter, but it does not have many references to Jihad.

The following is a quote from the Encyclopedia of Islam, op cit, with respect to the problems of Qur'anic chronology. At the end of the quote are its chronological lists taken from several different scholars of Islam:

> "The Kuran responds constantly and often explicitly to Muhammad's historical situation, giving encouragement in times of persecution, answering questions from his followers and opponents, commenting on current events, etc. Major doctrines and regulations for the Muslim community, which are never stated systematically in the Kuran, are introduced gradually and in stages that are not always clear. There are apparent contradictions and inconsistencies in the presentation of both the beliefs and the regulations, and the latter are sometimes altered to fit new situations. Thus it is essential to know the approximate dates or historical settings of some passages, and at least the chronological order of others, if they are to be understood fully. This problem was recognized by early Muslim scholars who devoted much attention to it in the first few centuries, until a fairly rigid system of dating was established and given the imprimatur of orthodoxy. In modern times the study of the chronology of the Kuran has been almost exclusively a domain of Western scholars, who have not however been able to reach a consensus on a dating system, or even on the possibility of establishing one".

The Egyptian standard edition gives the following chronological order of the Suras, with the verses said to date from a different period given in parentheses:

XCVI, LXVIII (17-33, 48-50 Med.), LXXIII (10 f., 20 Med.), LXXIV, I, CXI, LXXXI, LXXXVII, XCII, LXXXIX, XCIII, XCIV, CIII, C, CVIII, CII, CVII, CIX, CV, CXIII, CXIV, CXII, LIII, LXXX, XCVII, XCI, LXXXV, CVI, CI, LXXV, XCV, CIV, LXXVII (48 Med.), L (38 Med.), XC, LXXXVI, LIV (54-6 Med.), XXXVIII, VII (163-70 Med.), LXXII, XXXVI (45 Med.), XXV (68-70 Med.), XXXV, XIX (58, 71 Med.), XX (130 f. Med.), LVI (71 f. Med.), XXVI (197, 224-7 Med.), XXVII, XXVIII (52-5 Med., 85 during Hijrah), XVII

(26, 32 f., 57, 73-80 Med.), X (40, 94-6 Med.), XI (12, 17, 114 Med.), XII (1-3, 7 Med.), XV, VI (20, 23, 91, 114, 141, 151-3 Med.), XXXVII, XXXI (27-9 Med.), XXXIV (6 Med.), XXXIX (52-4 Med.), XL (56 f. Med.), XLI, XLII (23-5, 27 Med.), XLIII (54 Med.), XLIV, XLV (14 Med.), XLVI (10, 15, 35 Med.), LI, LXXXVIII, XVIII (28, 83-101 Med.), XVI (126-8 Med.), LXXI, XIV (28 f. Med.), XXI, XXIII, XXXII (16-20 Med.), LII, LXVII, LXIX, LXX, LXXVIII, LXXIX, LXXXII, LXXXIV, XXX (17 Med.), XXIX (1-11 Med.), LXXXIII

Hijrah, II (281 later), VIII (30-6 Mec.), III, XXXIII, LX, IV, XCIX, LVII, XLVII (13 during Hijrah), XIII, LV, LXXVI, LXV, XCVIII, LIX, XXIV, XXII, LXIII, LVIII, XLIX, LXVI, LXIV, LXI, LXII, XLVIII, V, IX (128 f. Mec.), CX.

The Encyclopedia of Islam, op cit, also details three Western Islamic scholars chronology of the Qur'an. (Noldeke was one of the greatest Qur'anic scholars from the West). This is the chronological order of the last Medinan Suras listed in their work:

Weil: 2, 98, 62, 65, 22, 4, 8, 47, 57, 3, 59, 24, 63, 33, 48, 110, 61, 60, 58, 49, 66, 9, 5.

Noldeke and Blachere: 2, 98, 64, 62, 8, 47, 3, 61, 57, 4, 65, 59, 33, 63, 24, 58, 22, 48, 66, 60, 110, 49, 9, 5.

[NOTE: Traditional Western dating breaks the chronological order of the Qur'an up into 3 or 4 groups. The last group (sometimes called "late Medinan") is presented above. There are earlier suras in both lists above, however, for space's sake, and editing time, only the last sura grouping is presented. Note that sura 9 is the second to last in all these three scholar's groupings.]

Canon Sell in "The Historical Development of the Qur'an", page 204, [8], details that Jalalu-d-Din as-Syuti (a great Muslim Qur'anic scholar) lists chapter 9 second to last, and Sir William Muir (a great Western Islamic scholar) lists chapter 9 as last. All of the above-mentioned references also list chapter 5 near the chronological end, if not at the very end.

The Hadith of Sahih Bukhari, volume 6, book 60, # 129 (or 5.59.650), [9], Hadith states: "The last Sura that was revealed was Bara'a..." So Sura 9 was considered by him to be one of the last, if not the last revealed chapters of the Qur'an.

Therefore, the works of six top scholars, (3 Muslim, 3 Western), all agree that chapter 9 is either the last or second to last chapter to be spoken or revealed by Muhammad. Consequently, since this chapter contains the largest amount of violent passages, this is our focus. In classical exegesis then, as a result of being the last Chapter revealed, Sura 9 would dominate, or abrogate, conflicting Qur'anic passages from earlier periods.

In "Milestones, Ideologue of Fundamentalist Islam in Egypt", Syed Qutb argues strongly for Jihad from select Qur'anic verses (4:74-76; 8:38-40; 9:29-32). These passages alone, he states, suffice to justify the universal and permanent dimensions of Jihad (pp. 53-76). All this being said, to be thorough and fair, we will also review other relevant earlier passages on Islamic violence and Jihad found in the Qur'an.

'JIHAD', the Real Meaning

'Jehad' (Jihad) is an Arabic word that literally means 'endeavor'. In the literal historical context, this Islamic doctrine clearly implies physically fighting in the way of the Arabic God 'Allah' to establish supremacy over unbelievers, until they relinquish their faith and become Muslims, or acknowledge their subordination by paying the 'Jaziya' (or Jizya) humiliation tax. As will be shown in subsequent chapters, Jihad historically has been a perpetual war against infidels (Buddhists, Hindus, Deists, Pagans, Atheists, Skeptics, Jews, Christians, etc). The 5 pillars (obligations) of Islam include Shahadah (the witness), Salat (mandatory daily prayers), Zakat (mandatory alms), Sawm or Siyam (fasting during Ramadan), and Hajj (pilgrimage to Mecca). As a practical matter (so as not to alert or advertise its methods and intents to potential adversaries), Jihad narrowly missed becoming a 'declared' pillar of Islam. Although not a declared pillar, amongst a majority of Muslims Jihad enjoys at least sympathy and support, if not active participation. It follows that Jihad then, in practice, serves as a functional pillar (obligation) of official Islamic theology. Indeed, any preview of Islamic written theology in relation to Jihad reveals that the practice is at least as important to the salvation of Muslims as are the other pillars. In many verses, the importance, and the promised benefits of Jihad (in both this life and the next) appear much larger than the more spiritual benefits associated with the other 5 pillars mentioned.

In the correct context of the Islamic sacred texts, '*Jihad*' means literally '*holy war*', but today there is an effort in some quarters to extend or redefine its meaning and scope. To some it essentially means, "struggle", and to those there are two types or divisions in Jihad: greater and lesser. "Greater Jihad," is the struggle within the soul of a person to be better, more righteous -- the fight against the devil within. "Lesser Jihad" is the fight against the devil without, the military struggle against those who subjugate Muslims or frustrate her aims. For those Muslims who ascribe to this differentiation, the struggle against the external oppressor waxes and wanes, but the fight to suppress the evil inclinations within is perpetual. When asked which is more important to Islam, greater Jihad or lesser Jihad, many 'moderate' Muslims tell infidels something like; "They don't call it greater Jihad for nothing". Unfortunatly, the rather small effort within some communities of Islam to redefine/reform Islam to exclude 'physical violence against non-believers' from the concept of Jihad, …is losing.

Amongst mullahs from Pakistan and Saudi Arabia to points across the globe, a somewhat different definition of the Greater and Lesser Jihad is now offered; "*They are of equal importance*", say even Moderate Muslims. "*Jihad against the oppressor of Muslims is an absolute duty. Islam is a religion that defends itself.*" The newer emphasis and message resonating now is as was described by a Pakistani Cleric interviewed in 2002; "*Both the Jihads have their importance. In one, we struggle to amend our inner self, and in another, we defend our religion. Islam is a religion of limits, except for Jihad, where there is no compromise. Jihad must be fought without limits*". This new emphasis places Jihad against 'the devil without' as more applicable today. Jihad against outside devils, in particular against the '*Great Satan America*', is waxing strong, assuming a permanent place of overriding importance. This is very disturbing with grave implications because once a Jihad has been declared and accepted by the followers of Muhammad, they tend to see it through to the end, even if that effort involves huge sacrifice and spans decades.

What follows are several classical definitions of Jihad. Thereafter we will examine passages from the Qur'an, Hadith, and Sira related to Jihad and violence in Islam. "Jihad" or other forms of the word occur in the Qur'an about 35 times. Additionally throughout the Qur'an there are other words used for various other forms of violence. References to all these terms (fighting, war, attack, Jihad, slay, kill, etc) are almost continuous.

From the "Concordance of the Qur'an", 1983[10] comes a definition, probably the simplest most straightforward found. Kassis essentially derived it from the Qur'anic context of the word:

JIHAD = JAHADA (verb). To struggle, strive, fight for the faith.

The following is a more detailed definition of Jihad from the Shorter Encyclopedia of Islam[11], page 89:

DJIHAD, holy war. The spread of Islam by arms is a religious duty upon Muslims in general. It narrowly escaped being a sixth "rukn", or fundamental duty, and is indeed still so regarded by the descendants of the Kharidjis. The position was reached gradually but quickly. In the Meccan Suras of the Kuran patience under attack is taught; no other attitude was possible. But at Medina the right to repel attack appears, and gradually it became a prescribed duty to fight against and subdue the hostile Meccans. Whether Muhammad himself recognized that his position implied steady and unprovoked war against the unbelieving world until it was subdued to Islam may be in doubt. Traditions are explicit on the point; but the Kuranic passages speak always of the unbelievers who are to be subdued as dangerous or faithless. Still, the story of his writing to the powers around him shows that such a universal position was implicit in his mind, and it certainly developed immediately after his death, when the Muslim armies advanced out of Arabia. It is now a "fard 'ala 'l-kifaya, a duty in general on all male, free, adult Muslims, sane in mind and body and having means enough to reach the Muslim army, yet not a duty necessarily incumbent on every individual but sufficiently performed when done by a certain number. So it must continue to be done until the whole world is under the rule of Islam."

Many Westerners have wondered in amazement at the number of men leaving safe and relatively comfortable lands to undertake a perilous journey and face death to fight superior forces in Afghanistan, Chechnya, and Iraq. Clearly, those who do so, do it out of a strong sense of religious duty, fully expecting to be rewarded for their sacrifice. The "Dictionary of the Qur'an", op cit, defines Jihad as;

"The literal meaning of Jihad is "to strive". Technically, Jihad is any endeavor that is made to further the cause of God, whether the endeavor is positive (e.g. promoting good) or negative (e.g. eradicating evil) in character, takes the form of social action or private effort, involves monetary expenditure or physical struggle, or is made against the enemy without or the enemy within (i.e. against "the bidding self"). The reduction of Jihad to "war" is thus unjustified, though war is an important form of Jihad, and a number of Qur'anic verses about Jihad (e.g. 8:74, 75, 9:44) refer primarily to fighting. The comprehensive nature of Jihad is evidenced by such verses as 29:69: "Those who strive in Us (= Our way), We guide them to Our ways." When Jihad takes the form of war it is know as qital ("fighting").

Regarding Jihad, the "Tafsir of Ibn Kathir", volume 2, pages 116, 117 on verse 2:191[12] states:

> As Jihad involves death and the killing of men, Allah draws our attention to the fact that the disbelief and polytheism of the disbelievers, and their avoidance of Allah's path are far worse than killing. Thus Allah says, "And Fitnah is worse than killing." This is to say that shirk (Polytheism) is more serious and worse than killing.

The classic manual of Islamic sacred law, *Reliance of the Traveler* [13], is one of the more respected, classical works in Islamic theology. This 1200+ page voluminous book on **Sharia** contains fundamentals of Islamic jurisprudence compiled by "the great 13th century Hadith scholar and jurisprudent", ***Iman Nawawi***, and others. This work was not written with a Western audience in mind. Nawawi wanted to produce a book on Islamic law that was precise and accurate, one that taught true Islamic values. There are additional statements regarding the rules of Jihad found in "Reliance of the Traveler", but we quote only one relevant statement that portrays Jihad's scope and application, from page 599:

> o9.0 <u>JIHAD</u>: "Jihad means to war against non-Muslims, and is etymologically derived from the word "mujahada, signifying warfare to establish the religion. And it is the less Jihad. As for the great Jihad, it is spiritual warfare against the lower self, (nafs), which is why the Prophet said as he was returning from Jihad.

Scholarly consensus by all reputable Islamic experts is sourced by scriptural basis for Jihad from such Qur'anic verses as: "Fighting is prescribed for you" (2:216), "Slay them wherever you find them" (4:89), "Fight the idolaters utterly" (9:36), and such Hadiths as the one related by Bukhari and Muslim that the Prophet said:

> "I have been commanded to fight people until they testify that there is no god but Allah and that Muhammad is the Messenger of Allah, and perform the prayer, and pay zakat. If they say it, they have saved their blood and possessions from me, except for the rights of Islam over them. And their final reckoning is with Allah."

A Hadith report by Muslim confirms this philosophy:

> "To go forth in the morning or evening to fight in the path of Allah is better than the whole world and everything in it."

> o9.1 <u>OBLIGATORY CHARACTER OF JIHAD</u>: Jihad is communal obligation. When enough people perform it to successfully accomplish it, is no longer obligatory upon others. ... and Allah Most High having said: *"Those of the believers who are unhurt but sit behind are not equal to those who fight in Allah's path with their property and lives. Allah has preferred those who fight with their property and lives a whole degree above those who sit behind. And to each Allah has promised great good."* Koran 4:95

> o9.3 Jihad is also obligatory for everyone able to perform it, male or female, old or young when the enemy has surrounded the Muslims.

> o9.8 The Caliph makes war upon the Jews, Christians, and Zoroastrians, provided he has first invited them to enter Islam in faith and practice, and if they will not, then invited them to enter the social order of Islam by paying the non-Muslim poll tax Jizya...in accordance with the word of Allah Most High: *"Fight those who do not believe in Allah and the Last Day and who forbid not what Allah and His messenger have forbidden – who do not practice the religion of truth, being of those who have been given the Book – until they pay the poll tax out of hand and are humbled."* Qur'an 9:29 The Caliph fights all other peoples until they become Muslim....

Finally, from Sahih Muslim, Book 1, Hadis #0033, and Sahih Bukhari, volume 1, Book 8, Hadis #387, comes a telling insight on the true meaning and scope of Jihad:

> Muhammad said, "I have been ordered to fight against people until they say that "there is no god but Allah", that "Muhammad is the messenger of Allah", they pray, and pay religious taxes. If they do that, their lives and property are safe."

The Qur'an says Jihad receives the highest reward and is the surest way to paradise if the "fighter" dies: "Think not of those who are slain in Allah's way as dead … they live … in the presence of their Lord" (Qur'an 3:169). "… To him who fighteth in the cause of Allah … soon shall we {God} give him a reward" (Qur'an 4:74).

According to Muslim doctrine, to deny Allah and Muhammad's exclusive right to be believed in and adored is a terrible crime. Having established the 'best religion' that abrogates all others, the Prophet undeniably prescribed that the correct course of action against non-believers is to fight them. Since the biggest crime any person or nation can commit is denial of Islam, it is quite clear the true solution to the problem has been dictated to be perpetual war (Jihad) against such renegades. Based upon Islamic scholars' writings, it appears undeniable that violent Jihad is permitted in Islam for both offensive and defensive purposes. It was commanded by, and praised by Muhammad as being one of the greatest forms of true Islamic spirituality. Further, some of the final direction from Muhammad was that that Jihad is to continue until all people are subjected to Islamic rule. Offensive aggression toward non-Muslims is clearly and unashamedly allowed, but prior to attacking, the Muslims are to offer them a choice: 1- Become Muslim; 2- do not become Muslim but pay the extortion (Jizya) tax; 3- defend yourself unto death.

Jihad embodies both an ideology and a jurisdiction, formally conceived by Muslim legal experts and theologians from the 8th to 9th centuries onward, based on their interpretation of Qur'anic verses and long chapters in the Traditions (the hadith). The consensus on the nature of jihad from all four schools of Sunni Islamic jurisprudence (Maliki, Hanbali, Hanafi, and Shafi'i) is clear:

Ibn Abi Zayd al-Qayrawani (Maliki),

Jihad is a precept of Divine institution. Its performance by certain individuals may dispense others from it. We Malikis (*one of the four schools of Muslim jurisprudence*) maintain that it is preferable not to begin hostilities with the enemy before having invited the latter to embrace the religion of Allah except where the enemy attacks first. They have the alternative of either converting to Islam or paying the poll tax (*jizya*), short of which war will be declared against them. [14]

Ibn Taymiyya (Hanbali)

Since lawful warfare is essentially jihad and since its aim is that the religion is God's entirely and God's word is uppermost, therefore according to all Muslims, those who stand in the way of this aim must be fought. As for those who cannot offer resistance or cannot fight, such as women, children, monks, old people, the blind, handicapped and their likes, they shall not be killed unless they actually fight with words (e.g. by propaganda) and acts (e.g. by spying or otherwise assisting in the warfare). [15]

From (primarily) the Hanafi school, as given in the Hidayah

It is not lawful to make war upon any people who have never before been called to the faith, without previously requiring them to embrace it, because the Prophet so instructed his commanders, directing them to call the infidels to the faith, and also because the people will hence perceive that they are attacked for the sake of religion, and not for the sake of taking their property, or making slaves of their children, and on this consideration it is possible that they may be induced to agree to the call, in order to save themselves from the troubles of war... If the infidels, upon receiving the call, neither consent to it nor agree to pay capitation tax, it is then incumbent on the Muslims to call upon God for assistance, and to make war upon them, because God is the assistant of those who serve Him, and the destroyer of His enemies, the infidels, and it is necessary to implore His aid upon every occasion; the Prophet, moreover, commands us so to do. [16]

al-Mawardi (Shafi'i)

The mushrikun (infidels) of Dar al-Harb (the arena of battle) are of two types: First, those whom the call of Islam has reached, but they have refused it and have taken up arms. The amir of the army has the option of fighting them...in accordance with what he judges to be in the best interest of the Muslims and most harmful to the mushrikun... Second, those whom the invitation to Islam has not reached, although such persons are few nowadays since Allah has made manifest the call of his Messenger...It is forbidden to...begin an attack before explaining the invitation to Islam to them, informing them of the miracles of the Prophet and making plain the proofs so as to encourage acceptance on their part; if they still refuse to accept after this, war is waged against them and they are treated as those whom the call has reached.... [17]

These consenting opinions are all in complete harmony. In the violent, nearly 1,400-year relationship between Muslims and non-Muslims, Jihad and dhimmitude were firmly established by the 8th century. Perhaps the preeminent Islamic scholar in history was Ibn Khaldun, a renowned philosopher, historian, and sociologist. In his writings in 1406, he summarized these opinions and five centuries of prior Muslim jurisprudence with regard to the uniquely Islamic institution of Jihad:

> In the Muslim community, the holy war is a religious duty, because of the universalism of the (Muslim) mission and (the obligation to) convert everybody to Islam either by persuasion *or by force*...The other religious groups did not have a universal mission, and the holy war was not a religious duty for them, save only for purposes of defense...Islam is under obligation to gain power over other nations. [18]

The simple terrible fact is that Jihad does not represent a mere excess or defect of Islam, but rather is an integral part of its timeless core. According to Muslim scholar Bassam Tibi,

> "Muslims are religiously obliged to disseminate the Islamic faith throughout the world.... If non-Muslims submit to conversion or subjugation, this call can be pursued peacefully. If they do not, Muslims are obliged to wage war against them. ... Those who resist Islam cause wars and are responsible for them"

World peace, according to his Islamic teaching, *"is reached only with the conversion or submission of all mankind to Islam."* So by Tibi's logic, when Muslims wage jihad, they are performing pious acts of worship to bring about the peace of universal Islam. So it is, by this convoluted logic, that when Muslims disseminate Islam through violent means it is not war (harb), but rather a sacred act of "opening" the world to Islam. In other words, by simply existing, the entire non-Islamic world is always responsible for any and all Jihadic acts against them.

All this official Islamic scripture and sacred writings shows that the official meaning, purpose, and scope of Jihad is in fact quite clear and unambiguous. Further evidence will be outlined in subsequent chapters and appendix laying out carefully and chronically both the permanent basis for violent Jihad today, and its application by Muhammad , his 'rightly guided Caliphs' who followed him, and all subsequent followers of Islam throughout history.

Bat Ye'or wrote in The Decline of Eastern Christianity "Jihad is a religious obligation. It forms part of the duties that the believer must fulfill; it is Islam's 'normal' path to expansion". It must now be noted that there is a deliberate effort underway by Islamists and their apologists to present the term Jihad differently. Some of these efforts may be genuine attempts to soften the religion and perhaps cause less military Jihad, but it seems most representations are simply propaganda efforts intended to disseminate misinformation for political purposes. The relatively new phraseology and interpretation is offered mainly to westerners, with the real meaning still taught in the vast majority of Islamic institutions around the world as it has always been. Obviously Islam does not want to alarm the intended audience with the truth, especially the Americans who have been acting badly of late.

In <u>Jihad: How Academics Have Camouflaged Its Real Meaning</u> *(by Daniel Pipes Ph.D. in history and director of the Middle East Forum)* Mr. Pipes states there is nearly universal falsification on the meaning of jihad amongst elitists. He cites an intellectual scandal wherein even scholars at American universities issue public statements that avoid or whitewash the primary meaning of Jihad in Islamic law and Muslim history. The result is obfuscation as we try to make sense of the Jihad declared on us and discover who the enemy is and what his goals are. Such apologists are dangerous because even people who think they know that jihad means holy war are susceptible to the combined efforts of scholars and Islamists brandishing notions suggesting Jihad means 'resisting apartheid' or 'working for women's rights'. To quote his article:

> ...through an examination of media statements by university-based specialists, they tend to portray the phenomenon of jihad in a remarkably similar fashion—only, the portrait happens to be false. ... from the more than two dozen experts I surveyed, only four of them admit that jihad has any military component whatsoever, and even they, with but a single exception, insist that this component is purely defensive in nature. ... To another half-dozen scholars in my survey, jihad may likewise include militarily defensive engagements, but this meaning is itself secondary to lofty notions of moral self-improvement. ... But an even larger contingent—nine of those surveyed—deny that jihad has any military meaning whatsoever. The trouble with this accumulated wisdom of the scholars is simple to state. It suggests that Osama bin Laden had no idea what he was saying when he declared jihad on the United States several years ago and then repeatedly murdered Americans in Somalia, at the U.S. embassies in East Africa, in the port of Aden, and then on September 11, 2001. It implies that organizations with the word "jihad" in their titles, including Palestinian Islamic Jihad and bin Laden's own "International Islamic Front for the Jihad Against Jews and Crusaders," are grossly misnamed. And what about all the Muslims waging violent and aggressive jihads, under that very name and at this very moment, in Algeria, Egypt, Sudan, Chechnya, Kashmir, Mindanao, Ambon, and other places around the world? Have they not heard that jihad is a matter of controlling one's anger? But of course it is bin Laden, Islamic Jihad, and the jihadists

worldwide who define the term, not a covey of academic apologists. More importantly, the way the jihadists understand the term is in keeping with its usage through fourteen centuries of Islamic history.

In the pre-20th century years (pre-modern times), jihad meant mainly one thing among Islamic majority Sunni Muslims. It meant the legal, compulsory, communal effort to expand the territories ruled by Muslims at the expense of territories ruled by non-Muslims. In this prevailing pre-modern view, the purpose of jihad is more political than religious. It aims first to extend sovereign Muslim power, and then by default to promote and spread the Islamic faith to those subjugated. The goal was boldly offensive, with its ultimate intent nothing less than to achieve Muslim dominion over the entire world. By winning territory and diminishing the size of areas ruled by non-Muslims, jihad accomplishes two goals: it manifests Islam's claim to replace other faiths, and it brings about the benefit of an Islamic 'just' world order. In 1955 (before political correctness conquered the universities), Majid Khadduri of Johns Hopkins University wrote that jihad is "an instrument for both the universalization of (Islamic) religion and the establishment of an imperial world state."

As for the conditions under which jihad might be undertaken—when, by whom, against whom, with what sort of declaration of war, ending how, with what division of spoils, and so on—these are matters that Islamic religious scholars over the centuries worked out in excruciating detail. But about the basic meaning of jihad—warfare against unbelievers to extend Muslim domains—there was perfect consensus in pre-modern times. For example, the most important collection of Hadith (reports about the sayings and actions of Muhammad), called Sahih al-Bukhari, contains 199 references to jihad, and every one of them refers to it in the sense of armed warfare against non-Muslims. To quote the 1885 Dictionary of Islam, jihad is "an incumbent religious duty, established in the Qur'an and in the traditions (hadith) as a divine institution, and enjoined especially for the purpose of advancing Islam and of repelling evil from Muslims." In the vast majority of pre-modern cases jihad signified one thing only: armed action against non-Muslims justified by both Allah and His messenger (Muhammad) as requisite for the advancement of Islam.

That said, jihad also had two variant meanings over the ages, one of them even more radical than the standard meaning and one quite pacific. The first, mainly associated with the thinker Ibn Taymiya (1268-1328), holds that born Muslims who fail to live up to the requirements of their faith are themselves to be considered unbelievers, and so legitimate targets of jihad. This tended to come in handy when (as was often the case) one Muslim ruler made war against another by portraying the enemy as not properly Muslim enough. The second variant, usually associated with Sufis, or Muslim mystics, was the doctrine customarily translated as "greater" or "higher" jihad. This Sufi variant invokes allegorical modes of interpretation to turn jihad's literal meaning of armed conflict upside-down, calling instead for a withdrawal from the world to struggle against one's baser instincts in pursuit of numinous awareness and spiritual depth. But as Rudolph Peters notes in his authoritative Jihad in Classical and Modern Islam (1995), this interpretation was "hardly touched upon" in pre-modern legal writings on jihad. Jihad is a concept has caused and continues to cause discomfort and untold human suffering. In the words of Bat Ye'or (the Swiss Islamic specialist), Jihad is responsible for "war, dispossession, dhimmitude (subordination), slavery, and death." As Bat Ye'or points out, Muslims "have the right as Muslims to say that jihad is just and spiritual" if they so wish; but by the same token, any truly honest accounting would have to give voice to the countless "infidels who were and are the victims of jihad" and who, no less than the victims of Nazism or Communism, have "their own opinion of the jihad that targets them."

… some deny that jihad has any martial component whatsoever, instead redefining the idea into a purely spiritual or social activity. But unfortunately for the rest of the world, most Muslims in the world today largely reject these moves away from the old definition and purpose of jihad. Instead, the classic notion of jihad continues to resonate with vast numbers of them, as Alfred Morabia, a foremost French scholar of the topic, noted in 1993: *"Offensive, bellicose jihad, the one codified by the specialists and theologians, has not ceased to awaken an echo in the Muslim consciousness, both individual and collective. . . . To be sure, contemporary apologists present a picture of this religious obligation that conforms well to the contemporary norms of human rights, . . . but the people are not convinced by this. . . . The overwhelming majority of Muslims remain under the spiritual sway of a law . . . whose key requirement is the demand, not to speak of the hope, to make the Word of God triumph everywhere in the world."*

… For usage of the term in its plain meaning, we have to turn to Islamists not engaging in public relations. Such Islamists speak openly of jihad in its proper, martial sense. Here is Osama bin Laden: Allah *"orders us to carry out the holy struggle, jihad, to raise the word of Allah above the words of the unbelievers."* And here is Mullah Muhammad Omar, the former head of the Taliban regime, exhorting Muslim youth: *"Head for jihad and have your guns ready."*

Pipes got it right, pointing out that the argument and issue is really a moot point. In fact it does not matter what propagandists, our educated elitists, Pipes, or all Islamic apologists claim Jihad means. What really matters is how millions of self-described devout Muslims understand it today and how they intend to act on their belief. What it has meant in the past (up to and including today) has already been fully defined by all previous actions of Muslim Militants in their conduct toward non-believers, and further debate to clarify or change that historical reality is just plain silly. Any honest review of Islamic history from 610 to 2004 answers the question of Jihadic definition quite convincingly, a portion of which will be reviewed in subsequent chapters. As far as majority Muslim understanding and use of the Jihad term goes, nothing much has changed through the last 1400 years. The lesser Jihad cannot be separated out from the greater Jihad and ignored; it appears they are both a part of unalterable core Islam. Anyone who suggests otherwise is either being deceitful …or has been deceived. The basic Islamic worldview sees all lands as either as Dar al-Islam (the abode of Islam), or Dar al-Harb (the abode of war). All those countries and societies not currently dominated by Islamic supremacy are by default the abode of war, where Jihad (and deception) is always fully justified. Those who contend that jihad war is not a main tenet of traditional Islam do so either deceitfully or in blissful ignorance.

The writings of two contemporary Muslim scholars of jihad, the late Majid Khadduri, and Bassam Tibi, confirm that Islam in our age is still in uniform compliance with the earlier sacred writings. The uniquely Islamic conception of "House of War" (Dar ul-Harb) and "House of Islam" (Dar ul-Islam) was a consensus formulation from the early classical period of Muslim jurisprudence.

Majid Khadduri's 1955 treatise on jihad remains one of the most respected analyses of this institution, summarizing the consensus views of these previous Islamic experts as follows:

> Thus the jihad may be regarded as Islam's instrument for carrying out its ultimate objective by turning all people into believers, if not in the prophethood of Muhammad (as in the case of the dhimmis), at least in the belief of God. The Prophet Muhammad is reported to have declared "some of my people will continue to fight victoriously for the sake of the truth until the last one of them will combat the anti-Christ." Until that moment is reached the jihad, in one form or another will remain as a permanent obligation upon the entire Muslim community. It follows that the existence of a dar al-harb is ultimately outlawed under the Islamic jural order; that the dar al-Islam (Islamic community) are permanently under jihad obligation until the dar al-harb is reduced to non-existence; and that any community accepting certain disabilities- must submit to Islamic rule and reside in the dar al-Islam or be bound as clients to the Muslim community. The universality of Islam, in its all embracing creed, is imposed on the believers as a continuous process of warfare, psychological and political if not strictly military. [19]

And in 1996, Bassam Tibi wrote this:

> At its core, Islam is a religious mission to all humanity. Muslims are religiously obliged to disseminate the Islamic faith throughout the world. "We have sent you forth to all mankind" (Q. 34:28). If non-Muslims submit to conversion or subjugation, this call (da'wa) can be pursued peacefully. If they do not, Muslims are obliged to wage war against them. In Islam, peace requires that non-Muslims submit to the call of Islam, either by converting or by accepting the status of a religious minority (dhimmi) and paying the imposed poll tax, jizya. World peace, the final stage of the da'wa, is reached only with the conversion or submission of all mankind to Islam…Muslims believe that expansion through war is not aggression but a fulfillment of the Qur'anic command to spread Islam as a way to peace. The resort to force to disseminate Islam is not war (harb), a word that is used only to describe the use of force by non-Muslims. Islamic wars are not hurub (the plural of harb) but rather futuhat, acts of "opening" the world to Islam and expressing Islamic jihad. Relations between dar al-Islam, the home of peace, and dar al-harb, the world of unbelievers, nevertheless take place in a state of war, according to the Qur'an and to the authoritative commentaries of Islamic jurists. Unbelievers who stand in the way, creating obstacles for the da'wa, are blamed for this state of war, for the da'wa can be pursued peacefully if others submit to it. In other words, those who resist Islam cause wars and are responsible for them. Only when Muslim power is weak is 'temporary truce' (hudna) allowed (Islamic jurists differ on the definition of 'temporary').[20]

Finally, as author Ram Swarup observed in *Understanding Islam through Hadis:* "Jihad is a divinely ordained institution in Islam. By many authorities it is counted as one of the pillars of Islam. Theologically, it is an intolerant idea: a tribal god, Allah, trying to be universal through conquest. Historically, it was an imperialist urge masked in religious phraseology."

Recent Muslim Views on Islam and Jihad

Several more modern Muslim leaders have put forward their reasoning describing when waging war is justified and allowed. From "The Qur'anic Concept of War", by Pakistani Brigadier S.K. Malik, it says (in the preface):

> "But in Islam war is waged to establish supremacy of the Lord only when every other argument has failed to convince those who reject His Will and work against the very purpose of the creation of mankind."

> "Many Western Scholars have pointed their accusing fingers at some of the above verses in the Qur'an to be able to contend that world of Islam is in a state of perpetual struggle against the non-Muslims. As to them it is a sufficient answer to make... that the defiance of God's authority by one who is His slaves exposes that slave to the risk of being held guilty of treason and as such a one, in the perspective of Islamic law, is indeed to be treated as a sort of that cancerous growth on that organism of humanity.... It thus becomes necessary to remove the cancerous malformation even if it be by surgical means, in order to save the rest of humanity."

That Muslim writer, from our ally Pakistan, states that those who reject Islam are viewed as a cancerous growth to be violently removed (i.e. murdered). Note that the writer basically agrees with "Western Scholars" observations that Islam is indeed "in a state of perpetual war" with non-Muslims. Indeed, reviewing conflicts worldwide today, it is Islamic militancy which is causing more death and despair in the world than any other religious or political ideology. Review the following news release from an Egyptian party newspaper issued after Sept 11th.

> The Middle East Media and Research Institute (MEMRI) www.memri.org

> Special Dispatch No. 280: Terror in America *(Posted Oct 3 2001)*

> The Egyptian newspaper, Al-Sha'ab, the mouthpiece of the Egyptian Islamist Al-Amal (Labor) party, ... in the cover story for the September 23, 2001 issue, which was dedicated to the attacks on N.Y. and D.C., by Dr. Muhammad Abbas Following are excerpts from his article:

> "I would have liked... to add to the flood of crocodile tears flowing from the four corners of the earth, as an expression of sorrow for America's victims... but I have found that my reservoir of tears ran dry a hundred years ago... Perhaps in another hundred years the time will come for me to cry over five thousand or even fifty thousand slain Americans." "Did I say five thousand? Did I say fifty thousand? By Allah, this number is miniscule..." "The tyrants of the world and of history (i.e. the Americans) suddenly discovered that their leader too could be attacked, and that the white Christian man can scream, suffer pain, bleed, and die..." "Do you want me to cry, right this minute, over two or three buildings? By Allah, that's ridiculous. How can someone who knows how you destroyed countries and obliterated cities from the face of the earth be sorry about two buildings..." "Despite all this, I did not exult. Death has glory and majesty, even when it is a dog that dies, let alone five thousand souls. I sat in front of the television and tears filled my eyes. I admit, I did not cry out of sympathy [for the victims]; [I cried] out of fear of Allah the powerful, the precious, the victor, the avenger, the just; how he takes the tyrants just when they think they rule the Earth and are capable of confronting Him..." "Islam is alive and well. The hero martyrs in Palestine are the ones who showed the world the incredible potential of the martyr's body. Whoever the perpetrators of the act [in the U.S.] may be, Islam is their teacher and their professor..."

Chapter 3
The Qur'an and Jihad

A small collection of passages is compiled in Appendix A regarding Jihad and fighting which make clear the specific nature of this combative ideology in Islamic scripture. The reading is somewhat labored, but well worth the insights, particularly if the reader has never been exposed to authentic Islamic 'holy writings'. For Westerners, who have not been raised on Islamic scripture, it is important to personally study the texts to decide with authority if Islamic spokespersons are shooting strait in their claims …or those who warn otherwise. If you don't discover for yourself, you risk becoming a pawn, played like a harp blindingly supporting someone else's agenda.

The passages outlined in Appendix A show how important Jihad and fighting are in Islamic scripture and history. Historically, Muhammad and his movement did not initially use force to induce the Jews, Christians and pagans to accept Islam, however force was justified for defense. Later, when he began to gather an army to himself and was able to go on the offensive, he did so. Appendix A shows that scripturally, Jihad is highly commendable, and those that fight are rated high in Allah's eyes, with constant promises that fighters will be greatly rewarded. They also show clearly the aggressive nature of Jihad. Muslims were allowed to attack non-Muslims and plunder their possessions.

A chronological review of the Qur'an's verses reveal that they widen in scope and offensive aggression. Muhammad's actions described therein show what could only be described as an ever broadening trail of blood conquest. Passage also clearly call for compulsion to Islam, it appears claims otherwise are just plain dishonest. There in nothing in the Qur'an that ever tells Muhammad's followers to stop attacking and subjecting non-Muslims, rather the direction is to continue until all the world is under Islam's rule. Please review the material in the afore mentioned appendix at this time, or at least read (and verify if necessary) until you are thoroughly convinced that you have sufficient knowledge such that you can no one can ever deceive you because of inexperience and ignorance of true Islamic scripture.

The Diary of Muhammad

Click here to preview Appendix B where there is a very griping and comprehensive diary of many of the recorded military/banditry exploits of Muhammad. It was written by Abul Kasem, an intellectual and former Muslim who managed to escape the intellectual/spiritual/moral bondage of Islamic theology. Abul wrote it using only authentic Islamic scripture and other sanctioned, sacred, and revered writings. As is shown therein, the great Islamic 'Seal of the Prophets' followed his own advice in 9:73 *"Prophet, make war on the unbelievers and the hypocrites and deal rigorously with them. Hell shall be their home"*. It documents that Muhammad's career of warring in the name of Allah began as soon as it became a viable option, and then did not cease. Those defeated by Muhammad's military actions were offered protection *if* they would submit to the dictates of Islam and pay tribute. Those that refused those options had no "choice" but to be put to death or, if Muhammad was feeling particularly merciful, banished after giving up all their worldly possessions (including their young women). Non-Muslims were *Dhimmis* (the people of obligation) and, as such, were to be "*utterly subdued*". Such a recipe guaranteed the expansion of Islam in all lands and with all peoples who were not able to withstand Jihad.

Probably few Muslims today understand that that many of their recent or distant ancestors entered Islam at sword point. As Arab dominance gripped cities and nations, many undoubtedly embraced Islam not only to survive, but to avoid payment of Poll Tax (Jaziya) and escape the humiliation reserved for the Zimmies (non-Muslims living under their Arab rulers). Except for those who joined for personal gain, probably most people were forced to join, accepting Islam solely for the purpose of survival for themselves and their children. Undoubtedly nearly all of those so forced hoped and longed for the opportunity to escape the grip of Islam at the time of their induction, but the grip of Islam on families, neighborhoods, and nations is very tight. Dreams of freedom became sad resignation, and after a generation or two none remember or recite the old hopes and dreams. It's interesting to take note that much of Islam today is made up from what essentially is a conscripted army. Islamic efforts to make that army tow the official line and become more responsive and obedient warriors (*Jihadists*) continue to this day. Calls to arms and Jihad seem constantly issued from various sources, and there seems to be a new crop of recently indoctrinated energetic young people ready to answer the call to prove their devotion, and to make teachers and family proud. Those who respond are also enthralled by the promise of glory, luxuries, and virgins in the next life. Properly incited, they depart on their dangerous journeys knowing nothing of the root causes and circumstances of their ancestral parents forced conversions. Their father's father's father, an entire previous lineage of many peoples, cry from the dust lamenting the choices of their progeny, but are unable to speak to hearts now filled with the same hatred and blood-lust that first drove them into bondage. It is a huge tragedy and travesty spanning generations, with little hope of redemption.

Because of its extensive and through sourcing, and its absolute accuracy in context and chronology, Abul's treatise cannot be refuted by any Islamic apologist no matter how slick and smooth. If you ever need to have complete picture of the life and heart of the great Muslim prophet, then Abul's article paints the most accurate, complete picture available. Next please read the following synopsis to Abul Kasem's article, then go to Appendix B and study it (or whatever portion you can stomach):

Synopsis:

This article (Appendix B) investigates the application of terror as a tactic that was used some fourteen hundred years ago by the very first Jihadists of Islam, to gain booty and become rich-quick through plunder. The main purpose of this essay is to probe whether a direct link exists among the *Modus Operandi* of the Jihadists (read Islamic Terrorists) of Muhammad's time and their counterparts operating today. In all, **one hundred** (100) cases of armed conflicts were investigated for their cause, timing, venue and the principal actor/s involved. The finding of this detail investigation is quite disturbing, …mind numbing, one may say. This exercise establishes, without any doubt whatsoever, that uncanny similarities exist between those Islamic fighters of Muhammad's time, and their counterparts operating today. We also find that, except for two or three cases, all armed conflicts were principally aggressive terrorist acts committed by the Muslim perpetrators. It was invariably the Islamic Jihadists who usually initiated the conflict, in many cases without any plausible reason/s and/or without or slightest provocation. As will be shown, the Muslim participants engaged in terror tactics with unbound savagery that often included gratuitous murder, genocide, ethnic cleansing, revenge killings, political assassinations, and in many cases, simply plain plunder and armed robbery. Muhammad followed this path of terror and pillage to reward his followers with easy and handsome booty, land, other goods and material benefits. The exercise of terror and its concomitant gain made the early Jihadists rich, self-supporting and this was crucial in the establishment of the authority of Islam in the entire Arabian Peninsula. Please make no mistake about it.

Most biographers of Muhammad have dealt at length with a handful of well-known wars fought between Muslim soldiers and the infidels' trained army. These major war-like combats number around thirteen in all and are well documented by many historians. Nonetheless, it is the so-called minor or smaller-scale skirmishes that stand out as the most important events to expose the true scale of savagery, cruelty, barbarism, unbound greed, treachery, guile and lasciviousness of the early converts of Islam-this, truly is a surprise discovery and is the well-kept secret amongst Islamists. It is rather sad to note that very few biographers/historians have attempted to investigate in detail these 'smaller less-significant' acts of terror. Many cruel Sha'ria or Islamic laws were formulated based on the examples set by Muhammad and his followers during all these violent armed conflicts/terror campaigns. Plenty Qur'anic verses also relate to these combative events.

This prolix article is based on information culled mainly from impeccable Islamic sources. We must first of all, realize that all these sources of 'immaculate' information were of course, carefully censored, filtered, cleaned, sanitized and any 'bad' and/or the 'horrendous' elements surgically removed before they were made public. Even then, we find enough mind-boggling, terrible, barbaric and utterly indigestible events/information buried deep inside those authentic Islamic books. If true freedom of information was practiced and no Islamic censorship was in place, imagine what would have been the content of un-sanitized, un-censored version of these Holy resources! A really worrying find of this study is that the latest English translated versions of the compilation of *Sahih Ahadith* have been organized by 'clinically' removing those 'bad,' 'terrible' and 'horrendous' sections of the *Ahadith* that make Islam look indeed, like a religion of terror and Bedouin barbarism. To gather the truth one must refer to the original *Sahih Ahadith* and their original translated versions. This latest attempt of 'surgery,' truly, is a clever ploy by the modern 'doctors' of Islam, to fool and beguile the world-now that everyone harbors absolute doubt that Islam is a religion of peace.

Finally, this study leads the author to the opinion that Islam and terrorism are completely inseparable. The root of terror *a la* Islamic fashion is in the divine command itself. It is deeply entrenched in the preachings, commands, injunctions, inspirations, practices and the examples set by Muhammad and his contemporary followers, who lived by the sword (read terror) and used it as a most potent weapon to subdue adversaries who happened to cross their path. If a Muslim follows 'Real Islam'-the unadulterated, pure Islam preached and practiced by Muhammad, he cannot be other than a terrorist, …plain and simple. Appendix B

Chapter 4
Muhammad's Actions, Speaking Louder than Words

Now, from the Muslim perspective using their own writings, let us examine in more detail some actions that Muhammad ordered. There are more incidents we could reference, but for the sake of time and space we have to limit the amount of detailed information (see Appendix B). This additional material is presented to facilitate honest evaluation and judgment of Muhammad himself, because it is only by his actions that he can and should be judged.

While reading the incidents below, we should continue to ask ourselves if real Islam, i.e. Muhammad's Islam, allows aggressive violence and terrorism. The following 13 events and incidents (occurring in the last years of Muhammad's life) will be examined:

1) The killing of Abu Afak.
2) The killing of Asma Marwan.
3) Attack upon the Banu Qaynuqa Jews.
4) The killing of Kab Ashraf.
5) The killing of Ibn Sunayna.
6) Attack against the Banu Nadir Jews.
7) The killing of the Shepherd.
8) Massacre of the Qurayza Jews.
9) The torture killing of Kinana.
10) The killing of a slave Wife and Mother.
11) The slaying of an old woman from Fazara.
12) The killing of Abdullah Khatal and his Daughter.
13) The attack upon Tabuk.

INCIDENT # 1 – The Murder of Abu Afak

This occurred around 2 A.H. In this incident Muhammad requested his men to kill an old Jewish man named Abu Afak. Abu Afak was 120 years old. He was a man with much experience and many years who probably became alarmed and concerned observing Muhammad and his followers. It is chronicled that Abu Afak spoke out and urged his fellow Medinans to question Muhammad. Below are the details from Muslim sources.

From "The Life of Muhammad, op cit., page 675,

SALIM B. UMAYR'S EXPEDITION TO KILL ABU AFAK

Abu Afak was one of the Ubayda clan. He showed his disaffection when the apostle killed al-Harith b. Suwayd b. Samit and said:

"Long have I lived but never have I seen

An assembly or collection of people

More faithful to their undertaking

And their allies when called upon

Than the sons of Qayla when they assembled,

Men who overthrew mountains and never submitted,

A rider who came to them split them in two (saying)

"Permitted", "Forbidden", of all sorts of things.

Had you believed in glory or kingship

You would have followed Tubba" [NOTE: Tubba was a ruler from Yemen who invaded that part of what is presently Saudi Arabia: the Qaylites resisted him]

The apostle said, "Who will deal with this rascal for me?" Whereupon Salim b. Umayr, brother of B. Amr b. Auf, one of the "weepers", went forth and killed him. Umama Muzayriya said concerning that:

You gave the lie to God's religion and the man Ahmad! (*Muhammad*)

By him who was your father, evil is the son he produced!

A "hanif" gave you a thrust in the night saying

"Take that Abu Afak in spite of your age!"

Though I knew whether it was man or jinn

Who slew you in the dead of night (I would say naught).

Additional information is found in the Kitab al-Tabaqat al-Kabir, (Book of the Major Classes) by Ibn Sa'd, Volume 2 [21] page 32:

> Then occurred the "sariyyah" [*raid*] of Salim Ibn Umayr al-Amri against Abu Afak, the Jew, in [*the month of*] Shawwal in the beginning of the twentieth month from the hijrah [*immigration from Mecca to Medina in 622 AD*], of the Apostle of Allah. Abu Afak, was from Banu Amr Ibn Awf, and was an old man who had attained the age of one hundred and twenty years. He was a Jew, and used to instigate the people against the Apostle of Allah, and composed (satirical) verses [*about Muhammad*].
>
> Salim Ibn Umayr who was one of the great weepers and who had participated in Badr, said, "I take a vow that I shall either kill Abu Afak or die before him. He waited for an opportunity until a hot night came, and Abu Afak slept in an open place. Salim Ibn Umayr knew it, so he placed the sword on his liver and pressed it till it reached his bed. The enemy of Allah screamed and the people who were his followers, rushed to him, took him to his house and interred him.

From a contemporary Muslim scholar - Ali Dashti's "23 Years: A Study of the Prophetic Career of Mohammad" [22] page 100:

> "Abu Afak, a man of great age (reputedly 120 years) was killed because he had lampooned Mohammed. The deed was done by Salem b. Omayr at the behest of the Prophet, who had asked, "Who will deal with this rascal for me?" The killing of such an old man moved a poetess, Asma b. Marwan, to compose disrespectful verses about the Prophet, and she too was assassinated."

Prior to listing all of the assassinations Muhammad had ordered, Ali Dashti writes on page 97: "Thus Islam was gradually transformed from a purely spiritual mission into a militant and punitive organization whose progress depended on booty from raids and revenue from the zakat tax." So here an aged man was apparently killed upon Muhammad's command. He was no apparent physical threat to Muhammad, and he did not urge people to commit violent acts against Muhammad or his followers. There was no discussion with Jewish leaders, no dialogue with Abu Afak, simply an apparent outright killing of one of Muhammad's weak and defenseless critics. The aged Abu Afak urged the people who lived in Medina to doubt and question Muhammad's words and acts. Muhammad's sayings probably seemed strange and dictatorial to the old man, and he chided the Arabs that put their faith in Muhammad with satirical verses. But apparently when Muhammad heard of this he viewed the 120-year-old man as a threat, not , not to his life, but to his credibility. Nowhere does it say that Abu Afak urged his fellow Arabs to attack or harm Muhammad. Yet for creatively speaking his mind for the benefit of his friends, this man was killed. Further understanding can be gleaned from the last statement in Umama b. Muzayriya's verse: "Though I knew whether it was man or jinn …who slew you in the dead of night (I would say naught)."

This statement displays that Muhammad's henchmen knew exactly what they were doing. They knew it was cold-blooded murder they were committing at Muhammad's request. They also intended to keep it secret, to hide their deeds from the populace at large, which is why Umama said he wouldn't reveal who murdered Abu Afak.

INCIDENT # 2 – The Murder of Asma Marwan

This incident immediately followed the murder of Abu Afak around 2 A.H.. The incident involves Muhammad's request for his men to murder a women named Asma b. Marwan. (Quoting from Guillaume, op cit, pages 675, 676)

UMAYR B. ADIYY'S JOURNEY TO KILL ASMA B. MARWAN

> "She was of B. Umayyya b. Zayd. When Abu Afak had been killed she displayed disaffection. Abdullah b. al-Harith b. Al-Fudayl from his father said that she was married to a man of B. Khatma called Yazid b. Zayd. Blaming Islam and its followers she said:

"I despise B. Malik and al-Nabit

and Auf and B. al-Khazraj.

You obey a stranger who is none of yours,

One not of Murad or Madhhij. [Note: Two tribes of Yamani origin]

Do you expect good from him after the killing of your chiefs

Like a hungry man waiting for a cook's broth?

Is there no man of pride who would attack him by surprise

And cut off the hopes of those who expect aught from him?"

Hassan b. Thabit answered her:

"Banu Wa'il and B. Waqif and Khatma

Are inferior to B. al-Khazraj.

When she called for folly woe to her in her weeping,

For death is coming.

She stirred up a man of glorious origin,

Noble in his going out and in his coming in.

Before midnight he dyed her in her blood

And incurred no guilt thereby."

> When the apostle heard what she had said he said, "Who will rid me of Marwan's daughter?" Umayr b. Adiy al-Khatmi who was with him heard him, and that very night he went to her house and killed her. In the morning he came to the apostle and told him what he had done and he [Muhammad] said, "You have helped God and His apostle, O Umayr!" When he asked if he would have to bear any evil consequences the apostle said, "Two goats won't butt their heads about her", so Umayr went back to his people.

> Now there was a great commotion among B. Khatma that day about the affair of bint [girl] Marwan. She had five sons, and when Umayr went to them from the apostle he said, "I have killed bint Marwan, O sons of Khatma. Withstand me if you can; don't keep me waiting." That was the first day Islam became powerful among B. Khatma; before that those who were Muslims concealed the fact. The first of them to accept Islam was Umayr b. Adiy who was called the "Reader", and Abdullah b. Aus and Khuzayma b. Thabit. The day after Bint Marwan was killed the men of B. Khatma became Muslims because they saw the power of Islam."

And now lets look at another quote, this time from Ibn Sa'd's, "Kitab Al-Tabaqat Al-Kabir" [op cit] volume 2, page 31:

> "SARIYYAH OF UMAYR IBN ADI"

> Then (occurred) the sariyyah of Umayr ibn adi Ibn Kharashah al-Khatmi against Asma Bint Marwan, of Banu Umayyah Ibn Zayd, when five nights had remained from the month of Ramadan, in the beginning of the nineteenth month from the hijrah of the apostle of Allah. Asma was the wife of Yazid Ibn Zayd Ibn Hisn al-Khatmi. She used to revile Islam, offend the prophet and instigate the (people) against him. She even composed verses. Umayr Ibn Adi came to her in the night and entered her house. Her children were sleeping around her. There was one whom she was suckling. He searched her with his hand because he was blind, and separated the child from her. He thrust his sword in her chest till it pierced up to her back. Then he offered the morning prayers with the prophet at al-Medina. The apostle of Allah said to him: "Have you slain the daughter of Marwan?" He said: "Yes. Is there something more for me to do?" He [Muhammad] said: "No two goats will butt together about her. This was the word that was first heard from the apostle of Allah. The apostle of Allah called him Umayr, "basir" (the seeing).

Now to sum this up and put it in perspective; Muhammad had al-Harith b. Suwayd b. Samit killed. This upset Abu Afak, so he spoke out against it. So, likewise, Muhammad had Abu Afak eliminated. This offended Asma b. Marwan, and she spoke out against that deed she deemed evil. She encouraged her fellow tribesmen to take action against Muhammad. When Muhammad heard of what she had said, he had her killed also.

Further note Hassan Thabit's poem as a response to her: "Before midnight he dyed her in her blood and incurred no guilt thereby." Even here his closest followers were fully aware of Muhammad's methods and understood that murder was allowed for Islam. There is nothing to refute that they had been murdering people all along, and Thabit rightly knew the she would be on Muhammad's hit list quite shortly. And, true to form, Muhammad dispatched his followers to kill her.

Now, at first glance, this order to kill Asma might seem justifiable to some. Asma was calling for someone to do away with Muhammad. But then, after all, he had been murdering her friends. But from Muhammad's viewpoint it is understandable that he might be troubled by her call. It is obvious that peaceful folks who are no threat to their neighbors normally have no reason to fear, but Muhammad's followers were practicing a hard-ball form of religion with no room for dissent or opposition. Today gang leaders, organized mobsters, drug cartels, and other criminal elements are similarly upset by those that expose and speak out against their murderous activities.

So let's look deeper at the event and examine the context of Asma's views, relationship to her tribe, and the threat she posed to Muhammad;

1. First, Asma had seen Muhammad in action. She had personal knowledge of several apparent cold-blooded murders. Of course, it seems reasonable by western standards that she should speak out against them.

2. Second, her tribe was not under Muhammad's rule. Perhaps they had a treaty with Muhammad, perhaps not. Either way, this woman was apparently free by local laws and norms to speak her mind. If a treaty existed, and she was out of line, Muhammad could have complained to her tribe's leaders, and they could have commanded her to be silent or dealt with the situation.

3. What's more noteworthy about this event is that after she was murdered, Muhammad said; "Two goats won't butt their head about her", meaning no one will care about her death. Obviously at a minimum her children, her family, and her friends felt differently, but that did not register as important to Muhammad any more than the value of her life as an unbeliever. Also note, that there were already people from her tribe who had become Muslims. Certainly these people were not going to listen to her.

The summary of these three points is this: if no one of significance really cared about her being murdered, then no one really cared about what she had to say. Her people also knew about Muhammad having Abu Afak murdered, and they didn't care about that either. In that light, it seems unlikely anyone would take her seriously enough to respond to her urgings to murder Muhammad, who was the leader of a powerful group of people. None of her own people were willing to put their lives on the line for her words. Although her stand seemed justified and principled, it had insufficient local support, which Muhammad perceived.

The bottom line is that Asma b. Marwan was not a legitimate threat to Muhammad. She was not a leader of her tribe and had little or no influence. As such she was neither a physical threat nor wielded power to command followers. She was little more than a nuisance, yet Muhammad had her murdered in premeditated cold blood anyway. It appears that both Asma and Abu Afak were killed simply because they rejected Muhammad, and their deaths chronicled to serve as examples in order to dissuade other would be critics. In our day, how would a society based on law and individual rights react to an organized group who murder sleeping civilians for the reasons and purposes just outlined, and what would happen to the leadership of that group?

INCIDENT # 3 – **Muhammad's Attack upon the Jews of Banu Qaynuqa**

Shortly after Muhammad arrived in Medina he had conflict with the Jews. There were a number of large and small tribes of Jews in and around Medina. The Banu Qaynuqa Jews were one of the larger tribes. Muhammad desperately wanted the Jews to believe in him, but almost to the man they refused. The more learned Jews perceived immediately that Muhammad's claim of being a prophet did not jibe with their traditions and earlier teachings of the prophets, and they quickly rejected him. Their rejection undermined Muhammad's credibility because they had the "Scriptures" (i.e. Torah or Old Testament). Thus, they were a threat to Muhammad and the theology he was in the process of establishing. From early on there were very ill feelings between the Jews and Muhammad. As Muhammad's power grew he began to confront the Jews.

Tabari places this incident with the Banu Qaynuqa as occurring in 2 AH. To set the stage, we will start with a quote from the esteemed collection of Hadith by Imam Muslim. The name "Abu'l-Qasim" is another of Muhammad's names. To quote Sahih Muslim, op cit, Book 019, Number 4363: *[NOTE: words in parenthesis are from the translator - Ahmad Sidiqqi].*

> It has been narrated on the authority of Abu Huraira who said: We were (sitting) in the mosque when the Messenger of Allah came to us and said: (Let us) go to the Jews. We went out with him until we came to them. The Messenger of Allah (may peace be upon him) stood up and called out to them (saying): O ye assembly of Jews, accept Islam (and) you will be safe. They said: Abu'l-Qasim, you have communicated (God's Message to us). The Messenger of Allah said: I want this (i.e. you should admit that God's Message has been communicated to you), accept Islam and you would be safe. They said: Abu'l-Qasim, you have communicated (Allah's Message). The Messenger of Allah said: I want this... - He said to them (the same words) the third time (and on getting the same reply) he added: You should know that the earth belongs to Allah and His Apostle, and I wish that I should expel you from this land Those of you who have any property with them should sell it, otherwise they should know that the earth belongs to Allah and His Apostle (and they may have to go away leaving everything behind).

Muhammad wanted them to submit to him. Note that the Jews rejected him and then how he threatened them: O ye assembly of Jews, accept Islam (and) you will be safe …

Notice how Muhammad's declaration – "You should know that the earth belongs to Allah and His Apostle,". So now Muhammad believed he co-owned the entire world with God. Some might say that his ego had already gotten the better of him. Also note that his intentions were well known with them – "You should know that the earth belongs to Allah and His Apostle, and I wish that I should expel you from this land." The enmity between them had grown and Muhammad was looking for a way to rid himself of those disbelieving Jews that he considered a threat to his credibility.

The Banu Qaynuqa Jews were primarily goldsmiths, tradesman, and craftsman. They were on his bad side and he waited for an opportunity to deal with them. He did not have to wait long. His opportunity arose following a problem between some Muslims and Jews. There are a lot of details surrounding this incident, but for length's sake we will limit our presentation. This incident in and of itself is a worthy subject for a separate in-depth investigation. However, what is important here is to display yet another facet of Muhammad's inclination to violence. Even at this stage of his ascent to power, attacking and killing numerous innocent people seems well within his character. In the eyes of the devout then and now, those that opposed or disagreed with Muhammad also opposed and disagreed with God, and thus faced God's wrath, expressed through Muhammad.

The entire set of details is not presented, save only those that pertain to the point. However, the source references from which those interested may look them up for study are; Sahih Muslim #4363, Guillaume, page 260, 364, 365, Ibn Sa'd, volume 2, page 32

The summary of the incident is as follows:

First, …Muhammad and the Qaynuqa were already at odds. They had rejected Muhammad and resisted his demand that they acknowledge his prophethood. Instead they made fun of him and vexed him. They treated him as some a false, ridiculous, egotistical man who claimed greatness and prophethood. Naturally, Muhammad could not long tolerate them.

Then, …after Muhammad's victory at Badr, he called the Qaynuqa Jews together and demanded that they now acknowledge his prophethood, or, they would end up like the defeated Meccans (see the Sahih Muslim quote above). The Jews still refused him, and stated they were ready to fight him if that was what he wanted. Their fate was set with this refusal.

Shortly thereafter, an incident occurred in a market place providing the convenient pretext for what was to follow. A Qaynuqa Jew played a bad joke upon a Muslim lady leading to her humiliation. Her male companion killed the Jew. His friends in turn killed the Muslim. This led to a confrontation between Muhammad and the Qaynuqa. Muhammad made no attempt to work things out with the Jews. Rather he received a visitation from a spirit named "Gabriel" - the same spirit that visited him for the first time in a cave (which caused Muhammad to attempt suicide). The timely "revelation" concerning those Jews can be reviewed in Sura 3: 12, 13. During this visitation, the ever reliable Gabriel provided the revelation

Muhammad needed to avenge his rejection. The details come from the "Kitab al Tabaqat al Kabir", op cit, vol 2, page 32:

> Then occurred the ghazwah of the Apostle of Allah against the Banu Qaynuqa on Saturday, in the middle of Shawwal, after the commencement of the twentieth month from the hijrah. These people were Jews and allies of Abd Allah Ibn Ubayyi Ibn Salul. They were the bravest of Jews, and were goldsmiths. They had entered into a pact with the Prophet. When the battle of Badr took place they transgressed and showed jealousy and violated the pact and the covenant. Thereupon Allah the Blessed and the High revealed to His Prophet: "And if thou fears treachery from any folk, then throw back to them (their treaty) fairly. Lo! Allah loves not the treacherous". [Sura 8:58] The Apostle of Allah had said: 'I fear the Banu Quynuqa' but after this verse it is stated that he marched against them.

With the altercation in the market place and the script from heaven, Muhammad now had full justification and divine permission from Allah to attack the Qaynuqa . He therefore didn't feel the need to engage in any kind of negotiations to work out the problems with the Jews, rather he immediately moved to rid himself of them. Muhammad besieged them for about fifteen days, and then the Qaynuqa surrendered. Another key piece of additional piece of information is provided by Ibn Sa'd:

> They shut themselves up in their fortress, so he (Prophet) strongly besieged them, till Allah cast fear in their hearts. They submitted to the orders of the Apostle of Allah, that their property would be for the Prophet while they would take their women and children with them. Then under his orders their hands were tied behind their backs. The Apostle of Allah appointed al-Mudhir Ibn Qadamah al-Slimi, of the Banu al-Silm, the tribe of Sa'd Ibn Khaythamah to tie their hands behind their backs. Abd Allah Ibn Ubayyi had a talk with the Apostle of Allah about them and entreated him (to release them). Thereupon he (Prophet) said: Leave them, may Allah curse them and curse him who is with them! He abandoned the idea of their killing and ordered them to be banished from Madinah.

Another critical set of details, relative to my argument is provided from Guillaume, pages 363, 364:

> My father Ishaq b. Yasar told me from Ubada - ..."when the B. Qaynuqa fought the apostle Abdullah b. Ubayy espoused their cause and defended them, and Ubada Samit who was one of the B. Auf, who had the same alliance with them as had Abdullah, went to the apostle and renounced all responsibility for them in favor of God and the apostle, saying, "O apostle of God, I take God and His apostle and the believers as my friends, and I renounce my agreement and friendship with these unbelievers: Concerning him and Abdullah b. Ubayy, this passage from the chapter of the Table came down [2 – Sura 5:56] "O you who believe, take not Jews and Christians as friends. They are friends of one another. Who of you takes them as friends is one of them. God will not guild the unjust people. You can see those in whose heart there is sickness, i.e. Abdullah b. Ubayy when he said, "I fear a change of circumstances." Acting hastily in regard to them they say we fear that change of circumstances may overtake us. Peradventure God will bring victory or an act from Him so that they will be sorry for their secret thought, and those who believe will say, "Are these those who swore by God their most binding oath?" [that they were with you], as far as God's words, "Verily God and His apostle are your friends, and those who believe, who perform prayer, give alms and bow in homage," mentioning Ubada taking God and His apostle and the believers as friends, and renouncing his agreement and friendship with the B. Qaynuqa...

There are a number of issues to be dealt with in relation to this incident. As a side note it is interesting to look at the "pact/treaty" that the Muslim writers claim to have existed between the various Jewish tribes and Muhammad. An analysis of this so-called "Charter of Medina", or "treaty", done by A. Wensinch, "Muhammad and the Jews of Medina" [23] page 70, reveals that this "treaty" was really more of an edict issued by Muhammad upon the Jews, rather than what might today be considered a "treaty". Muhammad laid a burden of regulation upon the Jews, which they had to accommodate, and with which they were apparently in full compliance. What is important is that Muhammad was at odds with the Jews because they had rejected him, and after his victory at Badr, Muhammad now felt confident that he could threaten, and then move against them, despite the earlier assurances in the Charter made at a time when Muhammad's forces were less dominant.

Accordingly, one of the more questionable and ugly actions committed by Muhammad against the Jews then occurred. The Jews shut themselves up in their fortress, then succumbed to the siege and submitted to the orders of the Apostle of Allah and agreed that their property would be for the Prophet while they would take their women and children with them. They were undoubtedly unhappy with both the earlier terms and the new surrender terms issued, but they resigned themselves to follow the dictates of this man with his powerful forces arrayed against them.

The Jews surrendered to Muhammad expecting to be expelled taking their families with them. However, as they surrendered, Muhammad ordered that their hands be tied behind their backs. Muhammad was preparing to massacre the males! It seems that they surrendered expecting acceptable terms, but now, when they were defenseless, Muhammad tied them up in preparation for wholesale slaughter. Then, an interesting exchange takes place, which seems a blot to Muhammad's claim of infallibility. A pagan confronts Muhammad and demands that the Jews not be massacred. Muhammad was challenged by a pagan to not commit the evil act, and in response Muhammad grew angered to the point where it was evident to all "shadows appeared upon his face". Tabari records:

> The Messenger of God besieged them until they surrendered at his discretion. Abd Allah b. Ubayy b. Salul rose up when God had put them in his power, and said, "Muhammad, treat my mawali well"; for they were the confederates of al-Khazraj. The Prophet delayed his answer, so Abd Allah repeated, "Muhammad, treat my mawali well." The Prophet turned away from him, and he put his hand into (the Messenger's) collar. The Messenger of God said, "Let me go!" - he was so angry that they could see shadows in his face (that is, his face colored). Then he said, "Damn you, let me go!" He replied, "No, by God, I will not let you go until you treat my mawali well. Four hundred men without armor and three hundred with coats of mail, who defended me from the Arab and the non-Arab alike, and you would mow them down in a single morning? By God, I do not feel safe and am afraid of what the future may have in store." So the Messenger of God said, "They are yours."

So, we see a pagan apparently shaming Muhammad, a religious man, to not carry out his brutal plan to murder 700 Jewish males. On this event alone, it could be argued that the pagan had more human compassion and a stronger sense of right and wrong, which is to say that his morality was superior to Muhammad's by any standard. Islam considers that when a young boy begins puberty, that he is an adult, so these males were probably aged from 14 on up. Abd Allah was apparently a warlord or mercenary who for political, military, and/or economic reasons allied himself with Muhammad's forces for this campaign. It should be noted here that for whatever reason the pagan later wisely counted himself amongst the 'believers' (as apparently all who survived the march of Islam in those days did in order to survive and prosper). His share of booty was undoubtedly increased in this and subsequent actions after his 'miraculous' conversion.

Another similar minor incident occurred between Ubayy and Ubada Samit. From Sir William Muir's work "The Life of Muhammad" [24] chapter 13, we read:

> Abdallah upbraided Obada (they were both principals in the confederacy with the Cainucaa,) for the part he had taken in abandoning their allies, and aiding in their exile: -- "What! art thou free from the oath with which we ratified their alliance? Hast thou forgotten how they stood by us, and shed for us their blood, on such and such a day? "- and he began enumerating the engagements in which they had fought together. Obada cut him short with the decisive answer, -- "hearts have changed. Islam hath blotted all treaties out."

Samit Ubada had an alliance with the Qaynuqa Jews. They had stood together at one time, and shed blood to defend Ubada and his tribe, but, because of the conflict between the Muslims and the Jews, Samit broke his alliance with the Jews. And, accordingly, there was yet another "revelation" for Muhammad justifying and supporting this, which will be further addressed.

This incident is documented so readers do not think that Muhammad only had a few people occasionally murdered. The record demonstrates that Muhammad was prepared to eliminate anyone, individuals or entire tribes, who in Muhammad's mind opposed him. All that was needed was a convenient event or any statement of opposition and the requisite revelation was generated to justify pulling the trigger.

These events, chronicled as they are, leads to legitimate questions:

1) If Muhammad and his followers were about peace, why didn't he try to work things out between himself and the Jews? There was no diplomacy as it progressed from an incident, to a "revelation," to an attack. Many nations and movements throughout history have suffered opposition from other nations without going straight to war; rather the norm is to try to work out misunderstandings. If Muhammad is an example for all mankind as claimed, why are his patience and peace making skills so terribly meager?

2) Was it really necessary to eradicate an entire tribe of people over an incident in which one Muslim was victimized after killing another? Is it reasonable that the most prominent members of a 'peaceful' religion destroyed an entire tribe of people?

<u>INCIDENT #4</u> – **The Murder of Kab Ashraf**

Muhammad continued to have problems with various people around Medina who refused to acknowledge his claim to prophethood. Kab Ashraf was a prominent local who made it known that he did not believe in Muhammad. Kab never lifted a weapon against Muhammad (or any Muslim) he only voiced his opinion against Muhammad, and allegedly made up some unsavory poems about Muslim women. Muhammad saw him as a threat, and therefore had him killed in the night. Tabari states that this murder took place in 3 A.H.

The following is from Bukhari, op cit, volume 5 #369: [Note, this is a very long Hadith, the actual killer is named Muhammad bin Maslama, but here we refer to him simply as Maslama

"Narrated Jabir Abdullah: "Allah's messenger said "Who is willing to kill Ka'b al-Ashraf who has hurt Allah and His apostle?" Thereupon Maslama got up saying, "O Allah's messenger! Would you like that I kill him?" The prophet said, "Yes". Maslama said, "Then allow me to say a (false) thing (i.e. to deceive Ka'b). The prophet said, "You may say it."

Maslama went to Ka'b and said, "That man (i.e. Muhammad) demands Sadaqa (i.e. Zakat) [taxes] from us, and he has troubled us, and I have come to borrow something from you." On that, Ka'b said, "By Allah, you will get tired of him!" Maslama said, "Now as we have followed him, we do not want to leave him unless and until we see how his end is going to be. Now we want you to lend us a camel load or two of food." Ka'b said, "Yes, but you should mortgage something to me." Maslama and his companion said, What do you want?" Ka'b replied, "Mortgage your women to me." They said, "How can we mortgage our women to you and you are the most handsome of the Arabs?" Ka'b said, "Then mortgage your sons to me." They said, "How can we mortgage our sons to you? Later they would be abused by the people's saying that so and so has been mortgaged for a camel load of food. That would cause us great disgrace, but we will mortgage our arms to you."

Maslama and his companion promised Ka'b that Maslama would return to him. He came to Ka'b at night along with Ka'b's foster brother, Abu Naila. Ka'b invited them to come into his fort and then he went down to them. His wife asked him, "Where are you going at this time?" Ka'b replied, "None but Maslama and my (foster) brother Abu Naila have come." His wife said, "I hear a voice as if blood is dropping from him." Ka'b said, "They are none but my brother Maslama and my foster brother Abu Naila. A generous man should respond to a call at night even if invited to be killed."

Maslama went with two men. So Maslama went in together with two men, and said to them, "When Ka'b comes, I will touch his hair and smell it, and when you see that I have got hold of his head, strike him. I will let you smell his head."

Ka'b Ashraf came down to them wrapped in his clothes, and diffusing perfume. Maslama said, "I have never smelt a better scent than this." Ka'b replied, "I have got the best Arab women who know how to use the high class of perfume." Maslama requested Ka'b "Will you allow me to smell your head?" Ka'b said "yes." Maslama smelt it and made his companions smell it as well. Then he requested Ka'b again, "Will you let me (smell your head)?" Ka'b said "Yes". When Maslama got a strong hold of him, he said (to his companions) "Get at him!" So they killed him and went to the prophet and informed him."

Now to repeat the story, this time as told by Ibn Ishaq, op cit, page 365;

He [Maslama] said, "O apostle of god, we shall have to tell lies." He answered, "Say what you like, for you are free in the matter."

Thereupon he and Silkan [Abu Naila], and Abbad, and Harith, and Abu Abs Jabr conspired together and sent Silkan to the enemy of God, Ka'b, before they came to him. He talked to him some time and they recited poetry one to the other, for Silkan was fond of poetry. Then he said, O Ibn Ashraf, I have come to you about a matter which I want to tell you of and wish you to keep secret." "Very well", he replied. He went on , "The coming of this man is a great trial to us. It has provoked the hostility of the Arabs, and they are all in league against us. The roads have become impassable so that our families are in want and privation, and we and our families are in great distress. Ka'b answered, "By god, I kept telling you O Ibn Salama, that the things I warned you of would happen." Silkan said to him, 'I want you to sell us food and we will give you a pledge of security and you deal generously in the matter." He replied, "Will you give me your sons as a pledge?" He said, "You want to insult us. I have friends who share my opinion and I want to bring them to you so that you may sell to them and act generously, and we will give you enough weapons for a good pledge." Silkan's object was that he should not take alarm at the sight of weapons when they brought them. Ka'b answered, "Weapons are a good pledge."

Thereupon Silkan returned to his companions, told them what has happened, and ordered them to take their arms. Then they went away and assembled with him and met the apostle."

Thaur told me the apostle walked with them as far as Gharqad. Then he sent them off, saying, "Go in God's name; O God help them." So saying, he returned to his house. Now it was a moonlight night and they journeyed on until they came to his castle, and Abu Naila called out to him. He had only recently married and he jumped up in the bedsheet, and his wife took hold of the end of it and said, "You are at war, and those who are at war do not go out at this hour." He replied, "It is Abu Naila. Had he found me sleeping he would not have woken me." She answered, "by god, I can feel evil in his voice." Ka'b answered, "Even if the call were for a stab a brave man must answer it."

So he went down and talked to them for some time, while they conversed with him. then Abu Naila said, "Would you like to walk with us to Shib al-ajmuz, so that we can talk for the rest of the night?" "If you like", he answered, so they went off walking together; and after a time Abu Naila ran his hand through his hair. Then he smelt his hand, and said, "I have never smelt a scent finer than this." They walked on farther and he did the same so that Ka'b suspected no evil. Then after a space did it for the third time and cried, "Smite the enemy of God!" So they smote him, and their swords clashed over him with no effect. Maslama said, "I remembered my dagger when I saw that our swords were useless, and I seized it. Meanwhile the enemy of god had made such a noise that every fort around us was showing a light. I thrust it into the lower part of his body, then I bore down upon it until I reached his genitals, and the enemy of God fell to the ground.

Harith had been hurt, being wounded either in his head or in his foot, one of our swords having stuck him. We went away, passing by the Umayya and then the Qurayza and then both until we went up the Harra of Urayd. Our friend Harith had lagged behind, weakened by loss of blood, so we waited for him for some time until he came up, following our tracks. We carried him and brought him to the apostle at the end of the night. We saluted him as he stood praying, and he came out to us and we told him that we had killed god's enemy. He spat upon our comrade's wounds, and both he and we returned to our families. Our attack upon god's enemy cast terror among the Jews, and there was no Jew in Median who did not fear for his life.

Further note: On page 442 there is a descriptive poem part of which deals with Kab's murder. A Muslim composes the poem, which in part says:

"…By Muhammad's order when he sent secretly by night

Kab's brother, to go to Kab

He beguiled him and brought him down with guile"

Ibn Sa'd's Kitab al-Tabaqat al-Kabir provides us with yet another interesting artifact related to this story. From the Tabaqat, vol 2, page 37: "Then they cut his head and took it with them. ... they cast his head before him [Muhammad]. He (the prophet) praised Allah on his being slain".

Note what happened here. Ka'b encouraged Muhammad's enemies, and made up some poems about Muslim women. Muhammad didn't like it, and had him murdered. To accomplish their action against Kab, Muhammad allowed them to lie to Kab in order to get him to lower his defenses and trust them. After they kill Ka'b, they behead him and brought the severed head to Muhammad. When Muhammad sees his head, Muhammad praises God for Ka'b being slain! Some obvious questions come to mind:

1) Did Muhammad abide by the treaty he had with the Jews? Was it lawful to dispatch men to commit the murder of one of their leaders under cover of night using deceit and cunning, or is no other law binding against the cause of Islam? If Kab were a real criminal, couldn't Muhammad have dealt with him according to the local law or agreements he had with the Jews?

2) What are the implications for societies today? In effect, do Muslims believe they can ignore local law and still murder in the night those who oppose them or Islam?

3) Are deceit and lies, when deployed against non-believers in the violent advancement of Islam, still acceptable behavior today?

INCIDENT # 5 – **The Murder of Ibn Sunayna**

Muhammad's problems with the various Jews were not over. They had rejected him, which he could not tolerate. His animosity towards them seemed to be ever increasing. Just after the murder of Kab Ashraf, and before the battle of Uhud (3 A.H.), Muhammad ordered his followers to "kill any Jew that comes under your power". Anti-Semitism is defined as; "an intense dislike for and prejudice against Jewish people". By that standard, Muhammad could be considered Islam's original anti-Semite.

From Guillaume, op cit, page 369:

"The apostle said, "Kill any Jew that falls into your power." Thereupon Muhayyisa b. Masud leapt upon Ibn Sunayna, a Jewish merchant with whom they had social and business relations, and killed him. Huwayyisa was not a Muslim at the time though he was the elder brother. When Muhayyisa killed him Huwayyisa began to beat him, saying, 'You enemy of God, did you kill him when much of the fat on your belly comes from his wealth?' Muhayyisa answered, 'Had the one who ordered me to kill him ordered me to kill you I would have cut your head off.'"

This story is also supported in the Sunan of Abu Dawud [25] Book 19, Number 2996:

Narrated Muhayyisah: The Apostle of Allah said: If you gain a victory over the men of Jews, kill them. So Muhayyisah jumped over Shubaybah, a man of the Jewish merchants. He had close relations with them. He then killed him. At that time Huwayyisah (brother of Muhayyisah) had not embraced Islam. He was older than Muhayyisah. When he killed him, Huwayyisah beat him and said: O enemy of Allah, I swear by Allah, you have a good deal of fat in your belly from his property.

Yet another murder committed upon Muhammad's command. Note that Muhayyisa would have killed a family member at the drop of a hat. Here Muhammad's 'revelation' and directions are clear and unambiguous, ordering all his followers to wantonly murder any and all Jewish people they may encounter. Hitler also did this, but in the name of Arian purity rather than in the name of a 'religion of peace'.

A quote from an Islamic scholar – Wensinck, op cit, writes in, "Muhammad and the Jews of Medina", page 113:

"It is remarkable that tradition attributes Muhammad's most cruel acts to divine order, namely the siege of Qaynuqa, the murder of Kab, and his attack upon Qurayzah. Allah's conscience seems to be more elastic than that of his creatures."..... Ibn Ishaq and al-Waqidi report that the prophet said the morning after the murder (of Kab Ashraf), "Kill any Jew you can lay your hands on."

Whether this is a display of the elastic conscience of a loving, merciful, and forgiving God, or simply a display of the elasticity of Muhammad's conscience is certainly debatable. Without question though, there is indeed something unique about Muhammad's conscience, as was the case with so many other leaders in history who engaged in wholesale killings to advance a cause. This incident shows that Muhammad had unsuspecting people, even those who had good relations with Muslims, murdered in cold blood simply because they were Jewish. There was no other apparent justification to murder these Jews other than they had chosen not to be Muhammad's followers. Undeniably the actions in this incident were the work of Muhammad's executioner committing murder at his explicit instruction.

Perhaps the reader might wonder the about the purpose of this incident being chronicled in the Islamic Holy works. The nature of the slaying, jumping upon an employer, an apparent innocent man whose only sin was being a Jewish, after being explicitly incited by Muhammad's instructions appears particularly barbaric and cruel. But to Muslims this incident serves to portray the conversion of the previously non-believing older brother, Huwayyisah. This story was archived not to document this brutal murder per se, but because it serves as a powerful example of the correct treatment of Jews. Apparently this is what passes for Islamic spirituality, implying that for some the path to conversion comes after following Muhammad's directions to kill unbelievers. One Muslim scholar I had an exchange with on the matter made it very clear he believes the story is not so much a tale of the death of a hapless Jew, but the wonderful conversion story of a brother which verifies to him that Allah is God. Of course, Huwayyisah may have converted out of fear and respect for raw power, since at that time apparently it was possible to kill non-believers indiscriminately, his brother having just mentioned he was prepared to do so…

INCIDENT # 6 – **The Attack against the Banu Nadir Jews**

Similar to the attack on the Qaynuqa, the attack on the Banu Nadir Jews arose from Muhammad's desire for an opportunity to move against those that rejected his authority. Tabari states the attack occurred during year 4 from the Hijrah. This event, like the attack upon the Qaynuqa has a large amount of detail, but we will only document the relevant portions for the argument at hand. However, the following references are provided should the reader wish to review the entire accounts.

References: Tabari volume 7, page 156+; Sahih Muslim, # 4324, 4347; Sunan of Abu Dawud, # 2676; Ibn Ishaq "Sirat Rasulallah" (translated by A. Guillaume) "The Life of Muhammad", pages 265 & 437+; Ibn Sa'd's, "Kitab al-Tabaqat al-Kabir", Volume 2, pages 68-71;

"The Life of Muhammad", by Muir, found:

This event, detained to show one aspect of Jihad, also displays Muhammad's unusual rational for attacking the Nadir. The incident started when Muhammad visited the Nadir to ask them to pay bloodwit - i.e. financial compensation, for a man who was murdered by one of their tribe. The Nadir agreed. While there, it is claimed that some of the Jews decided to kill Muhammad, by dropping a large rock upon him, from the roof of a nearby building. According to the sources, not all of the Jews agreed to attempt to kill him. However, Muhammad was given a "warning from heaven", that they were going to try to kill him so he quickly left the Nadir's area. Following that, Muhammad attacked them. He laid siege to their fort. During the siege Muhammad ordered his men to burn down the Nadir's date palm trees. This palm grove was very large and provided food and finances for the Nadir. As Muhammad destroyed their grove, the Nadir challenged Muhammad.

The Jews took refuge in their forts and the apostle ordered that the palm trees should be cut down and burnt, and they called out to him, "Muhammad, you have prohibited wanton destruction and blamed those guilty of it. Why then are you cutting down and burning our palm trees?"

The Jews said this because previously Muhammad had told his men that they were not to destroy food trees. But here, the Jews saw that Muhammad contradicted himself and went against his own teachings. As a response, Muhammad has yet another timely revelation:

"Whatsoever palm trees ye cut down or left standing on their roots, it was by Allah's leave Qur'an 59:5.

Tabari, op cit, volume 7, page 158 provides more details:

When the Messenger of God's companions returned they went to him and found him sitting in the mosque. They said, "O Messenger of God, we waited for you but you did not come back." "The Jews intended to kill me," he replied, "and God informed me of it. Call Muhammad b. Maslamah to me." When Muhammad b. Maslamah came, he was told to go to the Jews and say to them, "Leave my country and do not live with me. You have intended treachery." Muhammad b. Maslamah went to them and said, "The Messenger of God orders you to depart from his country." They said, "Muhammad, we never thought that a man of al-Aws would come to us with such a message." "Hearts have changed," he replied, "and Islam has wiped out the old covenants." "We will go," they said.

And an interesting verse is now revealed from The Sunan of Abu Dawud, op cit, Book 14, Number 2676. Narrated Abdullah ibn Abbas:

When the children of a woman (in pre-Islamic days) did not survive, she took a vow on herself that if her child survives, she would convert it a Jew. When Banu an-Nadir were expelled (from Arabia), there were some children of the Ansar (Helpers) among them. They said: We shall not leave our children. So Allah the Exalted revealed; "Let there be no compulsion in religion. Truth stands out clear from error."

In "The Qur'an and Its Interpreters" [26] volume 1, pages 252- 256, by Muhammad Ayoub, there are several differing Tafsir presented on this verse. Ayoub presents Wahidi's tafsir. Wahidi relates on the authority of Sa'id ibn Jubayr, who related it on the authority of Ibn Abbas:

"When the children of a woman of the Ansar all died in infancy, she vowed that if a child were to live, she would bring it up as a Jew. Thus when the Jewish tribe of al-Nadir was evicted from Medina [4/625], there were among them sons of the Ansar. The Ansar said, "O Apostle of God, what will become of our children!" Thus God sent down this verse." Sa'id ibn Jubayr said, "Therefore whoever wished to join them did so, and whoever wished to enter Islam did so likewise."

While Ayoub presents other tafsir on this verse, some of them supporting the concept that people are not to be forced into Islam, the only Hadith from a Sahih collection that I've found is the one above. And that context has nothing to do with not forcing people into Islam; rather, it allows captured Jews some limited family options. There will be more on this later.

INCIDENT # 7 - **The Murder of the Shepherd**

From Guillaume, op cit, page 673 an incident is detailed as occurring in 4 A.H. It involves another Muslim man named Amr Umayya, who was sent out by Muhammad to murder Muhammad's enemy Abu Sufyan. However, their assassination attempt failed. As he returned home, he met a one-eyed shepherd. The shepherd and the Muslim man both identified themselves as members of the same Arab clan. Prior to going asleep, the shepherd said that he would never become a Muslim. Umayya waited for the shepherd to fall asleep, and thereafter:

> "as soon as the badu was asleep and snoring I got up and killed him in a more horrible way than any man has been killed. I put the end of my bow in his sound eye, then I bore down on it until I forced it out at the back of his neck."

Umayya returned and spoke with Muhammad. He relates: "He [Muhammad] asked my news and when I told him what had happened he blessed me".

So, Muhammad blessed one of his men who brutally murdered a one-eyed shepherd while he slept. This shepherd did not assail Muhammad, but he did not believe in him. The shepherd did not invoke war against Muhammad. However, he wanted the freedom to choose his own faith and way, and he rejected Muhammad. Apparently Umayya was determined not to return empty handed following his failure to murder the individual Muhammad targeted, and his selection of the handicapped Shepherd appears to be a random accident. So we see another person who didn't want to follow Muhammad, and another justified murder - simply for casually mentioning without malice that he did not intend to follow Muhammad. Muhammad's trail of blood continued to grow, a pattern very familiar to all who followed him then and now.

Although with the citations in Appendix A and these descriptions we have covered a lot, we have not covered all of the Qur'an's verses related to Jihad, nor have we covered all of Muhammad's violent actions. However, it should be obvious that shortly after Muhammad's arrival in Medina, the concept of shedding the blood of those that opposed or refused Muhammad's rule was justified and ordained. Thus as soon as Muhammad had military power to force his will on others he began to put it to use, to spread his domination by any and all means available to him.

So far we've seen that Muhammad had people murdered, and that he even had whole tribes eliminated. Mothers, old men, friendly non-Muslim businessmen, handicapped shepherds, critics, all fell to his sword. He even would have massacred the adult males of an entire tribe of Jews, had not a pagan stopped him. Likewise he told another tribe (Banu Nadir) that they had ten days to leave or they would be beheaded. He allowed his followers to lie and deceive his enemies to murder them. We've seen him destroy the financial wealth of a tribe in order to defeat them. And those that followed Muhammad betrayed and broke former allegiances with friends and tribes in order to act against them.

After reading thus far, what should we think? Is it becoming clearer why there are so many devout Muslims who also espouse violent methods against non-brothers? Is it also becoming obvious why most Muslim peoples and nations are so feeble in their efforts to stop the extremists amongst them? In fact, the fastest and perhaps only way for Muslim terrorists in our day to be truly defeated, would be for them to first lose their grass-root local support, and then to be turned upon by 'peaceful' Islam, ... but it appears that would be contrary to the teachings and philosophies of Muhammad. Unfortunately, if true Islam deep down actually supports the twisted rationalization behind terrorism, then our hope for effective help from the Muslim community in the war on terror is not likely to be realized. The sad fact is that many 'moderate' true believers are content to support others to sacrifice themselves in Jihad and hope that their tactic support is sufficient to earn themselves a ticket to paradise riding the coattails of the martyrs. Additionally, to oppose Jihadist warriors is to guarantee a very unpleasant ticket to a fiery Muslim Hell, and out of fear few Muslims are willing to take that risk.

Now we continue our review of Muhammad's actions. Talk is very cheap, lets review more of what Muhammad actually did as he came into power?

INCIDENT #8 - **Muhammad's Massacre of the Qurayza Jews**

Muhammad lived among various Jewish tribes. He had issued an injunction or edict towards them where he expected them to fulfill certain conditions related to living in Medina. One of these was that the Jews were not to help Muhammad's enemies.

During A.H. 5, (i.e. 626, 627 A.D.), an important siege / battle took place, "The Battle of the Trench". During this time, Muhammad's enemies (Meccans and their allies), negotiated with the Jews of the tribe of Banu Qurayza to aid them against Muhammad. In the end the Jews did not betray Muhammad and did not allow the Quraysh to use their land to launch an attack, and they did not participate in any attack against Muhammad. Certainly they were not Muhammad's best friends, having seen the brutalities and murders he had carried out against so many of their own people, but they obviously feared the political/military realities after the Quraysh army departed, and did not want to be Muhamads targets.

The Quraysh eventually lifted the siege and returned to their homes. Following that, Muhammad claimed that the angel Gabriel came to him and ordered him to attack the Banu Qurayza. (Notice that it is this spirit "Gabriel" at work again, motivating Muhammad to attack). By this point in time the Muslims were aware that the Qurayza negotiated with the Quraysh. Though the negotiations did not result in the feared alliance, still they were of great concern to the Muslims and incited hatred towards the Jews, so refusal of the Quraysh to participate in action against Muhammad was about to be rewarded Islamic style. Sa'd Muadh, one of Muhammad's top lieutenants, who was severely wounded during the Battle of the Trench, proclaimed that he did not want to die until he had seen the Jews destroyed. As the confrontation began, a Muslim who was on good terms with the Qurayza told them that Muhammad intended to massacre the Jews.

Eventually, the Jews could not hold out and they surrendered, probably assuming their non aggressive stand during the battle of the Trench would prevent them from receiving a fate worse than previous cities he had conquered. By the time they realized their peril, it was too late, they were without weapons and their hands were bound behind their backs. Muhammad picked out one of his men to judge their fate: the very same Sa'd Muadh, who had made the previously mentioned death declaration, of which undoubtedly Muhammad was aware. Sa'd proclaimed that the adult males (any teenage boy who had started puberty) were to be beheaded, and, the woman and children enslaved. Thus Muhammad massacred 800 prisoners of war and enslaved their women and children.

The Sirat Rasulallah, op cit, page 464, records what one of the Jewish leaders said:

> Huyayy was brought out wearing a flowered robe in which he had made holes about the size of the finger-tips in every part so that it should not be taken from him as spoil, with his hands bound to his neck by a rope. When he saw the apostle he said, 'By God, I do not blame myself for opposing you, but he who forsakes God will be forsaken.' Then he went to the men and said, 'God's command is right. A book and a decree, and massacre have been written against the Sons of Israel.' Then he sat down and his head was struck off.

Muhammad massacred 800 men, not for making war upon him, not for aiding his enemies, but only because they were a threat to his further aims. They had rejected Muhammad and Islam, and they would not follow him as a prophet. Consequently, they would have to be removed. At this point in time, there were no more pagan leaders to plead for these Jews (as Ubayy had done for the Qaynuqa). There were no more Jewish tribes or allies nearby to lend them a hand, (they had all been expelled). Now Muhammad was free to do what appears he intended from the beginning: massacre those who threatened him and/or refused to become his followers.

Apparently some of these Jews were given the option of becoming Muslims but they refused. From the only records available, only four Jews are recorded as having converted - obviously to save their own lives. The Jews believed Muhammad was a false prophet, hence their leader accepted their massacre instead of yielding to him.

Edward Gibbon, in his classic history, *"The Decline and Fall of the Roman Empire"* described the aftermath of the assault:

> "Seven hundred Jews were dragged in chains to the market-place of the city; they descended alive into the grave prepared for their execution and burial and the apostle beheld with an inflexible eye the slaughter of his helpless

victims. Their sheep and camels were inherited by the Musulmans: three hundred cuirasses, five hundred pikes, a thousand lances, composed the most useful portion of the spoil."

Gibbon was a respected historian and not some Zionist. But even the Arab's own historians make no pretensions about their military conquests. There was no benevolence or spreading enlightenment as a motivation. It was all about rape and plunder. The History of Al-Tabari (pg. 166, 175), written in the 10th century clearly outlines the slaughter and pillaging and rapacious motivations of these forces. Even in recent history, the Arab tribes under the direction of Lawrence of Arabia weren't motivated to attack the Turks for anything other than simple plunder and gold.

INCIDENT #9 - The Torture and Death of Kinana

Previously we learned that Muhammad attacked the Jewish settlement of Khaibar following the treaty of Hudaybiyya. One particularly heinous incident among several stand out. Here is the material.

On page 515 of Ibn Ishaq's "Sirat Rasulallah", (The Life of the Prophet of God), the events of the conquest of Khaibar are detailed. This event occurred about 3 years before Muhammad's death due to poisoning. Khaibar was a large Jewish settlement about 95 miles north of Medina. The Jews there were primarily farmers. Khaibar was known to have some of the best date palms in the region. The Jews there were well to do because they had worked hard and earned it. They had good relations with the surrounding tribes of pagans, Christians, and Jews.

Prior to Muhammad's conquest of Khaibar, the Meccans had just stopped him from performing a pilgrimage to Mecca. Outside of Mecca, he also signed a humiliating treaty with the Meccans - a treaty that a number of his leading followers didn't like. This humiliated and embarrassed Muhammad and his followers, who then sought redemption in a different course of action. Apparently to placate his men, Muhammad claimed to have a "revelation" that God would give them the possessions of the Jews of Khaibar. Six weeks later he marched on Khaibar with the intent to conquer and plunder.

page 515 reads:

"Kinana al-Rabi, who had the custody of the treasure of Banu Nadir, was brought to the apostle who asked him about it. He denied that he knew where it was. A Jew came (Tabari says "was brought"), to the apostle and said that he had seen Kinana going round a certain ruin every morning early. When the apostle said to Kinana, "Do you know that if we find you have it I shall kill you?" He said "Yes". The apostle gave orders that the ruin was to be excavated and some of the treasure was found. When he asked him about the rest he refused to produce it, so the apostle gave orders to al-Zubayr Al-Awwam, "Torture him until you extract what he has." So he kindled a fire with flint and steel on his chest until he was nearly dead. Then the apostle delivered him to Muhammad b. Maslama and he struck off his head, in revenge for his brother Mahmud."

Many might find Muhammad's orders to torture Kinana to obtain "buried treasure" similar to what criminals do to obtain people's money or possessions. It is not difficult to picture organized crime figures beating some one or torturing them to make them talk. "Talk!, tell us where the money is!, or we'll make your pain even worse!". Finally, when he is near death, Muhammad has his head cut off. It appears that Muhammad's greed drove him to torture and then murder, for the sole purpose to obtain money.

Think about Muhammad's statement, "Torture him until you extract what he has". This is the prophet of Islam in action when he now has the power of the sword with no threat of external consequence. What kind of a man is this prophet of Islam, and what does this say about the people who choose to follow him, as all who do must also choose to justify and support all his deeds. Millions have gone to their death unwilling to risk their eternity on the man, but an even greater number have hitched their wagons to his destiny. It's an age-old dilemma and choice still being forced on many throughout the world today.

INCIDENT #10 - The Murder of a Slave Wife and Mother.

This incident involves a Muslim man who murdered his own slave wife and mother of his children. From the Hadith of Abu Dawud, Book 38, Number 4348: Narrated Abdullah Ibn Abbas:

A blind man had a slave-mother who used to abuse the Prophet and disparage him. He forbade her but she did not stop. He rebuked her but she did not give up her habit. One night she began to slander the Prophet and abuse him. So he took a dagger, placed it on her belly, pressed it, and killed her. A child who came between her legs was smeared with the blood that was there. When the morning came, the Prophet was informed about it.

He assembled the people and said: I adjure by Allah the man who has done this action and I adjure him by my right to him that he should stand up. Jumping over the necks of the people and trembling the man stood up.

He sat before the Prophet and said: Apostle of Allah! I am her master; she used to abuse you and disparage you. I forbade her, but she did not stop, and I rebuked her, but she did not abandon her habit. I have two sons like pearls from her, and she was my companion. Last night she began to abuse and disparage you. So I took a dagger, put it on her belly and pressed it till I killed her.

Thereupon the Prophet said: Oh be witness, no retaliation is payable for her blood.

To continue to quote from Abu Dawud. Note #3800 states:

"This shows that even if a Jew of any non-Muslim abuses the Prophet he will be killed. This is held by al-Laith, al-Shafi'i, Ahmad, and Ishaq."

We see that Muhammad allowed people to murder others simply for insulting him. Here, a slave woman, who was used as a concubine by her Muslim master, paid for her criticism of Muhammad with her life. The man murdered the mother of two of his children apparently in the presence of his young, and when the prophet hears of it he makes a special effort to sanction and justify the brutal act. It seems the opportunity to establish fear in the hearts of all should they disparage Muhammad simply could not be passed up.

Now then, was that slave a threat? Were Muslims going to leave Islam because of a slave women's criticism? Of course not, she was only an irritant to her husband. But Muhammad could not long tolerate any personal criticism. His ego could not allow his credibility undermined by anyone, no matter how insignificant and powerless, so he allowed and encouraged his followers to murder anyone who expressed different views. This incident also shows that Muhammad allowed his followers to even murder members of their own families.

INCIDENT #11 - **The Murder of the Old Woman from Fazara**

The incident involves the actions of Muslims who were sent out by Muhammad on a raid against the Fazara tribe. The Muslims were initially defeated in their first encounter with the Fazara. The wounded Muslim leader swore vengeance. After he recovered he went out and attacked the Fazara again. One very old woman was captured. Here is the account from Guillaume, op cit, and page 665:

"....and Umm Qirfa Fatima was taken prisoner. She was a very old woman, wife of Malik. Her daughter and Abdullah Masada were also taken. Zayd ordered Qays to kill Umm Qirfa and he killed her cruelly (Tabari, by putting a rope to her two legs and to two camels and driving them until they rent her in two.) "

Here, Muhammad's companions went out and attacked people, took some prisoners, then committed some brutal atrocities against their captives. These men were so destitute of basic human values, that they ripped an old woman in half by using camels! One wonders how many Muslims are intimately acquainted with the record of brutal killings Muhammad himself did or explicitly ordered, sanctioned, and justified. Muhammad and his followers seemed every bit as brutal as the worst humanity has ever produced.

INCIDENT #12 - **The Murder of Abdullah Khatal and his Daughter**

The incident involves another slave woman who was murdered, upon Muhammad's command because she had mocked Muhammad some time earlier. From Guillaume, op cit, page 550, 551:

"Another [to be killed] was Abdullah Khatal of B. Taym b. Ghalib. He had become a Muslim and the apostle sent him to collect the poor tax in company with one of the Ansar. He had with him a freed slave who served him. (He was Muslim). When they halted he ordered the latter to kill a goat for him and prepare some food, and went to sleep. When he woke up the man had done nothing, so he attacked and killed him and apostatized. He had two singing-girls Fartana and her friend who used to sing satirical songs about the apostle, so he ordered that they should be killed with him."

Let's pause and examine this paragraph. Muhammad ordered that an apostate man and his two slave girls to be killed. Khatal was ordered killed, not because he killed his Muslim male slave, but because he apostatized. Islamic law does not allow a Muslim man to be put to death for killing a slave. Muhammad also ordered two slave girls to be killed for singing satirical songs about him. They sung satirical songs about Muhammad probably at least a year or more earlier. Now, after Muhammad conquered Mecca, it was his time to pay those slave girls back. These slave girls were not threats to Islam, or to the new

Islamic State, they were only simple slave girls. They were ordered executed only because they sang a silly song about Muhammad. Page 551 finishes the story of the slave girls:

> "As for Ibn Khatal's two singing girls, one was killed and the other ran away until the apostle, asked for immunity, gave it to her."

Needless to say, if the second slave girl did not ask for immunity, Muhammad would have had her murdered also. Muhammad had her sister killed just for poking a little fun of him in song. A sense of humor was apparently not one of Muhammad's strong suits.

INCIDENT #13 - **Muhammad's Attack upon Tabuk**

There are many, many, violent incidents that could be drawn from. We conclude the incidents section with this event because it shows Muhammad's beliefs regarding Jihad and his mission of conquest for Islam. In one of his latest acts, it seems clear that Muhammad had no intention of living peacefully, side by side with non-Muslims, even with those who were far from his community's borders. The only conclusion that can be drawn is that non-Muslims were his enemies because they had rejected him. As recorded in the Qur'an, non-Muslims had these options: become Muslim, pay extortion tax, or fight and die.

Muhammad heard the Romans were going to attack him. He marshaled 30,000 of his troops and they went north to the town of Tabuk to do battle with the Romans. However, upon arriving, they found that there was no threat at all. Instead, Muhammad sent a detachment to Ayla, to give them the aforementioned options: convert, pay the Jizya extortion tax, or die. The Christian leader there decided to pay tribute. Details of the incident can be reviewed at http://answering-islam.org/Books/Muir/Life4/chap28.htm, from which the following is extracted:

> "To John ibn Rabah and the Chiefs of Aylah. Peace be on you! I praise God for you, beside whom there is no Lord. I will not fight against you until I have written thus unto you. Believe, or else pay tribute. And be obedient unto the Lord and his Prophet, and the messengers of his Prophet. Honor them and clothe them with excellent vestments, not with inferior raiment. Specially clothe Zeid with excellent garments. As long as my messengers are pleased, so likewise am I. Ye know the tribute. If ye desire to have security by sea and by land, obey the Lord and his Apostle, and he will defend you from every claim, whether by Arab or foreigner, saving the claim of the Lord and his Apostle. But if ye oppose and displease them, I will not accept from you a single thing, until I have fought against you and taken captive your little ones and slain the elder.

Think about what exactly is being said here; Do what me and my associates tell you, give us your finest merchandise, If my men are happy, I'm happy, pay me the money and you'll be protected, upset me or them and your family will not be safe. Frankly, Muhammad's words to John ibn Rabah read like a script strait from The Godfather.

Summary of these 13 actions by Muhammad:

We see how Muhammad's attack upon these people demonstrate his commitment to the teachings in Sura 9; "Make war upon the Christians and Jews, unless they convert or pay the extortion." Real Islam, Muhammad's Islam, is clearly taught in the Qur'an, and demonstrated by Muhammad's actions. Muhammad's actions speak loudly here. Committed near the end of his life, they clearly portray what he wanted his followers to continue to do: attack and conquer non-Muslim people. The vast majority of Islamic theologians today understand amongst themselves that these final acts and teachings abrogate all earlier more conciliatory verses. The fear of many is that the earlier more tolerant versus are repeated for western consumption only, so that the frog might not notice how hot the pot is becoming until it is too late…

Documentation shows many more people suffered a similar fate, but here is a summary of the 9 individual murders committed upon Muhammad's requests or efforts just outlined.

1) Abu Afak, a 120-year-old man, murdered while he slept.
2) Asma Marwan, mother of five, murdered while she slept.
3) A slave women and mother of two, murdered while she slept.
4) A one-eyed shepherd, murdered while he slept.
5) A very old women, ripped in half by Muslims who captured her on a raid.
6) A slave girl, who was murdered because she poked fun at Muhammad.
7) Murder of Kab Ashraf, a prominent local who did not believe in Muhammad.

8) Murder of Ibn Sunayna (Jewish merchant on good social/business terms with Muslims).
9) The torture and death of Kinana, to extract money.

If these descriptions shock the reader, consider that we can present these stories from the only source available ... the *'Islamic friendly'* written history of the events. Now there are always two sides to every story, but the victims' side of these incidents is simply not available, so the full story can never be known. One can only imagine just how far the truth may have been massaged to make the official record more palatable, or what additional important information has been omitted. The only thing that is certain is that the official account was never at risk of being challenged ... dead people generally don't talk very much. No one knows what other factors were at play beyond the data presented by those who wrote such history, but if we had the power to interview the victims and get their perspective on the events, they could easily turn out to be even more deplorable, gross, and inhumane. Even so, to most reasonable people, no further information is needed to deplore the actions of Muhammad and his followers in relation to these events.

One is also left wondering how many completely undocumented events may have not quite made it into the official record for reasons unknown. The question naturally arises, did all war-like and murderous actions of Muhammad and his close lieutenants get chronicled in the sacred works? Certainly we do not have an hour by hour accounting of the all Jihadic actions of the man and his people, and considering the 'inspirational' events that were chronicled, one can only imagine how many and what manner of horrific events occurred but were never documented. A study of more recent Islamic Jihadic relationships with her neighbors may help fill in the holes left by the Islamic writers.

History is written from the vantage point of the dominant victorious culture, and revisionist history seems a favorite pastime of Islamic scholars. Of course, most Muslims would be terribly offended at the suggestion that Islamic history may be slanted, but before you dismiss the possibility out of hand, consider Muslim revisionist history being written today. Amongst Muslims today there is a widespread belief that a worldwide Jewish conspiracy exists whose goal is to dominate the world, the outgoing Malaysian prime minister just stated that and received the applause of Muslim leaders worldwide. A book long since exposed plainly as pure fiction, Protocols of the Elders of Zion was initially spread by the intelligence services of the Russian czar in 1895. Leaders and lay alike in the Muslim world believe the work contains the actual minutes of conspiratorial meetings among Jewish leaders, who were plotting to take over the world. The book is gospel truth to these people, and no amount of logic or rational argument can steer those who believe this type of nonsense away from it. Even three years after 9/11, most in the Muslim Middle East, including the most educated and most intelligent, actually believe that Mossad (Israel's intelligence service) carried out the September 11 attacks on America. Then there is Monsieur Meysson who wrote a *bestseller* in France that claims no airplane crashed into the Pentagon, because no debris from the crash was ever found. To his mind, it was all a plot by the CIA and the U.S. military, who used an U.S. Air Force cruise missile to murder Americans in a conspiracy to justify a new Middle East war. Arab countries also regularly host conferences where Holocaust deniers masquerading as historians claim to be able to "prove" there was no massacre of Jews by the Nazis during World War II. Many Muslims worldwide praise Hitler for his services, yet almost in the same breath deny the Holocaust as "a big illusion of the Jews". Despite a history printing articles denouncing the holocaust as a farce, the second most influential Egyptian daily newspaper, Al-Akhbar, printed on April 18, 2001: "*Our thanks go the late Hitler who wrought, in advance, the vengeance of the Palestinians upon the most despicable villains on the face of the earth. However, we rebuke Hitler for the fact that the vengeance was insufficient*". Spin and violence seem the chief export of Islam, and simple reverse extrapolation using this kind of empirical data supports the suggestion there was much more murder and mayhem committed by Muhammad and his followers than Islamic scripture documents.

Chapter 5
Actions of the four "Rightly Guided" Caliphs

Previously it was mentioned we would review the actions of some of Muhammad's closest companions, particularly the four known as the "rightly guided" caliphs. Following Muhammad's death these men reigned over the Islamic empire, each one after the death of the previous one. These men are: Abu Bakr, Umar, Uthman, and Ali (Muhammad's son-in-law). Below is a brief timeline of some of their actions and conquests. We can not detail all their military actions here, as they are much too numerous. They ruled during a period of great Islamic expansion over other peoples and lands, and their writings describing the conflicts and glorious conquest are the quite prolific. This information is drawn from various volumes of the History of Tabari, op cit, the "History of Islam", by Robert Payne [27], and "Jihad", by Paul Fregosi [28]. These books will provide a more complete account of the Caliphs Islamic crusades. Of important significance it should be noted that all these conquests were not defensive in nature, but offensive. These men were conquering the world for Islam – exactly as Muhammad instructed. We should also add that during Ali's reign Islamic conquest paused slightly. The Islamic empire experienced its first civil wars during Ali's reign. All this occurred within a generation of Muhammad's death.

Note that these men are correctly called 'rightly guided', as opposed to 'wrongly guided'. This is because of the universal recognition that they always acted in full compliance of true Islam as guided by Muhammad's final clear teachings and example. A review of history reveals conclusively that they followed their prophets' instructions to the letter in advancing Islam through military conquest …through Jihad.

ABU BAKR'S REIGN

A.H. 11 (622, 623) Abu Bakr makes war upon the people of Yamana who wish to leave Islam.

A.H. 12 Muslim armies attack the Christians in Palestine.

UMAR'S REIGN

A.H. 13 Conquest of Damascus, Syria.

A.H. 14 & 15 Syria and Palestine conquered.

A.H. 15 – 21 Iraq, Southern Persia, and Egypt conquered.

UTHMAN'S REIGN

A.H. 24 Conquest in Northern Persia and Armenia.

A.H. 28 Attack on Cyprus.

ALI'S REIGN

During Ali's reign there were two civil wars. The first Islamic civil war occurred between Ali, Muhammad's son-in-law, and Aisha, Abu Bakr's daughter (a child Muhammad consummated a marriage with when she was 9 years old). 13,000 Muslims died killing each other as Ali defeated Aisha. Not long thereafter Ali fought Muwawiyya, Abu Sufyan's son. Muwawiyya was appointed governor of Damascus / Syria, and moved against Ali to take power. In the end, Ali won out as the two sides negotiated a peace of some sorts. Not long afterwards, Ali was murdered by Muslims, as was Uthman prior to him, and also Umar who was killed by a slave. In any case, after the 'rightly guided Caliphs had all met untimely violent deaths through murder and assassination, Muwawiyya then assumed power as Caliph.

As you can tell from that brief chronological summary, the Caliphs made war as aggressively as any conquering nation or people in human history. They went on conquest after conquest. The message the rightly guided leaders imposed with the sword at their hands was the same as Muhammad's: convert, pay extortion taxes, or die. Islam, real Islam, their Islam, was a religion of war, oppression, and conquest.

Below are Hadith dealing with the conquests and subjections of the Caliphs.

Bukhari 4.386: Narrated Jubair bin Haiya:

'Umar sent the Muslims to the great countries to fight the pagans. When Al-Hurmuzan embraced Islam, 'Umar said to him. "I would like to consult you regarding these countries which I intend to invade." Al-Hurmuzan said,

"Yes, the example of these countries and their inhabitants who are the enemies of the Muslims, is like a bird with a head, two wings and two legs; If one of its wings got broken, it would get up over its two legs, with one wing and the head; and if the other wing got broken, it would get up with two legs and a head, but if its head got destroyed, then the two legs, two wings and the head would become useless. The head stands for Khosrau, and one wing stands for Caesar and the other wing stands for Faris. So, order the Muslims to go towards Khosrau." So, 'Umar sent us (to Khosrau) appointing An-Numan bin Muqrin as our commander. When we reached the land of the enemy, the representative of Khosrau came out with forty-thousand warriors, and an interpreter got up saying, "Let one of you talk to me!" Al-Mughira replied, "Ask whatever you wish." The other asked, "Who are you?" Al-Mughira replied, "We are some people from the Arabs; we led a hard, miserable, disastrous life: we used to suck the hides and the date stones from hunger; we used to wear clothes made up of fur of camels and hair of goats, and to worship trees and stones. While we were in this state, the Lord of the Heavens and the Earths, Elevated is His Remembrance and Majestic is His Highness, sent to us from among ourselves a Prophet whose father and mother are known to us. Our Prophet, the Messenger of our Lord, has ordered us to fight you till you worship Allah Alone or give Jizya (i.e. tribute); and our Prophet has informed us that our Lord says:-- "Whoever amongst us is killed (i.e. martyred), shall go to Paradise to lead such a luxurious life as he has never seen, and whoever amongst us remain alive, shall become your master." (Al-Mughira, then blamed An-Numan for delaying the attack and) An-Nu' man said to Al-Mughira, "If you had participated in a similar battle, in the company of Allah's Apostle he would not have blamed you for waiting, nor would he have disgraced you. But I accompanied Allah's Apostle in many battles and it was his custom that if he did not fight early by daytime, he would wait till the wind had started blowing and the time for the prayer was due (i.e. after midday)."

Sahih Muslim, Book 001, Number 0029:

It is narrated on the authority of Abu Huraira that when the Messenger of Allah (may peace be upon him) breathed his last and Abu Bakr was appointed as his successor (Caliph), those amongst the Arabs who wanted to become apostates became apostates. 'Umar b. Khattab said to Abu Bakr: Why would you fight against the people, when the Messenger of Allah declared: I have been directed to fight against people so long as they do not say: There is no god but Allah, and he who professed it was granted full protection of his property and life on my behalf except for a right? His (other) affairs rest with Allah. Upon this Abu Bakr said: By Allah, I would definitely fight against him who severed prayer from Zakat, for it is the obligation upon the rich. By Allah, I would fight against them even to secure the cord (used for hobbling the feet of a camel) which they used to give to the Messenger of Allah (as zakat) but now they have withheld it. Umar b. Khattab remarked: By Allah, I found nothing but the fact that Allah had opened the heart of Abu Bakr for (perceiving the justification of) fighting (against those who refused to pay Zakat) and I fully recognized that the (stand of Abu Bakr) was right.

A Banquet of Hadith (which deals with Jihad and aggressive Islamic violence). We've examined many verses from the Qur'an, and associated context from Sira and Hadith, along with commentary from Islamic scholars regarding violence and Jihad. We also put together a list of violent incidents that demonstrate various facets of Islamic Jihad. Below is a selection of Hadiths regarding violence and Jihad to widen the reader's understanding of Islamic Jihad and violence. In some cases the Hadith is not quoted in full because of the length. Most of these hadith are available on the Internet and can be downloaded for further review. [NOTE. *Most of these Hadith come from the collections of Bukhari and Muslim. These two collections are regarded as absolutely reliable and truthful to the Sunni branch of Islam (85% of the Islamic world is Sunni). The collection of Abu Dawud is also held is high esteem, but not as highly as the other two*].

Sahih Muslim, Book 7, Number 3200:

Sufyan b. Abd Zuhair reported Allah's Messenger (may peace be upon him) as saying: Syria will be conquered and some people will go out of Medina along with their families driving their camels. and Medina is better for them if they were to know it. Then Yemen will be conquered and some people will go out of Medina along with their families driving their camels, and Medina is better for them if they were to know it. Then Iraq will be conquered and some people will go out of it along with their families driving their camels, and Medina is better for them if they were to know it.

Sahih Bukhari, 4.175: Narrated Khalid bin Madan:

That 'Umair bin Al-Aswad Al-Anasi told him that he went to 'Ubada bin As-Samit while he was staying in his house at the sea-shore of Hims with (his wife) Um Haram. 'Umair said. Um Haram informed us that she heard the Prophet saying, "Paradise is granted to the first batch of my followers who will undertake a naval expedition." Um Haram added, I said, 'O Allah's Apostle! Will I be amongst them?' He replied, 'You are amongst them.' The Prophet then said, 'The first army amongst' my followers who will invade Caesar's City will be forgiven their sins.' I asked, 'Will I be one of them, O Allah's Apostle?' He replied in the negative."

Sahih Muslim, Book 019, Number 4294:

"It has been reported from Sulaiman b. Buraid through his father that when the Messenger of Allah (may peace be upon him) appointed anyone as leader of an army or detachment he would especially exhort him to fear Allah and to be good to the Muslims who were with him. He would say: Fight in the name of Allah and in the way of Allah. Fight against those who disbelieve in Allah. Make a holy war, do not embezzle the spoils; do not break your pledge; and do not mutilate (the dead) bodies; do not kill the children. When you meet your enemies who are polytheists, invite them to three courses of action. If they respond to any one of these, you also accept it and withhold yourself from doing them any harm. Invite them to (accept) Islam; if they respond to you, accept it from them and desist from fighting against them. Then invite them to migrate from their lands to the land of Muhairs and inform them that, if they do so, they shall have all the privileges and obligations of the Muhajirs. If they refuse to migrate, tell them that they will have the status of Bedouin Muslims and will be subjected to the Commands of Allah like other Muslims, but they will not get any share from the spoils of war or Fai' except when they actually fight with the Muslims (against the disbelievers). If they refuse to accept Islam, demand from them the Jizya. If they agree to pay, accept it from them and hold off your hands. If they refuse to pay the tax, seek Allah's help and fight them...."

The following deals with the permissibility of killing women and children in the night raids *(provided it is not deliberate)*:

Sahih Muslim, Book 019, Number 4321:

It is reported on the authority of Sa'b b. Jaththama that the Prophet of Allah (may peace be upon him), when asked about the women and children of the polytheists being killed during the night raid, said: They are from them.

Bukhari 4.256: Narrated As-Sab bin Jaththama:

The Prophet passed by me at a place called Al-Abwa or Waddan, and was asked whether it was permissible to attack the pagan warriors at night with the probability of exposing their women and children to danger. The Prophet replied, "They (i.e. women and children) are from them (i.e. pagans)." I also heard the Prophet saying, "The institution of Hima is invalid except for Allah and His Apostle."

Sahih Muslim, Book 020, Number 4645:

It has been narrated on the authority of Abu Sa'id Khudri that the Messenger of Allah (may peace be upon him) said (to him): Abu Sa'id, whoever cheerfully accepts Allah as his Lord, Islam as his religion and Muhammad as his Apostle is necessarily entitled to enter Paradise. He (Abu Sa'id) wondered at it and said: Messenger of Allah, repeat it for me. He (the Messenger of Allah) did that and said: There is another act which elevates the position of a man in Paradise to a grade one hundred (higher), and the elevation between one grade and the other is equal to the height of the heaven from the earth. He (Abu Sa'id) said: What is that act? He replied: Jihad in the way of Allah! Jihad in the way of Allah!

Sahih Muslim, Book 020, Number 4646:

It has been narrated on the authority of Abu Qatada that the Messenger of Allah (pbuh) stood up among them (his Companions) to deliver his sermon in which he told them that Jihad in the way of Allah and belief in Allah (with all His Attributes) are the most meritorious of acts. A man stood up and said: Messenger of Allah, do you think that if I am killed in the way of Allah, my sins will be blotted out from me? The Messenger of Allah (pbuh) said: Yes, in case you are killed in the way of Allah and you were patient and sincere and you always fought facing the enemy, never turning your back upon him.

Sahih Muslim, Book 020, Number 4681:

The tradition has been narrated on the authority of 'Abdullah b. Qais. He heard it from his father who, while facing the enemy, reported that the Messenger of Allah (pbuh) said: Surely, the gates of Paradise are under the shadows of the swords. A man in a shabby condition got up and said; Abu Musa, did you hear the Messenger of Allah (pbuh) say this? He said: Yes. (The narrator said): He returned to his friends and said: I greet you (a farewell greeting). Then he broke the sheath of his sword, threw it away, advanced with his (naked) sword towards the enemy and fought (them) with it until he was slain.

Bukhari, 4.266A: Narrated Salim Abu An-Nadr:

(the freed slave of 'Umar bin 'Ubaidullah) I was Umar's clerk. Once Abdullah bin Abi Aufa wrote a letter to 'Umar when he proceeded to Al-Haruriya. I read in it that Allah's Apostle in one of his military expeditions against the enemy, waited till the sun declined and then he got up amongst the people saying O people! Do not wish to meet the enemy, and ask Allah for safety, but when you face the enemy, be patient, and remember that Paradise is under the shades of swords.", " Then he said, "O Allah, the Revealer of the Holy Book, and the Mover of the clouds and the Defeater of the clans, defeat them, and grant us victory over them."

Sahih Muslim, Book 020, Number 4597:

It has been narrated on the authority of Ibn 'Abbas that the Messenger of Allah (may peace be upon him) said on the day of the Conquest of Mecca: There is no Hijra now, but (only) Jihad (fighting for the cause of Islam) and sincerity of purpose (have great reward) ; when you are asked to set out (on an expedition undertaken for Islam) you should (readily) do so.

Bukhari 4. 79: Narrated Ibn 'Abbas:

On the day of the Conquest (of Mecca) the Prophet said, "There is no emigration after the Conquest but Jihad and intentions. When you are called (by the Muslim ruler) for fighting, go forth immediately." (See Hadith No. 42)

Sahih Muslim, Book 020, Number 4626:

It has been narrated on the authority of Abu Huraira that the Messenger of Allah (may peace upon him) said: Allah has undertaken to look after the affairs of one who goes out to fight in His way believing in Him and affirming the truth of His Apostles. He is committed to His care that He will either admit him to Paradise or bring him back to his home from where he set out with a reward or (his share of) booty. ...By, the Being in Whose Hand is Muhammad's life, if it were not to be too hard upon the Muslims. I would not lag behind any expedition which is going to fight in the cause of Allah. But I do not have abundant means to provide them (the Mujahids) with riding beasts, nor have they (i. e. all of them) abundant means (to provide themselves with all the means of Jihad) so that they could he left behind. By the Being in Whose Hand is Muhammad, I love to fight in the way of Allah and be killed, to fight and again be killed and to fight again and be killed.

Sahih Muslim, Book 020, Number 4652:

It has been narrated on the authority of Abu Sa'id Khudri that a man came to the Holy Prophet (may peace he upon him) and said: Who is the best of men? He replied: A man who fights in the way of Allah spending his wealth and staking his life. The man then asked: Who is next to him (in excellence)? He said: Next to him is a believer who lives in a mountain gorge worshipping hid Lord and sparing men from his mischief.

Bukhari 4.177: Narrated Abu Huraira:

Allah's Apostle said, "The Hour will not be established until you fight with the Jews, and the stone behind which a Jew will be hiding will say. "O Muslim! There is a Jew hiding behind me, so kill him."

Bukhari 4.180: Narrated Abu Huraira:

The Prophet said, "The Hour will not be established till you fight with people wearing shoes made of hair. And the Hour will not be established till you fight with people whose faces look like shields coated with leather. " (Abu Huraira added, "They will be small-eyed, flat nosed, and their faces will look like shields coated with leather.")

(The text note says these people are the Turks).

Bukhari 4.355: Narrated Abu Musa Al-Ashari:

A Bedouin asked the Prophet, "A man may fight for the sake of booty, and another may fight so that he may be mentioned by the people, and a third may fight to show his position (i.e. bravery); which of these regarded as fighting in Allah's Cause?" The Prophet said, "He who fights so that Allah's Word (i.e. Islam) should be superior, fights for Allah's Cause."

Bukhari 4. 41: Narrated Abdullah bin Masud:

I asked Allah's Apostle, "O Allah's Apostle! What is the best deed?" He replied, "To offer the prayers at their early stated fixed times." I asked, "What is next in goodness?" He replied, "To be good and dutiful to your parents." I further asked, what is next in goodness?" He replied, "To participate in Jihad in Allah's Cause." I did not ask Allah's Apostle anymore and if I had asked him more, he would have told me more.

Bukhari 4.792: Narrated Abu Said Al-Khudri:

The Prophet said, "A time will come when the people will wage holy war, and it will be asked, 'Is there any amongst you who has enjoyed the company of Allah's Apostle?' They will say: 'Yes.' And then victory will be bestowed upon them. They will wage holy war again, and it will be asked: 'Is there any among you who has enjoyed the company of the companions of Allah's Apostle ?' They will say: 'Yes.' And then victory will be bestowed on them."

Bukhari 1.387: Narrated Anas bin Malik:

Allah's Apostle said, "I have been ordered to fight the people till they say: 'None has the right to be worshipped but Allah.' And if they say so, pray like our prayers, face our Qibla and slaughter as we slaughter, then their blood and property will be sacred to us and we will not interfere with them except legally and their reckoning will be with Allah." Narrated Maimun ibn Siyah that he asked Anas bin Malik, "O Abu Hamza! What makes the life and property of a person sacred?" He replied, "Whoever says, 'None has the right to be worshipped but Allah', faces our Qibla during the prayers, prays like us and eats our slaughtered animal, then he is a Muslim, and has got the same rights and obligations as other Muslims have."

Abu Dawud, Book 14, Number 2635: Narrated Anas ibn Malik:

The Prophet said: I am commanded to fight with men till they testify that there is no god but Allah, and that Muhammad is His servant and His Apostle, face our qiblah (direction of prayer), eat what we slaughter, and pray like us. When they do that, their life and property are unlawful for us except what is due to them. They will have the same rights as the Muslims have, and have the same responsibilities as the Muslims have.

Bukhari 5.568: Narrated Usama bin Zaid:

Allah's Apostle sent us towards Al-Huruqa, and in the morning we attacked them and defeated them.

Bukhari 5.641: Narrated Jarir:

In the Pre-Islamic Period of Ignorance there was a house called Dhu-l-Khalasa or Al-Ka'ba Al-Yamaniya or Al-Ka'ba Ash-Shamiya. The Prophet said to me, "Won't you relieve me from Dhu-l-Khalasa?" So I set out with one-hundred-and-fifty riders, and we dismantled it and killed whoever was present there. Then I came to the Prophet and informed him, and he invoked good upon us and Al-Ahmas (tribe).

Bukhari 5.716: Narrated Ibn Abbas:

Thursday! And how great that Thursday was! The ailment of Allah's Apostle became worse (on Thursday) and he said, fetch me something so that I may write to you something after which you will never go astray." ... Then he ordered them to do three things. He said, "Turn the pagans out of the 'Arabian Peninsula; respect and give gifts to the foreign delegations as you have seen me dealing with them".

Abu Dawud, Book 14, Number 2478: Narrated Imran ibn Husayn:

The Prophet said: A section of my community will continue to fight for the right and overcome their opponents till the last of them fights with the Antichrist.

Abu Dawud, Book 14, Number 2493: Narrated Abu Malik al-Ash'ari:

Abu Malik heard the Apostle of Allah say: He who goes forth in Allah's path and dies or is killed is a martyr, or has his neck broken through being thrown by his horse or by his camel, or is stung by a poisonous creature, or dies on his bed by any kind of death Allah wishes is a martyr and will go to Paradise.

Abu Dawud, Book 14, Number 2496: Abu Hurairah reported the Prophet saying:

He who dies without having fought or having felt fighting (against the infidels) to be his duty will die guilty of a kind of hypocrisy".

Abu Dawud, Book 14, Number 2506: Narrated Abu Ayyub:

Abu Imran said: We went out on an expedition from Medina with the intention of (attacking) Constantinople. AbdurRahman ibn Khalid ibn al-Walid was the leader of the company. The Romans were just keeping their backs to the walls of the city. A man (suddenly) attacked the enemy. ...

Abu Dawud, Book 14, Number 2631: Narrated Ka'b ibn Malik:

When the Prophet intended to go on an expedition, he always pretended to be going somewhere else, and he would say: War is deception.

Abu Dawud, Book 14, Number 2632: Narrated Salamah ibn al-Akwa':

The Apostle of Allah appointed Abu Bakr our commander and we fought with some people who were polytheists, and we attacked them at night, killing them. Our war-cry that night was "put to death; put to death." Salamah said: I killed that night with my hand polytheists belonging to seven houses.

Abu Dawud, Book 14, Number 2664: Narrated Samurah ibn Jundub:

The Prophet said: Kill the old men who are polytheists, but spare their children.

Abu Dawud, Book 14, Number 2665: Narrated Aisha, Ummul Mu'minin:

No woman of Banu Qurayzah was killed except one. She was with me, talking and laughing on her back and belly (extremely), while the Apostle of Allah was killing her people with the swords. Suddenly a man called her name: Where is so-and-so? She said: I asked: What is the matter with you? She said: I did a new act. The man took her and beheaded her. I will not forget that she was laughing extremely although she knew that she would be killed.

Chapter 6
Early History of Peaceful Islam

Islamic leaders and politicians constantly tell us in English that "Islam is a peaceful religion", but one can't help wondering if they would say it quite so often if they were absolutely sure it was true.

Some recorded massacres in Muslim history: Joseph HaNagid, the Jewish vizier of Granada, Spain, was crucified on December 30, 1066 by an Arab mob, who then proceeded to raze the Jewish quarter of the city and slaughter its *5,000* inhabitants. Apparently, Muslim preachers objecting angrily to what they saw was inordinate Jewish political power, so they incited the riot. Similarly, in 1465, Arab mobs in Fez slaughtered thousands of Jews, leaving only 11 alive, after a Jewish deputy vizier treated a Muslim woman in "an offensive manner." The killings touched off a wave of similar massacres throughout Morocco. Other mass murders of Jews in Arab lands occurred in Morocco in the 8th century, where whole communities were wiped out by Muslim ruler Idris I; North Africa in the 12th century, where the Almohads either forcibly converted or decimated several communities; Libya in 1785, where Ali Burzi Pasha murdered hundreds of Jews; Algiers, where Jews were massacred in 1805, 1815 and 1830 and Marrakesh, Morocco, where more than three hundred Jews were murdered between 1864 and 1880.

Decrees were issued and ordering the destruction of synagogues in Egypt and Syria (1014, 1293-4, 1301-2), Iraq (854-859, 1344) and Yemen (1676). Jews were forced to convert to Islam or face death in Yemen (1165 and 1678), Morocco (1275, 1465, 1790-92) and Baghdad (1333, 1344). Some escaped, but the Jews of Arabia who remained were pretty much completely wiped out. Islamic revisionists claim they were killed because they were literally asking for it, is their apologetic rubbish propaganda. These Islamic revisionists (Islamaniacs) claim that the Jews demanded it as per their own law. I mean, that's like the Nazis claiming they were only accommodating the Jews demand to get warm by the ovens. Like Goebbels said, the bigger the lie, the easier it is for others to believe it.

Between 1894-96, the Ottoman Turks massacred over 200,000 (dhimmi) Christian Armenians, followed by the first formal genocide of the 20th century, in 1915, at which time they slaughtered an additional 600,000 to 800,000 Armenians. Contemporary accounts from European diplomats confirm that these brutal massacres were perpetrated in the context of a formal Jihad against the Armenians who had attempted to throw off the yoke of dhimmitude by seeking equal rights and autonomy. Regarding the 1894-96 massacres, the Turkish-speaking interpreter of the British embassy reported:

> [The perpetrators] are guided in their general action by the prescriptions of the Sheri [Sharia] Law. That law prescribes that if the "rayah" [dhimmi] Christian attempts, by having recourse to foreign powers, to overstep the limits of privileges allowed them by their Mussulman [Muslim] masters, and free themselves from their bondage, their lives and property are to be forfeited, and are at the mercy of the Mussulmans. To the Turkish mind the Armenians had tried to overstep those limits by appealing to foreign powers, especially England. They therefore considered it their religious duty and a righteous thing to destroy and seize the lives and properties of the Armenians..."

The scholar Bat Ye'or confirms this reasoning, noting that the Armenian quest for reforms invalidated their "legal status," which involved a "contract" (i.e., with their Muslim Turkish rulers).

> This ...breach...restored to the umma [the Muslim community] its initial right to kill the subjugated minority [the dhimmis], [and] seize their property...

Jihad was a key aspect of pre-modern (pre 20th century) Muslim life. According to one calculation, Muhammad himself engaged in 78 battles, of which just one (the Battle of the Ditch) was defensive. Within a century after the prophet's death, Muslim armies had reached as far as India in the east and Spain in the west. Though such a dramatic single expansion was never again to be repeated, important victories in subsequent centuries included the seventeen Indian campaigns of Mahmud of Ghazna (998-1030), the battle of Manzikert opening Anatolia (1071), the conquest of Constantinople (1453), and the triumphs of Uthman dan Fodio in West Africa (1804-1817). In brief, jihad as a doctrine and practice was fully integrated into pre-modern Muslim life. The decisive turning point in the Western Europe's long struggle against pre-modern Islamic conquerors came on the afternoon of Sept. 12, 1683, during the last Turkish siege of Vienna. The ever-heroic Poles marched to save Vienna while the French (*surprise!*) and other

Europeans looked away. Louis XIV and his Frenchmen had cut a deal with the sultan, because in their view humbling the rival Habsburgs trumped the fate of Western civilization (*sound familiar?*). But led by the valiant King Jan Sobieski, severely outnumbered Polish hussars - the finest cavalry Europe ever produced - charged into the massed Ottoman ranks with lowered lances and a wild battle cry. On that fateful afternoon, the Polish cavalry struck the Turkish lines with such force that 2,000 lances shattered. The charge stunned the Ottoman army, and a hundred thousand Turks ran for the Danube. No massed army from the Islamic world has since posed such an organized threat to the West. When the Muslim armies were stopped at the gates of Vienna, over a millennium of jihad had transpired. These tremendous military successes spawned many triumphant Islamic literary writings exalting Jihadic crusades. Muslim historians recorded in detail the number of infidels slain or enslaved, the cities and villages which were pillaged, and the lands, treasure, and movable goods seized. Christian (Coptic, Armenian, Jacobite, Greek, Slav, etc.), as well as Hebrew sources, and even the scant Hindu and Buddhist writings that survived the ravages of the Muslim conquests, independently validate this narrative and complement the Muslim perspective by providing testimonies of the suffering of the non-Muslim victims of jihad wars.

In the following chronology, note how closely Islam's inception is associated with war. From 623 to 777, a span of 154 years, there are 83 major military conflicts involving the Muslims.... Muslims tell us Islam is a religion of peace, but all historical facts seem to discredit that claim rather convincingly.

Chronology of early Islam

570 – Birth of Muhammad in Mecca.
577 – Muhammad's mother dies.
595 – Muhammad marries, starts to have children.
605 – Placement of Black Stone in Ka'aba.
610 – Mohammed, in a cave, hears an angel tell him that Allah is the only true God.
613 – Muhammad's first public preaching of Islam at Mt. Hira. Gets few converts.
615 – Muslims persecuted by the Quraish.
619 – Marries Sau'da and Aisha.
620 – Institution of five daily prayers.
622 – Muhammad immigrates from Mecca to Medina, gets more converts.
623 – Battle of Waddan.
623 – Battle of Safwan.
623 – Battle of Dul-'Ashir.
624 – Raids on caravans to fund the movement begin.
624 – Zakat becomes mandatory.
624 – Battle of Badr (see chapter on Badr).
624 – Battle of Bani Salim.
624 – Battle of Eid-ul-Fitr & Zakat-ul-Fitr.
624 – Battle of Bani Qainuqa'.
624 – Battle of Sawiq.
624 – Battle of Ghatfan.
624 – Battle of Bahran.
625 – Battle of Uhud. 70 Muslims killed.
625 – Battle of Humra-ul-Asad.
625 – Battle of Banu Nudair.
625 – Battle of Dhatur-Riqa.
626 – Battle of Badru-Ukhra.
626 – Battle of Dumatul-Jandal.
626 – Battle of Banu Mustalaq Nikah.
627 – Battle of the Trench.
627 – Battle of Ahzab.
627 – Battle of Bani Quraiza.
627 – Battle of Bani Lahyan.
627 – Battle of Ghaiba.
627 – Battle of Khaibar.
628 – Muhammad signs treaty with Quarish. (The Al-Hudaybiyya agreement was signed for a period of 10 years, which became the time limit for any agreement with non-Muslims. The agreement was broken after 18 months when Muhammad's army conquered Mecca)
630 – Muhammad conquers Mecca (Quarish).
630 – Battle of Hunsin.
630 – Battle of Tabuk.
632 – Muhammad dies. ...The reign of the Caliphs begins.

632 – Abu-Bakr (Muhammad's father-in-law) along with Umar, begin a military move to enforce Islam in Arabia.
633 – Battle at Oman.
633 – Battle at Hadramaut.
633 – Battle of Kazima.
633 – Battle of Walaja.
633 – Battle of Ulleis.
633 – Battle of Anbar.
634 – Battle of Basra.
634 – Battle of Damascus.
634 – Battle of Ajnadin.
634 – Death of Hadrat Abu Bakr. Hadrat Umar Farooq becomes the Caliph.
634 – Battle of Namaraq.
634 – Battle of Saqatia.
635 – Battle of Bridge.
635 – Battle of Buwaib.
635 – Conquest of Damascus.
635 – Battle of Fahl.
636 – Battle of Yermuk.
636 – Battle of Qadsiyia.
636 – Conquest of Madain.
637 – Battle of Jalula.
638 – Battle of Yarmouk.
638 – The Muslims defeat the Romans and enter Jerusalem.
638 – Conquest of Jazirah.
639 – Conquest of Khuizistan and movement into Egypt.
641 – Battle of Nihawand.
642 – Battle of Rayy in Persia.
643 – Conquest of Azarbaijan.
644 – Conquest of Fars.
644 – Conquest of Kharan.
644 – Umar is murdered. Othman becomes Caliph.
647 – Conquest of Cypress island.
644 – Uman dies, succeeded by Caliph Uthman.
648 – Byzantine campaign begins.
651 – Naval battle against Byzantines.
654 – Islam spreads into North Africa.
656 – Uthman is murdered. Ali becomes Caliph.
658 – Battle of Nahrawan.
659 – Conquest of Egypt.
661 – Ali is murdered.
662 – Egypt falls to Islam rule.
666 – Sicily is attacked by Muslims.
677 – Siege of Constantinople.
687 – Battle of Kufa.
691 – Battle of Deir ul Jaliq.
700 – Sufism takes root as a sect.
700 – Military campaigns in North Africa.
702 – Battle of Deir ul Jamira.
711 – Muslims invade Gibraltar.
711 – Conquest of Spain.
713 – Conquest of Multan.
716 – Invasion of Constantinople.
732 – Battle of Tours in France.
740 – Battle of the Nobles.
741 – Battle of Bagdoura in North Africa.
744 – Battle of Ain al Jurr.
746 – Battle of Rupar Thutha.
748 – Battle of Rayy.
749 – Battle of Isfahan.
749 – Battle of Nihawand.
750 – Battle of Zab.
772 – Battle of Janbi in North Africa.
777 – Battle of Saragossa in Spain.

As this chronology shows, in the 7th century A.D. Muhammad's Bedouins defeated the Persian and eastern Roman empires, and conquered the Middle East, North Africa, and Spain. This period, referred to as Islam's 'golden years', is what many Muslims aspire to be restored. The invaders eventually were stopped in the east in 718 at the city walls of Constantinople, and in the west in 732 some 200 miles from Paris. There followed another thousand years of seesaw wars on sea and land before the last Middle Eastern attack on a major European city, Vienna, which was repulsed in 1683. Those who expect Muslims to drop their belligerence toward the West, which has existed since Islam's founding in the 7th century, expect them to jettison core values of their faith - something for which there is no precedent in Islamic history. Although nowadays nothing seems less tolerated than pessimism, yet in relation to Islam this attitude is in fact simply just realism. While Muslims in the West live in peace, prosperity and religious liberty, Christians and other Infidels in Muslim lands have been, are now, and will continue to be persecuted, driven out, killed, or forced to convert and call themselves Muslims.

Non-Muslim Christian Violence

Undeniably, Christians have in the past also committed despicable acts in the name of their religion, and in recent history the Serbia conflicts and the Protestant-Catholic Northern-Ireland clashes stand out as examples. Detractors will continue to try to deflect criticism by pointing out such hatred and violence conducted in the name of Christianity. Though it is true that there has been many atrocities committed by misguided Christians (Spanish Inquisition, the Salem witch-hunts, and others), do not lose focus on the problem at hand today. Remember all those atrocities are diametrically opposed with Christian scripture and philosophy where the greatest commandment was affirmed by Christ to be:

> "Thou shalt love the Lord thy God with all thy heart, and with all thy soul, and with all thy mind. This is the first and great commandment. And the second is like unto it, Thou shalt love thy neighbor as thyself. On these two commandments hang all the law and the prophets" [Matt. 22:37-40].

So the basic tenet of the Christian faith is that people are the children of God, created in His image, and are all of value to Him. The basic tenet of Islam is that some people are chosen by God to be Muslim, but the rest are -not- the people of God, and that a Muslims duty is to expedite Allah's plan for non-believers to be converted ...or dispatched to hell! There are three major differences and distinctions that can be drawn between Christian crimes and the acts committed in Islam's name. The **first** difference is that the unfortunate events were limited in both time and scope ...they had an end. The **second** distinction is that terrorists acting from Christian cultures always did their vile deeds in violation its scriptural teaching (the words and example of Christ), not in fulfillment of it, as in Muhammad's Islam. The **third** dissimilarity is that people from Christian cultures who perform terrorist acts against others are recognized as criminals, not worshiped as heroes.

Shortly after Mohammed's death, the warriors of Islam struck out against Christians with enormous energy. Palestine, Syria, and Egypt -- once the most heavily Christian areas in the world -- quickly succumbed. By the eighth century, Muslim armies had conquered all of Christian North Africa and Spain. In the eleventh century, the Seljuk Turks conquered Asia Minor (modern Turkey), which had been Christian since the time of St. Paul. The Byzantine Empire was reduced to little more than Greece. In desperation, the emperor in Constantinople sent word to the Christians of Western Europe asking them to aid their brothers and sisters in the East. The 'Crusades' were the response to that desperate cry.

Due to disinterest, ignorance, and the tendency of Western societies toward excessive self-criticism, misconceptions about the Crusades remain common. Generally portrayed as a series of unprovoked holy wars against Islam, they are supposed to have been the epitome of self-righteousness and intolerance -- a black stain on the history of the Catholic Church in particular and Western Christian civilization in general. Since September 11, variations of this theme have been used to explain -- even justify -- Muslim terror against the West. Former president Bill Clinton himself, in a speech at Georgetown University, fingered Muslim anger at the Crusades as the "root cause" of the present conflict.

But the truth is that the Crusades were not religiously inspired unprovoked aggressions intended to forcibly convert the non-Christian world. In *A Concise History of the Crusades*, by renowned medieval historian Thomas F. Madden, the record is set straight. The Crusades, he shows, were not the brainchild of an ambitious pope, nor were they inspired by opportunistic, cold-blooded plundering knights. What they were was a much delayed response to more than four centuries of conquests in which Muslims had already captured two thirds of what was the old Christian world. At some point, Christianity as a faith and a culture had to defend itself or be subsumed by Islam. The Crusades were that defense. The story of the Crusades is one of Western reaction to Muslim advances -- they were no more offensive than was the American invasion of Normandy.

The Crusades did not accomplish their objectives, and unfortunately the end of the medieval Crusades and withdrawal of the Christian forces did not bring an end to Muslim Jihad. Islamic states like Mamluk Egypt continued to expand in size and power, and the Ottoman Turks built the largest and most awesome state in Muslim history. The Ottoman Turks proceeded to not only conquered their fellow Muslims, thus further unifying Islam, but also continued to press westward, capturing Constantinople and plunging deep into Europe itself. Under Suleiman the Magnificent the Turks came within a hair's breadth of capturing Vienna, which would have left all of Germany at their mercy. At that point Crusades were no longer waged to rescue Jerusalem, but Europe itself. By the 15th century, the Crusades were no longer errands of mercy for a distant people but desperate attempts of one of the last remnants of Christendom to survive. Europeans began to ponder the real possibility that Islam would finally achieve its aim of conquering the entire Christian world. In 1529, Suleiman the Magnificent laid siege to Vienna. If not for a run of freak rainstorms that delayed his progress and forced him to leave behind much of his artillery, it is virtually certain that the Turks would have taken the city.

It is often asserted that Crusaders were merely mercenaries and ne'er-do-wells who took advantage of an opportunity to rob and pillage in a far away land. Recent scholarship has demolished that contrivance. The truth is that the Crusades were notoriously bad for plunder. A few people got rich, but the vast majority returned with nothing. It is also often assumed that a central goal of the Crusades was the forced conversion of the Muslim world to Christianity, but nothing could be further from the truth. Muslims who lived in Crusader-won territories were generally allowed to retain their property and livelihood, and always their religion. It was not until the 13th century that the Franciscans began conversion efforts among Muslims, but those efforts were mostly unsuccessful and finally abandoned. In any case, such efforts were by peaceful persuasion, not the threat of violence.

Although there were undoubtedly opportunist bad-apples in the barrel, the typical Crusade soldier was motivated by the same spirit that drives the US today, the spirit of freedom and self-determination, the desire to live free of the horrors faced by non-Muslims in Muslim lands. They were defending their families, communities, and friends under siege as are we. Whether we admire the Crusaders or not, it is a fact that the world we know today would not exist without their efforts. Without the Crusades, Christianity might well have followed Zoroastrianism, another of Islam's rivals, into complete extinction.

"When accusing the West of imperialism, Muslims are obsessed with the Christian Crusades but have forgotten their own, much grander Jihad. In fact, they often denounce the Crusades as the cause and starting point of the antagonism between Christianity and Islam. They are putting the cart before the horse. The Jihad is more than four hundred years older than the Crusades". – Paul Fregosi, *Jihad in the West: Muslim Conquests from the 7th to the 21st Centuries*

Chapter 7
The Qur'an on Relations with Non-Muslims

The Qur'an's View toward Christians and Jews:

Muhammad's actions against the Jews of Banu Qaynuqa, the Banu Nadir Jews, the Qurayza Jews, and several individuals identified as Jewish in the Qur'an have been previously chronicled and will not be repeated here.

An important principal in the Qur'an holds that humanity is divided according to a strict hierarchy of worth. The "People of the Book" (Jews and Christians) come in behind all other Muslims, including Women and slaves, but they do come in slightly ahead of Pagans, Buddhists, Hindus, agnostics, atheists and others who are regarded as worthless and having no soul. In fact Muslims are forbidden to even have Jewish or Christian friends, which will be further studied in the chapter "The Psychology of Jihad".

> 58:19 Shaitan (Satan) has overtaken them (the Jews). So he has made them forget the remembrance of Allah. They are the party of Shaitan (Satan). Verily, it is the party of Shaitan (Satan) that will be the losers!

> 4:76 Those who believe, fight in the Cause of Allah, and those who disbelieve, fight in the cause of Taghut (Satan, etc.). So fight you against the friends of Shaitan (Satan); Ever feeble indeed is the plot of Shaitan (Satan).

With quotes referencing Christians and Jews from the Qur'an like: – *"Worst of Creatures, Perverse, and Friends of Satan"*, it seems impossible to characterize Islam as tolerant and harmless. By one widely accepted definition of a 'Religion' (*"An organization dedicated to raising the spiritual awareness, the moral standards, the civil conduct and actions of its members, and in improving peaceful relationships with all others"*), Islam seems to fall well short of qualifying. Clearly early Islam was neither harmless nor tolerant of non-believers. Intolerance seems the cruel norm in Islamic societies throughout history, while tolerance, charity and kindness towards different cultures and religions is glaringly absent. The fruits of orthodox Islam are bitter indeed, and it is by their fruits that they can and should be judged.

Christians and Jews then and now hold a special place in Islamic theology. In the end, they were regarded with contempt by Muhammad, and were presented in a hateful manner in the Qur'an and in modern Islamic theology today. The final direction appears to be this; When Muslims have the upper hand, they are not to seek peace, instead they are expected to be ruthless in the continued destruction of all their enemies.

> 47:35 So be not weak and ask not for peace (from the enemies of Islam), while you are having the upper hand. Allah is with you, and will never decrease the reward of your good deeds.

> 48:29 Muhammad is the Messenger of Allah, and those who are with him are severe (or ruthless, vehement) against disbelievers, and merciful among themselves.

The final words reported from the mouth of the dying Muhammad were a curse on the favored 'People of the Book'. From Ibn Sa'd page 322: When the last moment of the prophet was near, he used to draw a sheet over his face; but when he felt uneasy, he removed it from his face and said: **"Allah's damnation be on the Jews and the Christians who made the graves of their prophets objects of worship."**

His appetite to do violence to non-Muslims remained unquenchable his whole life, the final words coming from his mouth a curse on those he had spent his life destroying. Despite his victories and the multitudes he had murdered, he left this world bitter he could not have done more, with instructions to his followers to carry on in that effort. The bitterness of this final utterance from their beloved prophet, as he died a painful death at the hands of a Jewish girl, obviously *still* weighs heavy on the minds and hearts of all of Islam. With revenge a glorified mandate for Muslims, it seems unlikely they will ever collectively 'get over it'.

In its attitudes toward Jews today, the Muslim world resembles Germany in the 1930s. That was a time when state-sponsored insults, cartoons, conspiracy theories, revisionist history, and sporadic violence prepared Germans for the wholesale mass murder that was to follow. Outside Israel, violence against Jews is also persistent: Jewish buildings blown up in Argentina, France, and elsewhere, Daniel Pearl's murder in Pakistan and other Jews targeted for stabbings worldwide. The essential training of their young to vilify Jews and Westerners continues to serve as the psychological preparation for this kind of murder and mayhem against Jews, and now against Americans, and tomorrow against Japanese, Chinese, Australians, New Zealanders, Vietnamese, etc etc etc, …and on and on, …until the vision of the whole world as Islamic is achieved. To decide if Islam promotes bigotry and racism, the rules governing killing of non-Muslims should always be compared to the following Islamic rule governing the killing of brothers enshrined in the Qur'an:

> And whosoever killeth a believer intentionally, his recompense shall be Hell, he shall abide therein and God's wrath shall be on him and His curse, and (there) is prepared for him a great torment (4:93)

The Qur'an on Relations with Non-Muslim Family Members:

Earlier it was pointed out that Muslims broke ties of allegiance and friendship with allied tribes and near family members. The Qur'an takes this a step further. Sura 58:22 shows that family blood ties are broken. Islam has an anti-family element, causing Muslims to fight and kill relatives if they reject Muhammad's rule. The principals (and purpose) governing Muslim conduct with non-believing relatives will be further studied in the chapter "The Psychology of Jihad".

Muslims who Leave Islam

Just as Christians organizing against the core belief in Jesus Christ are no longer considered Christians, Muslims who actively oppose Muhammad's declarations and example of jihad would have ceased to be Muslims. But Islam goes well beyond that concept of losing fellowship. Sharia (Islamic law) is based on the Qur'an, the example of Muhammad (*sunna*) and the consensus (*idjmaa*). Under this law, anyone falling away from faith in Islam commits an "unforgivable sin". Such "apostates" must be taken into custody by force, and called on to repent. Anyone so confronted and who does not immediately repent and turn back to Islam has forfeited his life, and is to be put to death by the state. While this is not carried out on a regular basis in the many Islamic lands practicing Sharia, the threat is ever present. Sudan, and Mauritania address the issue of apostasy in their penal codes. In the Sudanese Penal Code of 1991, article 126. 2, we read: "Whoever is guilty of apostasy is invited to repent over a period to be determined by the tribunal. If he persists in his apostasy and was not recently converted to Islam, he will be put to death." The Penal Code of Mauritania of 1984, article 306 reads: "…All Muslims guilty of apostasy, either spoken or by overt action will be asked to repent during a period of three days. If he does not repent during this period, he is condemned to death as an apostate, and his belongings confiscated by the State Treasury".

In the Hadith there are many references demanding the death penalty for apostasy. According to Ibn Abbas the Prophet said, "Kill him who changes his religion", or "behead him". The only serious argument is as to the method and timing of death penalty implementation. There is a logical reason why Muhammad dictated that apostasy rank so high an offence as to be worthy of the death penalty. Muhammads Islam was largely a military movement in the 7th, 8th and 9th centuries, so he saw apostasy as a defection to the enemy. Traitors in military campaigns were always executed by military organizations of that region and others, and Islam was and is a warrior's faith designed to support military campaigns. One of Islam's most respected theologians and prolific writers in the last century, Pakistani Abu'l Ala Mawdudi, insists that both Qur'an and Hadith demand an apostate's execution. He quotes the Qur'an (9:11-12) and the canonized Hadith: "Any person, i.e. Muslim, who has changed his religion, kill him" (Al-Bukhari, Vol. 9, p. 45). The Islamic scholar, Majid Khadduri, agrees that Qur'anic commentaries say a believer who turns back from his religion must be killed if he persists in disbelief (p. 150).

Muhammad was not content to conquer by force, or kill those that merely opposed him physically or verbally; he also taught that Muslims who leave the Islamic faith are to be murdered. Here are some more quotes from Bukhari's collection of Hadith. Remember, Bukhari's Hadith is the second most important writing in Islam, following the Qur'an.

Bukhari, volume 9, #17

"Narrated Abdullah: Allah's Messenger said, "The blood of a Muslim who confesses that none has the right to be worshipped but Allah and that I am His Messenger, cannot be shed except in three cases: in Qisas (equality in punishment) for murder, a married person who commits illegal sexual intercourse and the one who reverts from Islam (Apostate) and leaves the Muslims."

Bukhari volume 9, #57

Narrated Ikrima, "Some atheists were brought to Ali and he burnt them. The news of this event, reached Ibn Abbas who said, "If I had been in his place, I would not have burnt them, as Allah's messenger forbade it, saying, "Do not punish anybody with Allah's punishment (fire)." I would have killed them according to the statement of Allah's Messenger, "Whoever changed his Islamic religion, then kill him."

Bukhari volume 9, #64

Narrated Ali, "Whenever I tell you a narration from Allah's messenger, by Allah, I would rather fall down from the sky, then ascribe a false statement to him, but if I tell you something between me and you, (not a Hadith), then it was indeed a trick (i.e., I may say things just to cheat my enemy). No doubt I heard Allah's messenger saying, "During the last days there will appear some young foolish people, who will say the best words, but their faith will not go beyond their throats (i.e. they will leave the faith) and will go out from their religion as an arrow goes out of the game. So, wherever you find them, kill them, for whoever kills them shall have reward on the Day of Resurrection."

"Narrated Anas: Some people from the tribe of Ukl came to the Prophet and embraced Islam. The climate of Medina did not suit them, so the Prophet ordered them to go to the (herd of milch) camels of charity to drink their milk and urine (as a medicine). They did so, and after they had recovered from their ailment they turned renegades (reverted from Islam, irtada) and killed the shepherd of the camels and took the camels away. The Prophet sent (some people) in their pursuit and so they were caught and brought, and the Prophet ordered that their hands and legs should be cut off and that their eyes should be branded with heated pieces of iron, and that their cut hands and legs should not be cauterized, till they die".

Not only did Muhammad teach that Muslims are to murder those that have left Islam, "wherever you find them", he further taught that a Muslim who commits this type of murder of fellow Muslims will also be doing God's service and will be rewarded. It is in this spirit that so many 'honor killings' continue to occur in Muslim communities. The following is a news release of one such killing that just happened to be recorded, whereas thousands of other incidents have occurred with no record (there are many such dark secrets to for Islam to hide).

November 1989 - **St. Louis, Missouri** - The FBI inadvertently tape-recorded the entire episode of a teenage girl being killed by her Palestinian father and Brazilian mother (the Feds were looking for evidence of terrorism, which they also found). Apparently their daughter had not lived according to their view of Islam. In a ghastly eight-minute sequence, Zein Isa stabbed his daughter Palestina thirteen times with a butcher's knife as his wife held the girl down and responded to Palestina's pleas for help with a brutal "Shut up!" The killing ends with Zein screaming; "Die! Die quickly! Die quickly! ... Quiet, little one! ... Die, my daughter, die!" By this time, she is dead. The 1989 killing in St. Louis was captured on a court-approved FBI telephone tap of a Palestinian, Zein Isa, who was suspected of supporting terrorist causes. Agents were not listening as the killing took place. The FBI ultimately handed over the tape, which was used to help convict the couple of murder. An egregious example of a family honor killing, permitted in some Islamic cultures, the murderous couple killed their daughter to insure she did not expose their terrorist plans and affiliations.

Islamic Dissent

The problem with attempting any real political reform in Muslim lands or with Muslim law is that anyone desiring change must first find fault with the 'perfect' Islamic government and judicial system. This usually leads to charges of blasphemy, which quickly puts the 'quash' on dissenters and their supporters. To document this dilemma, we look to our partner in the War on Terror. Those accused of blasphemy under Article 295/C of the Pakistan Penal Code may not obtain bail and are held until trial. If pronounced guilty, they face a mandatory death sentence. For those acquitted, the temptation to kill them anyway (and obtain the promised reward promised by Muhammad) seems too great for the 'innocent' to safely remain in the country, so survival dictates they escape to Europe. Many victims of the Pakistani blasphemy laws have failed to even survive prison, and even a number of those tried and then acquitted have been murdered following their release. As recently as July 2002, Mohammed Yousaf was shot dead inside the Central Gaol in Lahore while awaiting his appeal. On 7th February 2003, Mushtaq Zafar, a 55 year-old accused of blasphemy was shot dead on his way home from the High Court. And in June 2003, Naseem Bibi, a victim of a gang rape by police, was charged with blasphemy and murdered in prison before her trial could begin. Fundamentalists have also intimidated defense lawyers, and even a High Court judge was murdered after acquitting an accused man. In the city of Multan in Pakistan, Ayub Masih (Christian), who had previously been accused of insulting the Prophet Muhammad under the "Blasphemy Law", is being held in solitary confinement in a 4x6 foot cell. He also faces the death penalty with well over 100 others similarly accused as of this writing. Pakistan's infamous blasphemy laws are widely abused with devastating effectiveness to make false accusations against Christians and Ahmadis, as well as business rivals and political opponents. And Pakistan is a US ally with a relatively moderate government; one can only imagine the abuses that are occurring in more fundamentalist lands.

The Associated Press - Nov. 7, 2002 **TEHRAN, Iran** — A prominent reformist scholar has been sentenced to death on charges of insulting Islam's prophet and questioning the hard-line clergy's interpretation of Islam. A court in Hamedan in western Iran sentenced university professor Hashem Aghajari to death, Saleh Nikbakht told The Associated Press. Aghajari was detained in August after a closed hearing in Hamedan where he made a speech in June questioning the hard-line interpretations of the ruling clerics. Nikbakht said Aghajari, a top member of the reformist political party, Islamic Revolution Mujahedeen Organization, was also sentenced to 74 lashes, banned from teaching for 10 years and exiled to three remote Iranian cities for eight years. Iranian courts often impose such multiple sentences in cases where it wants to make an example of the accused. In cases where the death sentence is imposed, the others are not carried out. Nikbakht insisted his client had not said anything that insulted the Prophet Muhammad, as the charges alleged. "There has never been a word insulting the prophet in Aghajari's speech. This verdict is nothing but a rule against Iran's national interests," Nikbakht said. In his speech, Aghajari had said clerics' teachings on Islam were considered sacred simply because they were part of history, and he questioned why clerics were the only ones authorized to interpret Islam. Later, he was charged with insulting Islamic sanctities and the court described his speech as blasphemous.

The Herald - Jan 20, 2005 UK - Hizbollah threatens UK suicide attacks - HIZBOLLAH, the hardline religious group, yesterday threatened to carry out suicide attacks in London in an attempt to kill a UK-based Iranian exile television presenter said to have made insulting comments about Islam. Manouchehr Fouladvand, on the US-based Farsi language MA-TV, has been accused of mocking Mohammed and the Koran. There have been demands in Iran for the broadcaster's death. Mojtaba Bigdeli, spokesman for Iran's Hizbollah group, warned the British government must ban the satellite channel, run by Iranian exiles, within 30 days or face the consequences. "After one month, our commandos will carry out suicide attacks in London against the shameless presenter of the channel. He has crossed our red lines by insulting our prophet and Islamic values." Mr Bigdeli said Hizbollah had the approval of leading clerics to kill him. The case echoes the Iranian fatwa against the author, Salman Rushdie.
www.theherald.co.uk/news/31855.html

This should help explain the realities faced by good Muslims wanting reforms, justice, democracy, and other freedoms we take for granted. It should also help us understand that, although there are no real reform movements in staunchly Islamic lands, this does not mean that the people are content with their system of governance, or even with their Religion (which is the same thing). The lack of visible opposition is a reflection of the simple fact that the totalitarian control system in play is very *very* effective.

Suspected Collaborators

The Associated Press - April 23 2002 **HEBRON, West Bank** - Palestinian militiamen killed three suspected collaborators in Hebron Tuesday ... A mob strung up two of the battered, bullet-punctured bodies, and some brought their children to see the gruesome act of revenge. Hooded vigilantes shot the three alleged informers and dumped their bound and gagged bodies on the same spot where a missile from an Israel helicopter gunship killed Marwan Zalloum, a commander of the Al Aqsa Martyrs Brigades militia, in a targeted attack just hours before. The militia is linked to Palestinian leader Yasser Arafat's Fatah movement. "The fate of all collaborators will be like this," one of the masked men told reporters as he and the others sped away in a car. A similar action occurred in Ramallah on Monday, the public shooting of three alleged collaborators on the main square of Ramallah, while a large crowd watched as they lay on the ground, withering in pain. Bystanders tried to block approaching ambulances, but the three were eventually taken to a city hospital where one later died. ... several dozen alleged informers have been killed by fellow Palestinians in the past 19 months of fighting with Israel. In Hebron, a large crowd quickly gathered around the corpses lying in Salam Street. One of the bodies was strung up by one leg from an electricity pylon and stripped by the crowd down to his green underwear, his blood-soaked shirt pulled over his head to reveal deep cuts and bruises. Another body was strung up from a lamppost. People stuffed burning cigarettes in the bullet holes in the torso. Some kicked, spat and threw rocks at the corpses.

The three men suffered multiple gunshot wounds in the head and body, with their hands tied behind their backs. Their limbs also appeared broken, though it was not clear whether the injuries were inflicted before or after they died. Seven men in a car, all wearing woolen hoods or keffiyehs wrapped around their faces, claimed responsibility. The driver of the car, wearing a headband of the Al Aqsa Martyrs Brigade, told a reporter that the killings were in revenge for Zalloum's death (Zalloum and his bodyguard were killed in an Israeli missile attack). Thousands of people paraded past the bodies until a white municipal pickup truck came to take them away 3 hours later. As each body was thrown into the back of the truck, the crowd clapped, cheered, whistled, and chanted "Allahu akbar," or God is great. Some men lifted small children in the air for a better look. Others climbed up the stairs of a nearby mosque or onto rooftops for an unobstructed view. No one in the crowd objected to the violence. Many were smiling. Men whistled their approval on the street and women yelled from rooftops. Young children wandered past the sticky pool of blood on the ground and stared. "No problem," said a 16-year-old boy standing nearby. "They deserved it. They talked to Israel." But a 20-year-old woman who walked quickly past the crowd disapproved. "What will the world think when they see this?" she asked.

The Associated Press - Aug 7, 2003 **West Bank, Israel** - Palestinian militants executed a suspected collaborator with Israeli intelligence in the central square of the West Bank town of Ramallah. The Al Aqsa Martyrs' Brigades, linked to Palestinian leader Yasser Arafat's Fatah movement, carried out the summary execution not far from Arafat's office. Witnesses said three gunmen pulled the man into a car and drove to the center of town. Then one of the gunmen pulled the man from the car and shouted, "In the name of the Al Aqsa Martyrs' Brigades, we carry out the sentence of death," and shot him. He was identified as Samer Sharour, in his early 20s. Doctors said he was hit by six bullets in the head and chest. During the past decade, Palestinian militants have executed dozens of suspected collaborators, sometimes hanging their bodies in public squares, drawing criticism from human rights groups. The Palestinian Authority also has publicly executed several such suspects after quick trials.

Reuters – Aug 7, 2003 - **Srinagar, India** - Muslim separatist guerrillas in Indian Kashmir beheaded two people, one of them a teacher, in the latest violence in the disputed Himalayan region, police said. The teacher was abducted in the Anantnag district, south of Kashmir's main city Srinagar, and later beheaded because the rebels suspected he was an informer for the security forces. "Militants abducted and later beheaded Abdul Ahad Sheikh and his son," a police official said. The killings took place in Baramulla district in northern Kashmir. Militants also beheaded a villager in a neighboring district, also because he was suspected of being an informer, he said.

The Associated Press - Jul 12, 2004 **Sringar, India** - (Muslim) Militants Mutilate a Girl in Kashmir; Guerrillas chopped off the ears, nose and tongue of a teenage girl they suspected of helping police Monday, while other violence in Indian-controlled Kashmir left at least eight people dead, authorities said. The girl was held captive for eight days before the rebels abandoned her in a field outside the village of Manoh, about 200 miles southwest of Srinagar, the capital of India's Jammu-Kashmir state, a police statement said.

Reuters - Jul 26, 2004 **Jammu, India** - Separatist (Muslim) rebels decapitated a 55-year-old man and his two children in Indian Kashmir because they suspected them of being informers for security forces, police said on Monday. A group of nine militants barged into the home of Mohammed Shafi in a remote village in Rajouri district and beheaded him, a police officer said. They also killed his 22-year-old son and 15-year-old daughter, the officer said. "The militants thought he worked for security forces in the area," he said. The village, in the rugged mountains of southern Jammu and Kashmir, is a five hour trek from the nearest road. Militants fighting Indian rule in Kashmir have in the past killed men and women they believe to be working for the Indian army, along with their families, to deter others. In another incident, separatists aimed a grenade at soldiers visiting a hospital in northern Kashmir, wounding 26 civilians and two soldiers. "Militants lobbed a grenade near the outpatient department of a government hospital in Baramulla, where some Border Security Force personnel had come for treatment," a police officer said.

The Islamic exploitation of even believers has is well demonstrated by an incident in Pakistan the middle of April 1994:

> Hafiz Sajjad Tariq of Gujranwala in Pakistan accidentally dropped a copy of the Qur'an in a fireplace. As it caught fire, people of the locality became aflame with rage. Not caring that Sajjad was a pious Muslim devoted to exalt holiness of the Scripture (Qur'an), they alleged that he had desecrated the Word of God. As mullahs of the area heard of it, they instantly issued Fatwas of apostasy against Sajjad. Like hawks, the fundamentalists swooped down on him, each hoping that his blow would dispatch the victim to hell assuring him (the assailant) a seat in paradise. As they were hitting him, someone shouted that he was being dished out an un-Islamic punishment because he must be stoned to death. By then, they had broken his ribs and he was not able to walk. A gallant police officer intervened and locked him up with a view to saving him from mob-violence. As the news spread, a large crowd of frenzied Muslims appeared before the local police- station demanding his

immediate release. The Police Inspector, instead of enforcing the law, fell for the temptation of establishing himself as the champion of Islam and handed Sajjad to the attackers. They started stoning him mercilessly and thereafter set his body on fire. If this were not enough, they tied his corpse to a powerful motorcycle and dragged it through the streets for two hours! After this pious show of Islamic morality, they felt that they had done enough to avenge the honor of the Prophet to whom the Qur'an had been revealed.

Chapter 8
Islamic Honesty and Honor

With regard to honesty and lying, Islam has some semblance to other religions. There are sections in the Qur'an where honesty is praised as a virtue, and in a general sense lying is forbidden. The Qur'an says, *"Truly, Allah does not guide one who transgresses and lies."*[Surah 40:28]. In the Hadith, Mohammed was quoted as saying: *"Be honest because honesty leads to goodness, and goodness leads to Paradise. Beware of falsehood because it leads to immorality, and immorality leads to Hell."* This approach to communication and ethics is laudable, but unfortunately for many in the world, that direction appears to be intended as a standard limited to Muslim-to-Muslim relations, and does not necessarily apply to non-believers, whom the Islamic God *'does not love'*. Unlike most religions, within Islam there are certain provisions under which lying is not only tolerated, but actually encouraged. Bluntly stated, Islam permits Muslims to lie anytime that they perceive that their own well-being, or that of Islam, is threatened. The book "The spirit of Islam," by the Muslim scholar, Afif A. Tabbarah was written to promote Islam. On page 247, Tabbarah stated:

> "Lying is not always bad, to be sure; there are times when telling a lie is more profitable and better for the general welfare, and for the settlement of conciliation among people, than telling the truth. To this effect, the Prophet says: 'He is not a false person who (through lies) settles conciliation among people, supports good or says what is good."

Outlined in the Qur'an and other Islamic sacred works is a description of the murder of one "Kab Ashraf" (*see Chapter 4, Incident #4*). In this carefully chronicled event we learn that the Prophet Muhammad specifically sanctioned the use of deceit and lies to kill a troublesome opponent. For some time after his arrival in Medina, Muhammad continued to have problems with various people who refused to acknowledge his claim to prophethood, and had several critics murdered prior to this Kab Ashraf. Kab, a prominent local, made it known that he did not believe in Muhammad, yet never lifted a weapon against any Muslim. He only voiced his opinion against Muhammad, and allegedly made up some unsavory poems about Muslim women. Muhammad saw him as a threat, and had him killed in the night. When Kab's volunteer assassins sought permission from the Prophet to speak falsely to gain the trust of their victim, Muhammad replied: *"Yes. ... You may say it."* Ibn Ishaq quoted Him as answering, *"Say what you like, for you are free in the matter"*.

There are other events in the life of Mohammed where he lied and instructed his followers to do the same, rationalizing that the prospect of success in missions to extend Islam's influence overrode Allah's initial prohibitions against lying. An example similar to the assassination of Kab Ashraf just referenced can be found in the story of the killing of Shaaban Ibn Khalid al-Hazly. It was rumored that Shaaban was gathering an army to wage war on Mohammed. Mohammed retaliated by ordering Abdullah Ibn Anis to kill Shaaban. Again, the would-be assassin asked the prophet's permission to lie. Mohammed agreed and then even told Abdullah exactly what lie to tell. He instructed him to lie by stating that he was a member of the Khazaa clan. So when Shaaban saw Abdullah coming, he asked him, "From what tribe are you?" Abdullah answered, "From Khazaa ... I have heard that you are gathering an army to fight Mohammed and I came to join you." Abdullah then started walking with Shaaban telling him how Mohammed came to them with the heretical teachings of Islam, and complained how Mohammed badmouthed the Arab patriarchs and ruined the Arab's hopes. They continued in conversation until they arrived at Shaaban's tent. Shaaban's companions departed and Shaaban invited Abdullah to come inside and rest. Abdullah sat there until the atmosphere was quiet and he sensed that everyone was asleep. Abdullah severed Shaaban's head and carried it to Mohammed as a trophy. When Mohammed sighted Abdullah, he jubilantly shouted, "Your face has been triumphant (Aflaha al- wajho)." Abdullah returned the greeting by saying, "It is your face, Apostle of Allah, who has been triumphant. (Aflaha wajhoka, ye rasoul Allah)."

Most Muslims are familiar with the principles and concepts of Islam that justify lying in situations where they sense the need to do so. Principals taught by Muhammad such as *"War is deception"*, *"The necessities justify the forbidden"*, and, *"If faced by two evils, choose the lesser of the two"*, are derived from passages in the Qur'an and the Hadith. But when confronted with writings of their own revered scholars on the subject of dishonesty, Muslims hold true to form and in the spirit of what they know is allowed, will lie about lying. An example of Islamic deception is that Muslim activists always quote the passages of the Qur'an from the early part of Mohammed's ministry while living in Mecca. These texts are peaceful and exemplify tolerance towards those that are not followers of Islam. All the while, they are fully aware that most of these passages were abrogated (cancelled and replaced) by passages that came after he migrated to Medina. Another example is in the conduct of Saudi Arabia in the war on terror. Words of support and promises of reform flow easily to Americans, but actions to date demonstrate they are only words, meant for our consumption only.

Unfortunately, passages from the Qur'an clearly reveal that lying is permitted, particularly in reference to non-believers in conflict with Muslims. It is also clear that if forced to do so, Muslims may lie under oath and can even falsely deny faith in Allah, as long as they maintain the profession of faith in their hearts. In the Qur'an, Allah says: *"Allah will not call you to account for thoughtlessness (vain) in your oaths, but for the intention in your hearts; and He is Oft-forgiving, Most Forbearing."* Surah 2:225. The principal also has support in the Qur'an 3:28 and 16:106.

In the Hadith, Mohammed emphasizes the same concept. From "Ehiaa Oloum al-Din," by the famous Islamic scholar al-Ghazali, Vol. 3: PP.284-287:

> One of Mohammed's daughters, Umm Kalthoum, testified that she had never heard the Apostle of Allah condone lying, except in these three situations: 1) For reconciliation among people. 2) In war. 3) Amongst spouses, to keep peace in the family.

One passage from the Hadith quotes Mohammed as saying: "The sons of Adam are accountable for all lies except those uttered to help bring reconciliation between Muslims." The following quote demonstrates the broadness of situations in which the prophet permitted lying. *"The sons of Adam are accountable for all lies with these exceptions: During war because war is deception, to reconcile among two quarreling men, and for a man to appease his wife."* Considering that Islam has been in a perpetual state of war with non-believers, it appears there is neither accountability nor any practical limitation to deceiving non-Muslims.

The Arabic word, "Takeyya", means "to prevent," or guard against. The principle of Al-taqiyya (also called taqiah, Al-takeyya, Al-taqiyah, or kitman) conveys the understanding that Muslims are permitted to lie as a preventive measure against anticipated harm to one's self or fellow Muslims. This principle gives Muslims the liberty to lie under circumstances that they perceive as life threatening. They can even deny the faith, if they do not mean it in their hearts. Al-taqiyya is based on the following Quranic verse:

> "Let not the believers Take for friends or helpers Unbelievers rather than believers: if any do that, in nothing will there be help from Allah: except by way of precaution (prevention), that ye may Guard yourselves from them (prevent them from harming you.) But Allah cautions you (To remember) Himself; for the final goal is to Allah." Surah 3: 28

According to this verse a Muslim can pretend to befriend infidels (in violation of the teachings of Islam) and even display false adherence with their unbelief to prevent them from harming Muslims. Under this concept of Taqiyya, if under the threat of force, it is legitimate for Muslims to act contrary to their faith. The devout are taught that in such circumstances the following actions are acceptable: Drinking wine and alcoholic beverages, abandoning prayers, skipping fasting during Ramadan, renouncing belief in Allah and Muhammad, kneeling in homage to a deity other than Allah, and uttering insincere oaths and covenants.

Al-taqiyya and dissimulation refer to the practice of Muslims blatantly lying to non-Muslims, but the principal goes beyond mere lying for propaganda purposes. In accordance with this license to deceive, during time of weakness the Qur'an allows Muslims to have both a declared agenda and a secret agenda. The theological principle of Taqiyya means hiding one's true beliefs and intentions to confuse ones adversaries and enable mujahedeen to operate freely amongst enemies. The word comes from a root meaning "to guard against, to keep (oneself)". From the verb *Ittaqu*, it means linguistically to 'dodge the threat'. In this vein, a Muslim, if necessary, may eat pork, drink alcohol, and even verbally deny the Islamic faith, as long as it is with the tongue only, and he does not "mean it in his heart". A believer is taught he can make any statement as long as the 'heart is comfortable'. If the end result of the lie is perceived by the Muslim to be good for Islam or useful to bringing someone to "submission" to Allah, then pretty much any lie or act can be sanctioned. Indeed it is common practice for Muslims, especially leaders, to lie about any war or conflict involving Muslims vs. non-Muslims. Muslims reverting to deceptive tactics unashamedly do so with full knowledge they are adhering to Mohammed's words and example, so they operate without conscience believing they are absolved from any negative divine consequence. Even the Islamic God, Allah himself, is described in the Qur'an in the most literal translation from Arabic as; "the best of deceivers." [Surah 8:30] Another English translation goes; "They schemed - but God also schemed. God is most profound in His machinations". So it appears that the deity Muslims worship is a God of deception, or at least to non-believers. This Sura relates that when non-believers deceived and schemed, planning evil against Muslims, that Allah also schemed, and his deceptions were superior. If you can wrap your mind around the concept of a perfect lie, you can understand better the Muslim God.

In state-to-state relations Al-taqiyya political version is known as Kitman. Politically it means to project whatever image is necessary and advantageous in order to gain concessions from an adversary. The accepted principle of sanctioning lying for the cause of Islam bears grave implications in the sphere of international politics. The usual method of civilized diplomacy and negotiations might normally culminate in state treaties or other articles of agreement, but must be based on honesty, trust, and honored by both parties. But this principle of sanctioning lying for the cause of Islam implies that true lasting negotiated settlements may not be possible, as Muslims today seem to be taking ever greater liberty in expanding the parameters and scope of circumstances under which they are permitted to lie or use deceptive tactics. Knowing this, can non-Muslims expect anything more than deception and double-speak from Muslim leaders? Will nation-to-nation treaties with Islamic states yield the hoped for peace and benefits to the non-Muslim participants to such agreements? Unfortunately, when dealing with Muslims, one must keep in mind the implications of the principle of taqiyya, in that Muslims can communicate something with apparent sincerity, when in reality they may have in their hearts the opposite agenda. In AD 628 – Muhammad ongoing military conquests were not going well, and so for tactical purposes he signed a treaty with the Meccan Quarish tribe. (The Al-Hudaybiyya agreement between the Prophet and the Quarish was signed for a period of 10 years, which became, in Islamic tradition, the time limit for any agreement with non-Muslims). The Al-Hudaybiyya agreement was broken just 18 months later when Mohammed's army advanced and conquered Mecca. Arafat's signatures all had about the same value.

Have you noticed that every time militant Arab Muslim groups find themselves in a losing position in conflicts they initiated, they immediately proclaim they are ready to suspend hostilities and begin negotiations? They suddenly become concerned with victims, saying "Peace" so often it becomes meaningless, yet Westerners fall for it every time. Arab Muslims have an insidious habit of negotiating falsely, a tactic that is all too easy to pass off to ignorant Westerners longing for peace. Terrorists who rise up and kill (Saddam Hussein in his time, Yasser Arafat, Osama Bin Laden, the Janjaweed in Darfur, and now Iraqi terrorists Moqtada Sadr and al-Zarqawi) never stop or sue for peace when finding success. But when hit hard and causalities mount, they immediately plead for negotiations, only to start attacking again after resting and regrouping. In most prior wars involving nation states, Islamic countries howl for international intervention only when they start to lose battles they started. Nations need to start learning these rather transparent lessons of history. When they say they want to negotiate a fair ending to the conflict, it's a trick to call for a truce breather - called a "hudna". Perhaps it's forgivable for Western governments to make one or two mistakes in negotiations with Islamists, but when the same mistake is made time and again - then it is no longer mere error, its pure stupidity. Arafat frequently used this trick, relying upon the ignorance of the West. On May 10, 1994, 10 days after signing the First Gaza-Jericho agreement, Arafat spoke in English at a Johannesburg mosque explaining to his people why he was returning to the Peace table. He was unknowingly recorded to say; "This agreement, I am not considering it more than the agreement which had been signed between our prophet Muhammad and Quraysh..." To his own people in Arabic, Arafat had often repeated this illusion to the Hudaibiya Treaty. Although obscure to us, Palestinians understood perfectly well what he meant. Under the promise of peaceful 'accommodation' or 'truce', Arafat had made and broken many agreements over time. When Arafat's terrorists were stalking around the streets of Amman, Jordan in the 1960s, he made 26 separate agreements with King Hussein, breaking every single one. He went too far when he put out a contract on the King's brother, wherein the King finally declared war in September 1970 and slaughtered 7,000 of Arafat's Terrorists. Palestinians call that purge "Black September", often naming Terror attacks after it. To Israel and Westerners, the Oslo accords were supposed to provide the foundation for peace, but to Islamists they were never more than a temporary "hudna" intended to be broken from the beginning. Even after violating one cease-file, when the situation on the ground proves too dangerous for them, it is all too easy to follow it with another truce. This kind of "Bait & Switch" tactic harks back to Mohammed when he made the previously mentioned treaty with the Quarish he could not conquer, while he gathered a much stronger Muslim army and broke it 1 ½ years later. Because of the difficulty he had subduing them, after they surrendered Mohammed had all 600 men from the city slaughtered, and sold the women and children into slavery. This tactic is a template still in use because Muslims have enjoyed so much success with it.

As Muslims are instructed by the eminent Islamic scholar Imam Abu Hammid Ghazali (Al-Ghazali), who is one of the most famous and respected Muslim theologians of all time: *"Speaking is a means to achieve objectives. If a praiseworthy aim is attainable through both telling the truth and lying, it is unlawful to accomplish through lying because there is no need for it. When it is possible to achieve such an aim by lying but not by telling the truth, it is permissible to lie if attaining the goal is permissible."* (The Reliance of the Traveler, sec r8.2, pg 745[13]) By this logic, the praiseworthy, permissible goal of "making the whole world Islamic by Jihad" sanctifies any dishonest statement made to any non-Muslim opposing that effort. Muhammad said, *"War is deception"* and demonstrated this principal in his numerous Jihadic campaigns. Like Muhammad, it appears that a majority of Muslims consider the act of lying to non-Muslims in the advance of Islam to be a good work. This right to lie is not immoral in Muslim minds for the same reasons that give them the right to murder, rape and enslave infidels under the holy banner of Jihad. Amir Taheri, an Iranian author of ten books on the Middle East and Islam, said regarding taqiyya, "Muslims have every right to lie and to deceive their adversaries, and a promise made to a non-Muslim can be broken whenever necessary." [29]. Yasser Arafat was a master in the art of duplicity, and was respected by his fellows in part because he has enjoyed so many propaganda victories in his battle against the truth.

In a book of Arabic maxims, novelist Ayako Sono cites proverbs and truisms describing commonly understood principals of the Arabic culture[30]. The innate principals reduced to familiar sayings are hard for non-Muslims to comprehend, but are simply common sense for Arab Muslims. For instance, one popular saying goes, *"A man lacking in cunning is like an empty matchbox."* Another says, *"A well-told lie is better than an unbelievable truth."* Such guidelines and advice flow easily from a culture illuminated only by the Qur'an. This convenient morality is why few Muslims blink when they hear a spokesperson deceiving ignorant infidels claiming Islam is peaceful and tolerant. Westerners, accustomed to religious leaders and spokespersons that strive for accuracy and honesty, are inclined to assume pious Muslim representatives are similarly predisposed. Muslim representatives are aware of this inclination and delighted their task of verbally twisting Islam into a form acceptable to Americans is so easy. Although quite willing to take advantage of liberal sensibilities, behind our backs they are amused at our overall ignorance and poor awareness of Islam's mainstream goals and methods.

In mathematics, if A=B, and B=C, and C=D, then it is logical and correct to conclude that A=D. Now we know that Jihad is integral to Islam, and that war has always been a part of Jihad. We also know that for Muhammad and his followers 'War is deception'. Although not generally true in Muslim-Muslim relations, for non-believers the following same simple logic should always be kept in mind when dealing with Islamists.

Islam = Jihad, Jihad=War, War=Deception ...therefore; Islam = Deception.

It is often difficult to differentiate between "extremist" and "moderate" Muslims core values, as indeed it often appears to be more a matter of form than sustenance. But by listening carefully to their spokespersons, some conclusions can be inferred. The "extremists" tell the truth about the teachings of Islam, and have considerable, indeed overwhelming, textual authority on their side in the Qur'an, Hadith, and the Sira. The "moderates", so eagerly repeated and invoked, are actually more ill-defined, underanalyzed, and poorly understood, and have almost no textual authority on their side. The timidity of the supposed larger Muslim community has its roots in acute self-awareness that they are, to the degree that they disavow Jihad, incomplete or bad Muslims. As such this supposed majority, so weak in both foundation and conviction, can be nothing but inept at moderating the much more powerful and authoritive extremist elements amongst them. Most remain silent out of embarrassment, timidity, piety, fear, reverence, or sometimes a desire to support the deliberate religiously-sanctioned Islamic deception machine. More often than they care to admit, Muslims know all about what is expected of them by their religion, and much of what we hear from the Muslim mainstream is simple Taqiyya. After all, to go against true Islam is a death sentence in this life and the next. Although most Muslims will not participate in religiously sanctioned violence and treachery against their own country and neighbors, most are perfectly content to ride the coat tails of those willing to bloody their hands doing the dirty work of the God they worship, as taught by the word and example of His Messenger, Muhammad. Former Muslims often state that the idea of Moderate Islam is a myth, nothing more than a western illusion as such an idea presupposes rejection of some or all core tenants of Islam. Anyone who rejects, or wishes to reform even one single teaching of the Qur'an is considered to be a renegade and an apostate. Should we count on moderate Muslims coming to our rescue in sufficient numbers and strength? Survival dictates we not throw all our eggs in that basket until it becomes something more than an Arabian mirage.

Historically, Jihadic deception was a formidable weapon, even more powerful than Western methods. This is because it has a civilization/global dimensions versus the narrow State interest in classical Western methods of intelligence gathering and subversive tactics deployed on a much smaller scale. The original Fatah refers to the Arab-Islamic invasion and conquest of the upper Middle East and the outside world. In the early years of the Islamic conquest of the Arabian Peninsula, the concept of Al-taqiyya was devised to achieve success against the enemy (non-Muslims). Accordingly, Muslims were granted the right to infiltrate the Dar el-Harb (war zone), infiltrate the enemy's cities and forums, and to plant the seeds of discord and sedition. Such agents were acting on behalf of the Muslim authority at war, and therefore were not considered to be lying against or denouncing tenants of Islam, but were considered "legitimate" mujahedeen, whose mission was to undermine the enemy's resistance and level of mobilization. One of the major objectives of these early agents of sedition was to cause a split among the enemy's camp while downplaying any issues related to Islam. In many instances, they convinced their targeted audiences that the Jihad is not aimed at them. The indigenous people were more than happy to hear that they were not targeted. Local Muslims convinced many Jews that they will be protected from conniving Christians, and they convinced many Christians that Jews were the mortal enemies, because they killed Issa (Jesus). They convinced the Aramaics, Copts, and Hebrews that the enemy is Greece, and signed peace agreements with the Byzantines Greeks at the expense of Maronite Aramaics. Meanwhile the (allegedly) "un-Islamic" Muslims continued their attacks on the target's property and life. About the same period, they convinced the knitted diversity of India to degrade into civil war by introduction of a variant Buddhist/Mystical Islam called Sufism. Decried by most as "deviant Islam", it served a practical purpose to ease the transition of new recruits from local communities in India, resulting in divisions along Muslim/non-Muslim lines, and eventually fomenting unrest and chaos in the land. The net effect was to prepare the region for waves of armed Islamic invaders by Mohammad bin Qasim, Mahmud Ghaznavi, and others. This Jihadic method of deception and subversion was one of the most fascinating and efficient arms of the early Islamic conquests. As a result, in less than four decades, the Middle East fell to Arab-Islamic rule.

Al-taqiyya is still in use and widely practiced today. In the West, Arab-Islamic missionaries continue to succeed converting the uneducated, weak, disillusioned, and criminal elements by feeding them a Western "moderate" version of Islam, while at the same time denouncing the actions of militant Muslims in the rest of the world as 'un-Islamic'. This is done to prevent the new converts from seeing the real face of Islam, or at least until their faith or mental conditioning is strong enough to turn them against their own country, people, and even family. Today taqiyya and the Left have formed an unholy alliance, and are winning massively because of widespread ignorance of the nature of 'true Islam' amongst Westerners, both secular and religious. The dark family secret of the American far-Left is that its followers share one powerful trait with Osama bin Laden: They need to look down on others, to feel superior and just. The

Left complain and threaten claiming its racist or Islamophobic to hold the religion or its violent expansive civilization accountable for its own failures and the horrors it inflicts on others. Our domestic Left, and its representative media organizations, self-righteously shout and point to the excesses of a few renegade guards at Abu Ghraib prison, remaining completely silent on the industrial-scale massacres by Saddam Hussein, the government of Sudan, and so many active other terrorist regimes and organizations. Our liberal self-appointed "voices of conscience" fail to speak out against the beheading of Paul Johnson Jr. or Nick Berg, or the hundreds of Iraqi doctors, lawyers, engineers and educators brutally killed trying to build a humane government for themselves and their compatriots. Nor is there any mention of the countless Iraqi civilians killed by car bombs. For that matter, elites would prefer we forget all about the victims of 9/11. To them the only individuals worthy of sympathy and compassion are the downtrodden and oppressed terrorists themselves. In their minds, the terrorists' grievances and right to violent self-expression trump any victims' right to life and liberty. So now, to the weak-minded and easily manipulated, right has become wrong, good is evil, black is white, and the earth has become completely flat! To these morally challenged no amount of pain, death and loss will help them to see the truth about the theology determined to destroy the freedoms they use to spew such propaganda. These people will only see the light when they are personally faced with the 'convert or die' choice, and to save their own skins will likely be the first to declare; *"There is no God but Allah, and Muhammad is the prophet of Allah"*.

The very famous Greek philosopher, Aristotle (384-322 BC) made a simple observation that: *"Liars when they speak the truth are not believed"*. He may have been influenced by Aesop, the Greek fabulist (620-560 BC) who said; *"A liar will not be believed, even when he speaks the truth"*, or he may have simply repeated what his mother told him as a child after catching him in an adolescent fib. Either way, the advice is sound in any age, and tells us essentially that if an individual is known to practice deception, everything he/she states or claims is suspect. To continue to operate, all con-artists need first to be trusted. There has to be some degree of anonymity for a deceptive entity to continue to produce new victims. To successfully end the current Jihad declared against it, it is important that the non-Muslim world stop playing the gullible, willing victim quite so well. Islamic apologists, particularly the left-leaning mass media, need to re-access their agenda and decide if they want to continue advocating for a totalitarianism system masquerading as a religion aspiring to control freedom of religion, political affiliation, free speech, and the free press. Peter Jennings had been the sole anchor on ABC's *World News Tonight* since 1983. He, Ted Koppel, Dan Rather, and all the rest of the talking heads should make inquiries at Al-Jazeera as to positions available to independent journalists not willing to vilify Jews, Christians, Americans, and Infidels. These guys should be smart enough to connect the dots, draw the lines, infer the obvious, and then re-evaluate their alliances.

Chapter 9
The Battle of Badr

(Revised from an original article by Anwar Shaikh a renowned Indian Islamic scholar and historian)

The Battle of Badr is a tiny event by any stretch of the imagination, yet it has significantly influenced the course of human history. A deeper study of the March 624 event reveals that it served as the first successful exhibition of the Islamic doctrine known as Jihad. Emboldened by this small success, Jihad gained permanent foothold as a pillar of Islam, inspiring perpetual war against infidels ever since. Jihad served as the practical foundation of the Muhammad's Arabic Empire, and as a fundamental pillar of his Spiritual Empire, which sprang from the ashes of the Jihadic combat which first established his political Empire. Muhammad succeeded in transforming the concept of Allah into a new principal of Holy War, but this author claims that Jihad was ordained primarily for the purpose of establishing his vision of Islamic-Arab Cultural Imperialism. To establish if this is true, we must first look into the geographical and political background of Arabia, because the physical conditions of a land play a major role in determining its habits and culture.

At the time of Muhammad, the economic plight of Arabia created a pastoral society which had developed into two groups: firstly, the majority, known as the Bedouins, who had not only to keep wandering in search of pastures but also supplement their meager livelihood by resorting to brigandage, which meant raiding other tribes and commercial caravans. Though it was sheer looting, it assured them solace, security and survival, and so was not looked down upon as sinful but a source of power, pleasure and prestige. This institution of brigandage known as ghazwa (razzia) had existed long before the advent of Muhammad. The Umayyad poet al-Qutami has alluded to this custom in his two verses: "Our business is to make raids on the enemy, on our neighbor and on our own brother, in case we find none to raid but a brother."

It appears that even before Muhammad's time, robbing others was a compulsive trait of the Arab national character, considered more an act of honor and manliness than immorality. Realizing its significance, the Prophet converted this institution into a religious doctrine called 'Jihad', renaming it the Holy War against infidels, but in fact was just one mans effort to build an Empire. The Arab Empire built thereby was in essence exactly like any other empire, except in appearance it was designed to look godly. The doctrine of Jihad, then, is a derivative concept incorporating the Arab custom of 'razzia' (raiding for booty), and seeks ascendancy of Arabia and annihilation of non-Arabs in the name of Allah, the Most Merciful. What is really stunning is not the application of the doctrine to dominate and subjugate others, but that those so engaged believe in a man who told them God sanctifies murder, slavery, lying, rape, arson, and thievery against other human beings (non-Muslims) as acts of great piety to be rewarded.

Though we have already studied the nature of Jihad, in view of its complexity and emotional appeal, it is necessary to be repetitive for elucidating this bloodthirsty war mechanism. The first principle of Jihad is that a person loses his free will and becomes a slave of Allah "*Verily Allah has purchased the believers their lives and their properties; For theirs (in return) is paradise. They fight in His (Allah's) cause, so they kill (others) and are killed. It is a promise in truth which is binding on Him.*" (9:3). Now we know that Paradise is a place of luxury abounding in beautiful virgins and boys, where everything is available free and where toil, sickness, ageing and death are unknown. Moreover, we have learned that Allah's 'cause' is simply killing infidels. We read in <u>The Disputer</u> 58:20 ; "*Those (unbelievers) are Satan's party; why Satan's party, surely, they are the losers! Surely, those who oppose God and His Messenger, those are among the most abject. God has written 'I shall assuredly be the Victor, I and My Messenger....*" We have also already quoted Repentance 9:25 where Muslims get the specific command to wage a war against Christians and Jews "*until they pay the tribute out of hand and have been humbled*".

And what is Allah's cause? With regard to infidels, the cause of Allah is to convert or simply to kill them. And what is an infidel? He or she is someone who denies Muhammad; it does not matter a jot if he/she is a lover of God! So fond is Allah of murdering the unbelievers to glorify Himself and Muhammad that He has permanently divided humanity into two perpetually hostile groups. In a nutshell, it means that Muslims are God's party because they do not love their closest relations if they happen to be infidels. Owing to their belief, they are destined to be victorious against the unbelievers (who are Satan's party). The justification for Jihad has been constant for 1400 years; ...denying Muhammad is sufficient cause for a Muslim state to raid and subjugate non-Muslim territories. The Qur'an is specific in commanding the faithful to wage a war against non-Muslims. They must be fought until survivors surrender and pay tribute as a sign of their humiliation. Receiving tribute from unbelievers in the name of Allah is then the true purpose of Islam.

One can clearly see in this doctrine the Arab roots and custom of brigandage, newly sanctified in the guise of Muhammad's new religion. A religion wherein looting, murder and rape are no longer wicked acts attracting retribution, but instead made a pinnacle of piety deserving the highest reward that Allah can bestow. The Prophet made sure that brigandage no longer remained a low and haphazard affair, but a highly respected and disciplined process, now stamped with divine approval. Thus the battle of Badr served as a major inspirational source of this new Spiritual Arab Imperialism, which has been steadily rising in magnitude for the last fourteen centuries.

Throughout history many others have inspired the worship of men to fight others with the sword for gain. Muhammad's genius lay not only in sanctifying the sword but also finding the beneficial use for it with a view to magnetizing his own person for gathering crowds of followers around himself. An overwhelming majority of those who acknowledged him as their spiritual guide were hungry, haggard and hounded men; they would do anything to improve their economic plight and take revenge from their Meccan oppressors, who had forced them to leave their homes to seek refuge in Medina. This migration from Mecca to Medina had been necessitated by Muhammad's aggressive preaching of his faith, which annoyed unbelievers to the hilt. Bitterness of the refugees had been further aggravated by the fact that they had to rely on the local Muslim believers of Medina (Ansaars) for their sustenance. Though these refugees appreciated their brotherly hospitality, they resented their dependence, which custom held as a sign of disrespect, derision and degradation. Realizing his followers despondency, the Prophet turned it into a rage for vengeance, which then sought to plunder and persuade those who had inflicted torture on them and cast them out. However, these would-be predators did not have to bear the blemish of impiety like other brigands and assassins because they were told that although their acts might look putrid, they had been rendered pure, pious and perfect by the Almighty because He categorized them as Holy War against infidels.

This commandment of holy loot also served as an effective way of boosting their moral sky-high because they believed that they were doing all this to please Allah and not line their own pockets. Therefore, a soldier of God had to be at least twice as brave, boisterous and bullish as an ordinary fighter. Thus the Prophet revealed Allah's pleasure:

> "Assuredly, God will defend those who believe, surely God loves not any traitor. Leave is given to those who fight because they were wronged - surely God is able to help them - who were expelled from their habitations without right.... Assuredly God will help him who helps Him - surely God is All-strong, All-mighty." (The Pilgrimage: 22:38)

Note Allah's promise to help the Muslims in taking revenge from those who had wronged them. What is surprising is the fact that here vengeance means helping Allah! It smells of divine stratagem, which as we shall see, lays down the principle of looting and murdering non-Muslims as the righteous way of life; the Battle of Badr is the first precedent to this effect. Though small in size, it became a major event, which exerted an important influence in determining the course of history. It is therefore, interesting to know the details:

Muhammad's effort in spreading Islam had not borne much fruit until the summer of 621 A.D. when twelve men from Medina, visiting Mecca to perform the annual Hajj ceremony, embraced the faith that he preached. They undertook to propagate it among the fellow Medinites. Next year, in June, 622, a party of seventy-five pilgrims, including two women, came from Medina; they all had embraced Islam. Driven by the zeal of their new gospel, they invited the Prophet to come and live among them to avoid persecution. Muhammad, who had become safety-conscious, asked them if they would defend him as if he were one of their own. Their answer, though positively enthusiastic, was conditional: "What shall we get in return, if we suffer damage or death in the process?" "Paradise, of course," answered the Prophet.

These private meetings known as the two Pledges of al-Alaqba, encouraged the Prophet to persuade his Meccan followers to emigrate to Medina in small groups. When about seventy of them had done so, Muhammad himself quietly undertook the highly dangerous journey because his Meccan enemies had taken the oath of killing him before he could escape. Making use of the unfrequented paths, Muhammad reached his destination on September 24, 622. This flight is called HIJRAH and ranks as the traditional starting point of Islamic history, though the Islamic era begins on the first day of the Arabic year in which the HIJRAH or the flight took place i.e. July 16, 622. However, the significance of this date is believed to lie not in the act of emigration but "the belief that this day marks severance of kinship ties and announces unity of all Muslims, no matter where they come from."

To understand its background, one must realize that Muhammad belonged to the Quresh of Mecca whereas the people of Medina had their blood ties with other tribes. Thus, accepting common denominator of Islam, they all, including Muhammad, lost their tribal distinctions.

This understanding of the act of HIJRAH, though looks golden at first sight, becomes murky when subjected to investigation because when Muhammad grew strong, he declared emphatically that the right to rule belongs to the Quresh i.e. the people of his own tribe! This is the reason that all Arab caliphs both in the east and the west belonged to Muhammad's clan i.e the Quresh.

It took the Meccan emigrants eighteen months to settle in Medina. Muhammad was given a piece of land to build a house for himself. As he gathered power, he became a polygamist after the death of his first wife, Khadija, who also happened to be his employer. Around this house, eventually, were built several apartments to accommodate his nine wives and concubines.. As his followers met in his home to offer prayers, it came to be known as the Mosque of Medina.

Muhammad's followers, both the emigrants and Medinites expected rewards for embracing Islam, "the only true and exalted faith of Allah." The believers quite rightly expected favors from God at the expense of the Kafirs (unbelievers). The All-knowing Allah, responding to the prayers of the devotees revealed through Muhammad, the doctrine of Jihad i.e. murdering non-Muslims for possessing their wealth, property and women.

In essence, there was nothing new in it because the Arabs were customarily used to plundering the commercial caravans. To exploit this vice, Islam cleverly renamed brigandage and killing as Jihad, which was to be carried out to glorify Allah, the Great. By reshaping common robbery into a Divine pursuit, it inspired the lust for plunder with the spirit of untold devotion, discipline and desire that turned the looters into crusaders, who carried out their atrocities with greatly enhanced enthusiasm; in fact, they became ferocious robots who thought of pillage as piety and equated murder with melody.

The Quresh of Mecca were a trading community. In autumn, their commercial caravans proceeded to the Yemen and Abyssinia, and during spring to Syria. Among their merchandize were frankincense, gems, precious metals and leather. The last item was their major export, which had a high demand in Syria and Persia; it commanded high prices. These Meccan entrepreneurs exchanged them for piece-goods, silk and other items of luxury at Gaza and other marts. By the old standards, these caravans were really huge because they might consist of as many as 2,000 camels whose cargo could excel the value of 50,000 dinars or mithkals; the latter was a golden coin having the worth of a Byzantine Aureus, roughly equal to two-thirds of a pound sterling. Fourteen centuries ago, 50,000 dinars represented the same value which millions of dollars do today.

The special trait of these caravans was that they constituted the economic life of the Meccans because they were financed not only by the rich people of the community but also the small men, who might have saved a dinar or two, and wanted to profit, which usually amounted to 50%. These caravans represented communal investment, and because of their high value, were often the target of highway robbers. Therefore, they had to be accompanied by an 'army of defenders', whose size corresponded with the value of the goods. These commercial caravans had a good deal in common with the seafaring joint stock companies of old England, whose venture capital was contributed by many participants, entitled to profit according to their size of stake.

The successful journey of these caravans was a matter of special delight for the shareholders, but whenever, it succumbed to the attack of the plundering mafia, it created highly heart-rending scenes of women, beating their breasts, pulling hair and singing mournful songs to express their loss, that might also include the death of some defenders.

Enunciation of the doctrine of Jihad struck terror into the hearts of the Meccan traders, who were alarmed about their trade with the north because its route passed between Medina and the sea coast. It is baffling to realize that the Prophet, who prescribed hand-cutting as the punishment for stealing, personally led the Ghazawats i.e. pillage-expeditions (razzias) against the Meccan caravans in 623. Though he failed in all three attempts, in January, 624, he succeeded in robbing a caravan returning from Yemen as it reached Nakhlah near Mecca.

Failure of the Prophet's third razzia is actually a part of the famous battle of Badr. Abu Sufyan led a caravan to Syria in October, 623 A.D. (A.H.II). It carried huge loads of the Arab products demanded in the Syrian market. The Prophet asked for volunteers to join this predatory expedition. About 200 men came forward. They had only 30 camels, which they rode in turn. The plan was to attack the caravan at Osheira on its way to Yenbo, but it had passed this point by the time the holy plunderers reached there.

These rich cargoes were very important to the Muslims, who had hardly any effective equipment to fight the unbelievers for spreading Islam. So, Muhammad tried to enhance his influence in the territory of Osheira to make the caravan trade more hazardous for the Meccans. His efforts did bear fruit and a number of tribes living in the area entered into alliance with them. The initial escape of the caravan seems to have disturbed the apostolic plan and he became determined to waylay Abu Sufyan on his return journey. During the espionage activities, the Prophet found his son-in-law, Ali, asleep "on the dusty ground under the shade of a palm grove". Seeing his face soiled, the Prophet, in a pleasantry, said, "Sit up, O, Abu Turab", and he sprang up immediately, conscious of his neglect. This became his sobriquet during the rest of his life. This is why he is called "Ali, Abu Turab".

So alarming was the Prophet's resolve to rob the caravan that his Medinite opponents warned Abu Sufyan's people at Mecca of the impending danger. Damdam, a swift and efficient courier, was immediately sent to Mecca with the bad news.

As a reconnaissance, Muhammad dispatched two scouts, in early January, to the caravan station at Al-Haura. They were well received by the chief of the Juheina tribe, who took suitable measures to protect their identity. His services were thought so valuable that after the battle of Badr, he was rewarded with the grant of Yenbo.

It was Sunday, the 12th of Ramadan, when realizing the significance of the caravan, the Prophet set out on the predatory exercise without waiting for the return of his two spies, who were to brief him on the situation. It seems that the impatience to possess all that the caravan was carrying, played heavily on the minds of the Muslims. Hearing tales of the expected rich booty, even some non-Muslim citizens of Medina tried to join the expedition. Having noticed a couple of them, the Prophet called them to his camel that he rode and asked them about the nature of their business. They told him that they were heathen but as their city had extended protection to him, he ranked as their kinsman and they wanted to join him for plunder. The Prophet replied that it was meant for the believers only, and the unbelievers were not allowed to participate in such ventures. He emphasized in no uncertain terms: "Believe and fight". Since this was the only way to share the loot, they confessed that Muhammad was the Prophet of God. It is then that they got the permission to join his party.

His army, after necessary adjustments, contained 315 men; amongst them eighty were Refugees i.e. who had emigrated from Mecca with the Prophet, and of the remainder "about one-fourth belonged to the Aus, and the rest to the Khazraj". They had two horses and thirty camels which they rode in turns to overcome tediousness of the long hard journey. In terms of size and equipment, it may not be called an army, but in effectiveness, even the mighty hosts may not be compared with it because it had no equal in fervor, ferocity and fortitude. Their newly acquired faith was a novel specimen of moral justice and piety; being based on Jihad, it did not condemn but commended rapine, rape and ruination of unbelievers and held it as the way to secular success in this life and paradisiac comfort in the next world. The fervor of such a faith, which obliterated all thoughts of loss, defeat and sin, goaded Allah's warriors with an unequal zeal to march, seek and rob the precious cargoes that lawfully belonged to the investors.

For a couple of days, the holy warriors took a direct route to Mecca but reaching As-Safra, they moved in the direction of Badr, a resting station on the road to Syria. Through local gossip, Muhammad's spies came to know that Abu Sufyan's caravan was about to appear there any time. The report was correct but Abu Sufyan was a shrewd fellow. Realizing immediate danger, he at once dispatched a courier to Mecca asking for a strong defending force.

The Meccans having suffered losses at Nakhla were not prepared to see the repetition of similar humiliation. Again, it was the caravan of the year because the cargo it carried was worth more than 50,000 golden pieces. Its loss might render the whole community bankrupt. A mixed current of fear and fervor swept the Meccan society and every household contributed a warrior to the defense of the caravan according to the size of its stake. Soon an army of 800 men was raised, accompanied by a band of women, who specialized in singing war songs, which lent a lion's heart to a bleating lamb. Their battle-melodies accompanied by the sounds of their tabrets and footwork excited the Meccan soldiers to die for the honor of their city and ancestors.

As the army reached Al-Johfa, the envoy of Abu Sufyan appeared. He told Abu Jahl, the head of the army that Abu Sufyan had succeeded escaping Muhammad through stealth and rapid marches, and all was well. They heaved a sigh of relief, but the question arose if they should return without an engagement. A passionate debate took place among the chiefs of the army. One party argued that, since no harm had been done, there was no cause for a deadly contest. Moreover, it was argued that the people on the other side were their close relations: killing them would constantly torture their conscience. It was not only wise but also desirable to return home peacefully.

Abu Jahl, the head of the Makhzum clan, on the other hand, advocated a fight to the bitter end. He advocated that their return would be interpreted as a sign of their cowardice, and it was also politic to nip evil in the bud; otherwise, the specter of Muhammad would grow in potential threat all the time. His persuasion won the argument, and they passed three days making merry by the fountain.

On the other hand, Muhammad had also been advancing toward Badr. When he reached Al-Ruha, he heard that the Quresh, being aware of the danger, were marching on him. This necessitated a council of war. Unlike the Meccans, the Muslims showed contempt for blood ties and expressed a strong desire for an immediate contest.

Here the charisma of Muhammad's personality and political sagacity deserves mention. He had emigrated to Medina on the promise of his Medinite followers that they would defend him with their blood while he would be amongst them. Addressing the war council, and particularly to the men from Medina, he declared that their pledge neither induced his defense in any aggressive action nor had it any connection with the events that took place away from the city (Medina). Therefore, they were at liberty to leave him if they so wished.

Of course, a political mind would interpret this occasion differently but to the faithful this declaration conveyed a message of the Prophet's holiness, greatness and moral dignity hitherto unknown in the Medinite annals. How they were moved by this speech is expressed by their spokesman Sa'd Bin Moadh. He said, "Prophet of the Lord! march where you desire; encamp where you may choose; make war or conclude peace with whom you will. For I swear by Him (Allah) who has sent you with the truth, that if you were to march till our camels fell down dead, we would go forward with you to the world's end. Not one of us will be left behind."

It should also be noted that at the end of the meeting, the Prophet who claimed to be "Mercy of God to All Mankind", invoked Divine curse on the infidels, and prayed, "O lord, let not Abu Jahl, the Pharaoh of his people, escape. Let not Zama'a escape; rather let the eyes of his father run sore for him weeping and become blind".

This curse of the Prophet had a psychological purpose. Being fewer in numbers than the infidels, it made his followers believe that they already possessed the power to inflict death on their enemies. To the sincere believers of Muhammad, who had their own unbelieving parents and brethren as a sign of respect to the Apostle, it was unimaginable that his supplication against the unbelievers could go astray. Reinforced by this belief, they became even more determined to deliver them a dose of violence blended with the worst pillage.

Badr was chosen as the place of battle by the Prophet. It vouched for his martial skill as well as seriousness of purpose i.e. he wanted the battle to be decisive; neither party must escape lightly. He knew that the courage of his followers, which emanated from their religious convictions, was far more forceful than the strength that the superiority of numbers bestowed upon his enemy. A decimating blow to the unbelievers would lay the foundation of the Islamic Empire.

Badr is situated close to Medina, 'the City of the Prophet'. It is a valley which consists of a plain, having steep hills to the north and east; on the southern side is a low rocky range, and the west is closely dotted with sandy hillocks. A small stream also ran through it breaking into springs here and there. The Prophet chose the most useful reservoir for his army and destroyed the rest. This was a wise military maneuver, which assured him mastery of the water sources of the battlefield.

The day before the engagement took place, Muhammad had placed the banner of the refugees (the emigrants) in the hands of Mus'ah; ensign of the Khazrajite was given to al-Hobab and the flag of Aus was handed to Sa'd Bin Moadh.

Here one again sees the tactical wisdom of Muhammad in choosing the fighting spot. As the Quresh army, comprising a thousand men advanced toward Muhammad, the glaring rays of the Arabian sun struck their eyes, making their movements troublesome. Also, the vastly numerical superiority of the enemy was hidden by the fall of the ground behind. Knowing the gravity of the situation, the Prophet again resorted to the device of praying to Allah for harnessing the superstitious energies of his followers' belief into a combating force. Raising his hands upward, he solicited the Maker, *"O Allah, accomplish for me what Thou hast promised me. O Allah, bring about what Thou has promised to me. O Allah, if this small band of Muslims is destroyed, Thou wilt not be worshipped on this earth"*. (Muslim, Vol. 3, 4360)

The historian may find it strange that a man is telling his Creator what will happen if He does not listen to him, and the Almighty agrees to his suggestion for fear of losing worshippers, but his followers intoxicated by the promises of heavenly virgins and boys had no such qualms. They believed that Allah is directed by Muhammad and, therefore, the battle shall end in a resounding victory for them.

It was customary among the Arabs to enter single combats before starting the battle. As Sheiba, his brother Otba and Al-Walid (son of Otba) moved forward to challenge for single duels, three Citizens (the natives of Medina as distinct from the Emigrants) came out from the Muhammadan ranks to encounter them.

Here we notice the tribal tendencies of the Prophet, who did not want the honor of starting the contest go to anyone but his own kith and kin. Calling them back, he turned to the fellow Emigrants and shouted "you sons of Hashim, arise and fight, according to your right."

However, this pro-Quresh leaning of the Prophet is well balanced by the choice of his combatants. Out came three warriors, known for their valor, courage and fighting skills. They were Ali (the Prophet's adopted son and son-in-law), Hamza (the Prophet's uncle) and Obeida. As the infidels saw their heroes become sacrificial lambs at the Muslim altar, their spirits began to sink. Even more daunting was the bravery displayed by the Prophet, who recited verses from the Koran, and brandishing his sword stood by his followers like a lofty granite and assured them that paradise was the reward for martyrdom.

The story of Omeir, a sixteen-year-old Muslim boy, who was allowed to participate in this battle, is worthy of note. He was hungry and eating dates, when he heard the prophet associate paradise with martyrdom. Looking at the dates scornfully, "is it these", he cries ruefully "that hold me back from paradise? Verily, I shall taste no more of them until I meet my Lord". Motivated by the force of belief, he rushed upon the enemy and tasted the wine of martyrdom loathed by many and loved by a few.

Yet another story worthy of narration is that of Moadh, who slew Abu Jahl, and was attacked by his son Ikrima. In this catastrophic action, Moadh's arm was nearly severed from his shoulder. Martyrdom was also his goal, which he coveted, and believed that a second rate action was not compatible with the dignity of such a heavenly prize. Since his best performance was being checked by his dangling arm, he put his foot on it, and ripping it off with the courage of a divine knight, he attacked the enemy to achieve his most cherished aim.

Was it the valor of his followers that won the day? Of course, it was a great factor in securing the field, but the inspiration that the Prophet provided was the paramount reason of success. Though he is considered 'illiterate' by his followers, he was the master of mob psychology and excelled in operating this mechanism.

The day, i.e. 17 Ramadan, the second year of Hijrah (623 A.D.) when the battle took place, was punctuated with sharp gales. As the first violent blast swept across the valley, the Prophet told his followers that the Angel Gabriel had arrived with one thousand angels to help the Muslim cause. The following two piercing blasts were interpreted by him as the arrival of the angel Michael and the angel Israpheel, each heading a reinforcement of 1,000 angels to fight on the side of the Muslims!

Nobody stopped to think why were they not visible to the crusaders, but to Muhammad only? Again, the angels must be very weak creatures if three thousand of them were required to fight just 1,000 Meccans. The Koran testifies to this event:

"And Allah most surely helped you at Badr, when you were utterly abject. So fear Allah, and happily you will be thankful. When you saidst to the believers: 'Is it not enough for you that your Lord should reinforce you with three thousand angels sent down upon you, Yea: if you are patient and god fearing, and the foe come against you instantly, your Lord will reinforce you with five thousand swooping angels". (The House of Imran: III:120)

By this statement Muhammad secured the entire credit for his Prophethood, which had been honored by Allah with a reinforcement of 3,000 heavenly fighters, and a promise of 5,000 belligerent angels in any future engagement against the infidels.

One ought to know the attitude of the Prophet toward his chief adversary, Abu Jahl, who was presented to him when he was about to breathe his last. As he lay at his feet, the Prophet looked at him and said, "it is more acceptable to me than the choicest camel in Arabia".

Now, we come to booty, the goal of the Islamic warfare, which Allah Himself sanctioned to strike terror in the hearts of those who refuse to bow before the Islamic Imperialism and claim their right to human dignity.

By modern standards the booty acquired from the Battle of Badr may look trivial but by then prevailing economic conditions of Arabia, its psychological effects, and the part it played in building the Arab Empire, was simply terrific; "the loot consisted of 115 camels, 14 horses, a great store of vestments and carpets, articles of leather, with much equipage and armor". The famous sword of Abu Jahl, known as 'Dhul-Fikr' fell to the share of the Prophet.

The Battle of Badr was fought on the doctrine of Jihad, which essentially means building the Arab Empire by denying non-Muslims all rights except the right to serve their Arab masters, which servitude is perpetual humiliation of non-Muslims through a system of subjugation and payment of tribute (i.e. imperialism). When we delve deeper into this doctrine, it transpires that its tentacles equally spread to the non-Arab Muslims, who are converted to Islam with the force of arms; they are, of course, exempted from the payment of Jaziya i.e. poll tax, but are treated as second-class citizens and may be exploited economically as well as psychologically through the hegemony of faith, which favors the Arab Muslims against the non-Arab Muslims. I shall return to this point later.

To further explain the novelty of Jihad as the Doctrine of Struggle against the infidels, the following point should be made: A Muslim nation requires no particular reason to attack a non-Muslim country. It is in itself a heinous crime not to acknowledge Muhammad as the last Prophet of God. According to the Koran all religions are false except Islam. Thus Allah is the enemy of non-Muslims, who are regarded as the worst kind of beasts under the sun. It is a myth that the Jews and Christians being 'People of the Book' are exempt from this restriction. Having abrogated all other religions, the Prophet prescribes the course of action against them as Jihad. Muhammad's solution for the problem of any person or nation denying Islam is a perpetual war against them until the infidels are killed or subdued.

All previously imperial nations, as they became civilized and conscious of human dignity, realized that it is morally wrong to maim, mutilate and murder other people for personal or collective gain and abandoned imperialism tendencies. In fact, gradually, they upheld human rights through a code of justice and economic improvement and the concept applied to all people irrespective of race and color. Today, we live in a world where murder, rape, robbery, denial of justice and usurpation of rights are considered the greatest moral vices, ...but this standard of morality is utter nonsense in the world of Islam because denial of Islam is considered a serious crime justifying stripping of human rights and subjecting them to perpetual abuse until he/she acknowledges the Prophethood of Muhammad. Faith in Islam is considered the only true virtue. This is the reason that a Muslim, no matter how wicked, shall go to paradise, whereas a highly righteous non-Muslim irrespective of his piety, shall be thrown into hell! Practicing this sort of discrimination is a basis of Islamic culture, so small wonder that Jihad is a fundamental Islamic doctrine. Jihad teaches that murder, rape, and plunder are considered the loftiest of virtues which increases a Muslim's piety, and which is also a sure guarantee of paradise. However, its prominent attraction is booty, which acts as the greatest predatory motive and which is considered by all other accomplished cultures and advanced civilizations as highly impious. This ruinous man-hating Islamic philosophy is deeply ingrained in the Battle of Badr which still serves today as a guiding precedent for all Muslims. The obvious contradiction between Islamic doctrines and universally accepted principals of human rights, dignity, and equality are not lost on Muslims, they are just simply ignored. To them, Islamic doctrine simply abrogates all contradicting principals and virtues not based on Muhammad's words and example.

The Arabs have never treated non-Arab Muslims as equals in their countries. For example, no Indian, Pakistani or Bangladeshi Muslim holds an important ministerial or administrative post in any Arab country. Their practical status is equivalent to that of infidels: when non-Muslim subjects broke chains of the Arab domination, they became free, and even their superior, over a period of time, but the non-Arab Muslims even when they are politically independent, remain spiritual and psychological slaves of Arabia. This is the specialty of the Arab Imperialism, which vouches for the patriotism and wisdom of Muhammad. This is not a fiction but a fact because Islam is essentially the ambassador of Arab national interest, seeking to perpetuate it as Arab Imperialism in the guise of religion. One cannot help applauding the genius of the Prophet, who made his own country the center of Divine reverence and then persuaded his followers all over the world, under the threat of hell, to prostrate toward Mecca to qualify for paradise!

Look at the underlying stratagem for yourself. The Prophet declared:

- God, the Creator of the world had Kaaba (Mecca, the center of Arabia) built as His own House by Adam, and then rebuilt by Abraham. Thus the land of Arabia, being the Home of Allah, is superior to all other lands.

- On death, the body of a Muslim must be buried facing Mecca (to show his devotion to Arabia), otherwise, he shall not be admitted into paradise.

- So sacred is Mecca (the birth-place of Muhammad) that nobody must defecate facing this City. He who does so, is an infidel and shall go to hell.

- Arabic is not only the language of the Koran but also of Allah. So all Muslims must learn and speak Arabic to be godly.

- The hadith no. 5751 (Mishkat, Vol. 3) reports the Prophet saying: "Love the Arabs for three reasons because (1) I am an Arab (2) the Holy Koran is in Arabic, and (3) the tongue of the dwellers of paradise shall also be Arabic.

- Every Muslim, no matter where he lives, must come to Mecca for pilgrimage a least once in a life-time, if he has the means to do so. This religious duty of the Muslims has been an important economic artery of (Saudi) Arabia for centuries and serves as a substitute for the tribute that the Prophet laid on non-Muslims to glorify the Arab Imperialism.

What really proves Islam to be the ambassador of Arab Imperialism is the fact that it demands non-Arab Muslims to follow the Arab cultural and moral lead blindly. How is it done? This impossible goal has been made possible by the Divine Command that states Allah has made Muhammad the model of Behavior for every believer, which he must follow to avoid the fire of hell and qualify for the luxuries of paradise:

In Islam, the 'Last Day' is the Day of Judgment when a person's fate shall be decided in terms of heaven and hell: the basis of verdict shall be whether or not he or she has followed the Prophet as the Model of Behavior. In simple language, paradise is meant only for those who believe, feel, think, walk, talk, sleep, eat and drink as Muhammad did. We all know that Muhammad was a great Arab patriot and practiced the Arab culture. Therefore, every non-Arab Muslim must adore Arabia like Muhammad and adopt all Arab cultural, moral and spiritual values.

This is not a wishful interpretation, but is actually happening in all countries that lie within the pale of Islam: this principle is the foundation of the Arab Imperialism, and it perpetuates itself through the force of faith irrespective of whether the Arabs are politically ascendant or not!

Again, Islamic Arab Imperialism is different from Roman, Iranian, Turkish, Japanese, or British Imperialism because it is not based on political or economic power, but exploitation of human weakness, emanating from instinctive fear of uncertainty, which makes man feel that he is drowning and must clutch at a straw to survive, irrespective of how irrational this act might be. By imposing dictatorship of faith on its followers, Islam has crucified their rational and inventive faculties, leading to the degradation of their national cultures; this has become the major cause of their backwardness, and all the evils that spring from it.

To assess the significance of the Battle of Badr, one must realize that had the Prophet lost it, the doctrine of Islam would have been laid to rest along with the bodies of its crusaders. This little event, in fact, proved to be a vigorous seed, whose branches spread into both the east and west. However, the west checked its growth in the Battle of Tours. At this pivotal event a great contribution was made by brave and outnumbered Polish freedom fighters, which insured the survival and advancement of western civilization against the murderous onslaught and momentum of the Islamic crusades. Westerners owe a great debt of gratitude to those great men and their descendents.

Note: Ali Sina, an Islamic scholar and intellectual, further illuminates the dynamics of this pivotal event in his article 'The examples of Muhammad' (http://www.faithfreedom.org/Articles/sinaawa40621.htm). The following is from that article:

This battle marks the begging of Muhammad's rise to power, the Meccans lost 49-70 men, with about the same number taken hostage. How Muhammad dealt with the injured and the captives in this and other battles set the tone for subsequent Islamic savagery, which has lasted to this day. It's only by knowing these personal accounts of Muhammad that we can understand terrorist obsessions to cut off the heads of their victims, and why Muslim mobs cry out "Allah is great" while in the very act of committing gruesome murder. They do this because of the numerous examples by the Prophet himself.

Among the people who were slain was Aba Hakam (Abu Jahl, as derogatorily he came to be called by Muslims). Aba Hakam was severely wounded but still alive when Abdullah, the servant, of Muhammad, ran up, put his foot on Aba Hakam's neck, got hold of his beard and started insulting the fatally wounded man whom his own people had named the father of wisdom. Abdullah cut off Aba Hakam's head and carried it to his master. *"The head of the enemy of God!"* exclaimed Muhammad joyously; ---- *"God! There is none other God but he!"* - *"Yea There is no other!"* responded Abdullah, as he cast the severed head at the Prophet's feet. *"It is more acceptable to me;"* cried Mohammad, hardly able to contain his joy, *"than the choicest camel in all Arabia"*.

According to some historians, Muhammad is said to have given orders for Aba Hakam's body to be mutilated and disfigured. (Waqidi, p. 85) Another man who fell in Badr and whose body was mutilated was Umaiya bin Khalaf. The reference to his mutilation can be found in the Book of Bukhari (Volume 5, Book 58, Number 193). These were men with whom Muhammad had personal enmity. According to one Hadith, Muhammad had vowed to kill Umaiya long time before the battle of Badr. (Bukhari Volume 4, Book 56, Number 826, and Volume 5, Book 59, Number 286). After three days the bodies of the slain were dragged and dumped in a well. Muhammad stood by the well and looked on triumphantly, as the bodies were brought up and cast in. Abu Bakr stood by, and examining their features, called aloud their names. Unable to contain his joy Muhammad started calling them by name and bragged to the corpses about his victory. The following account can be found in Sahih Muslim Book 040, Number 6869:

Anas b. Malik reported that Allah's Messenger (may peace be upon him) let the dead bodies of the unbelievers who fought in Badr (lie unburied) for three days. He then came to them and sat by their side and called them and said: O Abu Jahl b. Hisham, O Umayya b. Khalaf, O Utba b. Rab'ila, O Shaiba b. Rabi'a, have you not found what your Lord had promised with you to be correct? As for me, I have found the promises of my Lord to be (perfectly) correct. Umar listened to the words of Allah's Apostle (may peace be upon him) and said: Allah's Messenger, how do they listen and respond to you? They are dead and their bodies have decayed. Thereupon he (the Holy Prophet) said: By Him in Whose Hand is my life, what I am saying to them, even you cannot hear more distinctly than they, but they lack the power to reply. Then he commanded that they should be buried in the well of Badr.

The "promise" that Muhammad was talking about was a curse that the vindictive prophet had laid on these men when he was in Mecca and they had derided him when someone dumped the manure of camel on his back. On that occasion Muhammad said: "*O Allah! Punish Abu Jahl, 'Utba bin Rabi'a, Shaiba bin Rabi'a, Al-Walid bin 'Utba, Umaiya bin Khalaf, and 'Uqba bin Al Mu'it.* (Bukhari Volume 1, Book 4, Number 241)

The following story can cast more light on the revengeful and implacable character of Muhammad. Among the captives was Abul Bokhtari. He had shown kindness to Muhammad and was especially instrumental in procuring his and his followers release from the quarters of Abu Talib, in a time that the Quraish had boycotted him and his family and they were living in a state of self-imposed house-arrest, Muhammad, mindful of this favor, proclaimed that he should not be harmed. However, Abul Bokhtari had a companion whom Muhammad did not want to let go. He pleaded for his friend's life but Muhammad would not budge. So he exclaimed: *"The women of Mecca; shall never say that I abandoned my comrade through love of life. Do thy work upon us both."* Thus, feeling released from all moral obligations, Muhammad killed both of them. Here we see a man not only murdering prisoners of war, but also killing someone to whom he owed a personal favor simply because he could not let go of the pleasure of taking revenge on a personal enemy.

On their way back to Medina from the raid at Badr, one of the prisoners put to death was a devoted father named Uqbah bin abi Muait. Before his execution the man pleaded with Mohammed saying, *"Who, then, will take care of my little girl?"* Mohammed's 'merciful' answer: *"Hell-fire."*

So who exactly was this Muhammad, the man hundreds of millions are striving to emulate? As has been shown, the face he showed his enemies was not nearly so beautiful and pleasing as the face shone to believers. Muhammad was a man of war who sent out or went out on at least 74 expeditions and raids in only a ten year period (622-632), and who personally conducted 24 major military campaigns. His carnal lusts for young flesh (wives, sex-slaves, and even children) are legendary, but it was through violence and murder where he gained power and wealth. He was wounded in battle (Battle of the Trench) and undoubtedly personally slew victims. By promising virgins and bounty in this life and the next, he inspired men to his self-serving cause. Through Jihadic war he unified the Arab tribes, further consolidating his power through personally ordered assassinations of individual opponents as well as murder, exile, or enslavement of all defeated peoples.

Tabari (AD 839-923) was an early Muslim historian considered largely reliable by scholars today. Tabari lists Muhammad's assets at his death (horses, camels, milch sheep, and so on), including his weapons. In fact Tabari records the nicknames Muhammad's had lovingly given those instruments which were such a large part of his life. Muhammad nicknamed three swords that he took from the Qaynuqa Jewish tribe after banishing them from Medina: "Pluck Out," "Very Sharp," and "Death". Two other swords from elsewhere are named: "Sharp" and "That is wont to sink" (presumably into human flesh). After his Hijrah (Emigration) from Mecca to Medina in 622, he owned a sword called "Having the vertebrae of the back." which he collected as booty from his victory at the Battle of Badr. Muhammad also named bows: "Most conducive to ease, or wide," "white," and "of nab wood". The name of a coat of mail implies "ampleness" or "redundant portions," probably because Muhammad was portly (cf. Ibn Ishaq, Life of Muhammad, trans. Guillaume, p. 383). Finally, Muhammad himself had a few nicknames. After Tabari lists several positive ones, he matter-of-factly provides one that is particularly telling: "The obliterator". (*Tabari; Volume 9, pp. 153-55, trans. Ismail K. Poonawala.; University of New York Press*)

Chapter 10
The American Muslim

In the face of sure outcry, we now must ask the question: 'What about Muslims living with us here in America'? Of course, not many Muslims here have inclinations to commit terrorist acts. Undoubtedly the majority of Muslims living in America are nominal citizens living without the essential political dimensions of orthodox Islam, and are certainly (or hopefully) not bent on terrorist actions. Many are content to continue to raise their families and prosper with the rest of us and do not want violence, being people with a better moral code than the militants and their view (right or wrong) of what Muhammad expects today. They try to follow a path dictated by personal conscience as exemplified by Shirin Ebadi, the Iranian lawyer and human-rights fighter who was awarded the Nobel Peace Prize. Ebadi insists that no one, least of all the mullahs, has the right to tell others how to live and practice their faith. "There are no priests and no church in Islam," she repeats. "As Muslims we are alone responsible for our deeds and shall face Divine Judgment as individuals. Because we are not robots no one could programme us with his version of religion. … All human beings are of equal worth simply by existing". That kind of statement, of course, is in direct opposition to the basic principles and articles of Islam, which hold that humanity is divided according to the strict hierarchy of worth outlined in 'The Psychology of Jihad' chapter. Additionally, Ebadi is a woman, and as such is regarded by Iran's Khatami and other mullahs as, at best, half of a human being.

There are many moderates like Ebadi who say they are Muslims, but in fact the Qur'an condemns them all as Muslim-wanna-bes, hypocrites, and pretenders who do not obey the commands of their god and his messenger. The Qur'an commands Muslims to kill infidels if they wish to join the faithful in Paradise: 47:4-6, *"When ye encounter the infidels, strike off their heads till ye have made a great slaughter among them, . . . And whoso fight for the cause of God . . . he will bring them into the Paradise"*. The fundamental, orthodox, true Muslims will continue to teach and pressure nominal Muslims like Ebadi towards obeying Muhammad's commands to establish the rule of Islam, if necessary through the use of violence. Nominal Muslims in America and elsewhere only need to awaken to the actual call of the Qur'an, Hadith, and Sira, to perhaps transform their faith and begin to use violence for Islam's sake. It appears more and more that they are awakening, as evidenced by the fact that their violence is increasing along with the number of Muslims involved in violent activities. Shiite Muslims in Iraq are currently coming under violent pressure to join foreign and Sunni jihadiats against the elected government and the Americans.

The hope that a everlastingly peaceful form of Islam might take permanent root in any country is wishful thinking. The gravitational pull of the Qur'an towards fundamentalism is like the force from a 'black-hole' and will eventually swallow-up every effort to reform her. Remember the Qur'an is 'perfect' and cannot be re-interpreted, re-written, nor reformed. As far as the Qur'an is concerned, literalists are Muslims and all Muslims are literalists. Even minor deviation from the Qur'an would in fact invalidate the entire faith. As such, any local or regional successes at ignoring Islamic fundamentals are destined to be temporary.

Although the vast majority of Muslims in America are not terrorists, and many even abhor the actions of their Muslim brethren around the world …still, since Islam teaches world domination these moderate Muslims rarely raise their voices in protest to their own brethren. If the Israelis bomb Hezbollah camps in Lebanon or Hamas camps in Syria, Muslims in New York, Detroit, and Los Angeles will organize a mass demonstration. But getting Muslims to condemn the terrorist actions of a brother … say of those in Sudan, Egypt, Algeria, Afghanistan, Iraq, and more recently in Turkey… is like pulling teeth. While the Muslims worldwide continually condemn Israel, few Muslims have ever raised their voices in protest over Palestinian homicide bombers or Saddam Hussein's genocidal war upon the Kurds. None ask why Bin Laden failed to help the Kurds (reports now indicate that he was working with Saddam Hussein to kill them).

There are very few Muslims in the Syracuse, NY area compared to many cities in the country, only about 5000. Yet since 9/11 several negative incidents have occurred including an arson case at a Jewish

Synagogue involving two Muslim men, raids centering on Muslim-owned stores selling counterfeit DVDs, and a high profile case involving an Iraqi doctor accused of illegally funneling funds to Iraq thru his charity. The latter two in particular resulted in claims of profiling and bigotry from the Muslim populace. Rather than working to foster an atmosphere of trust, this tiny Muslim community acts in such a way as to only cause further mistrust. Then there is an organization called the Syracuse Peace Council. These left-wing activists attempt to cover their anti-American agenda by claiming to be advocates for world peace. However they have rightfully earned the nickname "The Syracuse Hate Council" by witnesses of their demonstrations against the American government several times this year. This angry organization of social malcontents calling for radical Socialist change within America happens to draw support from the likes of Magda Bayoumi of the Islamic Society of CNY. Ms. Bayoumi is not a strong supporter of the war on terror, but since she is against the destruction of terrorists, then is it unreasonable to expect her to be nice enough to persuade her fellow Muslims to stop trying to kill us instead of trying to bring down our government? Just recently Magda Bayoumi penned a letter to the editor of the Syracuse Post Standard to complain about what she perceived as discriminatory and bigoted reporting concerning a Post Standard article. The article discussed an investigation on whether Islamic Society of CNY may be illegally channeling funds to Iraq for other than the claimed Bam Iranian earthquake relief, possibly to support terrorism. This defensive attitude, crying foul and pretending to be a victim over every perceived injustice and slight, does not help the Muslim cause in America today. As we face new terror alerts American citizens continue to wonder whether Muslims in America are with us or against us. After reading this book one must accept the fact that within their very secretive society radical elements exist that wish to cause America great harm. It's not Christians or Jews who are releasing audiotapes weekly calling for Jihad; it's the radical followers of Islam. The American Muslim community could choose to be a great asset in this fight, as surely they would be able to easily identify the radicals living amongst them. But alas, to the degree that they have assimilated the Qur'an is the degree to which they will continue to support Jihad against infidels.

Although virtually all terrorists working to destroy Americans are in their own minds devout Muslims, it needs to be re-emphasized that hopefully not many Muslims in America are terrorists. Most of them are undoubtedly good people, but the seeds of terrorism are planted deep within the theology of Islam. This theology, when free to grow and blossom, shows itself in the actions normal Muslims take when they feel that Islam is challenged. Mob attacks in Pakistan, and the attacks by Muslim mobs in Nigeria and Indonesia, are examples of Islamic violence and mob mentality from 'peaceful' moderate Muslims. And as was demonstrated in "Not Without My Daughter", who knows when a peaceful, liberal or moderate Muslim will be persuaded, enticed, or incited to turn to fundamentalism and embrace the violence of Islam?

Stephen Schwartz stated in his June 2003 testimony to the U.S. Senate's Subcommittee on Terrorism and Homeland Security:

> "Shia and other non-Wahhabi Muslim community leaders estimate that 80 percent of American mosques out of a total ranging between an official estimate of 1,200 and an unofficial figure of 4-6,000 are under Wahhabi control ... Wahhabi control over mosques means control of property, buildings, appointment of imams, training of imams, content of preaching including faxing of Friday sermons from Riyadh, Saudi Arabia, and of literature distributed in mosques and mosque bookstores, notices on bulletin boards, and organizational and charitable solicitation ... The main organizations that have carried out this campaign are the Islamic Society of North America (ISNA), which originated in the Muslim Students' Association of the U.S. and Canada (MSA), and the Council on American-Islamic Relations (CAIR)."[31]

Representative Peter T. King said publicly while promoting his book "Vale of Tears" that he estimates 80-85% of the Muslim leadership in America supports "Islamic fundamentalism". Indeed, there have been increasing instances where Wahhabi Muslims have successfully penetrated key U.S. institutions, such as the military and our prison system. As recent media reports have noted, the two groups that accredit and recommend Muslim chaplains to the military have long been suspected of links to terrorist organizations by the federal government (The Graduate School of Islamic and Social Sciences and an organization under the umbrella of the American Muslim Foundation). Recently, one of the key architects of the U.S. military's chaplain program, Abdurahman Alamoudi, was arrested and charged with an illegal relationship with Libya, long a state sponsor of terror. Federal investigators also have detained Captain James Yee (a Muslim clergymen), once stationed at Guantanamo Bay, Cuba, and who is being investigated for potential ties to al Qaeda. A 'moderate' Muslim employed by the FBI even refused to take part in a surveillance of a suspected Al-Qaeda operative because he said, "Muslims do not spy on Muslims".

The Graduate School and 'The Islamic Society of North America', another group with ties to Islamic extremists, also refer Muslim clerics to the U.S. Bureau of Prisons. The New York State prison system promoted a Muslim cleric to a position that allowed him to supervise the hiring and firing of all prison chaplains. He was later removed from his job when officials discovered he was an al Qaeda sympathizer who incited prisoners against America. Jose Padilla, a terrorist accused of trying to build a "dirty bomb" to unleash in the United States, was exposed to radical Islam in the U.S. prison system. Richard Reid, the so-called "shoe bomber", was converted to fundamentalist Islam while serving time in a British prison.

A Senate subcommittee has been formed and an inquiry is underway to analyze and scrutinize (for terror-related activities) the procedures used by the military and prison system to recruit Muslims clerics. The senators are looking into whether the instances of Wahhabi infiltration at key U.S. institutions may be part of a larger pattern. In response, many pundits have been quick to accuse investigators of Muslim bias. These same Muslim organizations and their supporters (the 'convenient masses') are falsely charging "bigotry".

Muslim groups in America such as the Muslim Public Affairs Council, CAIR and the AMC let it be known in the 2004 election that they intend to vote as a bloc for any Democrat in order to defeat President Bush. They fawned over Dennis Kucinich because he was the only Democrat to call for the immediate abandonment of Iraq by U.S. troops. This attitude speaks volumes concerning the Muslim population in America and its laissez-faire attitude towards terrorism. Instead of stepping up to the plate and doing more to help us protect the country that has welcomed them with open arms, they whine about being profiled. Said Omar Ahmed, chairman of the Board of CAIR in a speech to California Muslims; *"Islam isn't in America to be equal to any other faith, but to become dominant. The Qur'an should be the highest authority in America, and Islam the only accepted religion on earth"* [32]

Militant Islamists continue plotting and carrying out acts of terror with renewed vigor despite Western military successes in Afghanistan and Iraq. This is because militant Islam is an ideology, not an individual, and remains largely unchallenged. Now ideologies do not fall out of the sky contaminating men by accident, rather they are pushed and taught by its devoted followers. The chief place where Islam is taught is in mosques. The method of instruction is by self anointed indoctrination experts through 'sermons' sourced from authentic Islamic script contained in the Qur'an, the Sira and the Hadith. These motivation experts are adept at crowd psychology and emotional manipulation. If we want to avoid new domestic terror attacks, radical mosques all need to be monitored. Imams and clerics espousing anything close to treason and terror against -any- nation or individual will need to be identified and expelled. It is sheer folly that even after all that has happened, and all we know about the history and theology of Islam, mosques remain safe havens due to a overabundance of political correctness enforced by the suicidal left along with groups like the ACLU. All the while radical mosques remain the center of radical Islamic indoctrination, serve as the center for terrorist recruitment, a hub for paramilitary and explosives training, and of course collection points for terrorist financing.

Years ago in New York City, the FBI's Joint Terrorism Task Force began monitoring some men attending the Brooklyn Farooq Mosque. Agents watched in 1989 as men converged on the mosque in the early morning, loaded up their cars, and traveled to Calverton, Long Island, pausing only for prayer breaks. Once there, they would spend hours shooting handguns and AK-47s at targets on a range. These men included Mahmud Abouhalima, Mohammed Salameh and Nidal Ayyad, an Egyptian and two Palestinians who went on to bomb the World Trade Center three years later. Another participant of this cell was Egyptian Sayyid Nosair, who would later murder Rabbi Meir Kahane at a New York City hotel. Fortunately, Nosair was captured after attempting to murder a federal police officer and a 70-year-old man, but he would later help plan the WTC attack from his jail cell. An excerpt from Nosair's notebook, written three years before his jihad cell carried out the first WTC attack, demonstrates the imperative to monitor mosques:

> Before announcing the establishing of the state of Abraham in our holy land[,] to break and to destroy the morale of the enemies of Allah. And this is by means of destroying the structure of their civilized pillars. Such as the touristic infrastructure which they are proud of, and their high world buildings which they are proud of, and their statues which they endear, and the buildings in which gather their leaders. And without any announcement of our responsibility as Muslims for what had been done. And therefore, the enemies of God will be busy in rebuilding their infrastructure and rebuilding their morale. And they will not care much about what goes on around them more than [they] care about rebuilding their morale; and therefore, the chance will be available for the Muslims to repossess their sacred lands from the enemies of God, the traitors and hypocrites who will be at this moment in a very psychological weakness from what they see around them. And this is because the forces on which they were depending were crushed into pieces and are in a tragic collapse.

Another player in the Farooq jihad gang included an American named Clement Hampton-El (a.k.a. "Doctor Rasheed"), who, like Mahmud Abouhalima, was a veteran of the Afghanistan jihad. Clement would later conspire with other mosque associates - Egyptians, Sudanese, and a Palestinian - in a failed plot to bomb the United Nations complex, the Lincoln and Holland Tunnels, and the FBI's Manhattan headquarters.

No one at the time monitored sermons delivered on Fridays or their mosque planning meetings, but they themselves saved some reports to their chosen imam, Sheikh Omar Abdel Rahman, the blind cleric and leader of Egypt's deadly Islamic Group, 'Gamaat al Islamia'. Sheikh Omar would later relocate to the United States in mid-1990 and take up preaching in Farooq and other mosques in New York and New Jersey. These sermons by the Blind Sheikh and other radical imams were sometimes recorded and distributed for recruitment and fundraising purposes. Typical of such motivational sermons was the one Sheikh Omar gave just a few weeks prior to the first WTC bombing, where after explaining to his followers that "*God has obliged us to perform jihad*", he elaborated that "*[if] those who have the right [to jihad] are terrorists, then we are terrorists. And we welcome being terrorists. And we do not deny this charge to ourselves. The Qur'an makes it among the means to perform jihad for the sake of Allah, which is to terrorize the enemies of God and our enemies too. ... Then we must be terrorists, and we must terrorize the enemies of Islam, and frighten them, and disturb them, and shake the earth under their feet*".

We simply cannot afford to continue ignoring such clear and present potentially lethal threats to our infrastructure and citizenry. Experts tell us that 80-90% of even US mosques are at varying stages of radicalization, but even monitoring a hundred mosques to identify and expel a single radical imam inciting jihad would likely save US lives and be well worth the effort. Expelling a handful of radical clerics would also force the rest to at least tone-down overt public incitement. By such proactive actions we could prevent 100's to 1000's of otherwise nominal US Muslims from becoming Jihadists. Removing the Jihadist imperative from a young man is much more difficult than preventing the brainwashing process in the first place.

Despite an ever-growing body of evidence, many individuals, groups, and nations continue to function as a propaganda machine deceiving much of the American public, academia, and even our government. The stakes are becoming too great to continue our naïve and gullible habits. A tolerant, welcoming nation has given Islam the benefit of the doubt, but too many have already proven unworthy of that hope and confidence. Many of those spewing the incorrect or incomplete propaganda are aware they are not telling the whole truth about Muhammad and Islam, knowing the purpose of the misinformation is to weaken our resolve and keep us from instigating effective counter-measures. Despite the continuing rivers of blood flowing all over the world, they want to calm our fears that Islam is not a violent religion and that Muhammad was not a terrorist, proclaiming he was a lover of peace. But history (recent and distant) speaks for itself, and it would be unwise for any to welcome the kind of peace that Muhammad and his modern day followers seek. Those that defend Islam, or try to portray it in only a positive light, are deliberately or ignorantly misleading us and causing us to be inadequately prepared for their next deadly strike. Even the Muslim terrorists who flew the planes into the NY towers would undoubtedly have declared that Islam was a religion of peace, and Muhammad was a benevolent, merciful leader. Someone saying something is true does not make it true, and that cause is not helped if a million or even a billion repeat the lie. Truth is truth, to the end of reckoning!

After Pearl Harbor and the tragic internment of Japanese-Americans, those same persecuted people sent their Sons in large numbers to join the fight in Europe against Hitler. Those volunteers were amongst the fiercest, bravest, and most loyal patriots to join the conflict, and none today question their (or their parents) loyalties. Through such contributions and actions they proved that the suspicion and paranoia was unjustly heaped upon the Japanese Americans. The jury is still out on whether the religious convictions and political leanings of the many large American Muslim communities justify the hope and brotherhood they have been offered in contrast. When we see the vast majority of American Muslim communities sacrificing for this country in like manner, then we should welcome those communities in full faith and welcome Islam into the great melting pot that is our nation. Think of what these individuals could accomplish in terms of penetrating and to bring down terrorist groups and all their supporters. I hereby render the invitation and challenge to American Muslims to become full partners in this war. An effective on-site intelligence section and a division or two of properly equipped, fierce, devoted, patriotic Muslim American men with social and language skills from the region would quickly penetrate and make short work of the kind of terrorists we are currently facing in Iraq and Afghanistan. But alas, I fear that is a dream based on pure fantasy. Please American Muslims, prove me wrong!

MSNBC Oct 23, 2003 — On Wednesday, NBC News reported on a man who helped the Pentagon develop the Islamic chaplains program for the U.S. armed forces, a man who was later stopped with hundreds of thousands of dollars in his possession — and some serious questions about his background. Now there is more, and if federal prosecutors are right, this is a man who moved from the shadowy world of terrorism to the centers of power in Washington and back again. Federal Prosecutors have indicted the founder of the Islamic chaplain program on charges he illegally dealt with Libya and laundered money. But there are even more serious allegations about him in some new documents. Abdurahman Alamoudi, a consultant to the Pentagon on the chaplain program for more than a decade, is now accused of helping Osama bin Laden and Hamas. Court documents filed late Wednesday night claim Alamoudi has provided "financial support to Hamas" and "financial support to fronts for al-Qaeda."

One of the groups allegedly tied to Alamoudi is a charity that gave a Virginia post office as its address. Alamoudi was the charity's vice president. Who founded it? Abdullah bin Laden, Osama bin Laden's nephew. Also ringing alarms: Alamoudi's Palm Pilot, which the government claims included the names and numbers of six designated global terrorists. Terrorism expert and NBC News analyst Steve Emerson said, "The public face of Mr. Alamoudi was 180 degrees different from the private face. And the private face clearly showed that he was involved or directed fund-raising for Hamas, fund-raising for other terrorist groups." The government also alleges Alamoudi had a Swiss bank account and $2.2 million in unreported income, on which he failed to pay taxes. …in an audiotape of a conversation obtained by NBC News, Alamoudi seems to embrace violence and suggests al-Qaida should choose better targets: (Translated) "I prefer to hit a Zionist target in America or Europe or elsewhere." Alamoudi's lawyer said her client doesn't remember saying such a thing and questioned the tape's authenticity.

Over the years, Alamoudi has been a familiar face in Washington. Among other activities; the Pentagon chose him to help select Muslim chaplains. He met with President Clinton. He made six trips to Muslim nations as a goodwill ambassador for the State Department and even met with presidential candidate George W. Bush. Last year, FBI Director Robert Mueller even spoke to an organization founded by Alamoudi, over the objections of some agents. *"Alamoudi himself was able not only to insinuate himself, but he put other people in place",* according to Steve Emerson. These new allegations are contained in court documents arguing that Alamoudi should be held without bond until he goes on trial. There are already at least three investigations of the chaplain program Alamoudi helped develop that are under way. Some individual Muslim chaplains also are under scrutiny…

Reuters - Jun 25, 2004 SEATTLE - A National Guard soldier captured on videotape telling undercover agents posing as Muslim extremists how to cripple U.S. battle tanks declined to enter a plea at his arraignment on treason charges on Friday, the Army said. Specialist Ryan Anderson, a 26-year-old Muslim convert and gun rights advocate who was arrested last February as his unit prepared to ship out to Iraq, faces a court-martial beginning Aug. 16 at Ft. Lewis near Tacoma, Washington, where his unit is based. Anderson's charges -- attempting to give intelligence and other aid to two men he thought were al Qaeda operatives -- carry a maximum penalty of death, though Army officials said earlier this week they will not seek a death sentence in the case. Several accused al Qaeda abettors have been released in recent months for lack of evidence, including Brandon Mayfield, an Oregon lawyer and Muslim convert jailed for two weeks in May while officials tried to tie him to train bombings in Madrid, on March

11,which killed 191 people. Muslim Army chaplain Capt. James Yee, also based at Ft. Lewis, was accused of spying, mutiny, sedition, and aiding the enemy at Guantanamo, Cuba, but the Army dropped those charges in May.

Chapter 11
Worldwide Islam Today, by Country

Unfortunately, even long recent centuries of social/economic/military failures have not removed the jihadist imperative from the souls of Muslims. Far from having fallen into remission, jihad remains an ever-present threat, the default mode of operation whenever Muslims find themselves in close and sustained proximity with non-believers. All over the world today, there are many stories to be found detailing Muslim terrorists, operating for Islam's sake, attacking, bombing, and murdering those they feel inhibit their aims. Islamists are attacking non-Muslims along a vast arc extending from Nigeria to Indonesia. Violence occurs between Muslims and Orthodox Serbs in the Balkans, Jews in Israel, Hindus in India, Buddhists in Burma and Catholics in the Philippines. It is no accident that from its inception, Islam has always had bloody borders, as violence has always been integral to Islam. How can it possibly be otherwise with Quranic direction like sura 9: 73,122-123 *"Prophet, make war on the unbelievers and the hypocrites and deal rigorously with them. Hell shall be their home: an evil fate"* … *"Believers, make war on the infidels who dwell around you. Deal firmly with them. Know that God is with the righteous"*. It appears a majority of Muslims in the world today may indeed view America as the last great wall preventing the natural advance of Islam. In their mind, America must be destroyed or brought down, by any means necessary, to facilitate the end goal of all true Islamists, the total domination of all people and places. This is what motivated Sheik Rahman to try and blow up the New York towers. This is what motivates many Muslims throughout America to speak of a day when America will fall to Islam's power.

The Abu-Hafs al-Masri Brigades, a group linked to al Qaeda, took credit for the Nov 2003 Istanbul, Turkey synagogue attacks stating: *"The remaining operations are coming, God willing, and by God, Jews around the world will regret that their ancestors even thought about occupying the land of Muslims."* Does the God of Islam urge his people to kill other people who are gathered to worship? If not, we would hear Muslims speaking out clearly stating that the God of Islam does not urge the children of Ishmael to murder the children of Isaac, and not just Islamic politicians issuing statements to westerners, but clerics, imams, teachers, ayatollahs, and common lay members who regularly drop to their prayer rugs and fill mosques for worship.

Many Muslims might be peace loving and thoroughly disgusted with the acts of Islamic terrorism, but it is a sad fact that most of them are afraid to do anything about it. They know better than anyone the number, strength, and probable consequences of opposing the extremists. Also, it should be pointed out that many Muslims do not know in any detail the historical facts surrounding their own prophet. But in contrast, Muslim terrorists are usually very well educated in Islamic history, doctrine, and theology. They are the pious members of the 'religion' … spiritual leaders, and they operate with full confidence knowing they are following the example of their prophet. So often we hear of the fire-breathing clerics, even in this country, spewing hateful sermons inciting followers to act against many perceived enemies. The western expectation is that 'moderate' Muslims sanction them and appoint/elect better teachers and representatives, but to hope for such is naïve. To become a pious leader in Islam is to become fully acquainted with the real Muhammad and real Jihad. There are in reality relatively few religious leaders who teach a doctrine different than the one taught by Muhammad, and those are rightly considered apostate or corrupt teachers by most Islamic bodies in the world. In most parts of the Muslim world, there are the fire-breathing types of leaders who make no bones about their violent leanings, and then there are the more savvy diplomatic types who speak conciliatory tones when non-Muslims are near. But to their own people and in their native tongues, often those same diplomats can be heard praising all terrorists who act in Islam's name calling them Heroes and Martyrs. Remember that lying and deceiving non-brothers is explicitly allowed by Islamic doctrine set down by Muhammad himself.

Recent Islamic Terrorism Actions, by Country

ALGERIA - Approximately 130,000 people have been killed in Algeria during the last 9 years or so. The incidents are too numerous to report in any detail, and continue today. Below is one story from one of the survivors of an Islamic terrorist attack. The Muslim terrorists are not responsible for all the deaths; the

Algerian police and Army have also killed many. However, the Muslim terrorists frequently target civilians, children, and those that are unable to defend themselves. By one account Muslim terrorists stabbed to death 4 French nuns.

> BLIDA, Algeria - <u>Islamic guerrillas hold captive brides hostage to terror</u> by *Martin Regg Cohn Toronto Star Middle East Bureau.* In the dead of night, in the name of Islam, four terrorists burst into the home of 17-year-old Salima Amina Zenagui. Accusing her of loose morals, the Islamic fundamentalists ordered Zenagui to cover her auburn hair with a hijab head-scarf. Then they abducted her at gunpoint to their underground hideout, where the teenager was forced to marry a terrorist twice her age. After a religious wedding ceremony, he raped her - with a warning that any resistance would mean certain death. The bleeding didn't stop for 15 days. The mental torture, and the physical cruelty, continued for another five months. During the long nights and endless days, Zenagui slowly lost her sanity. And the will to live.
>
> Zenagui is one of thousands of young women and teenage girls believed to have been kidnapped by fundamentalist terrorists during Algeria's five-year Islamic insurgency. Forced into so-called temporary marriages that are a religious license to rape, their screams are soon silenced. Most of the victims have their throats slit, their bodies dumped in wells like the one discovered last week in Bentalha, just outside Algiers. Police were drawn by the stench of death to the 40-metre-deep well, where they found about 30 badly decomposed corpses of women and girls believed to have been abducted and raped after a massacre in the area a month ago.
>
> Known as "zawaj al mutaa", or "marriage of pleasure," the controversial practice is disdained by mainstream Muslims today. It dates from Islam's early years, when fighters in a holy war helped themselves to single women during periods of hardship or isolation. Zenagui believes her captors were fundamentalist terrorists from the GIA, who rationalize rape as a way of motivating their men to sacrifice themselves for Islam. Even as they mistreat their captive women, they worship their God. In their hideout, Zenagui watched them pray toward Mecca five times a day. They read the Koran, Islam's holy book, and often played inspirational cassette tapes about the Prophet Mohammed.

ARGENTINA - In March 1992, Muslim terrorists blew up the Israeli embassy in Argentina, killing 29 people. On July 18, 1994 a car bomb blew up the Argentine-Israeli Mutual Association, killing nearly one hundred people.

BANGLADESH - Islamists in this 83 % Muslim country aspire to establish a true "Islamic Republic" much like the Taliban. Members of minority religions have been under constant attack for decades. Some reports indicate Buddhists and Christians were blinded, had fingers cut off, or had hands amputated, while others had iron rods nailed through their legs or abdomen. Women and children have been gang-raped, often in front of their fathers or husbands. Pakistani Muslim soldiers raped 250,000 Bangali women in 1971 after massacring 3 million unarmed civilians. Hundreds of temples were desecrated and statues destroyed with thousands of homes and businesses looted and/or burned. The human rights organization 'Freedom House' reports native Hindus have been subject to "rape, torture and killing with the destruction of their cultural and religious identity at the hands of Muslims."

CHINA - Uighur Muslim separatist terrorists are active in Western China's Xinjiang Province. It is known that bombings and attacks have taken numerous lives, but the Communist regime suppresses most news and reports.

EGYPT - In Sept 1991, in Imbaba, a district of Cairo, hundreds of Muslims attacked the minority Christians there, burning down a church with a Pastor's wife inside. Other churches were attacked, and Christians were beaten. The government had to send in 3000 troops to stop Muslims from continuing to attack Christians. For years on-end in Egypt, Muslims have murdered hundreds of Coptic Christians. Muslims welding automatic weapons have even sprayed worshippers in church with bullets. In the deadliest attack on tourists in 1997, it was reported that at least 60 people were killed, including children, when unidentified gunmen opened fire at the world famous temple site of Luxor in southern Egypt. Islamist gunmen opened fire indiscriminately on tourists after the tourists got off a bus and were about to enter a temple in the morning. They were machine-gunned down by men shouting, 'Allahu-Akbar'. According to one eye-witness, two kids were holding down to their mothers' skirts when brutally torn into pieces with bullets. After the killing, the Islamists boarded a bus and prayed at a nearby mosque. Tourists from Egypt, Switzerland, Germany and Japan were among those killed in the attack. State television issued a brief statement saying "attackers hit a number of foreigners, Egyptians, and policemen who exchanged fire with them..." and the statement added that six attackers were killed in the shoot-out with police. Prior to the event, attacks by Muslim militants had killed 34 international tourists in the past five years. 34 people were killed in attacks on two Sinai resorts at Taba and Ras Shitan Oct 2004. July 23, 2005 terrorists set off multiple bombs that killed at least 88 in the SHARM EL-SHEIK Red Sea resort packed with Jew, European, and Arab vacationers.

ENGLAND - In August 1994 two car bombs blew up in London, one at the Israeli Embassy and another at a Jewish charity shop. An Iranian expatriate by the name of Manoucher Motamer indicated that Iran was responsible for the bombings. London's 9/11 awakening occurred 7/7/05 in the underground and on a signature double-decker bus. The investigations into the 7/7/05 tube/bus terrorist bombings, with the failed attempt 2 weeks later by 4 more would be homicide bombers, continues as of this date.

FRANCE - Several years ago, Muslim terrorist began bombing innocent French civilians. Here is one article:

> TERROR Campaign widens; Bomb in Paris Subway - July 25, 1995 --At least four (4)people were killed and another 35 wounded in an afternoon terror attack that took place today in the Paris Saint-Michel underground station, near the Latin quarter. Police officials are investigating and wouldn't immediately comment, but French Prime Minister Alain Juppe is quoted by the Reuters News service as saying that he believes that "there is a very strong suspicion of a (terrorist) attack".

These attacks were similar to bombings carried out by Muslim terrorists in France in 1986, in which dozens of people were killed. On August 26, 1995, a militant Islamic group led by a twenty-four-year-old French Muslim named Khaled Kelkal attempted to blow one of France's high-speed trains off its rails. Luckily, the bomb's detonator failed. Later that fall, other bombs would go off: two in double-decked metro rail cars in suburban Paris, one in a trash can along the very bourgeois Avenue de Friedland, another in a Parisian open-air market, and one more in a provincial Jewish school. In all there were nine attacks in three months, which killed ten people and wounded 114. Nearly 100 anti-Semitic incidents were reported in France in 2000, including the fire-bombing of a Paris synagogue and a Jewish shop in Toulon, and a near-fatal stabbing of a religious man on a bus in London. The bus victim, a young man wearing a yarmulka, was stabbed at least 17 times in the face, neck and chest by a 27-year-old man from Algeria. There were 135 physical acts -- vandalism, arson, assault, and attacks or attempted attacks -- against Jews in the first half of 2004, compared to 127 for all of 2003, according to statistics. The growing attacks and anti-Semitism led Israeli Prime Minister Ariel Sharon in July 2004 to call for all Jews to flee France and repatriate in Israel.

INDIA - The scale of 'loss of life' and 'social upheaval' caused by militant Islam may be worse in India than any other land, simply by virtue of the number of individuals involved. By some estimates, over 60 million have died in conflicts with Muslims over the centuries. Jihadists have destroyed all native Hindu, Sikh and Buddhist communities from five of India's provinces (including North Kashmir, now called Pakistan and Bangladesh). Islam first came into India as a Military force in the year 715 C.E., in the Province of Sindh, but it made inroads into the country proper between 1020 and 1194 after which Mohammedan power became dominant in north India. The people of Kerala had their violent introduction to Islam in the 18th century, when Tipu Sultan, the usurper of the Mysore Principality marched into Kerala attacking the Zamorin Raja of Calicut and began 'converting' people to Islam. Tipu went about with a Koran in one hand and a sword in the other giving the subject people of Kerala a choice of accepting Islam or death. Doing this, he marched from Calicut up to Alwaye where he was forced to retreat because of stiff resistance. In 1669 Aurangzeb issued a general order for the destruction of Hindu temples, and it is estimated that about 3000 temples were destroyed and converted into Mosques in the 750 years of Muslim rule in India. During the sultanate and later under Aurangzeb, many hundreds of thousands of Hindus were forcibly converted to Islam. The sentences of criminals and prisoners of war were ruthlessly executed with mercy and allowances only available to individuals embracing Islam. The Jaziya tax was both a heavy financial -burden and a badge of inferiority borne by the Hindu, which also stimulated conversions to Islam. In the 1860s a Muslim cleric in the Punjab region of India launched a murderous jihad initially against Sikhs, and then against all non-Muslim groups. In South India in 1921, jihadists carried out massacres, the forced conversion of Hindus, and the desecration of Hindu temples. The number of casualties over the centuries are at least and order of magnitude greater than suffered by the Jews in the holocaust, and the ongoing conflicts have been key to the economic and social disadvantages of Indian society. Although Indians are an industrious and educated people, the social, political, and economic costs of the ongoing conflicts are the cause of its poor economic performance compared to other industrialized nations.

INDONESIA - The Voice of the Martyrs Magazine writes that, "around 280 churches have been burned, demolished, stoned, attached and closed since 1991 in Indonesia (Sept 1996 issue). [That number is up to around 500 churches today.] The article continues, "The June 9, 1996 attack in Surabaya, the second largest city in the country was the worst yet as 10 churches were simultaneously razed by Muslim mobs." The article further records that 5,000 Muslims took part in the riots. Again, these actions are not the work of a few select terrorists, they are the work of normal Muslims who know what Islam expects of them, and as Muslims they exercised their faith to attack and destroy Churches in Jihad for Allah. Since the country is majority Muslim and has been for decades, no one knows the extent of the killings, rapes, and beatings. The peaceful Buddhists who previously occupied the region would have many stories to tell. Buddhist cultures seem particularly at risk to Islamic methods of conquest, and the appetite for violence for those performing the genocide is seemingly never quenched. Although 99% Muslim, non-Muslims are hit again and again. In August 2003 a blast at the JW Marriott hotel in Jakarta killed 12, and again with a suicide car bombing outside the Australian embassy in Jakarta in 2004 which killed 10 people. One of Indonesia's islands is Bali where most of million inhabitants are Hindu. Jemaah Islamiah, is the name of the terrorist Islamic flavor preferred by devout Muslims in that region. In 2002, the bombing of two nightclubs on that resort island of Bali killed 202 people, most of them foreign tourists (the infidel targets). It was, at the time, the worst terrorist attack anywhere in the world since Sept 11, 2001.

ISRAEL - Muslim actions against the Jews of Israel would fill volumes. I mention only one series of incidents here of particular significance. In 1921, the first British High Commissioner of Palestine, Sir Herbert Samuel, appointed one Haj Amin al-Husseini as the Grand Mufti of Jerusalem (1921-1937), in an attempt to appease Arab nationalism. After a series of violent riots against Jews, the Arab Hebron riots in 1929 resulted in the rape and massacre of most of that Jewish community, the chief instigator being the very same Haj Amin Al-Husseni. The Jews of Hebron were nearly all exterminated, with men's testicles cut off, women raped, their breasts cut off, and babies slashed to death. Following his early release from a British prison in connection with the Hebron massacres, Husseni started issuing fatwas against all Jews. In 1937, the Grand Mufti's violence reached such a crescendo that he had to escape from Palestine. He found sanctuary in Lebanon, where he was welcomed by the French (surprise!). In 1941 he helped organize a revolt of the Arabs in Iraq against the British with the encouragement of the Germans. When that failed, the Grand Mufti made his way to Berlin, where he remained from 1941 until the end of World War II as the guest of Adolf Hitler. While in Berlin he broadcast propaganda on behalf of the Nazis to the entire Middle East. He organized the Moslems in Albania and Kosovo (including the SS Khanzar Muslim division) for the German war effort on the Eastern Front and against the Jews. He constantly encouraged the Nazi death machine to exterminate the Jews of Europe at a faster pace. The Mufti surpassed even Adolf Hitler in his hatred for Jews. At the 1946/47 Nurenberg War Trials, Adolf Hitler's deputy, Dieter Wisliceny, testified that "the Mufti was one of the instigators of the systematic extermination of European Jewry and had been a collaborator and adviser of Eichmann and Himmler in the execution of this plan." The Grand Mufti became an international figure and a rallying point for the Arabs of the Middle East and fascists around the world. At that point in time he had a valid claim to have been instrumental in killing more Jews than anyone else. Yasser Arafat was known as Mufti's relative, and was seen by many Arabs as his spiritual heir.

ITALY - A Muslim stabbed, but failed to kill, Ettore Capriolo, the man who translated "The Satanic Verses" into Italian. The attack occurred in Milan Italy. A bomb blast Feb 26, 2002 damaged parked cars and shattered windows near the Interior Ministry in downtown Rome. Investigators believe the bomb was planted on a moped around the corner from the ministry, the headquarters of Italy's national police and security services. The attack, while largely symbolic, reflected a rising tide of Islamic terrorism that seems to be focused on Italy. Only days earlier the police uncovered a tunnel that suspected Muslim terrorists were digging in the vicinity the U.S. embassy in Rome, apparently intending to carry out a chemical attack or blow it up.

JAPAN - In July 1991, a Muslim murdered Hitoshi Igarashi, the Japanese man who translated "The Satan Verses" into Japanese. He was stabbed to death in Tokyo. A Muslim living in Britain - Abdul Quddus, who is a senior vice president of Britain's Muslim league, said, "The attacks are justified because people translating the book are also insulting the faith."

NIGERIA - In Oct. 1991, thousands of Muslims attacked Christian churches, businesses, and homes in Kano, Nigeria. Kano is in northern Nigeria, which is predominately Muslim. It was estimated that 300 Christians were murdered by Muslim mobs. Muslims were upset because Christian evangelists had been converting Muslims in the region to Christianity.

In northern Kaduna state, more than 400 people were killed in rioting instigated by Muslim religious leaders who recently committed themselves to peace and reconciliation, and hundreds of homes and businesses, and at least six Anglican churches were destroyed by arson. Enraged after a Nigerian newspaper ran an article claiming Muhammad would probably have married one of the contestants of the Miss World contest, Muslims burnt down the newspaper offices. Rioters chanting "Allahu Akbar" barricaded streets with burning tires, and began looting and burning homes and businesses. Christian citizens were stabbed, beaten to death and even burnt alive. At the height of the riots Muslim youths operated roadblocks, checking the religious identity of motorists and viciously attacking any Christians they found." Our people are being shot, butchered and roasted," Bishop Josiah Fearon of the Diocese of Kaduna reported to a friend. Bishop Josiah believes the 'Miss World' article merely provided an excuse for the violence, which in reality was instigated for more sinister political reasons. Across North and Middle Belt Nigeria Muslim activists have successfully lobbied for the expansion of Shari'ah. Eleven states have now adopted full Shari'ah to the detriment of their non-Muslim minorities who have begun to see their freedoms eroded. However in Kaduna state, where Muslims and Christians are roughly equal in numbers, Governor Alhaji Ahmed Mohammed Makarfi has resisted the demands for full Shari'ah instead allowing for a more limited expansion applying it only in Muslim-majority areas. This has infuriated Islamic religious leaders who are trying to oust him from office. The article provided Muslim leaders with just the excuse they needed. By unleashing terrible violence against Christians they hope to instigate a crisis which will result in the governor's removal.

In Dec. 2003 a student-led Islamic sect (Al Sunna Wal Jamma) launched an armed uprising with the aim of setting up a Taliban-style Muslim state in northern Nigeria. The group attacked the police stations in Kanamma and nearby Geidam, killing two policemen, stripping the buildings of guns and ammunition and burning them to the ground. They then retreated to a primary school in Kanamma where they hoisted the Taliban flag of Afghanistan. At least 18 people were killed.

> Guardian Unlimited UK – Jos, Nigeria - Feb 26, 2004 - At least 48 people have been killed in the latest outbreak of religious violence in Plateau state, central Nigeria, the police said to Reuters yesterday. They were hacked down on Tuesday when Muslim warriors attacked Yelwa town in the mainly Christian district of Shendam. The Plateau police commissioner, Ilozuoke, told reporters: "The victims were pursued to a church they ran to for refuge and were killed ... forty-eight of them died instantly." Security sources said the attackers' guerrilla tactics suggested that they were hired mercenaries from Nigeria's northern neighbors, Chad and Niger. Mr Ilozuoke said troops and police had been sent to the area to try to contain the violence, but no arrests had yet been made. More than 100 people have been killed in clashes between Christians and Muslims in southern Plateau in the past two years: in 2001 more than 1,000 were killed. And about 10,000 have died in communal and religious violence in Nigeria since 15 years of military rule ended in 1999.

PAKISTAN - When the Muslims in Pakistan found a torn up Qur'an in a mosque, 30,000 Muslims attacked the only majority Christian town (Shanti Nagar) in Pakistan and destroyed over half of it in 1996. Churches were burned, businesses were destroyed, and women and girls were raped. The army had to come in to stop the Muslims. A worldwide outcry against the action prompted Pakistan's Prime Minister to help rebuild the Christian homes, churches, and businesses that were destroyed.

[Note: This action was not the work of an organized terrorist group; rather it was a display of pure, real Islam as the majority of average simple Muslims in the region understood it. There was no Bin Laden leading the effort, no Hamas or Hezbollah orchestrating the action, it was ordinary Muslims, 30,000 of them, attacking a Christian village, because they thought that some Christian had torn up a Qur'an.]

PHILIPPINES - In the Philippines, the Abu Sayyaf specializes in kidnappings and beheadings of hostages in their terrorist campaign against the predominantly Catholic central government. In mid-1972, partisan political violence was generally divided along religious lines and gripped all of Mindanao and the

Sulu Archipelago. In 1973-75, the Moro National Liberation Front (MNLF) fielded some 30,000 armed fighters. Destruction and casualties, both military and civilian, were heavy; an estimated 50,000 people were killed. Talks between the government and the Moros began in late 1976 under the auspices of the Organization of the Islamic Conference to which the Moros looked for support. The talks led to an agreement between the government and the MNLF signed in Tripoli. After a lull in the fighting, the truce broke down in 1977 amid Moro charges that the government's autonomy plan allowed only token self-rule. Conflict between the autonomous south and government has been on-again, off-again ever since, characterized by military defeats, followed by signed truces, then after a short period the breaking of the agreements by the southern Muslims on some pretext. On Jan 4th, 2004 a bomb killed over 10 people at a gymnasium in the southern Philippines, with up to 30 hurt. The target of the attack on the southern island of Mindanao was Vivencio Bataga, the Christian mayor of the largely Muslim town of Parang, who had survived several attempts on his life. Mindanao has been racked by more than three decades of violence as Muslim rebels battle to establish an Islamic state in the south of this overwhelmingly Roman Catholic country.

The Abu Sayyaf and the Moro Islamic Liberation Front (MILF), an offshoot of the MNLF, continues to seek Muslim self-rule through Jihad (murder and terrorism). Nearly two decades after the government in Manila created the Autonomous Region in Muslim Mindanao, its five provinces remain among the poorest in the country as its population remains focused on war versus development. The rebellion in the south has killed more than 120,000 people since the late 1960s and stunted development of an area rich in minerals, rice and other natural resources.

RUSSIA - Many more recent attacks are chronicled in Appendix C. What could collectively be described as Russia's Sept 11th occurred late Aug, 2004, when homicide bombers brought down two commercial airliners, followed a week later by a bloody hostage incident at a school killing hundreds of women and children. The incident at Beslan, Russia is so significant that a special chapter has been dedicated to its description. A notable fact is that the community targeted in the town of Beslan is a predominately Christian enclave in the mostly Muslim south Caucasus region.

SPAIN - Spain's 9/11 occurred on March 11, 2004 when militant Islamists bombed several commuter trains, causing widespread death and injury, just prior to national elections. The people of Spain, in a state of shock, voted for appeasement and withdrew support forces from Iraq, as demanded by the militants. Spanish white hands raised in surrender brought great satisfaction to Islamic groups worldwide. But neither Islamic nor Western peoples feel respect for Spain's capitulation, as the eventual destiny of any nation not willing to fight militant Islam is more speedy servitude to the Islamic masters manipulating them.

SUDAN - Separate from the earlier Christian and animist purges in the South, the Darfur genocide has recently left an estimated additional 30,000 people dead and 1.4 million displaced in Sudan and Chad. A State Department report, based on interviews with 1,136 refugees in neighboring Chad, said 67 percent of refugees reported witnessing aerial bombardment by (Islamic) Sudanese government aircraft; 61 percent reported the killing of a family member; 16 percent reported rape; and 33 percent reported hearing racial epithets. In months of interviews across Darfur, scores of Sudanese have described horrific atrocities committed by Janjaweed and Sudanese soldiers, including systematic gang rapes, summary executions, and male children being thrown into burning huts or onto pyres. The abuses seemed designed to erase the collective identity of the mostly Muslim black Africans, survivors said. Survivors testify that they often called the victims 'slaves', before raping women to create `Arab babies' and castrating the men. The Janjaweed killed male babies, apparently to wipe out future generations, the survivors said.

THAILAND - Four soldiers were killed Jan. 4, 2004 during the armory raid in Narathiwat province and more than 300 weapons were stolen. Over 20 schools were torched in what officials believe was a diversionary tactic. Two days later 2 monks, aged 65 and 13, were attacked with machetes and killed by four men on two motorcycles as they left a temple in Yala, about 1,000 km south of Bangkok. Since the armory raid, a series of hit-and-run assaults have killed at least 43 people in the Muslim-dominated southernmost provinces in this Buddhist majority country. Government officials blame the violence on Muslim separatists with possible links to terror networks like al-Qaeda. Most of the victims have been police officers, soldiers, Buddhist monks and village leaders, with at least 60 police killed in 2002 and 2003. A bloody struggle was waged in the 1970s and 1980s by violent Islamic separatist groups, some seeking reunification with Malaysia, costing thousands of lives. Muslims fighting for a separate Islamic nation are suspected of countless bombings, arson attacks, shootings and other assaults during the past several years in southern Thailand, in a bid to destabilize Bangkok's grip and allow Islamic "Sharia" law to dominate. Relentless arson attacks on government schools in the south during the past decade, has been blamed on Muslims who want to cripple the official education system so more Muslim children end up in local Islamic schools or fundamentalist institutions in the Middle East.

Mohammed's faithful followers also wiped out the Syrian and Moroccan cultures, Christianity in Turkey, Jewish cultures in Syria and the rest of Middle East, the Zoroastrian Faith in Iran, Buddhism in Afghanistan and Indonesia. This section is by no means a complete list of Islamic conflict with current or past nations, and some may feel slighted to discover their countries conflict and struggle with Islamic militants is not represented here. Please forgive me if I have misplaced emphasis or omitted important events and struggles other innocent societies have had with Islam. My intent is to cite sufficient history to establish reality firmly and permanently into the minds of cognizant, honest adults. All history, news, and data would simply be overwhelming, and much too numerous to cite in a single chapter, book, or even in many volumes of works.

In previewing Islam's domino-like conquests worldwide, the modus operandi appears to be triggered when they establish a "critical mass" of about 10 percent of a given population. At about that point Muslim leaders and politicians begin to become bellicose and intimidating in their demands. The Jihadist arm in unison actively foments violence, revolt, murder, kidnappings, and other criminal activities. This in-turn cowers peace loving peoples and many leave for safer regions, further accelerating Islam's demographic conquest. Absent strong National leadership and will, no individual or neighborhood can withstand such onslaught for long. Europe should be terribly worried, by 2020 Muslims will account for 10% of its overall population. In population Islam is exploding, while the West is dying.

Muslims could easily prove to the world that Islamic nations are willing to fight against supposedly misguided Muslims practicing terror and genocide, by forming a united military force and using it to stop the genocide against South Sudanese Christians and black Muslims in Darfur sponsored by the Sudanese Muslim government. Will Peace-loving Muslim nations come forward to stand with infidels against Islamic murderers, or will we get more of the same old tired English only lip service when expediency calls for it, while their Imams and Clerics in Arabic inspire ever more young zealots to join jihads against Israel, the USA, Russia, India, Philippines, and elsewhere. With notable exceptions like the action Musharraf government is taking against Arabs in Eastern Pakistan, what will be seen is the usual active and passive support for various Islamic militant groups, the families of their 'martyrs', and, of course, playing the US/Israel blame game at the UN.

It is a curiosity to repeatedly hear of incidents when Muslims go on violent murderous rampages immediately after religious services on their Sabbath. In stark contrast to genuinely peaceful religions, young men stream out of Mosques going strait to work taking vengeance against some perceived slight or injustice. When Muhammad got offended, he murdered.... today, Muslims get offended, they murder. It is motivated by one and the same spirit and philosophy - the same malevolent spirit that appeared to Muhammad which caused him to attempt suicide, then talked him out of it, and started him on a path of violence. The same spirit that had him massacre 800 Jewish men and adolescent boys, then enslave their women and children (*those Jews had never clashed swords with Muhammad or his followers until he attacked them*). The spirit that drove Muhammad and his followers had a thirst for conquest, and during Muhammad's last 10 years of life the blood flowed freely.

Not only have Muslims attacked non-Muslims in Pakistan, but also the religious strife between Sunni and Shia Muslims has taken the lives of hundreds during the last few years. Bombings of each other's mosques and gunfights outside of Mosques have taken place. Even inside of the Mosques, people have been shot. It is probably safe to assume that even if Islam succeeded in conquered the whole world, the bloody peace of Muhammad would continue unabated between nations and tribes. Islam seems capable of justifying violence and war against anyone, anywhere, anytime, for almost any reason.

Though the devout continue to kill to bring about a day when the entire world is under the thumb of Islam, it is certain that wars and conflict would not end if that day were to ever arrive. Since the Islamic prescription for any hearsay, sacrilege, or misstep is violence, a world full of Muslims would undoubtedly be a world of continual tribal, regional, or economic war. Interactions between various Islamic peoples and sects today have demonstrated that conclusively. All Islamic visions of peace and utopia are unrealistic, nothing more than the unrealizable inventions of infantile magical thinking.

Chapter 12
Todays News from Peaceful Islam

The near and far history of a people and culture is certainly telling, but the acts and behavior of its members today are inescapably revealing. Through this chapter and its associated Appendex C, we will attempt to identify exactly that, *'true Islam'*, as it is being practiced by large numbers of its devoted followers *today*. Not 1400 years ago, not a few hundred years ago, not fifty years ago, not even a decade ago, but right now. Even as you read this, ever more newsworthy events are being played out somewhere in the world, probably in several places simultaneously. Undoubtedly many many smaller-scale events and actions are also at play, in places nearby and in remote lands which none of us will ever hear about. Because of the prolific, abundant material in this chapter, due to the extraordinary energy and efforts of Islamic extremists worldwide, the actual citations are separated out into Appendex C. The amount of source material is overwhelming and mind numbing, as is the material presented regarding the actions of Islamists throughout all history. As the reader reviews the material here, there is one question he/she should keep in mind. If Islam were truly a religion guided by compassion, mercy, patience, balance and peace as claimed, could the acts recorded in this chapter and Appendex C have taken place?

There is constant bloodshed with Jihad disseminating death and terror. In Southern Sudan alone, Jihad has caused the death of some two million people and generated an even larger number of refugees. The Arab government in Khartoum, Sudan has for decades been conducting a genocidal campaign against the Christian and animist blacks in the south -- a campaign that includes mass starvation, the bombing of hospitals, and slavery. Tens of thousands have been sold into slavery. The Muslim Government of Sudan in February 1998 imposed a veto on humanitarian aid flights to the southern predominantly Christian province of Bahr el-Ghazal, and up to 60,000 men, women and children died of starvation in a matter of weeks. On July 14, 1999 it repeated the ban, leaving 200,000 people starving and trapped without food. Some claim that the Muslim King of Libya, Moamar Ghadafi, is paying Billions of Dollars to Sudan and other African Countries, to kill Christians and make Africa an all Muslim Continent.

In 2003 armed Islamists, some from Pakistan, have been infiltrating the Indonesian isle of Sulawesi. Coinciding with the anniversary of the 2002 Bali bombing, they have attacked five villages, burning churches and homes. The Muslim regional chief of police, brigadier general Taufik Ridha, claims that he does not know the motive of these crimes, even though the attackers separated out Christians (including a six year old girl) and then shot them in the head or hacked them to death; and despite the fact that many of the weapons used were the same as those used by the Laskar Jihad group, responsible for the massacres of Christians in 2000. The Laskar Jihad, under pressure from the Islamic government responding to American demands, claims to have disbanded, which really now seems to be a new Islamic euphemism for *'reorganizing under a new Jihadic banner'*.

This culture of hate has multiple heads from Algeria to Afghanistan, to Indonesia, via Gaza and the West Bank, Damascus, Cairo, Khartoum, Teheran, Turkey, and Karachi. It scatters the seeds of terrorism from one end of the earth to the other. Muslims in Indonesia slaughtered at least 200,000 Christians in East Timor (*a former Portuguese colony annexed by Indonesia in 1975*) and another 100,000 Christians have been killed in Indonesia proper. Moslem fighters returning from fighting the Russians in Afghanistan murdered over 100,000 in Algeria in the '90s. Christians have been pursued, and massacred, and their churches burned down by Jihadists in the Moluccas and other Indonesian islands. The additional death toll in those violent attacks is over 10,000, while an additional 8,000 Christians have been forcibly converted to Islam. Atrocities are also being committed by Jihadists in both the Philippines, and some northern Nigerian states. Hundreds of innocent people died when Jihad struck at the Jewish Community Center of Buenos Aires in Argentina, and the U.S. embassies in Kenya and Tanzania. In Egypt, Jihadists have massacred Copts (native Egyptians) in their churches and villages, and murdered European tourists. Christians in Pakistan and in Iran live in terror of accusations of blasphemy, which, if "proven", can yield a death sentence. And a cataclysmic act of Jihadic terror resulted in the slaughter of 3,000 innocent civilians of multiple faiths and nationalities in New York, on September 11. As in all offensive Jihadist acts, none of those victims were guilty of any crime. They were murdered and mutilated out of hatred inspired by a destructive and ambitious religious/political philosophy (AKA 'Radical Islam').

Realize that the news releases outined in [Appendex C](#) in no way represent the entire scope of current Jihadists acts against those they target worldwide. Most activities are generally never reported or suppressed by a media who normally prefer to not mention the religious motivations or affiliations behind the stories. Rather these postings are cited to demonstrate the general trend of ongoing activities in support of 'pure Islam' for the benefit of those who do not always follow world events closely. Even those who try to keep up with news and trends will learn from this linear presentation of various events all following the same general topic. This first entry separated out has special significance to Americans, as it is regarding an icon of the US Democratic Party, which should always be remembered. Subsequent entries represent some of the major stories starting in Algeria in 1997, with more space given to the more recent activities, up to the date of this writing. Please take the time to review the material in [Appendex C](#), at least until you are thoroughly convinced of the facts of much of mainstream core Islam today.

US History - Jun 5, 1968 **Los Angeles, California** – Robert Francis Kennedy (Attorney General of the United States, U.S. Senator – Presidential Candidate), was shot dead in 1968 at Los Angeles' Ambassador Hotel by Sirhan Sirhan. At the time, Kennedy was a Democratic senator and presidential candidate. A Palestinian Arab, Sirhan Sirhan, stepped forward and fired a .22-caliber revolver at Senator Kennedy. Although he was quickly tackled, Kennedy and five others were wounded. Sirhan Sirhan was arrested at the scene and later convicted of first-degree murder and given a life sentence. Senator Robert F. Kennedy died the next day. Sirhan Bishara Sirhan is a 25-year-old Palestinian Muslim immigrant who said he felt betrayed by Kennedy's support for Israel in the 1967 Mideast war. As Yitzhak Rabin wrote in his memoirs: "The American people were so dazed by what they perceived as the senseless act of a madman that they could not begin to fathom its political significance." What was its political significance? According to a report made by a special counsel to the L.A. County District Attorney's office, Sirhan shot Kennedy for his support of Israel, and had been planning the assassination for months. In an outburst during his trial, he confessed, "I killed Robert Kennedy willfully, premeditatedly, and with twenty years of malice aforethought." (Twenty years, of course, date back to Israel's declaration of nationhood in 1948). When Yasser Arafat's Black September terrorist stormed the Saudi Embassy in Khartoum in March of 1973 and took US Ambassador Cleo Noel, Charge d'Affaires George Curtis Moore, and others hostage, Sirhan's release was one of their main demands. On March 2, 1973, after Nixon rejected that demand, Arafat was overheard and recorded by Israeli intelligence and the U.S. National Security Agency giving the code words for the execution of Noel, Moore, and Belgian diplomat Guy Eid, who were shot to death. James Welsh, a Palestinian analyst for the N.S.A., went public with charges of a cover-up of Arafat's key role in the planning and execution of these kidnappings and murders. (There is no statute of limitations on murder.) If Sirhan had acted independently of the PLO, why were they willing to kill Americans to try to gain his freedom?

Chapter 13
Real Islam; a Case Study

The information and data presented thus far is overwhelming, to the point of desensitizing a reader deluged with it over a relatively short period. The process of reading leaves insufficient time for contemplation and normal human emotion. So much has happened; so many lives have been forever altered or snuffed-out as a result of Islamic Jihadic actions throughout the world. It is simply impossible to digest and properly consider on a personal human level the full impact of Islam's deeds yesterday and today. The reader is encouraged in this section to put him/her self into the shoes of someone and thus more intimately consider the personal impact of the violent acts performed against them by the energetic Muslim militants. A personal case study is given from the perspective of one victim and witness in Indonesia, which gives us the true human context to the many historical and current-news accounts cited herein. The pain, trauma, confusion, terror, and sorrow felt by this victim is representative of all victims of zealous Islamic militants acting on their religious convictions. In the end it doesn't matter if the victim dies from beating, having their throat slashed, shot, stabbed, burned, blown up, run down, or forced to jump off a burning sky scraper, the terror is the same, and the feelings and experiences of both the victim and victimizer are roughly identical. What matters is that just before the attack the victims were largely at peace with their attackers, having no designs to harm them in any way, and that the perpetrators carry out their acts feeling absolutely no empathy towards their victims.

Joel-News-International: 21 June, 1998 **Jakarta, Indonesia** – 'CHINESE GIRLS RAPED' (reported by a missionary to Indonesia, Bill Hekman: "Here I submit a victim's account of being raped during the May riots here in Jakarta".) Reference to Huaran Bulletin Board June 12, 1998.

"My name is Vivian, and I am 18 years old. I have a little sister and brother. As a family we live in what is supposed to be a "secure" apartment. At 9.15 am, May 14th, 1998 a huge crowd had gathered around our apartment. They screamed, "Let's butcher the Chinese!", "Let's eat pigs!", "Let's have a party!" We live of the 7th floor and we got a call from a family on the 3rd floor saying that the crowd had reached the 2nd floor. They even chased some occupants upstairs. We were all very frightened. In our fright we prayed and left everything in God's hands.

Afterward we left our room and went upstairs to the top floor, as it was impossible to go downstairs and escape. We got to the 15th floor and stayed with some friends. Not long afterwards we were surprised because some of the crowd coming out of the elevators right before we entered the room. We hurried into the room and locked the door tightly. At that time we heard them knock at the other rooms loudly and there were some screams from women and girls. Our room was filled with fear.

We realized that they would come to us. So we spread throughout the room hiding in the corners. We could hear girls of 10 to 12 years old screaming, That time I didn't know that these little girls were being raped. After about half an hour the noise diminished and we had some guts to go out and check. It was indescribable. A lot, some of them young girls, were lying on the floor. "Oh my God, what has happened?" Seeing all of this we screamed and my little sister Fenny, screamed hysterically and hugged her father.

Tears started coming down from my eyes. With our friends, a newlywed couple, we started going downstairs. Reaching the 10th floor, we heard a scream for help. The scream was very clear and we decided to go down and see. But as we turned we saw a lot of people. I saw a woman in her 20s being raped by 4 men. She tried to fight back but she was held down tightly.

Realizing the danger we ran as hard as we could. But unfortunately the mob caught Fenny. We tried to rescue her, but could not do anything. There were about 60 of them. They tied us up with ripped sheets, myself, my father, my mother Fenny, Donny, Uncle Dodi and my Aunt Vera. They led us to a room. Uncle Dodi asked what they wanted, but they did not reply.

They looked evil and savage. One of them grabbed Fenny roughly and dragged her to a sofa. At that time I knew she was in great danger. I screamed loudly but one of the mob slapped me in my face. My father who also screamed was hit with a piece of wood and he fainted. My mother has fainted when Fenny was dragged to the sofa. I could only pray and pray that disaster would not befall us.

Uncle Dodi kept trying to stop them by offering money. His efforts were fruitless. And in the end 5 people raped Fenny. Before beginning with the raping they always said "*Allahu Akbar*" (an Islamic phrase in Arabic meaning "*God is great*"). They were ferocious and brutal.

Not long afterward, around 9 men came to the room and dragged me. I also saw them forcing and dragging my Aunt Vera. But at that time I passed out and everything went blank. I became conscious at around 5 or 6 pm. My head hurted and I realized I had no clothing on my body. I cried and realized my family was still there. My father was hugging my mother and little bother Doni. I also saw uncle Dodi lying on the floor and Aunt Vera was crying over his body. I felt so weak and fainted again.

The next day I was in the Pluit hospital. My father and mother were beside me. With all the pains on my body I asked, "Mom, why Fenny …Mom?" I felt a stinging pain as I said these words. My cheeks were swollen. My mother cried again and couldn't speak any words, while my father, holding back his tears, managed to smile at me. After 4 days in treatment, my condition has improved. With a sad look, my father told me then what had happened. After I fainted 7 people raped me. At that time my father still couldn't see well after being hit with a piece of wood.

They raped me repeatedly. Then my father said "Vivian, Fenny is gone…" I was confused and cried out, "Why Dad?" My father couldn't answer. He told me to rest and went out of the room. I cried over and over again, feeling that my life had no meaning any more. A week ago, after I was released from the hospital I was told everything that had happened.

When Fenny was raped she kept on fighting and so she was repeatedly slapped by her rapists. The last time she fought Fenny spitted on one of them. Offended, the man grabbed a knife and stabbed Fenny's stomach over and over again. Finally she died with blood over her whole body.

My father told me that uncle Dodi had the same fate watched by aunt Vera who was also raped. "God…why should all of this happen? Where are you God? Are you still alive?" My aunt Vera now stays with her parents. She is in shock. Her face is blank and she refuses to eat. Almost every hour my mother and I cry over all these happenings. I can never forget. These mobs of people are monsters."

Additional comments from Bill Hekman: This is one of many victims. Hundreds of women and children were raped, mutilated and killed by Muslim mobs. Some had their vaginas ripped apart, their bodies cut into pieces. Over 5000 of the Chinese Indonesian's shops were looted and burned down. A few days ago another 63 shops were burned in Tegal, Central Java. The city of Solo is burned down. There is no protection and no justice in this country any more. Yesterday I was in the Kelapa Gading area and that area was spared from destruction. The police and military had guarded all the entry roads. The people there had collected large sums of money from door to door and paid for their protection. A similar situation took place in the Pondok Indah area. For the people who cannot pay millions to the armed forces there is no protection. Right now the hundreds of thousands of thugs, robbers, rapists, and killers live all around us. They are our neighbors. There is no punishment for the criminals and no justice for the victims. Yet, all Indonesians call themselves believers in God almighty. Some Christians are putting signs on their shops "Owned by Muslim".

The next article attempts to describe the indescribable. It delves into the spirit and mentality and family support structure that is the force behind homicide bombers. All involved are completely void of empathy, a key characteristic of a certain personality dysfunction better known by its technical term 'narcissistic personality disorder'.

The killing mantra (Washington Post 6/21/2002) by Diana West   ---   And Palestinian mothers? … The sickening fact is, the strongest desire of certain Palestinian parents is for their children to die, killing as many Jews as possible, from infants to old people, in the process. Take Mariam Farhat. When she got word her 19-year-old son, Mohammed, had been shot dead after murdering five Israeli teens and wounding 23 others, she told the Saudi-owned daily Al-Sharq Al-Awsat: "I began to cry, 'Allah is the greatest,' and prayed and thanked Allah for the success of the operation. I began to utter cries of joy and we declared that we were happy. . . . I encouraged all my sons to die a martyr's death." (Translation by Middle East Media Research Institute.)
The maternal death wish may seem freakish, but Mrs. Farhat is not alone. "May every bullet hit its target and may God give you martyrdom," Naima el Abed tells her son, Mahmoud, on a video released by Hamas that records the 23-year-old college student's preparations for a rampage against Israel. "This," she says, "is the best day of my life." Almost as good, no doubt, as the day of her son's funeral. This came after Mrs. el Abed's little terrorist was shot dead attempting to infiltrate a Jewish community, killing two Israeli soldiers. Consider the Palestinian scene of bereavement that followed: "All around her were women, clapping and celebrating his death, while his father Hassan quietly received congratulations," the Associated Press reported. "Several of their nine other children handed out candy to visitors. 'I wish all my children would be like him and carry out operations like that,' Naima el Abed said." Chances are excellent that they will —and not just to please mom. The Palestinian Authority may blindly blame Israel for creating a generation of suicidal maniacs, but it is the PA itself that has helped nurture—if such a word applies—such taboo-breaking evil through its relentless propaganda machine.
With subtitled clips from Palestinian-controlled television (available through WorldNetDaily.com), MSNBC's Alan Keyes this week gave American viewers an eye-popping look at the pernicious role the PA plays in teaching young people to kill and be killed. It starts with state-sponsored sing-alongs for the romper-room set—ditties about blood-drenched soil and warriors of Jihad. It continues with shows featuring girls in party dresses delivering bloodthirsty harangues: "When I wander into the entrance of Jerusalem, I'll turn into a suicide warrior! I'll turn into a suicide warrior! In battle-dress! In battle-dress! In battle-dress!" And it goes on through the seemingly continuous loop of

government-broadcast sermons. From one tele-imam comes, "Bless those who wired themselves, putting the belt around his waist or his sons, and who enter deeply in the Jewish community and say, 'Allah is great.' " Or: "Wherever you are, kill these Jews and these Americans who are like them and support them."

Mr. Keyes pointed out a young boy in one congregation. Can a child thus indoctrinated ever make peace? This same boy is probably now caught up in the latest Palestinian craze — trading charms, Pokemon-style, that feature the faces of suicide bombers. Maybe he'll go on to Al-Najah University in Nablus, alma mater of this week's bus bomber, Mohammed "How beautiful it is to kill and be killed" al-Ghoul. Al-Najah, it must be noted, was the scene of last fall's commemoration of the Sbarro pizza-parlor attack, complete with fake pizza slices, plastic body parts and play explosions. ...That PA sure teaches its children well.

As an experiment, every Internet savvy individual should go to Yahoo or Google and do searches (in any language) of sites containing the word "Muslim" or "Islam", and which also must contain one of the following words; "violence, attack, terrorism, militant, murder, bombing, or riot. Make note of the number of hits, and preview some of the writings, then repeat the experiment using the other major religions of the world, Hindu, Jew, Christian, Buddhist, and any others you care to explore. This sort of quantitative macro research does not reveal the details of the nearly innumerable postings, but it is a good indicator of the past, and extrapolations into the future may be inferred thereby. The only predictions into the future that can be counted on are ones based solidly on the past.

This body of evidence is sickening, overwhelming, and undeniable. Can a thinking man deliberate on these facts and come to any kind of reassuring conclusion other than Islam has not quite finished its bloody conquests? Unfortunately, even electing a pacifist President and locking the door will not protect our children from the designs Islam has upon this people. Buddhism, a peaceful religion and pacifist way of life, was once the dominate religion and culture in Afghanistan and Indonesia, but today it is near impossible to find even artifacts of the culture now completely conquered by Islam. Pacifism operates on the assumption that non-threatening postures will eventually be recognized and not be attacked or destroyed. Sadly, such assumptions have not (and will not) work against Islamic militants who throughout history have demonstrated little empathy and less tolerance towards others. Whether the perceived opponents are pacifist or openly oppositional makes no difference, Islamic Jihad has shown little or no deference in its actions, conduct, and options presented to all types of peoples and cultures. Islamists prefer pacifists, they are much less trouble to kill, enslave, and/or convert. If you want to help the Islamist cause, then by all means, be a pacifist.

Chapter 14
Islamic Psychology 101

Various mental malformations are usually at play when an individual goes 'Postal' and kills randomly, but those kinds of disorders do not represent the Islamic character. With one fifth of the world's population Muslim, it is impossible to characterize the appeal of Jihad to hundreds of millions as a psychological disorder. On the other hand, mental and emotional forces at play leading to large groups becoming brainwashed to a single cause have been characterized in other gang, tribal, nationalistic, and religious cults, and extrapolations of those 'cause and effect' examples certainly appear to apply to Islam.

It is no accident that many rituals practiced in Islam are centered on violent or war-like activities. Eid al-Adha (Feast of Sacrifice) is one of Islam's most important annual holidays where every family participates in the ritualistic slaughter of animals by slicing the creature's throat. While western men might help a son with the distasteful task of cleaning a fish, Muslim fathers involve their young sons in the bloody gruesome practice of slaughtering a large animal. Such a spectacle desensitizes its participants to the sight of pain, blood and death, serving to prepare young Muslims to carry out the very nasty work of Jihad against human beings. A 10-day festival called Ashura also appears designed to prepare Shiites for martyrdom. In it, participants of all ages slash their foreheads with swords, beat their breasts in penance, and flagellate themselves with chains and whips until the streets are stained with their blood. An attempt to describe other factors that induce a devout Muslim to kill in the cause of Jihad will be further outlined in this chapter.

The Victim de-Humanization factor:

The principals governing Muslim relationships with others is vital to militant Islam because in all genocidal activities to date, grooming killers to first dehumanize victims in their minds is an important prerequisite. The indoctrination in sacred script and official publications and media creates the erroneous belief that Americans, Jews, Hindus, and other non-Muslims are not human beings in the same sense as Muslims, and can and should be slaughtered with impunity.

With regard to the concept of equality, the idea is unacceptable to Islam. For in all forms of Islamic thought and practice, the non-believer cannot be the equal of the believer. A basic principle of Islamism holds that humanity is divided according to a strict hierarchy of worth. At the top of this hierarchy are free Muslim males, the cream of humanity. Below them, in descending order of humanity, are: Muslim male slaves, free Muslim women, Muslim female slaves, the males of the "People of the Book" (*Jews and Christians*), and, then, the female of the 'People of the Book'. Finally, the rest of humanity comes in dead last (excuse the pun); because they lack a soul they are regarded as worthless having no rights whatsoever. This unfortunate final grouping includes Buddhists, Hindus, atheists, agnostics, and others. But before Jews and Christians celebrate escaping last-place in this uniquely Islamic popularity contest, the fine print should first be carefully studied. Quotes referencing Christians and Jews from the Qur'an include: – "Worst of Creatures, Perverse, and Friends of Satan". The clear direction from Muhammad appears to be that Muslims are not allowed to even be friends or take favors from Jews and Christians, unless that devotion/tax is extracted by force or threat of force. Christians and Jews then and now hold a special place in Islamic theology, and are presented in a hateful manner in the Qur'an and in modern Islamic theology today. In the end they were regarded with contempt by Muhammad, the final words reported from the mouth of the dying Prophet were a curse on them *"Allah's damnation be on the Jews and the Christians ...."*

> 98:6 Verily, those who disbelieve (in the religion of Islam, the Qur'an and Prophet Muhammad) from among the people of the Scripture (Jews and Christians) and Al-Mushrikun will abide in the Fire of Hell. They are the worst of creatures.

> 5:51 O you who believe! Take not the Jews and the Christians as Auliya' (friends, protectors, helpers, etc.), they are but Auliya' to one another. And if any amongst you takes them as Auliya', then surely he is one of them. Verily, Allah guides not those people who are the Zalimun (polytheists and wrong­doers and unjust).

Many who have known devout followers of Allah have felt the distance between themselves and their associates. This anti-social philosophy also goes a long way to explain the experiences of many women who have married Muslims, only to be turned into slaves or otherwise treated harshly. In the officially 'state sponsored' Wahhabi controlled elementary schools in Saudi Arabia (our alleged ally in the war on terror), there is a fifth-grade lesson book that reads as follows: *"It is forbidden for a Muslim to be a friend of one who does not believe in Allah and his Messenger or who fights the Islamic religion. God has severed the [link of] friendship between Muslims and infidels. The Muslim, even if he lives far away, is your brother-in-belief, while the infidel, even if he is your brother of kin, is your enemy by religion."* It is the Qur'an itself that directs Muslims to break friendship and business ties and other allegiances. The Qur'an even takes this a step further.

> 58:22 You (O Muhammad) will not find any people who believe in Allah and the Last Day, making friendship with those who oppose Allah and His Messenger (Muhammad), even though they were their fathers, or their sons, or their brothers, or their kindred (people). For such He has written Faith in their hearts, and strengthened them with Ruh (proofs, light and true guidance) from Himself. And We will admit them to Gardens (Paradise) under which rivers flow, to dwell therein (forever). Allah is pleased with them, and they with Him. They are the Party of Allah. Verily, it is the Party of Allah that will be the successful.

This shows that even family blood ties are to be broken in the cause of Islam, sometimes causing orthodox Muslims to fight and kill their own relatives if they reject Muhammad's rule. Family ties, devotions, and sensibilities form the backbone of Western civilizations, from which we derive our strength and teach morality. In Islam, even normal, natural family bonds are subservient and must yield to Muhammad's vision of Islam. This explains why, in many Muslim communities and households, family member are expected to police the acts, thoughts, and expressions of other household members. On a slightly broader scale, communities are expected to monitor the conduct of families in their neighborhoods. So in Islamic lands, the control structure in place extends from the highest branches of the government (including the Judiciary), to the lowliest family member. The consequences imposed for failure to support the official family, neighborhood, tribal, national policy with respect to violent Jihad vary by tribe and region, but are often quite brutal. Here is some more supporting Muslim opinion on the subject:

> "O believers, do not treat your fathers and brothers as your friends, if they prefer unbelief to belief, whosoever of you takes them for friends, they are evil-doers." (Repentance: 20)

> "Let not the believers take the unbelievers for friends.... whoso does that belongs not to God." (The House of Imram: 60)

> "O believers, do not make friends with the Jews and Christians; whoso of you makes them his friend is one of them." (The Table: 55)

When one takes into consideration all that Muhammad asks of the faithful, the direction to have no Muslim friends makes perfect sense. It's all part of the psychology of violence. Built-in natural human feelings of empathy and all impulses of conscience must first be overcome before an individual can perform an act of violence or treachery upon another. Normal feelings of affection, respect, and trust toward a friend would get in the way of a Jihadic action that might require the killing of that same friend. When Muhammad specifically tells followers not to develop personal relationships others it serves to dehumanize all non-Muslims. This philosophy and psychology, when internalized, is designed to groom the Muslim believer into becoming an effective, non-thinking, non-feeling Jihadist warrior (i.e. a killing machine). Objects of disdain are much easier to kill than real live, feeling human beings. Not exactly in line with their oft repeated claim that 'Allah is most merciful, most forgiving, most loving and charitable', but for some reason that contradiction does not seem to register. Certainly any personal dilemma resulting from such contradictions are easily dismissed once fully immersed in the blood-lust and lynch-mob mentality of Islamic militants. Apparently 'most-merciful' in their minds only applies to fellow Muslims and is not proffered to infidels, except perhaps to survivors who agree to pay the eternal 'survivor tax' (*assuming you can wrap your mind around the concept of 'kind enslavement' or 'merciful indentured-servitude'*). From the perspective of non-brothers however, the Muslims personification of Allah seems awfully cruel, unforgiving, unmerciful, and unfeeling.

Islamic dehumanization of non-Muslims results in people innocently taking a tube in London, a train in Madrid, a plane in Washington, a bus in Jerusalem, or going to the theater in Moscow or a school in Beslan, to be wantonly murdered with nary a Muslim afterthought. Indeed videos like the beheadings of American civilians or mutilating their corpses invokes excitement, pleasure, and celebration in the Arab world, where they are replayed over and over to a demanding audience. The graphic video of the decapitation murder of Nick Berg, while his faithful Muslim murders chant 'Allah Akbar' sickens human beings capable of empathy and normal human emotion, ...but is a spiritual religious experience to Islamists. It is pure stupidity to expect reform from individuals or cultures excited and thrilled at the images of such wanton violence and brutality as has been perpetrated by Osama and his ilk. One can study the culture and religion to understand in an abstract intellectual level the process of Islamic corruption of the individual psyche, but one cannot truly 'understand' the depth of animal depravity gripping the hearts and minds of these 'new barbarians' without trying to put yourself in their place and trying to think and feel as they do, but any attempting such methods of full immersion risk losing humanity in the journey, if not sanity.

The Full Immersion and Education factor:

The first step in any process wherein an individual surrenders personal will over to any cause is full immersion into the alternate doctrine and philosophy demanding the devotion, and separation from all competing realities. In keeping with this rule, the secrets of Islamic extremist group's successes lie in the effectiveness of Islamic schools worldwide. The secret is embodied in millions of poor and impressionable boys kept entirely ignorant of the world and, for that matter, largely ignorant of all but one interpretation of Islam. These schools often manufacture young men who are the perfect Jihad machines. With support from governments, family, and cultural traditions, such schools continue to serve as Islam's primary method of indoctrination. The Qur'an is recited, memorized, and then recited again. Considering the source material memorized, it is a simple, natural act for those so brainwashed to step out of such schools, pick up a weapon, and start killing infidels.

We all know (because it's true and because it has been repeated so many times) that 'repetition is the best teacher'. Repetition and consistency are indeed the best teachers, of which Islamic students receive heavy doses along with further reminders five times a day when called to prayer. For Muslims, daily prayers are not personal supplications where questions are asked or answers expected. The Islamic God is unapproachable and unknowable, and certainly above considering anything as mundane as individual needs or personal revelation. All instructions and answers are already contained in the scripture, word, and example of Muhammad, and it is the duty of Muslims to accept the Cleric or Imams explanation of how these unalterable revelations apply to their life issues today. As such daily prayers represent more declarations of compliance than typical supplications seeking help on a personal level. These personal devotionals, repeated five times a day, seem designed to be more chants to reinforce commitment to all Islamic principals and aims. Then there is the socio-emotional power of 'group-think' events. In many other Muslim group settings (Friday sermons, funerals, protests), the rapture of large gatherings raising arms and chanting 'Allah Akbar' have the same socio-emotional effect as the huge crowds in the early 1900's raising arms, clicking heals and proclaiming 'Heil Hitler!' The otherwise weak and powerless individual gains power, acceptance, and respect by surrendering self to the group, thus cloaking that weakness with the perception of power that comes from affiliation with a group drunk on a sense of superiority and a divine mandate to make war.

The Overcoming Empathy factor:

Man is born with internal mechanisms intended to further both the individual and the species. Some of those mechanisms are emotional, including the natural tendency for empathy towards others. Empathy is the ability to see and feel things from the viewpoint of another. Empathy plays a critical role in persuading individuals to conduct their activities so as not to cause undo harm or pain in others. A person who has not lost the ability to feel empathy and compassion actually "*feels*" a portion of the anguish and pain experienced by a victim. A person so in tune with others responds by seeking relief for the victim, and in doing so also consoles his own empathetic suffering. Empathetic feelings are quite natural in children, increase with cognitive development, and are further sharpened when children are born and natural parental instincts become more active. A person who has lost the ability to feel empathy feels nothing at the sight and sound of fellow beings in anguish, and those who take pleasure at the suffering of others have deteriorated further into depravity and are said to suffer a dangerous form of mental and/or emotional illness (*narcissism is a dangerous personality disorder characterized by the lack of empathy and self-deceit, which malady most of the worst despots in history have suffered from*).

The Over-riding Conscience factor:

Other innate internal tendencies are also programmed in the human spirit, including longing for freedom, and our *conscience*. Conscience is defined as that internal moral sense which enables us to differentiate between right and wrong, and which lights the way for moral conduct. It is the gut feeling of rightness or wrongness, which grips ones heart as we act on the varied daily impulses that drive us. Normal empathy certainly plays a part in this internal compass, but conscience is cognitively and spiritually more significant than simple empathy. All these codes are ingrained in our minds and hearts and serve us individually and as a species, for without subjecting behavior to a common standard of vice and virtue, social evolution is not possible. This is the reason that even primitive societies have always had words denoting a differentiation between good and bad. Although societies do not all practiced universal standards of vice and virtue, yet it is well known that almost all communities have always had codes to acknowledge what was good and bad. Codes, for example, respecting others and their property, mutual fidelity, speaking the truth, keeping promises, respecting family ties, helping the poor, weak, and handicapped. These codes come into being in response to our innate conscience, and are generally considered signs of good morality. Since every one desires security of person and property, liberty to worship, fair trial, freedom of speech etc., these facts, over a period of time, rose to become what is called Human Rights. He who violates these rights is considered by developed nations to be an enemy of humankind.

The Islamic Superiority factor:

For a person to abandon internal standards guiding proper behavior towards others, forces or factors must first be applied to break down those natural internal clocks. There are many ways this can be accomplished in individuals and societies, and proven methodologies continue to be applied today with predictable results, as has indeed been the case with every political, national, or religious sect, which has ever behaved badly toward non-members or the non-privileged (including Islam). Islamic fundamentals preach innate superiority of Muslims over non-Muslims, social segregation, hatred of unbelievers, and elimination of dissenters through dominance, death and destruction. We turn to more quotes from the Qur'an to verify that conclusion:

- Do not let non-Muslims enter mosques. They will go to hell. -Repentance: 17
- ye who believe! The non-Muslims are unclean. So let them not come near the Inviolable Place of Worship. -Repentance: 28
- ye who believe! Murder those of the disbelievers ...and let them find harshness in you. -Repentance: 123
- Humiliate the non-Muslims. -Repentance: 29
- Certainly, God is an enemy to the unbelievers. -The Cow: 90
- God has cursed the unbelievers, and prepared for them a blazing hell. -The Confederates: 60
- Let not the believers take the unbelievers for friends.... whoso does that belongs not to God. -The House of Imram: 60
- Moslems are hard against the unbelievers, merciful to one another. -Victory: 25
- Muhammad has been sent by God with the religion of Truth, that He may cause it to prevail over all religions. -Private Apartments: 28
- Muslims are the best of all nations. -House of Imram: 110

A Muslim naturally believes in all such Qur'anic verses, pounded into his mind and spirit from childhood, which then warps his social outlook as he quickly becomes a narrow-minded sectarian. This psychological approach is the fountain of all fundamentalisms. It is a myth to say that Islam advocates good relationship with People of the Book (Jews and Christians). If this were not enough, one could refer the matter to the sayings of the Prophet. Hadith, Chapter 71 of SAHIH MUSLIM clearly states that Islam is the religion for all humanity and abrogates (overrides, replaces) all others. Simply stated it means that Muslims are superior to non-Muslims and have the birthright to dominate them. This is why Islam calls itself *Din-e-Ghalib*, the religion of dominance.

Obviously, believers from the best religion are superior to other people, and Muslim fundamentalists must fully assimilate this sense of superiority before they can act without natural conscience against inferior beings or objects. As previously mentioned, step-1 for any murderer is to first dehumanize the victim in his or her own mind. This fundamental Islamic sense of superiority, then, is step-2, and becomes the foundation of Islamic morality, over time supplanting or abrogating all superior natural or built-in instincts.

The Sex/Lust factor:

For the entire history of mankind, pirates, bandits, and armies have attracted young men to their ranks implicitly or explicitly advertising opportunities for rape and plunder, but Islam adds a twist to this base attraction. To succeed in Jihad is not only to gain honor, booty, and privilege in this life, but also in the next. To further illuminate the powerful force that is driving young men to Jihad we must ask …what is this hoped for paradise? Muslim scholars are usually embarrassed by this question and some even pretend that it is not physical but a condition of the mind. But in truth 'Islamic Paradise' is the chief temptation for enjoining active participation in Jihad, especially for young men. The reason that the Qur'an explains it so well and in such detail is that it was (and is) intended as a primary recruitment tool. The 'revelations' came at the beginning of Muhammad's prophetic journeys, as he was starting the process of gathering young men into armies to do his bidding. Descriptions of Paradise describe luxurious surroundings dwelt in by Houris and also Ghilman. Houris are the most beautiful ever-young virgins with wide, flexing eyes and swelling bosoms. Ghilman are the immortal young boys, pretty like pearls, clothed in green silk and brocade an embellished with bracelets of silver (apparently to satisfy those preferring the 'alternate' lifestyle). Allah guarantees every believing man no fewer than seventy Houris and many Ghilmans. To make sure that the lucky fellow can cope with them, Allah will increase his virility a hundred-fold! Individual lust and desire to dwell in such surroundings is a driving force justifying Islamic morality, and why Muslims (usually depressed and deprived as a result of Islam), are ready to practice a twisted morality based on violence. Those who surrender their psyches to the seduction of Jihadic violence fully expect to eat celestial food, drink pure wine, and enjoy the carnal company of divine consorts. Their staunch belief in the intercessory powers of the Prophet Muhammad (his authority to accommodate his followers in paradise irrespective of what they may have done), inspire them to follow his example into the ranks of Jihadic warriors. It's a win-win proposition … succeed and enjoy the carnal benefits of power, rape and plunder in both this life and the next, …or fail and enjoy all you lust after in the next life. Either way your reward is sure and guaranteed. Allah has promised all sorts of rewards, gluttony, and unlimited sex to Muslim men who kill unbelievers in his name. He promises that in the fight for His cause whether a man kills or is killed he will return to the garden of Paradise, where Allah will "wed us with Houris (celestial virgins) pure beautiful ones", and unite us with large-eyed beautiful ones while we recline on our thrones set in lines. In that glorious place Jihadists are promised to eat and drink pleasantly for what they did, and have sex with "boys like hidden pearls", and "youth never altering in age like scattered pearls". (See Qur'an 9:111, 56:54, 56:20, 56:19, 56:24, 76:19, and The Tidings: 30)

The only way to miss out on all this great stuff (and end up in fiery hell) is to fail to engage in Muslim violence against non-believers. Allah warned that: *"Unless we go forth, (for Jihad) He will punish us with a grievous penalty, and put others in our place"* (Qur'an 9:39). In these ways, through fear, false faith, greed, and lust, Islam is driven and inspired into the conscience of individuals, manifesting itself in gross crimes against humanity worldwide. After the people of Taif - the last major Arab City to resist Islam - surrendered in February, 631 C.E., to escape horrors of the siege, Muhammad was presented with three beautiful women; he gave one of them "to Ali, another to Usman and the third to Omar." To realize the significance of this episode, one ought to remember that both Ali and Usman were his sons-in-law and Omar was his father-in-law.

Muhammad constantly promised men fighting for his fledgling movement that if they die fighting Allah will reward them with a "virgin-rich" Garden (Suras 44:51-56; 52:17-29; 55:46-78). The more fighters he lost in battle, the more explicit the descriptions became. The heavenly trick worked then, and amazingly still works today, despite the impossibility of enjoying the physical sex act with no physical body. But will the God of all men comply with murderers demands for heavenly consorts upon their arrival into the spirit world after death, or will they simply be laughed at as they are escorted to their spiritual prison cells? You do the math.

The Self Loathing factor:

With their carefully cultivated sense of superiority, a gnawing sense of inferiority persists. As described in the chapter on Islamic Politics and Economics, it remains impossible for Islamic lands to compete with western economies and political freedoms. All attempts to 'catch up' within any Islamic context continue to fail. But for all their hatreds of the West, most Muslims are westernized to some degree, which leads to some degree of self-hatred. Western wear is the preferred dress for mass events involving chanting "Death to America", and those same young men can be found cuing at embassies seeking a better life in Western lands. Even Osama dresses half-Western, with his reliance on Western inventions total. Islamists are totally dependant on Western inventions and even democracy itself for the means to organize, communicate, and attack its benefactors. So there is day to day humiliation of individuals, with no practical way out, whose rage and jealousies become further amplified by officially sanctioned conspiracy theories. Within these constructs and this mindset, an element of personal self-loathing exists and grows in Muslim minds. When combined with the idea that victims are always already guilty by virtue of unbelief and/or opposition to Muhammad, otherwise rational Muslims transform themselves into Jihadists when they readily accept that the correct response to this conundrum is murder.

Blind Allegiance to Muhammad factor:

As every student of psychology knows, the purpose of any fundamentalism is to secure blind following from its adherents. This is possible when one is conditioned to a certain object or goal which begins to rank as the sole purpose of their lives. As a result, the purpose begins to overrule the method of acquisition; whatever secures it is good and whatever obstructs it is bad. In a nutshell, people must stop thinking for themselves, especially in terms of morality. As the Marxists brainwashed people in the name of proletarianism and what it stood for, Muslims have been conditioned to the person of the Prophet Muhammad, who is projected as the savior of his followers, having complete power to find them permanent residence in paradise (the abode of luxury, love making and lasciviousness). For total obedience, they are at liberty to indulge in the most convenient morality such as dishonesty, rape, murder, theft, and treason without losing their chance of entering a paradise that has been absolutely guaranteed by their faith in the Prophet.

For those properly conditioned, the use of violence for securing territorial and political advantage over non-Muslims then becomes the sole standard of Islamic morality against which such acts can be favorably judged (which explains the Palestinian prison systems 'revolving-door' concept for fellow Muslims caught committing crimes against Israelis). Islam declares Muhammad as the final and greatest of all prophets, and reverence for him and his methods has become an article of faith. A Muslim unwilling to force Islam on others is considered deficient in belief. As a result, every Muslim looks for an opportunity to demonstrate the magnitude of his faith by molesting non-Muslims, and even attacking fellow-brothers who express less bigotry. More Qur'anic verses clearly states that Jihad is a definite exchange proposition for Muslims (i.e. paradise for killing non-Muslims or getting killed in the process of Jihad).

> "Allah has bought from the faithful theirselves and their belongings against the gift of paradise; they fight in the way of Allah; they kill and are killed." (Repentance: 110)

> A HADITH (the saying of the Prophet Muhammad) declares: "Know that Paradise is under the shades of swords." (Sahih Bokhari, Ch. 22: 73)

Islamic terrorist organizations are among the most self-defeating and destructive because they send their own young to be killed under the guise of martyrdom while attacking and murdering the innocent.

Leaders and Imams promote such brutality consciously as a tactical tool, but the vicious psychological undercurrent supporting such vile behavior comes from strait from Islam.

The Group-think factor:

Because no good can come from outside Islamic tenants and peoples, without Islam a Muslim is in danger of losing his sense of belonging to anything of value. With everything else outside of Islam shut-out due to being unclean or unworthy, Muslims would be completely lost if deprived of their Islamic identity and connections, and so do not dare even think of abandoning their 'faith'. Along with the threat of fiery hell, a possible death sentence in this life awaits Muslims who oppose Islamic methods and goals, which is why even the thought of such heresy invokes feelings of sheer panic to most Muslims. Being a member of the Islamic Umma gives him strength, confidence, and a sense of purpose and superiority that otherwise he wouldn't have. This false sense of superiority then becomes an emotional and psychological trap. Those caught in this web are saddled with a self-image propped up only by words and bravado having no foundation in truth. When coupled with fear and insecurity, this image is what leads otherwise normal human beings into egregious thinking errors resulting in poor judgment, including decisions to engage in or support bigotry, and eventually ...murder.

History teaches us that groups of people, or sometimes even an entire nation, can suffer from dangerous delusions. One need only cast a look back at the last century when millions of Germans believed they were the "Master Race" and the Japanese believed their emperor was a living god and the conquest of Asia was their destiny. For several decades, most Russians were brainwashed into believing that Communism was the ideal social/economic system, oblivious or ambivalent of the millions who died in Soviet gulags and their own spiritual bankruptcy. Now, despite an even longer history of defeat and despotism, fundamentalist Muslims around the world are experiencing pretty much the same kind of mass delusion, believing that it is Islam's destiny is to dominate and rule the entire world.

The 'Resistance is Futile' factor:

As will be seen in subsequent chapters on Islamic politics and economics, there also exists within its economic and political structures, along with these psychological and social forces at play, a certain system of interdependency which guarantees the perpetuation of the Islamic order. These interdependencies act to compel continued individual participation in a society so organized. To put it another way, the entire social, political, psychological, economic, and religious structures and practices exert significant force to coerce involvement of its members, and to perpetuate its existence. It is literally a trap; in any way you view it, with options for escape nearly impossible. For poor Muslims who know no other way, it seems the only way to escape the kind of despair guaranteed to exist in Islamic societies is by and through the sword. Consider the following points collectively:

- Hate is taught from birth, and Muslims are mandated to expand Islam.

- You live in continual fear because someone might accuse you of collaborating, or of being a 'bad Muslim'.

- You must support and fund your cleric and his causes, because not supporting the organization will certainly mean your family being economically/socially cut off, if not brutally dealt with.

- You can't leave the organization and 'best' social order to join another; such treason is punishable by death.

- Any act or expression of dissent is tagged as an insult to Muslims, or blasphemous, with perilous repercussions.

- Fear destroys faith, without faith nothing permanent is begun or built and everyone is guaranteed to live in a miserable impoverished fearful condition.

- Unable to criticize the 'best religion' your miserable condition must be blamed on unbelievers.

- The only way to remain safe, or to gain any advantage in Islamic lands, is to support and/or participate in the process of Islam's often-violent methods of expansion.

- Killing unbelievers (or bad Muslims) or being killed in the process is the only offer that guaranties paradise, and so is the only way out of your miserable existence.

In summary, Muslims suffer from a strong sense of superiority, despite technical and intellectual inferiority. This leads to Self-hatred caused by recognition of their actual state of inferiority as well as the impurity of their own desires. No practical means of escape from genuine and never ending humiliations, combined with the promise of rewards (monetary, honor, and sensual), in this life and/or the next.

So it is, with personal free agency surrendered to Islamic causes, Muslims find themselves between a rock and a hard place. In reality they can escape the spiral of despair, but they do not know it. They are held to their limited and perverse options by a combination of fear and ignorance. Did the one God of the universe create this social order that removes both personal choice and culpability for killing others, and which perpetuates misery and despair forever? Is this the final, best, and greatest religion Muslims claim it is? If not God, then who created this perfect secret society where you must kill or be killed to be saved?

Chapter 15
Islamic Politics 101

History occurred Jan 2005 in the Middle East with the initial Iraqi elections. Emotions ran high with the large turnout, with purple stained fingers now a symbol of democratic success. Iraqis and Americans alike sacrificed dearly for the future hopes of a suppressed, persecuted people. The chief question now is whether principals of freedom, tolerance, and equal rights can take permanent root in Islamic lands and reform Jihadists. Unfortunately, the possibility exists that such aspirations may be naïve in the long term. The Mullahs in Iran continue to demonstrate that a violent, unpopular, ruthless minority *can* successfully frustrate the hopes and aspirations of the majority. Lebanon has also shown that it takes just a handful of Islamic anarchists to ruin a society, even when most citizens want progress and prosperity. Even the hold of secularists in Turkey remains tenuous. Democratic regimes built up in Afghanistan and Iraq will likely remain only as long as Western troops are present to protect them, and are in danger of quickly evaporating without that massive support. Any future prediction not firmly founded in actual history is simply a wish.

Any review of the Qur'an and history shows that Muhammad taught and led a totalitarian movement (enforced by the sword) strikingly similar to those led by other fascists and despots in recent history. Political Islam compares very well to any totalitarianism system of government including fascism, communism, and imperialism. It is simply indisputable that Islamist fundamentalism shares with other totalitarian movements a commitment to centralized political power and economic control. Islam, by its own definition and design, is a growth industry designed to mobilize the masses to score political victories, subvert host governments, and establish Islamic domination. Although it attempts to appropriate a particular religious look and feel, at bottom all forms of Islamist totalitarianism are not religious (spiritual) movements. Pure Islam is first and foremost a political movement – a quest for political power for the express purpose of physically subjugating all people everywhere. In both its totalitarian methods and global goals, fundamentalist Islam is even more intimidating than both fascism and communism, and so political Islam is the true successor to those largely spent movements. Militant Islam rises in full ascendancy from the ashes of earlier 20th century failed/discredited systems like the fabled Phoenix. This is happening before our eyes due in no small part to the fact that both good manners and the PC police prohibit disparaging certain religions, and Islam in particular.

Islamic totalitarianism is obsessed with worldly power and influence. Islamic governments desire not only to dictate regional politics, but also to dominate the West at every game of worldly success and power. Radical fundamentalists are not content with mere rejection of the West's alleged vices. If that were all there was to it, they might simply do what the Amish have done and stage a retreat from wickedness. But the Islamic mandate is not about building a few mosques, schools, clinics, or community centers to meet the needs of Muslim congregations, but rather to change existing societies into Islamic societies, to make Islam both dominate and supreme. Islam's totalitarian mantra and credo strikingly similar to pure secular ideologies more easily identified.

Islam's goal is to overthrow all competing governments and establish the Khalifat. The utopian fantasy of one seamless totalitarian state is a common thread that unites all radical movements of all ages. The Islamic utopian blueprint calls for a Caliph (a glorified Mullah) to wield the Islamic sword of power in one seamless totalitarian worldwide state. This outrageous fantasy pre-dates and has survived all relatively more modern failed political experiments. Today, extremists easily extract the appropriate language (found throughout all Islamic sacred texts) to sell the concept that the Qur'an insists that all nations must be fought until they embrace Islam. Despite claims otherwise, the most violent passages have not been abrogated by more recent doctrine from Muhammad. The Qur'an is the immutable and unalterable word of God, so the movement has been permanently cast into the cement of an unalterable mandate, which is what has given it unusual durability. The doctrine of Jihad and Jizya essentially means building the Islamic Empire by denying infidels all rights except the right to serve their Muslim masters. The secret of Islam's survival and longevity lies in both the deceptive cloak it wears in the form of a religion, and in the fact that economic weakness is always inherited by states based on its tenants. Up until the age of oil this has made Islamic countries appear relatively unthreatening compared to more modern industrialized countries with more powerful economies and the armies that can be built thereby.

By any historical definition, bin Laden, the Taliban, and all other Islamic militants can be accurately described as fascists. As violent devotees of Islam, they believe in the innate superiority of a fanatical elite, anxious to torture, jail, and kill any who disagree. Non-Muslims of any religion, women, homosexuals, are all dehumanized as their innate and natural inferiors. Hitler also believed he was the leader of the master race destined to rule the world, blaming all Germany's problems on Jews and Western governments. Hitler for a time managed to convince most Germans it was not a crime to kill all who did not fit into his Arian mold of the 'perfect human', because they were inferior and sub-human, thus leading to millions of deaths and destruction previously unimaginable. Hitler was a threat to the world many years before a world blinded by pacifism and relativism finally realized that self-preservation dictated he must be fought and destroyed. Hitler justified heinous acts in his efforts to make the Third Reich the 'only' Reich, just as Muhammad and militants justify anything to make the entire world bow to Islam. The Nazis cleverly manipulated the German people's collective frustration into a pervasive sense of victimization. Once this victimization psychosis was fully accepted, the Nazis then offered the answer; entitlement, under the guise of superiority and social justice. Properly indoctrinated and incited, Germans readily embraced their inherent superiority and forcefully claimed their entitled power, obliterating or enslaving all opposition. As Germany became more powerful and acted more and more irrationally towards neighbors, elitists and appeasers of the day refused to properly identify the gathering threat. Seventy years later ...it's Deja vu, all over again. In the twentieth century, genocidal totalitarian maniacs wore swastika armbands and herded members of supposedly inferior races into death camps shouting, "Heil Hitler!" In the twenty-first century, they wear black pajamas and masks, decapitate civilians, shoot children in the back, and plow hijacked airplanes into buildings shouting, "Allahu Akbar!"

1400 years of history also demonstrate that Islam is imperialist, in that it seeks perpetual humiliation of non-Muslims through a system of everlasting subjugation and payment of tribute. This method of dominating and subjugating a people for national gain (through booty and tribute) is what is known as pure Imperialism ...by definition! Imperialism is the campaign to establish of economic and political hegemony over her conquered. Murder and plunder of other nations for booty by the Romans, the Persians in Iran, the Mughals, the Turks, the Spanish in Central/South America, or the British, was horrific for the exploited. Though dressed in religious garb and chanting 'God is Great!' ...the Islamic beast of Imperialism is just as ugly and evil as any other in the history of man. Though Islamic leaders claim to be pious representatives of God acting on divine instruction, it does not change the practical facts and consequences to the conquered peoples and lands. Of course, the practice of Imperialism is not an Arabian invention, murder and plunder of other nations for booty pre-dates Muhammad's adaptation of the practice for 'religious' purposes. But where all other imperialist movements have waned with enlightenment, the decay of regional powers, or the death of individuals, Islam's imperialist movement has amazingly survived and thrived these last 1400 years, which is the only thing that makes it unique. Everything about Imperialism is self-serving and at other nations expense, nothing about it is isolationist, self-protective, pacifist, or harmless. Though presenting itself in religious garb demanding respect and protection, Islamic Imperialists practice Jihad more to expand Islam than to protect it. Islam has one goal, and that is to overthrow all competing governments (including European) and establish the Khalifat. Nothing is more dangerous to weaker competing forms of governance than Imperialism.

There are also many similarities between fundamental Islamists and die-hard communists. Both of these groups abhor highly educated thinkers and scholars, essentially forbidding rational thinking that does not support their ideologies. In the early 1960s, as part of the 'Cultural Revolution', the Chinese Maoist regime killed many intellectuals and scholars, virtually suppressing most higher education for decades. In place of rational thought and real education, they set up institutions to study Marxism and Maoism. Mao's "Red Book" became a Bible to his subjects, a focus of education with memorizations required. Contrast this with Iran, where Ayatollah Khomeini's regime killed millions of intellectuals, scholars, and rational thinkers right after the Islamic revolution. Like the communist Chinese, the Iranian fundamentalist government closed universities for three years and in their place advanced schools emphasizing religious indoctrination. Memorization of the Qur'an became a national imperative. Because communists possess a hatred of the capitalist West, they supported the Iranian fundamentalists in their rage against America. Despite similarities in their methods and anti-western / anti-capitalist rhetoric, these two competing ideologies did get along very well once their common enemy was removed. In the aftermath of Shah's removal from Teheran, the Mullahs and their Islamic henchmen killed nearly all communist who helped bring them into power, right along with other infidels and intellectuals. To Islamists in Iran, communism was simply a tool to be used to secure power. While they were being used by Islamists, poor communists did not imagine they would be killed by their Islamic 'comrades'. Although most were killed, in a twist of irony a few were able to save themselves by escaping to the evil capitalist West. Remaining and emerging thinkers and intellectuals now struggle to escape their own homeland. *[Note: Islamists are currently using liberal democrats in the same way in their efforts to bring down conservatives acting in opposition to Islamic hegemony.]*

Though they differ in their methods of control, German Nazism, Italian Fascism, Japanese Imperialism, Stalinist/Maoist Communism, and now Islamic Fundamentalism are all cut from the same totalitarian cloth. The Columbia Encyclopedia, 2001 Sixth Edition defines totalitarianism as follows:

> "A modern autocratic government in which the state involves itself in all facets of society, including the daily life of its citizens. A totalitarian government seeks to control not only all economic/political matters, but also the attitudes, values, and beliefs of its population, erasing the distinction between state and society. The citizen's duty to the state becomes the primary concern of the community, and the goal of the state is the replacement of existing society with a perfect society".

In Berlin in 1939, you would be hard pressed to find a German who did not sincerely believe in the superiority of Arian genetics. The Japanese similarly all originally truly believed in the divinity of their emperor and superior rights/standings of their native people, as did comrades following Iosif Stalin, Pol Pot, Mao Zedong, and Genghis Khan at the peak of their influence. Another common thread in all these theologies is the fundamental belief of the superiority of their system of living -***and***- their inherit right to impose it on others by any means necessary. This thread is duplicated perfectly in the fundamental practices and beliefs of all of Islam, moderate and extremist. Such thinking errors are rampant, and unfortunately at this stage in cultural development, probably completely intractable.

Unlike Constitutional democracy in the US, there is no cultural or legal mandate for separation of church and state in Islamic states, making all forms of secular democracy an alien and hostile concept to Muslim culture and law. Women have few rights, even against their husbands, who may legally beat their wives and concubines. Enslaving infidels and raping infidel women are also justified under Qur'anic law (and still occur in some Muslim lands). Grotesque punishments for crimes (beheadings and such) are not medieval holdovers; on the contrary, they will forever be part of authentic Islam as long as the Qur'an is revered as the perfect Word of Allah. The problem is that for all its schisms, sects, and multiplicity of voices, Islam's (often-violent) expansionist elements are firmly rooted in its central texts. Following these tenants strictly, Islam cannot be other than a religion of violence, and any system of governance based on it must always be oppressive by Western standards (no principles of tolerance, no religious freedom, and no laws protecting equality or individuality). In Islam, all aspects of personal, religious, and political life become merged. This template has resulted in a series of various despots, and corrupt monarchies or Mullahs, and a few Soviet-style state autocracies imposed on tribal societies in the Arab world. Any attempt to throw off the prescribed and accepted Islamic templates are fought vigorously by Jihadists. Beirut Lebanon was briefly a shining example of co-existence between Muslims and other ethnic groups, and a showcase of prosperity, until the fundamentalists took control and turned it into a nightmarish quagmire of terror and oppression. As the people slid backward in every way imaginable, affluent educated Lebanese seemed powerless to prevent the calamity. Few dared risked life, limb, and eternal Islamic hell to resist fundamentalist goals.

We seek out and fight terrorists, yet overall we ignore the religious infrastructure that created them. Three and ½ years since 9/11, the theology remains largely immune from challenge because it calls itself a religion. If Adolph Hitler had called Nazism a religion, would we have been similarly disposed and refrained from criticizing Nazi credos? Note that in previous conflicts success meant we did not support or excuse 'moderate' Nazis, Fascists, Imperialists, or Communists …all followers *and* supporters of the dangerous philosophies were brought low in total war. From 1933 onward, anyone wearing a swastika and reciting from *Mein Kampf* would be immediately recognized as a potentially dangerous enemy of freedom and democracy. Americans need to become fully acquainted with the aspirations, methods, and political philosophy contained in the Qur'an adopted by those who worship the man who wrote *that* manifesto, which unfortunately are no less dangerous.

Another point that needs to be made is that Islam is not initially opposed to democratic processes in non-Islamic countries. To orthodox Muslims in non-Muslim lands, democracy represents a convenient tool, not an enemy. Remember both Hitler and Khomeini came to rule through democratic means, but once in power they killed the process that elevated them to power. Now, instead of opposing democracy, the Shiite Mullahs of Iraq have wisely made good use of the elections to secure near total power and control. Through democratic means Islam seeks opportunity through discontent, deception, conversions, and/or demographics to seize control of government institutions, and then gradually to introduce 'reforms' until the region is subject to every form of Islamic manipulation and governance. In democracies under siege, non-Muslims are not mistreated initially. But as Islamists power grows, freedoms and protections quickly erode and then persecution begins. This modus operandi is the template Muhammad taught by example in conquering the indigenous people in Medina and Mecca. This is peaceful Islam. Those countries that prove resistant to such methods are subject to more violent forms of Jihad to weaken them to the point that they accept and submit to the dictates of Muslim political ambitions. Ultimately, Islam offers only three options to non-believers ...convert, pay Jizya (become slaves to superior Islamic masters), or die. The term "Islamic democracy" is an oxymoron, like "Tolerant Bigot", "Honest Falsehood", "Capitalistic Communism", or "Humane War". Although democracy has room for a defanged Islam not bent on destroying it, unfortunately real Islam leaves no room for democratic principals. When principals of free speech and human rights are genuinely adopted, the baby it delivers is free-will and free-enterprise, which then promotes and protects individual progress. All of these positive progressive concepts represent a direct threat to the elaborate control structures ensuring Islamic power over the masses.

Until it becomes the dominant political force controlling courts, police, and the military, the form Islam takes appears as a harmless religion to the uninformed, but in reality the faith is contaminated with all the perversions, lusts, and control mechanisms of its secular cousins. Cleverly masked by religious trappings, Islamic totalitarianism in democracies is easily able to hide behind the extended civil liberties and protections offered to actual religions. In this setting it has found fertile ground and has had a free hand to continue its mischief, since criticizing a 'religion' is considered 'bad form' and unacceptable in all societies. However, as its worldwide members continue in unison to act in treasonous and warlike ways, the movement will likely eventually be reclassified as the dangerous political movement it actually is. When that reclassification is finally made, it will signal the 'beginning of the end' to Islamic deception and expansion. As their prophet Muhammad correctly observed, "*War is deception*", and removing an opponent's ability to succeed at deceit renders it much less potent and successful in warlike activities. The biggest deception of all being played out on the West is the claim that Islam represents a benevolent religion deserving of the usual respect and protections.

Once taking power through whatever means, the grip of Islamic politics is iron tight. Instead of clicking heals and proclaiming "*Heil Hitler*", Muslims must bow and recite requisite prayers five times a day and proclaim "*Allahu Akbar*" on demand (the prayers are not supplications, simply recitations designed to reinforce complete devotion to Islam and all her ways). The first things to go in conquered lands are certain freedoms of speech, writ, and religion. German Nazism, Italian fascism, Japanese militarism, Stalinist Communism, and now Islamic fundamentalism have always been and will always be enemies of free speech and religious tolerance, because those concepts represent a direct threat to indoctrination and control of the masses. Control and power are what is at stake, and evil knows very well that Truth and Knowledge are the antithesis and antidote of totalitarianism. Final and permanent victory in the War on Islamic terror cannot occur until the dangerous ideologically is recognized and fought with the same vigor Islamic militancy is opposed militarily. As a first step, schools and universities need to start teaching American kids (including Muslims) all about real history and real Islam, instead of the propaganda it currently sells our children. Tenured or not, Communist, Islamist, and all apologists promoting misinformation and propaganda need to be exposed and expelled. The last thing we need is colleges and universities pumping out more Islamic brown shirts. In the case of Islam, excessive diversity is irresponsible and means only one thing ...national suicide.

Until -all- Muslims abandon the philosophy of violent Islamic Jihad, survival dictates that we must protect ourselves from militants committed to, and engaged in, such vile activities. To do so we must seek and apply the rule of law, but it would also be wise to present alternate social, religious, economic and political options to the many good, kind-hearted Muslims living among us still bound to what amounts to a totalitarianism system deliberately disguised as a religion of peace. But in its conduct with non-Muslims over time, that religious disguise is becoming paper-thin, becoming even more translucent daily as the evidence against it continues to mount.

Islamic Economics 101

The renowned scholar Bernard Lewis tells us that Arabia was once, by middle-age standards, a great civilization. For reasons to be explored here, the hard facts on the ground today are that economies in predominately Islamic lands have been in steady decline for at least the last four-centuries. It is common knowledge that the economic performances of Islamic lands are pathetic when compared to Western industrialized nations. The July 2002 U.N.'s "Arab Human Development Report," written by Arab intellectuals, painted a surprisingly accurate picture of Arabic societies. With a collective population roughly that of the United States, the 22 Arab states have:

- A total GDP less than Spain's, with exports (without oil) less than Norway's, and per capita income less than one-sixth that of Western democracies (sorry, no credit for terror exports).

- Fewer Internet connections per person than even Sub-Saharan Africa, and fewer books translated into Arabic over the past 100 years than even Spain translates in an average year.

- No visible presence in main arenas of human excellence today — Nobel-prize winners, World Cup finalists, Olympic medal-winners, breakthrough scientists, leading historians, international business successes, internationally recognized leaders like Gandhi or Martin Luther King.

- No democratic civil or political rights, sub-standard human rights for her own peoples, virtually none for women or infidels. No political visionaries of any kind. Instead what we see produced are more dictators and despots.

- Dismal standard of living, few legitimate business or economic opportunities, poor health care, and education systems that churn out religious fanaticism and little else.

These sad facts are the hallmarks of a civilization devoid of legitimate, democratic government and free-market economies. Despite all the claims otherwise, neither quality nor longevity of life are by-products of fundamental Islam. The reasons for this poor performance is obvious to everyone except the poor inhabitants of these areas. Numerous human social experiments in communism and pure socialism have shown convincingly that when you remove freedom and economic incentive, productivity and innovation languish. If it were not for the oil in the ground, the productive output of Arab lands would be at the bottom of undeveloped third-world countries. Except for a handful of fortunate countries with massive natural resources (oil), all majority Muslim countries fall into the category of economically "less developed nations". But the reasons for this go beyond the lack of free-market opportunities and mechanisms. The continuing lack of Muslim economic success is a direct result of a culture and practices dictated by oppressive Islamic principals. The lack of innovation and growth is a direct result of incompetence, corruption, or over-regulation on the part of 'religious' governments. The condition is obvious, even to Muslims, but the root causes are not so easy for otherwise intelligent Muslims to identify. The usual reaction is both typical and predictable, ...the West must be at fault, nothing bad could possibly come from the worlds 'best' religion. Within this construct, the only solution which can be proffered is to return to more pure Islamic values, and to attack Western hegemony with Jihad. As such, the erroneous diagnosis and prescription guarantees a continuation of the patients predicament. This culture of blame can not produce either introspection nor reform. Indeed, in terms of achievement, Arab leaders lack standing to criticize any country, culture, or society. Without excellence in any endeavors today, Arabs look silly as they continue to disparage others and export misery and terrorism. This destructive cycle continues endlessly, ensuring only the continuing economic disadvantage, frustration, and misery of its participants.

By contributing to order, honesty, and fairness, a progressive religion can be an asset to the economic well being of citizens. But when a 'religion' propagates ignorance, inefficiency and poverty it becomes a liability to host societies. Like other totalitarianism systems, Islam acts as an economic hindrance, placing barriers to ambition, prosperity, and fulfillment of human potential. With Islamic education focused (as a political necessary) on indoctrination, and with other Islamic control mechanisms in society, the kind of education which might lead to significant economic reform is not offered. Only a tiny minority of the most privileged escape to western institutions, and then usually choose to stay in the open societies who host them. Then there is the fact that half the population (women) are prevented from getting an education, entering the workforce, and contributing to industry. Instead women are regulated to being nothing more than servants to their husbands and baby factories for Islam.

Paying large percentages in alms is also a heavy burden, as is the personal and social burdens associated with caring for large numbers of minors. Contributing to support local and distant Jihads is also expected. In fact the opportunity to donate sons and money is irresistible to many Muslims, the following reveals why;

Allah will give "a far richer recompense to those who fight for him" (Sura 4:96). The Prophet said: "Whatever one spends to facilitate Jehad, Allah shall give him a reward which will exceed his contribution 700 times." (Tirmzi, Vol.1, p.697) "He who reared a horse for the sole intention of using it in a Jehad, then he will be rewarded one virtue for each grain he gave the horse as a feed." (Ibn-E-Majah, Vol. 2, p. 172) "A martyr (in Jehad) is dressed in radiant robes of faith: he is married to Houris and is allowed by Allah to intercede for seventy men (i.e. he is authorized by God to recommend seventy men for entry into paradise, and his intercession is sure to be granted.) (Ibn-E-Majah, Vol. 2, p. 174)

Consider also the productivity effects of a limited workforce who are interrupted 5 times a day for rather lengthy compulsory prayers, and who fast all day for weeks on end (40 days/year). Then for merchants, there is undoubtedly fear of providing services or products not in complete conformity with rigid, canonical Islamic restrictions. Such realities are not exactly conducive to market expansion and employment.

Because of the Islamic prohibition to usury (interest rates attached to monetary loans), any who manage to acquire wealth in Islamic lands have no incentive to invest in or otherwise finance new businesses ventures. This prevents the flow of capital to fund other companies or start-ups, effectively killing the entrepreneurial spirit.

Of even more significance is the general Islamic disrespect when contracting to non-Muslim entities. Non-Muslims quickly learn of the propensity of Muslims to break contracts for self gain, and act instead to protect their own capital investments by avoiding such adventures in financial recklessness. Opportunities for cooperation and profit disappear when comes to be known that Muslims are taught my Muhammad himself that covenants with infidels can be broken with impunity if it serves the best interest of Islam. But business behavior between Muslims also suffers from an Arabic culture which is tribal and hegemonic. All such self-destructive business conduct flows as a natural extension of the example exemplified by the caravan raiding Muhammad. The Islamic and/or Arab morality that glorifies dishonesty and cunning to get gain results in suspicion instead of trust. It is a fact that when you remove trust from business relationships, nothing much will happen. Because personal or institutional risk becomes untenable, things like long-term-investment, shared-vision, common-goals, cooperative-projects, and group-achievement become impossible.

The net result of all these Islamic cultural effects on markets and industry make economies based on it much less than competitive in a world economy based on open markets, freedom, and business law not based on the Qur'an. Lands hamstrung by Islamic principals and culture seem guaranteed to fail competitively, producing only the kind of desperate uneducated, unenlightened core material required to produce ever more Jihadic foot soldiers. Another consequence of the Muslim model is that the trappings of superior economic models in adjoining non-Muslim lands are thereby guaranteed to be superior, which more often than not produces jealousy and bitter animosity, if not fodder inspiring conquest and plunder.

It is a bitter pill for Muslims to see inferior 'Infidels' enjoying bountiful fruits of their industry while large numbers of 'brothers' and their families flounder in relative poverty. Such feelings of jealousy and outrage also further stoke the flames of angry, expansionist Islam. The restricted, repressive economic model of Islam is the root cause of poverty and economic stagnation in societies based on it, but the blame is easily shifted to 'repressive' neighboring peoples and religions. So Islam itself seems designed to perpetuate both the root neediness, and the goals and methods which the political movement must employ to satisfy those needs (conquest and plunder) …how terribly convenient.

But what else can we hope from the example of a man who could only show his followers how to assassinate and plunder enemies to get gain. Muhammad never created wealth through legitimate means, yet he became very wealthy, but only at the expense of a host of hard-working innocent victims. His example and revelations were intended more to help himself in recruitment efforts aimed at men he sought to participate in his core business. His cut of the exploits were profitable whether he participated in the murder and plunder or not. Of course, not everyone can be a bandit, much larger numbers must toil the soil and produce/improve the lands and merchandise to make the system work for the few thugs who benefit from such an unsustainable system.

If good-hearted, intelligent, and hard-working Muslims can not quite find enough humanistic reasons in the example of Muhammad and his devout followers worldwide to leave the religion, then one might hope that pure economic self-interest will do the trick. On almost every plane of human existence (spiritual, economic, intellectual, emotional, physical) Islam is a heavy ball-and-chain preventing both individual and economic progression. Forced obedience to any cult through fear, coercion, ignorance, and lust creates vice instead of virtue, stagnation instead of growth. My heart goes out to all the good families trapped in Islam. May they all find the means and support necessary to survive the ordeal until enough of their fellows gain sufficient enlightenment and strength to wrest their lands and families from the blight.

The Women of Islam

We have seen clearly into the mind and heart of male Islamic terrorists and the 'moderate' Muslims who actively or passively support them, but what about the women of Islam. What could possibly drive them to continue their allegiance to the causes of Muhammad? There are many women who have escaped Islamic bondage who have written quite eloquently about the ordeals of women in the Muslim world. The author must defer to those numerous testaments and will not explore the details of living as a Muslim woman in Muslim lands. This work is dedicated to understanding the motivations of Muslims on Jihad, and so Muslim men in particular. The author admits that his insights into the feminine Muslim culture is very limited, and that he is not qualified to say what makes Muslim women become or remain devoted followers of Muhammad. I will, however, express an opinion without the usual evidentiary backing.

A former Muslim woman has provided care for my young children, and her good nature and strong sense of family values are beyond reproach. She sacrifices and works for her family, and genuinely cares for others in general. Her work ethic and dedication to family seems to exceed the maternal instincts of many Christian women I have known. My suspicion is that Muslim women participate in Islam out of necessity, because there are no alternate options, and because they have a strong natural maternal instinct and have great love for their children. Beyond that, I can't imagine why they practice the religion, as it seems to this author that Islam has little to offer women. It's a mystery wrapped in an enigma, but I hope to understand it one day.

Islamic paradise, that very carnal place envisioned by Islamic Jihadists, does not seem to apply to Muslim women. Indeed, it would seem that even if their husbands virility were increased a hundred fold, that the 70+ virgins, all the pretty little boys running around, the other wives, and the slave-concubines, might leave a Muslim girl wondering if she will be the beneficiary of any attention at all from an adoring (if not exhausted) husband. When you speak of paradise to Muslim women, they seem at a loss to characterize their afterlife in any but very nebulous abstract terms. What is very carnal, visual, and well defined for men is much less than clear for poor Muslim women. Muhammad's revelations were obviously intended more to help in his recruitment efforts, aimed at men he sought to participate in his exploits. Another potential problem in the logic of Islamic paradise is this; as Muslim men practice their new found virility on the Houris (celestial virgins) there would seem to be a constant need in Muslim heaven for replacement untouched young girls to replenish the somewhat more soiled originals, but in any case most Muslim women would certainly not qualify for that particular position as described. Once you scratch the words 'untouched, unspoiled virgin' off your resume, my understanding is that it's near impossible to put them back.

Burquas symbolize to westerners the outwardly manifestation of repression for tens of Millions of Muslim Women living in what amounts to Islamic bondage. This all-encompassing garment separates women from all but close relations. They may not speak to others, travel alone or in the company of non-relations, hold leadership positions, vote, drive, attend school, or speak freely. Their lives consist of servitude to their masters, at deadly peril. Some societies are less limiting, with women only confined to wearing a hair covering and veil with other restrictions less pronounced, but even in these societies' women's rights and opportunities cannot be compared to western standards. All women in Islamic lands subject to Sharia are subject to horrific punishments for promiscuity or adultery. Even in Saudi Arabia, one of the more advanced, wealthy, and educated Arab Islamic lands, it is a common ploy for husbands to end arguments with their wives by raising their finger and proclaiming *"I divorce you, ...I divorce you, ...I ...."* Usually at about the second invoking of the official *'three strikes and your out'* Islamic method of divorce, women are on their knees begging the angry man for forgiveness and imploring them not to repeat the fateful third *'I divorce you'*. These poor women degrade themselves because they know full well how utterly alone they are in Islamic society without the benefits of property, rights, and substance that they enjoy only through their continued association with their husband. At-Talaq is the title of Sura #65 dealing with divorce. In its primitive sense, the Arabic word 'talaq' means 'to dismiss'. Instant divorce by uttering the word three times is a rampant practice in many Muslim lands. Under Muslim law sending a talaqnama (a statement of divorce) is also enough to end the marriage, without seeking the wife's opinion or consent, similar to saying talaq thrice. In an ever so subtle concession to worried wives, in August 2001 Singapore's highest Islamic authorities declared that Muslim men may not accomplish 'talaq' via cell phone text messages. However, July 27th 2003 the Malaysian government decreed that a man may indeed divorce his wife via text message.

Are there women who join Islam without either being born into the cult, forced into the organization, or deceived into believing it is something entirely different? What inspires women to join? I really can't imagine.

As for women, the Qur'an 4:34 states that "men have authority over women". Sura 4:34 instructs that that woman must be obedient to their husbands or be admonished (verbally abused), banished from the bed (psychologically abused) and beaten (physically abused via wife-beating). This and other passages clearly claim that women are inferior to men and their husbands have the right to scourge them if they are found disobedient. It advises men to take a green branch and beat their wives (because a green branch is more flexible and inflicts greater pain). (Qur'an 38:44). It teaches that women will go to hell if they are disobedient to their husbands (66:10). It maintains that men have an advantage over the women (Qur'an 2:228). It not only denies women equal rights, it decrees that their witness is not admissible in courts of law (Qur'an. 2:282). This means that a woman who is raped cannot accuse her rapist unless she can produce a male witness.

There are further suras that make a woman's inheritance (4:11-12) worth half of a man's. These are actual Islamic teachings which provide the basis for numerous misogynic cultural practices. The Qur'an also states that if a women becomes captive in a war, her Muslim master is allowed to rape her (33:50), and that women are "tilth" (property to cultivate) for their husbands (2:223). There are also numerous hadiths which reflect poorly on women, including one in which Muhammad declares that most of hell's population is female and that women are deficient in intelligence and piety (Bukhari, I:6:304). The Holy Prophet allows men to marry up to four wives, and is licensed to sleep with slave maids and as many 'captive' women as he can acquire (Qur'an 4:3) even if those women are already married (as He himself did). Furthermore, by the example of Muhammad, a man may take a pre-pubescent wife as young as 9 years old to his marriage bed. Although most countries limit such marriages to children 11-13 years old, the practice of bedding younger girls is not unknown in some regions. Further, the insane practice of genitalia mutilation and honor killings continues today in many Islamic lands and families.

[A word of warning for those who find their version of the Qur'an translated differently than the verses quoted herein. Almost all English translators of the Qur'an have deliberately tried to soften many harsh verses. Yusufali in particular goes out of his way to twist words to hide the harshness of the real Qur'an. For example he translates the verse (Qur'an 38:44) that says plainly in Arabic "take a green branch and beat your wife" to "take a little green grass and strike therewith". He translates a different verse (Qur'an 4:34) that states "beat your wife" correctly, but he cannot help but add the word (lightly) in parenthesis.]

Since the Qur'an can not be altered, these practices are not likely to be influenced by Western norms. As the preceding text demonstrates, Muslim women are often considered by Westerners to be victims of Islam, and as such receive almost blanket immunity from the more violent and inhumane acts of their sons, brothers, husbands and fathers. However common sense tells us that nurture, instruction, encouragement and support by the women folk must play some role for an entire culture to support such vile activities. Although not generally true for all Muslim women, the following article speaks volumes of the feminine mindset fully immersed in Islam.

The Guardian - Jul 20, 2004 - **Arab women singers complicit in rape**, says Amnesty report. (www.guardian.co.uk) While African women in Darfur were being raped by the Janjaweed militiamen, Arab women stood nearby and sang for joy, according to an Amnesty International report published yesterday. The songs of the Hakama, or the "Janjaweed women" as the refugees call them, encouraged the atrocities committed by the militiamen. The women singers stirred up racial hatred against black civilians during attacks on villages in Darfur and celebrated the humiliation of their enemies, the human rights group said. "[They] appear to be the communicators during the attacks. They are reportedly not actively involved in attacks on people, but participate in acts of looting." Amnesty International collected several testimonies mentioning the presence of Hakama while women were raped by the Janjaweed. The report said: "Hakama appear to have directly harassed the women [who were] assaulted, and verbally attacked them." During an attack on the village of Disa in June last year, Arab women accompanied the attackers and sang songs praising the government and scorning the black villagers. According to an African chief quoted in the report, the singers said: "The blood of the blacks runs like water, we take their goods and we chase them from our area and our cattle will be in their land. The power of [Sudanese president Omer Hassan] al-Bashir belongs to the Arabs and we will kill you until the end, you blacks, we have killed your God." The chief said that the Arab women also racially insulted women from the village: "You are gorillas, you are black, and you are badly dressed."

The Janjaweed have abducted women for use as sex slaves, in some cases breaking their limbs to prevent them escaping, as well as carrying out rapes in their home villages, the report said. The militiamen "are happy when they rape. They sing when they rape and they tell us that we are just slaves and that they can do with us how they wish", a 37-year-old victim, identified as A, is quoted as saying in the report, which was based on more than 100 testimonies from women in the refugee camps in neighboring Chad. Pollyanna Truscott, Amnesty International's Darfur crisis coordinator, said the rape was part of a systematic dehumanization of women. "It is done to inflict fear, to force them to leave their communities. It also humiliates the men in their communities."

The UN estimates that up to 30,000 people have been killed in Darfur, and more than a million have been forced to flee their homes. Peace talks between the Sudanese government and two rebel movements broke down on Saturday when the rebel groups walked out, saying the government must first disarm the Janjaweed. Another human rights organization, Human Rights Watch, today publishes alleged Sudanese government documents showing that it was much more closely involved with the Janjaweed than it has so far admitted. The documents, which Human Rights Watch said it had obtained from the civilian administration in Darfur and are dated February and March this year, call for "provisions and ammunition" to be delivered to known Janjaweed militia leaders, camps and "loyalist tribes". One document orders all security units in the area to tolerate the activities of Musa Hilal, the alleged Janjaweed leader in north Darfur interviewed by the Guardian last week. Peter Takirambudde, the executive director of Human Rights Watch's Africa division, said: "These documents show that militia activity has not just been condoned, it's been specifically supported by Sudan government officials." The official government line is that it did not arm or support the Janjaweed, though its presence was useful in helping to combat rebels in Darfur.

BBC- 18 June, 2002- **The Gaza Strip, Israel:** By Middle East correspondent Orla Guerin. The mother of a Palestinian suicide attacker who killed two Israelis before being shot dead has spoken of her feelings about her son's actions. A video released by Hamas shows a proud mother taking up arms beside her favorite son. First a warm embrace, then a loving kiss. Naima al-Obeid was saying goodbye to her 23-year-old Mahmoud, a college student on his way to carry out a suicide attack. "God willing you will succeed," she says. "May every bullet hit its target, and may God give you martyrdom. This is the best day of my life." Mahmoud says: "Thank you for raising me".

Naima got her wish... Mahmoud was shot dead attacking the Jewish settlement of Dugit in the Gaza Strip on Saturday. Two Israeli soldiers were killed in the ambush. Their deaths are being celebrated near Mahmoud's home.

We found crowds coming to the mourning tent - and not just because of him. People here aren't just remembering Mahmoud - they are honoring his mother. She has become a heroine, being talked about on the streets, praised in the local papers. Some Palestinians are taking a great deal of pride in a mother who saw her son go to kill and die without shedding a tear. They are already saying she will inspire other women to do the same. In her home, in Gaza, she showed me pictures of the son she calls "my heart". She had no sympathy for the dead Israelis, no regrets over the loss of her own son. "Nobody wants their son to be killed. I always wanted him to have a good life. "But our land is occupied by the Israelis. We're sacrificing our sons to get our freedom," she told me. I asked her if it mattered whether her son killed women and children. "The women and children are also Jews," she said, "They're all the same for me. "And I want to tell Jewish mothers - take your children and run from here because you will never be safe. We believe our sons go to heaven when they are martyred. When your sons die they go to hell." Naima is surrounded by well-wishers, no one asking why she gave her son a license to kill. She has nine more children, whom, she says, all have a duty to fight the Israeli occupation.

Chapter 16
The Infidel POW

An increasingly popular trend among Islamic terrorists worldwide is to post videos of Muslims beheading infidels. Non-Muslims have been beheaded in the Philippines, Chechnya, Kashmir, Iraq, Pakistan, and elsewhere. The Qur'an's Sura 47:4, has been cited as the theological basis for such acts: "When you meet in battle those who have disbelieved, smite their necks; and after the slaughter fasten tight the bonds, until the war lays aside its burdens. Then either release them as a favor, or in return for ransom." Sura 8: The Spoils of War, section 12 also states that Allah will throw fear into the hearts of the disbelievers, and directs faithful Muslims to 'smite their necks and fingers', with section 67 informing that "A prophet may not take captives until he has made a slaughter in the land".

The beheading of Daniel Pearl in 2002, followed by the killings of Nicholas Berg, Paul Johnson Jr., Kim Sun-Il, and Eugene Armstrong, as well as the killing of other nationals and threats to behead a growing list of captives, have garnered major media attention for the terrorists as Arab satellite channels rush to air the pictures and videos to customers eager to see them. Yet Saudis Arabia's Prince Sattam issued a statement to Westerners that Johnson's beheading was a malicious crime rejected by Islam, declaring, "This has happened for the first time in the Kingdom". But according to a Jun 25 2004 CBS News report, the Saudi government ordered and carried out 52 beheadings in 2003, for crimes including robbery, drug smuggling, and homosexuality. In the kingdoms largest cities such beheadings (with other gruesome punishments) are regularly performed in the courtyards of mosques following Friday prayers.

The terrorists are not primarily using the various beheadings as a technique to make us cower and drive us out. The beheading films are first and foremost a recruitment tool, and have been around for a long time. The first generation of vile home-movies depicting the gruesome slaughter of infidels were circulated in North Africa decades ago. The purpose, now and then, is to demonstrate to orthodox Muslims their bona fide status as true emissaries of Muhammad, and to excite homicidal fanatics and lure them into the local Islamist gang. These recruiting films are aimed at subhuman homicidal maniacs who revel in bloody brutality, an emotion that passes for spirituality to them. Thanks to the Internet and comrades at Arab satellite stations, Muslim Jihad marketing and distribution methods have now improved dramatically.

Today's Jihad movement, like so many before, continues to draw its foot soldiers from people who dream of beheading infidels, a fantasy that flows naturally after receiving a proper education consisting of memorizing the Qur'an and studying the life, words, and example of their 'prophet'. It is quite clear that they see us all as animals deserving slaughter. These vile sub-human acts discredit any notion that our enemies are normal human beings driven to desperation by injustice, misery, and oppressive US hegemony. It is pure folly to think terrorists and their masters are people trying to avenge some injustice or remedy old grievances, yet some people still fall for this sort of complete rubbish. The only way sensible people could possibly begin to believe such garbage, is to first carefully censor all evidence showing the true nature and source of terrorist acts. Islamic propagandists (including our own left leaning liberal media elitists) accomplish this by taking the scenes of 9/11 and the beheading videos off the air, and journalistically by filtering the utter barbarity of these people through the use of 'sensitive' words designed to have no emotional impact. This censor effort has become an imperative of Islamists and their apologists because they know the beheadings truly define and bring into clear focus not only the hearts and minds of terrorists, but also the core values of the parents and communities who raised them, not to mention the 'religion' that inspires them.

The scenes we saw Sept 11 were every bit as horrible as the beheadings, which briefly unified us in the realization that we were facing an enemy that would have to be fought to the finish. Videos of the people who jumped to their death from the Twin Towers, or those burned or crushed in New York and Washington provide clear documentation of what awaits us all if we fail to win. Now the beheading videos both confirm and deepen that evidence. We cannot wage an effective war unless we understand the true nature and objectives of our enemy. We jeopardize prolonging the agony if we do not grasp that terrorists' ranks are full of people who are there primarily because they are thrilled by the prospect of beheading us, and who believe such acts are pious and will win them a ticket into Muslim heaven where scores of virgins await, anxious to provide them an orgasmic eternity. Survival dictates we not be oversensitive to the point we avoid viewing the actual history being played out before our very eyes. To 'Know Thine Enemy', we need to see, feel, and understand these creatures, to solidify national support and bring our full military might to bear to end this thing as quickly as possible.

The fact that Jihad means obligatory war for devout Muslims has been previously discussed in earlier chapters, proved using authentic Islamic sources. Muslims who commit acts of violence and terror against infidels can find ample justification for their actions, based on the teachings of the Qur'an and, more importantly, the example of their prophet. The prophet himself left a trail of assassinations and other bloody acts behind him until his own death, all of which are recorded by Muslim historians, which become a tradition among Muslims in the early centuries of its development. The growing body of Islamic internet site proud postings of violent videos/pictures makes it disgustingly clear the practice is continuing through today. We now attempt to further clarify the mind and rational of Islamic militants carrying out so many terrible instances of beheadings. Unfortunately these cruel rituals are neither new, nor isolated incidents or aberrations.

It is a perilous fact that the practitioners of the Muslim religion are taught a philosophy that encourages terrorism against civilians, and does not differentiate between innocent civilians and soldiers. The Geneva Conventions and conventional rules of war have no validity and are simply rejected by Jihad warriors, who believe they are immune because they operate under a higher law. Accordingly, all infidels without a treaty of protection (i.e. not already subdued and paying the Jizya tax) can be dealt with at the pleasure and discretion of the fighter. Options at his disposal include kidnapping and ransom, slavery (including sex slavery), or to simply torture and kill the poor soul.

This review highlights some additional Islamic direction on the subject. The citations herein are but a small portion of the enormous amount of evidence indicating that killing noncombatants or captives appears supported by both Islamic principles and history. What is outlined herein should give Westerner civilians caught up in Jihad a clear idea of what he/she can expect from Islamic warriors, as well as what prisoners of war can expect from their Muslim captors.

Many of the remaining citations were taken from an article by Andrew G. Bostom, Jihad Killings of POWs and Non-Combatants, first published September 9, 2004 at frontpagemagazine.com.

W.H.T. Gairdner, the renowned early 20th century scholar of Islam, wrote the following discussion of Muhammad's treatment of POWs, based exclusively on Muslim sources:

> "After Badr, especially, the greatest vindictiveness and bloodthirstiness were manifested. Many prisoners were slaughtered in cold blood, at least two of them at the personal insistence of Muhammad who had a special grudge against them. The most famous Companions (except Abu Bakr) were then the most truculent. One of them was for burning the prisoners en masse! [Gairdner's emphasis] The Prophet checked these excesses. But the very words in which he did so, the very limits set up, show clearly that defenseless prisoners might always be slaughtered in cold blood if they could not get anyone to redeem them. The Sura produced after the event (Q.8:67-68) explicitly commands the slaughter of prisoners on occasions when it is advisable to make an impression by 'frightfulness': on such occasions the sin would be to grow rich by accepting ransoms! And there is a whole series of traditions which make out that the 'leniency' shown at Badr was a sin, that Mohammed had been against that sin, humane Abu Bakr was the chief offender, and that had that sin been punished, only the whole-hoggers who had urged the slaughter of all the prisoners ('Umar and Sa'd) would have escaped...the Koran itself recommended the ransoming of war-captives as a form of charity suitable for rich Muslims. But the Badr alternative is always there in the background, and on suitable occasions may always be brought into the foreground. The prisoner of war is mubah damuhu: his life's essentially forfeit." [33]

A review of Egyptian high school textbooks in 2002 reveals the classical exegesis on these Qur'anic verses which is still being taught to students in non-Azharite (i.e. non-religious) as well as Azharite schools.

> "Studies in Theology: Tradition and Morals, Grade 11, (2001) pp. 291-92 ...This noble [Qur'anic] Surah [Surat Muhammad]... deals with questions of which the most important are as follows: 'Encouraging the faithful to perform jihad in God's cause, to behead the infidels, take them prisoner, break their power, and make their souls humble - all that in a style which contains the highest examples of urging to fight. You see that in His words:

"When you meet the unbelievers in the battlefield strike off their heads and, when you have laid them low, bind your captives firmly. Then grant them their freedom or take a ransom from them, until war shall lay down its burdens.'"

"Commentary on the Surahs of Muhammad, Al-Fath, Al-Hujurat and Qaf, Grade 11, (2002) p. 9 ...When you meet them in order to fight [them], do not be seized by compassion [towards them] but strike the[ir] necks powerfully.... Striking the neck means fighting, because killing a person is often done by striking off his head. Thus, it has become an expression for killing even if the fighter strikes him elsewhere. This expression contains a harshness and emphasis that are not found in the word "kill", because it describes killing in the ugliest manner, i.e., cutting the neck and making the organ - the head of the body - fly off [the body].' "

Although chilling to our modern sensibilities, particularly when being taught to children, these are merely normative interpretations of the rules for jihad war, based on over a millennium of Muslim theology and jurisprudence. And the context of these teachings is unambiguous, as the translator makes clear that:

"[the] concept of jihad is interpreted in the Egyptian school curriculum almost exclusively as a military endeavor... it is war against God's enemies, i.e., the infidels... it is war against the homeland's enemies and a means to strengthening the Muslim states in the world. In both cases, jihad is encouraged, and those who refrain from participating in it are denounced."

Ibn Hudayl, a 14th century expert and author of an important treatise on jihad, explained forthrightly, sanctioned procedures and methods which contradict Islamic apologists erroneous assertions that certain war crimes, including razing beheading, are not sanctioned by Islam:

"It is permissible to set fire to the lands of the enemy, his stores of grain, his beasts of burden – if it is not possible for the Muslims to take possession of them – as well as to cut down his trees, to raze his cities, in a word, to do everything that might ruin and discourage him, provided that the imam (i.e. the religious "guide" of the community of believers) deems these measures appropriate, suited to hastening the Islamization of that enemy or to weakening him. Indeed, all this contributes to a military triumph over him or to forcing him to capitulate. [34]

The late, seminal 20th century scholar of Muslim Spain and North Africa, Charles Emmanuel Dufourcq, characterized the impact of these repeated attacks, indistinguishable in motivation from modern acts of jihad terrorism (like 9/11/01 and, perhaps even more geographically relevant, 3/11/04):

"It is not difficult to understand that such expeditions sowed terror. The historian al-Maqqari, who wrote in seventeenth-century Tlemcen in Algeria, explains that the panic created by the Arab horsemen and sailors, at the time of the Muslim expansion in the zones that saw those raids and landings, facilitated the later conquest, if that was decided on: 'Allah,' he says, 'thus instilled such fear among the infidels that they did not dare to go and fight the conquerors; they only approached them as suppliants, to beg for peace.' " [35]

Al-Mawardi, a significant 11th century (Shafi'ite) jurist from Baghdad, wrote regarding the treatment of jihad POWs. The real issues at hand: what does Muslim Law actually instructs regarding jihad POWs in various campaigns conducted throughout Muslim history, and how does the spate of contemporary beheadings of prisoners of jihad terrorism comport with these rulings. Al-Mawardi's writing makes clear that killing of jihad POWs is a primary (i.e., "first") option based solely upon what is most expedient for the Muslims:

"As for the captives, the amir [ruler] has the choice of taking the most beneficial action of four possibilities: the first to put them to death by cutting their necks; the second, to enslave them and apply the laws of slavery regarding their sale and manumission; the third, to ransom them in exchange for goods or prisoners; and fourth, to show favor to them and pardon them. Allah, may he be exalted, says, 'When you encounter those [infidels] who deny [the Truth=Islam] then strike [their] necks' (Qur'an sura 47, verse 4)"....Abu'l-Hasan al-Mawardi, al-Ahkam as-Sultaniyyah." [36]

Al-Mawardi was hardly unique, the views of this Shafi'ite jurist being nearly identical to those of key jurists representing the three other main Sunni schools of Islamic jurisprudence, including the Hanafites, who prevailed in Ottoman Turkey:

Abu Yusuf (from the Hanafi school of jurisprudence, d. 798):

"...that one can even ...finish off the wounded, or kill prisoners who might prove dangerous to the Muslims.. As for the prisoners who are lead before the imam, the latter has the choice, as he pleases, of executing them, or making them pay a ransom, for the most advantageous choice for the Muslims, and the wisest for Islam. The ransom imposed upon them is not to consist either of gold, silver, or wares, but is only in exchange for Muslim captives..." [37]

Ibn Abi Zayd Al_Qayrawani (d. 996), head of the North African Maliki school at Qairuan:

"There is no inconvenience to kill white non-Arabs who have been taken prisoner". [38]

The famous Syrian jurist Ibn Taymiyya (d. 1328) of the Hanbali school under the Mamluks:

"...If a male unbeliever is taken captive during warfare or otherwise, eg., as a result of a shipwreck, or because he has lost his way, or as a result of a ruse, then the imam may do whatever he deems appropriate: killing him, enslaving him, releasing him or setting him free for a ransom consisting in either property or people. This is the view of most jurists and it is supported by the Koran and the Sunna..." [39]

These rulings had tangible consequences. For centuries, from the Iberian Peninsula to the Indian subcontinent, jihad campaigns waged by Muslim armies against infidel Jews, Christians, Zoroastrians, Buddhists and Hindus, were punctuated by massacres, including mass throat slittings and beheadings of captives. Here are but a few examples. Non-Muslim (i.e., Christian) prisoners were beheaded, summarily, during a jihad campaign against Tripoli in the mid-7th century, as chronicled by Ibn Khaldun in his, History of the Berbers and the Moslem Dynasties of Northern Africa:

"Abd-Allah set siege to the city [Tripoli]; but later, unwilling to let himself be diverted from the goal that he had in mind, he gave the order to break camp. While we were making our preparations, we spied some vessels that had just landed on the shore; immediately we attacked them and threw into the water anyone who was aboard. They put up some resistance, but then surrendered, and we tied their hands behind their backs. They were four hundred in number. Abd-Allah then joined us, and he had their heads cut off." [40]

During the period of "enlightened" Muslim rule, the Christians of Iberian Toledo, who had first submitted to their Arab Muslim invaders in 711 or 712, revolted in 713. In the harsh Muslim reprisal that ensued, Toledo was pillaged, and all the Christian notables had their throats cut. On the Indian subcontinent, Hindu combatants captured during jihad campaigns were killed in orgies of brutal violence, on a simply staggering scale, as documented by Muslim chroniclers. After Muhammad bin Qasim took the fort of Brahmanabad in Sindh following a 6-month siege, around 711-712 C.E.

"...When the plunder and the prisoners of war were brought before Qasim, and enquiries were made about every captive, it was found that Ladi, the wife of Dahir, was in the fort with two daughters of his by his other wives. Veils were put on their faces, and they were delivered to a servant to keep them apart. One-fifth of all the prisoners were chosen and set aside; they were counted as amounting to twenty thousand in number, and the rest were given to the soldiers...(Qasim) sat on the seat of cruelty, and put all those who had fought to the sword. It is said that about six thousand fighting men were slain, but according to some, sixteen thousand were killed..." [41]

And Amir Timur, during his jihad campaigns through Northern India (1397-99 C.E.) conducted what may have been the greatest mass slaughter of prisoners ever chronicled:

"Next day, Friday the 3rd of the month. I left the fort of Loni and marched to a position opposite to Jahan-numa where I encamped... I now held a Court... At this Court Amir Jahan Shah and Amir Sulaiman Shah and other amirs of experience, brought to my notice that, from the time of entering Hindustan up to the present time, we had taken more than 100,000 infidels and Hindus prisoners, and that they were all in my camp...I asked their advice about the prisoners, and they said that on the great day of battle these 100,000 prisoners could not be left with the baggage, and that it would be entirely opposed to the [Islamic] rules of war to set these idolaters and foes of Islam at liberty. In fact, no other course remained but that of making them all food for the sword. When I heard these words I found them in accordance with the rules of war, and I directly gave my command for the tawachis [drumbeaters] to proclaim throughout the camp that every man who had infidel prisoners was to put them to death...When this order became known to the ghazis of Islam, they drew their swords and put their prisoners to death. 100,000 infidels, impious idolaters, were on that day slain. Maulana Nasiru-d-din 'Umar, a counselor and man of learning, who, in all his life, had never killed a sparrow, now, in execution of my order, slew with his sword fifteen idolatrous Hindus, who were his captives..." [42]

Lastly, Babur (1483-1530), the founder of the Mughal Empire, who is revered as a paragon of Muslim tolerance by modern revisionist historians, recorded the following in his autobiographical "Baburnama", about infidel prisoners of a jihad campaign:

"Those who were brought in alive [having surrendered] were ordered beheaded, after which a tower of skulls was erected in the camp." [43]

Other historical examples from jihad campaigns abound demonstrating a philosophy and conduct violating basic standards of Human rights. Recent jihad-inspired decapitations of infidels by Muslims have occurred across the globe- Christians in Indonesia, the Philippines, and Nigeria; Hindu priests and "unveiled" Hindu women in Kashmir.

Any contention that Islam does not sanction the killing of non-combatants is highly questionable, as any claim is clearly contradicted by the repeated actions of Muslims during jihad campaigns yesterday and today. Both Muslim and non-Muslim sources document countless episodes of the pillage and massacre of non-combatants during jihad conquests and raids. And there is ample juridical justification for such acts. For example, the great Maliki jurist and philosopher Averroes (d. 1198) asserted,

"Most scholars agree that fortresses may be assailed with mangonels, no matter whether there are women and children within them or not. This is based on the fact that the Prophet used mangonels against the population of al-Ta'if." [44]

The much lionized Sufi theologian Al-Ghazali (d. 1101) made a similar pronouncement. The lauded Al-Ghazali's wrote plainly on acceptable behavior during jihad war, and the treatment of the vanquished non-Muslim [dhimmi] peoples:

"...one must go on jihad (i.e., warlike razzias or raids) at least once a year...one may use a catapult against them [non-Muslims] when they are in a fortress, even if among them are women and children. One may set fire to them and/or drown them... " [45]

The Hanbali jurist Ibn Taymiyya (d. 1328) provided this caveat, which allowed for killing those who would otherwise be classified as non-combatants, if they merely engaged in verbal or written propaganda:

"As for those who cannot offer resistance or cannot fight, such as women, children, monks, old people, the blind, handicapped and their likes, they shall not be killed unless they actually fight with words [eg. by propaganda] and acts [by spying or otherwise assisting in the warfare]. Some jurists are of the opinion that all of them may be killed, on the mere ground that they are unbelievers, but they make an exception for women and children since they constitute property for Muslims" [46]

Contemporary Muslim theologians like Yusuf Al-Qaradawi, hailed as a moderate voice in Britain, sanction homicide bombings against all Israeli citizens using jihad criteria consistent with those iterated by these classical jurists.

Unfortunately, historical examples of the killing of non-combatants during jihad campaigns abound, beginning with the very earliest Muslim conquests. The 7th century Chronicler John of Nikiou describes the jihad conquest of Fayyum and Nikiou, including the massacre of non-combatant women and children:

"[In Fayyum] The Ishmaelites attacked, killed the commandant, massacred all his troops and immediately seized the town...Whoever approached them was massacred; they spared neither old men, nor women, nor children...Then the Muslims arrived in Nikiou. There was not one single soldier to resist them. They seized the town and slaughtered everyone they met in the street and in the churches – men, women and children, sparing nobody. Then they went to other places, pillaged and killed all the inhabitants they found... But let us now say no more, for it is impossible to describe the horrors the Muslims committed when they occupied the island of Nikiou, on Sunday, the eighteenth day of the month of Guenbot, in the fifteenth year of the lunar cycle, as well as the terrible scenes which took place in Cesarea in Palestine." [47]

John Cameniates provided an eyewitness account of the jihad capture and pillage of Thessaloniki in 904 C.E. Cameniates, his elderly father, and his brother, taken prisoner while they tried to escape by the ramparts, were spared their lives because they promised their captors a large amount of money. They were marched as prisoners through the city, and thus witnessed the terrible carnage of their fellow townspeople who had sough refuge in the church of Saint George. A summary, and excerpts from Cameniates narrative reveals that:

"The Thessalonians tried to escape through the streets, pursued by the Saracens, who were unleashed like wild beasts. In their panic, men. women, the elderly, and children, 'fell into each other's arms to give each other one last kiss.' The enemy hit with no mercy. Parents were killed while trying to defend their children. No one was spared: women, children, the elderly, all were immediately pierced by the sword. The poor wretches ran through the town, or tried to hide inside the caves; some of them, believing they could find refuge inside a church, would seek shelter inside, while others tried to scale the walls of the ramparts, from where they jumped into the void and crashed to the ground. Nuns, petrified with fear, with their hair disheveled, tried to escape, and ended up by the thousands in the hands of the barbarians, who killed the older ones, and sent the younger and more attractive ones into captivity and dishonor… The Saracens also massacred the unfortunate people who had sought refuge inside churches."

"The church [of Saint George] was full of wretches who had sought safety within it. There were about three hundred of them, as we learned later. A great number of murderous enemies came in. Immediately their leader bounced onto the holy altar, where the divine offices are held by the priests: there, crouching down with his legs crossed, in the manner of the barbarians, he sat, full of rage and arrogance, looking at the crowd of those people, full of the evil spirit of what he intended to commit. After grabbing my father and my brother with his hands, and after ordering that we be guarded in an area near the entrance by some of his men whom he had chosen, he gave a sign to his men to do away with the crowd. Like wild wolves when they meet their prey, they began to massacre the poor creatures quickly and mercilessly, and, overflowing with rage, they inquired with their eyes as to what the terrible judge wished to do with us: but he stopped them from doing anything against us, for the moment… After the end of the massacre of those poor people, the entire floor was covered with bodies, with a lake of blood in the middle. Then, as the murderer could not get out, he ordered that they pile up the bodies one on top of the other, on the two sides of the church; then he quickly jumped down from the altar, came up to us, and grabbed my father and my brother with his hands." [48]

Professor J.B. Segal reviewed the jihad destruction of the Christian enclave of Edessa in 1144-1146 C.E., during the Crusades, using primary source documentation, including a contemporary account by Michael the Syrian.

"Thirty thousand souls were killed. Women, youths, and children to the number of sixteen thousand were carried into slavery, stripped of their cloths, barefoot, their hands bound, forced to run beside their captors on horses. Those who could not endure were pierced by lances or arrows, or abandoned to wild animals and birds of prey. Priests were killed out of hand or captured; few escaped. The Archbishop of the Armenians was sold at Aleppo…The whole city was given over to looting, '..for a whole year..', resulting in '…complete ruin..'. From this disaster the Christian community of Edessa never recovered." [49]

Michael the Syrian (Patriarch of Antioch from 1166-1199) chronicled the two devastating jihad attacks (1144 and 1146 C.E.) by the Seljuk Turks, which included the mass murder of non-combatants, as follows:

"The Turks entered with their swords and blades drawn, drinking the blood of the old and the young, the men and the women, the priests and the deacons, the hermits and the monks, the nuns, the virgins, the infants at the breast, the betrothed men and the women to whom they were betrothed! …Ah! what a bitter tale! The city of Abgar, the friend of Christ, was trampled underfoot because of our iniquity: the priests were massacred, the deacons immolated, the subdeacons crushed, the temples pillaged, the altars overturned! Alas! what a calamity! Fathers denied their children; the mother forgot her affection for her little ones! While the sword was devouring and everyone was fleeing to the mountaintop, some gathered their children, like a hen her chicks, and waited to die together by the sword or else to be led off together into captivity! Some aged priests, who were carrying the relics of the martyrs, seeing this raging destruction, recited the words of the prophet: "I will endure the Lord's wrath, because I have sinned against Him and angered Him."[8] And they did not take flight, nor did they cease praying until the sword rendered them mute. Then they were found at the same spot, their blood spilled all around them…."

"The Turks descended from the citadel upon those who had remained in the churches or in other places, whether because of old age, or as a result of some other infirmity, and they tortured them, showing no pity. Those who had escaped from being suffocated or trampled [in the crush] and had left the city with the Franks were surrounded by the Turks, who rained down upon them a hail of arrows which cruelly pierced them through.

O cloud of wrath and day without mercy! In which the scourge of violent wrath once again struck the unfortunate Edessenians. O night of death, morning of hell, day of perdition! which arose against the citizens of that excellent city. Alas, my brethren! Who could recount or hear without tears how the mother and the infant that she carried in her arms were pierced through by the same arrow, without anyone to lift them up or to remove the arrow! And soon, [as they lay] in that state, the hooves of the horses of those who were pursuing them pounded them furiously! That whole night they had been pierced by arrows, and at daybreak, which was for them even darker, they were struck by the swords and the lances!... And then the earth shivered with horror at the massacre that took place: like the sickle on the stalks of grain, or like fire among wood chips, the sword carried off the Christians. The corpses of priests, deacons, monks, noblemen and the poor were abandoned pell-mell. Yet, although their death was cruel, they nevertheless did not have as much to suffer as those who remained alive; for when the latter fell in the midst of the fire and the wrath of the Turks, [those barbarians] stripped them of their clothing and of their footwear. Striking them with rods, they forced them – men and women, naked and with their hands tied behind their backs – to run with the horses; those perverts pierced the belly of anyone who grew faint and fell to the ground, and left him to die along the road. And so they became the prey of wild beasts, and then they expired, or else the food of birds of prey, in which case they were tortured. The air was poisoned with the stench of the corpses; Assyria was filled with captives." [50]

Professor H.Z. Hirschberg includes this summary of a contemporary Judeo-Arabic account by Solomon Cohen (which comports with Arab historian Ibn Baydhaq's sequence of events), from January 1148 C.E, describing the Muslim Almohad conquests in North Africa, and Spain:

"Abd al-Mumin...the leader of the Almohads after the death of Muhammad Ibn Tumart the Mahdi [note: Ibn Tumart was a cleric whose writings bear a striking resemblance to Khomeini's rhetoric eight centuries later] ...captured Tlemcen [in the Maghreb] and killed all those who were in it, including the Jews, except those who embraced Islam...[In Sijilmasa] One hundred and fifty persons were killed for clinging to their [Jewish] faith...All the cities in the Almoravid [dynastic rulers of North Africa and Spain prior to the Almohads] state were conquered by the Almohads. One hundred thousand persons were killed in Fez on that occasion, and 120,000 in Marrakesh. The Jews in all [Maghreb] localities [conquered]...groaned under the heavy yoke of the Almohads; many had been killed, many others converted; none were able to appear in public as Jews [emphasis added]...Large areas between Seville and Tortosa [in Spain] had likewise [emphasis added] fallen into Almohad hands." [51]

The mid-15th century Hindu chronicle Kanhadade Prabandha included descriptions of a wave of jihad attacks at the end of the 13th century, and first three decades of the 14th century. These campaigns vanquished extensive regions [Malwa, Gujarat, Ranthambhor, Siwana, Jalor, Devagiri, Warangal, Ma'bar, and Ramesvaram], and resulted in the death or enslavement of perhaps millions of Hindus. [52] The devastating nature of such attacks, which included deliberate targeting of non-combatants, is captured in this account:

"A farman (firman) was now given to Gori Malik (to sack Bhinmal)...The Turkish [Muslim] invaders entered the town making dreadful din and clamor. Orders were issued clear and terrible: 'The soldiers shall march into the town spreading terror everywhere! Cut down the Brahmanas [Brahman priests], wherever they may be- performing homa or milking cows! Kill the cows- even those which are pregnant or with newly born calves!' The Turks ransacked Bhinmal and captured everybody in the sleepy town. Thereafter, Gori Malik gleefully set fire to the town in a wanton display of force and meanness." [53]

Ibn Battuta (1304- 1368/ ? 1377), one of the world's most famous travelogue writers, witnessed this display of murderous brutality towards Hindu prisoners, and their non-combatant wives and children, during a jihad campaign in southern India in the mid 14th century conducted by the Sultan Ghayasuddin:

"All the infidels found in the jungle were taken prisoners; they had stakes sharpened at both ends and made the prisoners carry them on their shoulders. Each was accompanied by his wife and children, and they were thus led to the camp... In the morning, the Hindus who had been made prisoners the day before, were divided into four groups, and each of these was led to one of the four gates of the main enclosure. There they were impaled on the posts they had themselves carried. Afterwards their wives were butchered and tied to the stakes by their hair. The children were massacred on the bosoms of their mothers, and their corpses left there. Then they struck camp and started cutting down trees in another forest, and all the Hindus who were made captive were treated in the same manner." [54]

Both Turkish and Christian chroniclers provide graphic evidence of the wanton pillage and slaughter of non-combatants following the Ottoman jihad conquest of Constantinople in 1453. First from the Turkish sources:

"Sultan Mehmed (in order to) arouse greater zeal for the way of God issued an order (that the city was to be) plundered. And from all directions they (gazis) came forcefully and violently (to join) the army. They entered the city, they passed the infidels over the sword (i.e. slew them) and...they pillage and looted, they took captive the youths and maidens, and they took their goods and valuables whatever there was of them..." [Urudj] [55]

"The gazis entered the city, cut off the head of the emperor, captured Kyr Loukas and his family...and they slew the miserable common people...They placed people and families in chains and placed metal rings on their necks. " [Neshri] [56]

And Vryonis summarizes the key contents of letters sent by Sultan Mehmed himself to various Muslim potentates of the Near East:

"In his letter to the sultan of Egypt, Mehmed writes that his army killed many of the inhabitants, enslaved many others (those that remained), plundered the treasures of the city, 'cleaned out' the priests and took over the churches...To the Sherif of Mecca he writes that they killed the ruler of Constantinople, they killed the 'pagan' inhabitants and destroyed their houses. The soldiers smashed the crosses, looted the wealth and properties and enslaved their children and youths. 'They cleared these places of their monkish filth and Christian impurity'...In yet another letter he informs Cihan Shah Mirza of Iran that the inhabitants of the city have become food for the swords and arrows of the gazis; that they plundered their children, possessions and houses; that those men and women who survived the massacre were thrown into chains." [57]

The Christian sources, include this narrative by Ducas who gathered eyewitness accounts, and visited Constantinople shortly after its conquest:

"(Then) the Turks arrived at the church [the great church of St. Sophia], pillaging, slaughtering, and enslaving. They enslaved all those that survived. They smashed the icons in the church, took their adornments as well as all that was moveable in the church...Those of (the Greeks) who went off to their houses were captured before arriving there. Others upon reaching their houses found them empty of children, wives, and possessions and before (they began) wailing and weeping were themselves bound with their hands behind them. Others coming to their houses and having found their wife and children being led off, were tied and bound with their most beloved...They (the Turks) slew mercilessly all the elderly, both men and women, in (their) homes, who were not able to leave their homes because of illness or old age. The newborn infants were thrown into the streets...And as many of the (Greek) aristocrats and nobles of the officials of the palace that he (Mehmed) ransomed, sending them all to the 'speculatora' he executed them. He selected their wives and children, the beautiful daughters and shapely youths and turned them over to the head eunuch to guard them, and the remaining captives he turned over to others to guard over them...And the entire city was to be seen in the tents of the army, and the city lay deserted, naked, mute, having neither form nor beauty." [58]

And finally from the contemporary 15th century historian Critobulus of Imbros:

"Then a great slaughter occurred of those who happened to be there: some of them were on the streets, for they had already left the houses and were running toward the tumult when they fell unexpectedly on the swords of the soldiers; others were in their own homes and fell victims to the violence of the Janissaries and other soldiers, without any rhyme or reason; others were resisting relying on their own courage; still others were fleeing to the churches and making supplication- men, women, and children, everyone, for there was no quarter given...The soldiers fell on them with anger and great wrath...Now in general they killed so as to frighten all the City, and terrorize and enslave all by the slaughter." [59]

Remarkably similar descriptions of jihad massacres of non-combatants in both the pre-modern and modern eras have been recorded from Greece and the Balkans, Asia Minor, Africa, the Indian subcontinent, and the Far East (Malaysia and Indonesia). Indeed the 20th century opened and closed with frank jihad genocides- the Armenian genocide committed by the Ottoman Turks during the initial two decades, and the genocide of southern Sudanese Christians and Animists committed by the Arab Muslim Khartoum government during the final two decades.

Muslim conquerors, spurred on in their missionary zeal by the doctrine of jihad, sought to impose Islamic rule globally, either by conversion of infidels under threat of war, or at minimum, submission to the Shari'a, with acceptance by the vanquished non-Muslim populations of unequal and servile status. This classical conception of indefinitely warring blocs of humanity has been taught continuously, through the present, at the leading centers of Islamic learning for both Sunni and Shi'ite Muslims. Yusuf al-Qaradawi even used such unfettered Medieval terminology (i.e., Dar ul-Harb and Dar ul-Islam) during a 1998 interview about the meeting between the Chief Rabbi of Israel and the Rector of Al Azhar University. Perhaps even more disturbing, "secular" Turkey itself is a signatory to the 1990 Universal Declaration of Human Rights in Islam, a document that incorporates jihad war ideology in its triumphal proclamation that the Shari'a has primacy over the Universal Declaration of Human Rights, including the specific statement that God has made the umma (Islamic community) the best nation, whose role is to "guide" humanity. ("The Islamic Shari'ah is the only source of reference for the explanation or clarification of any of the articles of this Declaration"). One must question whether well-intentioned platitudes that ignore or obfuscate Muslim theological-juridical institutions, and the violent history of Islamic jihad, can really offer a pathway to meaningful reform.

More recently, a prominent Islamic Cleric based in the UK gave an interview to *The Sunday Telegraph* on 05/08/2004, 5 days after the Beslan Russia massacre of women and children, while promoting a "celebratory" conference in London the following Saturday (9/11) to commemorate the third anniversary of the September 11 attacks. In the interview he indicated he would support hostage-taking at British schools if carried out by terrorists with a just cause. Omar Bakri Mohammed, the spiritual leader of the extremist sect al-Muhajiroun, said that holding women and children hostage would be a reasonable course of action for a Muslim who has suffered under British rule. In the interview, Mr Mohammed said: "If an Iraqi Muslim carried out an attack like that in Britain, it would be justified because Britain has carried out acts of terrorism in Iraq". This learned cleric, I suspect, is fully aware of the jurisprudence cited here and fully aware of the example of Muhammad, and he aspires to follow in his footsteps. The terrorists who massacred the Russian children those first three days of September felt no empathy in their pitiless acts, thinking only of how proud their God and his prophet will be of their sanctified pious acts of murder and mayhem. They fully believe, as do all devoted and learned, that their brutal acts are an offering acceptable to their God that will earn them a place in heaven with the great ones, with their virility increased a hundred fold so they can exercise eternal lust chasing around scores of virgins and boys. The fact that they will be dead, and have no penis with which to copulate, and no sperm to ejaculate, is lost on them. As terrorists die and enter next state of existence, I imagine they go fairly quickly from a state of rapture and delusion, to a state of confusion and frustration, if not severe anguish.

Chapter 17
Beslan, Russia & Islam

Aside from India and Israel, probably no modern industrialized nation has suffered to the degree that Russians have at the hands of Islamic terrorists. Having held the "Great Satan" title long before it was transferred to the USA, Muslim militants have taken particular glee in tormenting Russians. Muslim sites have posted movies depicting the beheading of Russian soldiers long before such acts became a spectacle to Westerns. What could collectively be described as Russia's Sept 11th occurred late Aug, 2004, when homicide bombers brought down two commercial airliners, then a suicide bombing targeting commuters in Moscow, followed a few days later by a bloody hostage incident at a school killing hundreds of women and children. On Sept 3rd, 2004, Russians saw up close and personal the spectacle of children being mowed down by automatic fire at School No. 1 in the southern Russian town of Beslan, bringing the nation's worst hostage crisis to a shattering end of gunfire, explosions, ...and death. Ten Russian commandos also died trying to prevent the slaughtering frenzy, as crying children tried to flee through the explosions and gunfire, some naked and covered in blood. Though the dead Islamic terrorists will be worshiped with other suicide/homicide extremists in large parts of the Muslim world, only those Russian commandos, with the parents and teachers who also died trying to save the children, will be accepted into heaven for their bravery and good deeds. Worldly praise and worship by peers notwithstanding, the reward waiting for the Muslim cowards for their behavior is not 72 virgins, boys like pearls, mansions, riches, and unbounded food and gluttony. If it takes an eternity, the unbending demands of Justice will be fully satisfied for the horrible Men and Women, and all others remotely culpable for acts against the innocent, divinely created, and loved children of Beslan.

Sept 1st 2004, a gang of men and women stormed into the secondary school in Beslan (North Ossetia province) during a ceremony to mark the first day of the new school year. According to The New York Times, when the terrorists took over the Russian elementary school, they shouted "Allahu akbar" (Allah is Great). The terrorists had previously stockpiled weapons and explosives at the school in the well-planned operation. In the aftermath a cameraman for the British network ITN reported seeing around 100 bodies in the gymnasium where many of the hostages were held, mostly women and children. Russia's Interfax news agency reported the assault was triggered following several explosions after which panicked hostages made a break for freedom, possibly driven by extreme thirst. The explosions went off as the emergency personnel went to get bodies of people killed early in the raid, as the militants had agreed. As the desperate hostages began to flee, Militants then opened fire and security forces were compelled to returned fire. The Interfax new agency reported some terrorists then split into three groups to blend in with the fleeing hostages and took refuge in a nearby home. The scene around the school was chaotic, with people running through the streets, the wounded carried off on stretchers. An Associated Press reporter saw ambulances speeding by, the windows streaked with blood. Huge columns of smoke billowed from the school, where windows were shattered, part of roof gone and another part charred. Four armed men in civilian clothes ran by, shouting, "A militant ran this way." Soldiers and men in civilian clothes carried children, some naked or clad only in underpants, some covered in blood, to a temporary hospital set up behind an armored personnel carrier. The children drank eagerly from bottles of water given to them once they reached safety. One unidentified woman freed Thursday told Izvestia that during the night children occasionally began to cry, adding: "then the fighters would fire in the air to restore quiet". Prosecutor-General Vladimir Ustinov said 326 hostages were killed and 727 wounded in the attack, with some still unaccounted for. Soon after Beslan, a message attributed to Chechen rebel leader Shamil Basayev was posted on his Kavkaz-Center Web site. In it he proposed to exchange Chechnyan independence for security, threatening more attacks. "...we are not bound by any circumstances or by anybody, and will fight by our rules, as is comfortable and beneficial for us," he wrote. He also put the ultimate blame for the school siege on Putin, and appealed to the world to recognize the righteousness of the Chechen cause.

Negotiators said the hostage-takers had repeatedly refused offers of food and water throughout the standoff. "They are very cruel people, we are facing a ruthless enemy," said Leonid Roshal, a pediatrician involved in the negotiations. Correspondents say many of those released were desperate for water when they came out, and some were barely able to stand. Many of the children were only partly clothed because of the stifling heat in the gymnasium where they had been held since the militants took the building on Wednesday. By Friday morning conditions were so bad that people could hardly breathe. Hostage Salimat Suleimanova said: "So many children lay unconscious without food and water." Others reported: "Most of kids were almost unconsciousness. Those who could move started to pee into shoes and then drink urine. They would make several sips of urine and then would stop and cry because their lips were chapped and the urine stung their skin."

Indira Dzetskelova, the mother of one of the child hostages in Beslan, Russia, reports that "several 15-year-old girls were raped by terrorists." Her daughter "heard their terrible cries and screams when those monsters took them away." Her traumatized daughter Dzerase sobbed as she added: "When the assault started, some of us were running out through the school dining room. "The terrorists started to shoot from the roof, then one of them ran into the dining room and started to shoot from the window. "I saw kids and women falling to the ground. And I saw that vermin's face. I saw his smile as he killed my friends." Diana Gadzhieva, 14, was held with her sister Akinba, aged 11. She told how the rebels executed all the adult men in a room upstairs. "We saw groups of men hostages going out and never coming back." Other survivors told how screaming teenage girls were dragged into rooms adjoining the gymnasium where they were being held and raped by their Chechen captors. An 18-month-old baby had been repeatedly stabbed by a black-clad terrorist who had run out of ammunition.

A just rescued mother described the hostages' three days of hell in the Russian School Gymnasium. She told reporters of the terrorists holding up the corpse of a man just shot dead in front of hundreds of hostages, his pockets stuffed with ammunition and grenades, warning: "If a child utters even a sound, we'll kill another one." When children fainted from lack of sleep, food and water, their masked and camouflaged captors simply sneered. In the intolerable heat of the gym, adults implored children to drink their own urine. Hours after escaping alive, a woman who had been taken hostage with her 7-year-old son and her mother spoke of three days of unspeakable horror of children so wired with fear they couldn't sleep, of captors coolly threatening to kill hostages one by one, of a gymnasium so cramped there was hardly room to move. "We were in complete fear," said Alla Gadieyeva, 24, who spoke to an Associated Press reporter, as she lay collapsed in exhaustion on a stretcher outside a hospital. "People were praying all the time, and those that didn't know how to pray we taught them".

Alla told reporters that she and her mother, Irina, were in the school courtyard Wednesday seeing off her son, Zaur, on his first day of school when they heard sounds like "balloons popping." She thought the noise was part of school festivities. But then five masked gunmen burst into the courtyard, shooting in the air and ordering people to get inside the building. Children, parents and teachers Alla estimated there were about 1000, were herded into the gymnasium. Alla said children whimpered in fear, and all around there was screaming and crying. The hostages were forced to crouch, their hands folded over their heads. For the rebels, the first order of business was confiscating cell phones. They smashed the phones, then delivered a warning: "If we find any mobile phones, we will shoot 20 people all around you." The gymnasium was quickly transformed into an arsenal of explosive bombs dangling from the ceiling, set on the floor, strung up on walls. She said they seemed to be homemade, primitive packages containing bolts and nails. On the first day, people got a tiny bit of water to drink, but no food. After that, Alla said, nothing. When she asked the rebels for water for her mother, they laughed at her. "My mother was terrified, and I thought she was having a heart attack. When I saw my son, my mother ... go unconscious, so tired, so thirsty, I wanted it all to come to an end," she said. "When children began to faint, they laughed," Alla said. "They were totally indifferent." During the ordeal, Zaur became so traumatized that he would flinch whenever someone touched him, or even brushed by him, she said. As with most of the other children, his only spells of sleep were the times he fell unconscious from thirst and exhaustion. When asked how her son would remember the ordeal, Alla replied: "How can a person ever forget it? Would you ever forget it?" As Alla spoke under a grove of spruce trees, she had not yet been reunited with her mother or son, although authorities confirmed to her that they were alive. She recounted how the hostage-takers eventually took off their masks. They had beards, long hair, and spoke with Chechen accents, she said. "They're not human beings," Alla said. "What they did to us, I can't understand."

As the battle intensified, the rebels betrayed agitation for the first time. "We'll shoot until our guns stop," a rebel announced to the crowd. "And when our guns stop, we'll blow up the building." The hostage-takers began pushing people out of the gym and into the basement. That created an opening for the hostages: They began breaking windows and fleeing. Some pushed children outside. Alla said she helped her son and mother through a window. She didn't manage to get out. For some reason, a 6-year-old boy whom she didn't know was drawn to Alla. She held him in her arms. He clung to her, she said, "as if he would never let go." A group of hostages, including Alla and the boy, finally made a rush for a set of doors in the gymnasium. As they fled, she saw bodies of captives strewn on the floor as rebels fought with Russian security troops swarming around school compound. Some Russian soldiers appeared as they reached the doors. "At first I didn't believe it," Alla said. "I thought they were Chechens." Her doubts soon vanished. It's OK, the soldiers told her. "You're home now." As Alla told her tale, townspeople kept coming up, asking her about the fate of their loved-ones. A man, around 20, asked Alla if she knew what had happened to one of the captives, a woman. She's dead, Alla replied. The man bit his lip, ...nodded, ...and then turned away. The tragedy and travesty, though thousands of miles away, might just as well have happened at the school in your neighborhood. Those killed and maimed students, parents, and teachers kept for days without water or food in a sweltering school building before being butchered were, in essence, ...our children, ...our sisters, ...our wives, ...and our parents!

Officials told FOX News that 10 of the 31 terrorists killed by Russian soldiers were Arabs. Jihadists from the Middle East are known to have joined the Chechen uprising. Decent human beings feel great outrage at the involvement of the "peaceful" Muslim religion with the mass killings of innocent children, in yet another wake-up call for the civilized world. In Chechnya and other Muslim lands, as in Palestine after Sept 11th, celebrations are ongoing. Many not passing out sweets smile, somehow gaining sick affirmation that the servants/warriors of their private God 'Allah' are finding such success destroying infidels. Continuing to practice Al-taqiyya (also called taqiah, Al-takeyya, Al-taqiyah, or kitman), spokespersons speaking in Russian and English condemn the attacks, then in unison raise their fists with the usual Friday chants as Clerics and Imams praise the terrorists as martyrs and call for more Jihad against the 'decadent' West. The hypocrisy dripping from the words, as obvious as blood flowing from an open wound to us, can not be seen by any in these primitive cultures steeped in violence. On Sept 7th, President Putin angrily responded to reporters questions regarding possible inquiries and negotiations saying: "Why don't you meet Osama bin Laden, invite him to Brussels or to the White House and engage in talks, ask him what he wants and give it to him so he leaves you in peace?" Putin said in a meeting with foreign journalists late Monday. "You find it possible to set some limitations in your dealings with these bastards, so why should we talk to people who are child-killers?" he said, ruling out a public inquiry into the operation to retake the school. Across Russia's 11 time zones, hundreds of thousands rallied to denounce terrorism, as if such words could have any impact influencing Islamists to abandon methods perfected in 1400 years of Jihad. The Urals city of Yekaterinburg saw its largest-ever public demonstration as 20,000 people took to the streets, while Russian television showed several thousand massing in driving rain in the Pacific port of Vladivostok. At least 100,000 people joined a rally in Moscow bolstering Putin against critics of the authorities' handling of the bloody siege. Putin, in an unprecedented burst of candor told the Russian people, "We were weak, and weak people are beaten." Already, he is reaching out a tentative hand, looking for help from us and from the Israelis, and Israel and the US will generously respond, as long as the much-maligned Israeli Right retains its shaky hold on power, and as long as strong republicans continue to lead us.

The southern town of Beslan buried more of the 335 people -- half of them children. Every few meters a new grave was being dug or filled with a coffin in a new cemetery created to deal with the deaths. "The whole town is crying, wailing for the pain that can never ease," said Masha, neighbor of four-year-old Rada Solkazanova and her mother Larisa, buried together Tuesday. "Now all people want to do is find their loved ones and bury them. Can you imagine the pain of never knowing what happened and never burying your children?" she added. "They're not people, they're animals," said Assiya, another neighbor. "They call themselves Muslims, but what have they got to do with any kind of religion if they can kill children?". They were the chosen victims of the global Islamic terror network, and all Russia watched in horror, day after day, as they were shot, stabbed, raped, and blown-up, along with their helpless parents and teachers, while other little ones perished in slow agony from thirst, dehydration, and heat stroke inside a Russian school, where the water fountains ran but dying captives were not allowed to drink anything but their own urine. One thing is now clear, not just local Chechens, but also international Islamofascist barbarians with imperial designs carefully planned the attack on the children and mothers of Beslan. The child rapes and executions demonstrate that the operation was planned as a suicide mission from the beginning.

In the bloody summer of 2004, millions of Russians learned the same hard lessons we learned on September 11: That we are at war with a vicious global enemy, an Islamist enemy that hates not just Jews, but also Secularists, Christians, Jews, Hindus, Buddhists, Agnostics, Atheists, Feminists, Liberals, Communists, Republicans, Democrats, and even progressive Muslims. Russians have found that Muslim militants are an enemy that cannot be appeased, bought off, or safely accommodated or supported against others. To prevent having our own heads severed, or those of our children cut off and handed to us, we must unite to cut them down first. Russia must fight with us again, as it did in the 1940s. This time, with a free Poland, a democratic Italy, with England, Australia, the recently liberated states in Eastern Europe, and with Latin America and parts of Asia joined with us, victory is certain. All will retain their God-given liberties, and even Spain, Germany, France, and other weak nations will benefit, but will forever suffer the shame of being on the wrong side of history, and (rightly) suffer in both prestige and prosperity. Middle Eastern and other Islamic countries will be left to suffer and wallow in the despair they have wrought upon themselves and the rest of the world, and will scratch out an existence behind ever growing measures found effective to prevent Islamic ideologies and peoples from further contaminating the civilized world. Muslims in free lands will finally get a real education, and leave the violent tenants of Islam in huge numbers. A coordinated alliance of Russia, Australia, the United States, England, Poland, Italy, Japan, and South Korea will quickly defeat the Imperial designs of Muslim Imams and leaders worldwide. They will do so not with proportionate response, a method of weakness and failure, but with education for all, and unbridled methods of 'total war' where needed, showing no mercy against a foe that shows no mercy to us as they shoot our children in the back, raping, pillaging, torturing, mutilating, beheading, terrorizing innocents gleefully while chanting "Allah Akbar". Al Sadr and his ilk, Osama bin Laden's all, and all who sympathize and worship them as heroes and martyrs, must be wiped from the face of the earth forever.

The left has pretty much silenced rational discussion of any kind with its knee-jerk over-reaction to anything that might possibly offend any groups' delicate sensibilities. Now making sensible observations or drawing correct inferences based on pure fact is 'Islamophobic'. Challenging questions are dismissed as "Muslim bashing" or, even more absurdly, as "racist" (as if religion were a race). To smug self-righteous elitists, the rest of the world must forever bow to the 'Politically-Correct Gods' and forever put up with Islamic inspired murder without complaint. The Sept 11 commission found faults everywhere, except with any part of pure Islamic religious philosophy and its role in brainwashing those acting or acquiescing in its name. In politics the saying is: "It's the economy, stupid!". While the world pretends that Islam is a non-violent religion, modern and ancient history begs to differ, screaming: "It's the religion, stupid!" The macabre act of Islamic terror in Russia is both immoral and illegal. Article 51 of the Protocols Additional to the Geneva Convention prohibits combatants from using civilians to: "shield military objectives from attacks or to shield, favor or impede military operations." Moreover, the International Criminal Court considers "conscripting or enlisting children under the age of 15 years, or using them to participate actively in hostilities in both international and non-international armed conflicts" to be a war crime. Thus, even if other attacks that deliberately slaughter civilians are excluded from the equation, Islamic terrorist organizations, and the Muslim leaders and lay people (read: the nearly invisible 'Moderate Muslim' having no tongue) that tolerate them, are war criminals twice over. It is long past time to unbind the corset of political correctness that suffocates so much of our public discourse, and to state some self-evident truths. How can any human being with a shred of conscience dismiss what occurred in that school as anything less than pure evil, scorned though the word may be by our own elite? At its root, the attack in Beslan was not really about Russia's war against noble separatists in Chechnya fighting for an "Islamic" state. Words like 'separatists', and 'freedom fighters' simply provide the immediate 'feel good' cover words accepted by sympathizers in the media worldwide. In fact the fight is all about simple, profound religious bigotry and the rule of the Caliphate, versus Russian nationalism and territorial integrity and the rule of democratic law based (since the 1990's) on equality and human rights. Its not about intolerant and undemocratic Russians trying to prevent Chechens from practicing religion or be free, …but it is about intolerant and undemocratic Chechens trying to eliminate all religions but Islam, to conquer and govern the land and enslave infidels. In other words, Russia is fighting the same threat faced by non-Muslims all over the world, with full moral, national, and territorial justification.

Update: *Reuters* - Aug 26, 2005 - Moscow, Russia - Shamil Basayev, the man behind Russia's Beslan school siege, has been appointed the new first deputy prime minister in Chechnya's outlawed separatist government. Basayev considers Russian civilians legitimate targets and makes common cause with Islamic radicals elsewhere. Basayev has claimed openly that he organized the raid on Beslan, in southern Russia. Russia's most wanted man, he describes himself as "a bad guy, a bandit, a terrorist". He was also behind dozens of other violent acts, often targeting Russian civilians. In an interview aired by U.S. television network ABC News Aug 2005, Basayev said he accepted he was a terrorist but said his violence was justified.

Chapter 18
Persia-Egypt and Islam

Egyptian and Iranian natives have much more in common than they realize. Hadrat Umar Farooq was the Caliph who succeeded Abu Bakr in 632. Umar's armies were very active, taking Damascus in 635, Antioch in 636, Jerusalem in 638, Syria in 640. Drunk on conquest and plunder, his armies then completed Islam's conquest of both Egypt and Persia in 641. Umar's marauders were especially merciless in their persecutions of the Zoroastrian "*heathens and idolaters*" of Persia. In the ninth century, the continuing persecutions of surviving Zoroastrians pushed some to migrate to more tolerant lands in Hindu India, where to this day they form a respected minority known as 'Parsis'. To those unable to escape, the horrors on the Muslim conquest were only exceeded by the next several hundreds of years, as they continued suffering one humiliation after another. One fact not often discussed: conquered natives were periodically forced to give up a portion of their children by kidnap (later by a process known as '*devshirme*') into slavery. Once taken and converted to Islam, male children 14-20 were trained to be janissaries (infantry men), and then compelled to fight, kill, and subjugate ever more victims. Girls had other 'duties'. It is a terrible tragedy that these manipulated youngsters grew up knowing nothing of the sorrow and loss their parents experienced at their departure. Neither they nor their progeny understood how they were used, and denied the warmth and love of true family. Islam's followers in Iran and Egypt natives need to develop awareness that their family/spiritual roots and national heritage are truly engendered in Persia and Egypt, NOT in Muhammad and Islam. Muslim conquers killed, burned, and destroyed superior cultures, but still spiritual family ties tug at the hearts and soul of these once great people. An avalanche or pride and healing await these good people as they discover and reunite with their true heritage.

Today, Islam continues to advertise itself as a religion of peace in an effort to attract the masses, but in the 7th century no such pretenses preceded the armies of Umar. Today Islamic proselyters are seldom disappointed as they continue to count on the general ignorance regarding the fact that Islam and Jihad comprise more a doctrine of war than of peace. Wherever Islamic governments are dominant, it subjugates and suppresses women, even while its apologists present it as the perfect champion of women's rights. Indeed, Muhammad himself was the worst example of a misogynist, claiming Allah had given him rights to rape innumerable women of conquered peoples, and otherwise basically help himself to any poor girl he took a fancy too, including a 9 year old little girl. While making excuses for such vile behavior, defenders of the Qur'an also claim the book promotes scholarly leaning, when in fact it is filled with nonsensical fantasy usually in direct contradiction to scientific fact. Muslims present Islam as a religion which encourages learning, reminding others that Muhammad said "*seek knowledge even if it is China*", while at the same time any book of knowledge perceived as contradicting the Qur'an is considered satanic. The direction remains for such heresy to be destroyed forthwith, as was the practice of Muslim marauders since the movements inception. The Royal Library of Alexandria in Egypt, founded at the beginning of the 3rd century during the reign of Ptolemy II, was once the largest in the world, at its peak storing up to 700,000 scrolls. In 640 AD Moslem marauders took the city, and upon learning of "a great library containing all the knowledge of the world" the conquering general asked Khalifa Omar for instructions. Omar is quoted as saying of the Library's holdings, "*they will either contradict the Qur'an, in which case they are heresy, or they will agree with it, so they are superfluous*", whereupon he ordered the library to be destroyed and the books burnt. Although a cultural travesty and crime against knowledge and learning, at the time the burning scrolls were the least of the worries of the surviving native Egyptians.

Islam's methods of war perpetrated great suffering to the ancestors of today's devout Egyptian Muslims. By 659 AD Egypt was completely conquered and subdued. Islam raped Egypt's women, killed many of her men, took many slaves, and applied the heavy yoke of Dhimmi to her survivors. Once the greatest civilization in the region, still nothing could match or oppose the fanaticism and brutality of the marauding Islamic hordes. Out of necessity, survivors migrated to Islam. With elders, intellectuals, records, and all opposition obliterated, Egyptians were soon enough oblivious to the facts surrounding their ancestor's tremendous prior achievements, and of facts surrounding the treatment of their fathers, mothers, and grandfathers in the Jihad which annihilated them. That kind of evil bloodletting does not obliterate the reality of the existence of the murdered, however, their blood still cries from the dust, and will continue to rise up to the heavens until the full measure of justice is served upon those who tortured and killed them and caused their children to live in ignorance. It has been a common tragedy in conquered lands for surviving young to go on ignorantly serving the Islamic masters who slew and subjugated their own parents. All this should serve to give notice to today's great civilizations …Education, knowledge, even great cultural, scientific, technological, and economic achievements notwithstanding; all can fall to marauding Islam hordes if not dutifully defended.

Earlier in Persia, the religion was forced upon natives in what is known today as Iran. The invading Arabs raped Persian women, massacred the population, and looted their lands and wealth. They burned all books and permanently destroyed both the cultural/scientific knowledge and written history of the people. The imperative to rape young infidel women is not always well understood outside of Muslim circles. You see, according to Islamic way of understanding, virgin girls get a 'free-pass' to heaven. *(kind of makes sense in a sick sort of way, really, considering the logistical need to keep innumerable dead martyrs constantly supplied with fresh virgin material)*. So an underlying sinister intent of Muslim marauders (Jihadists), besides satisfying their lusts in an expression of power and hatred, is through rape to make sure vile infidel woman don't make it to heaven by denying them their virgin 'free-pass'.

Native peoples of Egypt and Persia, remnants of two great civilizations, forever bonded by their mutual experience with Islam about the same time. By design and necessity, most calling themselves Muslims in these lands have been denied even the knowledge of their own ancestry, let alone the particulars of what there female and male ancestors suffered at the hands Islam. These two separate accomplished civilizations were built by a skillful, educated, and hard-working great and proud people. Natives in these lands today unknowingly have many loving ancestors, obviously on the other side of the veil separating the living from the dead, who still care deeply about their progeny. Their grand-parents and other relations from prior generations, speak with one voice from the grave. They are joined by more recent ancestry, who have learned since death that they were lied-to and used, and also had their heritage stolen from them by Islam. Both the living and dead in these lands, especially native Moslems, have more to avenge for the way Islam harms their families today, and has hurt generations of their ancestors in the past. Many more 'spiritual' natives feel the cries, as if from the dust, yet are not quite sure how to respond to answer family promptings from the other side. Many sons and daughters still struggling in this life, find their hearts impulsively turning towards their fathers and mothers, as those same lost parents and grandparents hearts feel the tug to reach out across the veil to connect with their heritage. If these feelings and urges were given voice, the words they speak to loved ones are these, *…escape Islam, escape hatred, escape violence, become worthy to join loving family in the next life and beyond. Stand true and faithful to your family, to your true heritage, and to your conscience. Offer no more loyalty to that pathologic madman, Muhammad, nor his deceived followers. Be true to your own heart, and your family.* There are no Moslems in the next life, there is no Ummah, there are only brothers and sisters, mothers and fathers, truth, and inescapable justice. There is no Qur'an, no celestial sluts to satisfy physical or spiritual lusts, and absolutely no-one worships or respects one certain small withering spirit named Muhammad. That diminutive creature spends all his time wracked with the clear knowledge of his crimes, and avoiding facing his millions of victims.

Some are beginning to understand that that many of their recent or distant ancestors entered Islam at sword point. As Arab dominance gripped cities and nations, most undoubtedly embraced Islam not only to survive, but to avoid payment of Poll Tax (Jaziya) and escape the humiliation reserved for the non-Muslims living under Arab rulers. Undoubtedly nearly all of those so forced hoped and longed for the opportunity to escape the grip of Islam at the time of their induction, but the grip of Islam on families, neighborhoods, and nations is very tight. Dreams of freedom became sad resignation, and after a generation or two none remember or recite the old hopes and dreams. It's interesting to take note that much of Islam today is made up from what essentially is a conscripted army. Islamic efforts to make that army tow the official line and become more responsive and obedient warriors *(Jihadists)* continue to this day. Calls to arms and Jihad seem constantly issued from various sources, and there seems to be a new crop of recently indoctrinated energetic young people ready to answer the call to prove their devotion, and to make teachers and family proud. Properly incited, they depart on their dangerous journeys knowing nothing of the root causes and circumstances of their ancestral parents forced conversions. Their father's father's father, an entire previous lineage of many peoples, cry from the dust lamenting the choices of their progeny, but can not speak to hearts filled with the same hatred and blood-lust that first subdued their parents. It is a huge tragedy and travesty spanning generations. An enlightenment, or awakening, is feared and fought against by Islamic fundamentalists as they fight to ensure the continuation of their rightful place as overseers of conquered peoples deliberately and carefully kept in the dark.

If Islam really were a great and peaceful religion, we might expect peace, prosperity, and enlightenment to break out all over in lands it has subdued and governed for so long. Instead, everywhere Islam goes, all the locals get is poverty, oppression, corruption, murder, rape, and thievery. The facts on the ground confirm this, notwithstanding the vigorous, often threatening denials of Islamists. "*How beautiful the Emperors robe*", they exclaim, while the rest of the world sees the ugly nakedness of the violent culture consuming all in its path to serve today's Islamic elite. "*Islamophobic bigot!*" they scream, as they sharpen their blades and plan their next vile act in the name of their hateful God *Allah*. Today's Middle East is a region where even words have been systematically corrupted. Dictatorship is called "*nationalism*", stealing is called "*Jizya*", terrorism is called "*holy war*", murder is called "*martyrdom*", and terrorists have become "*insurgents*". In truth Islam is a hateful cult all about dominance of the weak, and destruction of anything outside of it's own putrid shell of bigotry. Islam's shrill rhetoric is dangerous for sure, but the cries from loved ones long lost pierce to the very soul of long lost children. These quiet whisperings offer both sorrow and healing to the children of Egypt and Persia, and are also a force to be reckoned with.

Chapter 19
Islamic Aid (Jizya)

Many misguided pundits, having no specific knowledge of the philosophy of Islam, continue to attribute the core cause of terrorism to poverty and desperation, proffering the solution of undermining terrorists support base by providing increased aid. They assert that recipients of significant food, material, and cash will experience gratitude and begin to love us, or at least hate us less. Such assumptions are wishful 'magical' thinking at its worst. Any review of empirical evidence and history of radical Islam suggests that all such assumptions are delusional if not dangerous. As outlined in Islamic Economics 101, the nature of Islam guarantees inferior prosperity in Islamic nations, which since its inception has inspired only envy, lust, and often sanctimonious plunder. Muslims, convinced of their superiority over non-believers, are incapable of feeling gratitude for that which they sincerely believe is owed to them. Muslims are Masters by divine decree, whereas all dhimmi are slaves whose very lives are at the disposal of their masters. When Moslems find infidels enjoying greater prosperity, influence, or power than themselves, calls for Jihad become louder. This is true even in more affluent Islamic lands punch-drunk on oil wealth. As has been demonstrated in Saudi Arabia, even widespread prosperity does not prevent either Jihad or the creation of terrorists…it simply better funds it. The lack of gratitude we see today from Islamic recipients of massive aid is likely because they view the donations as a Jizya tax, which Muhammad instructs Muslims are fully entitled to.

When a charitable man knows of a family's need for food, he will do the neighborly thing and impart of his substance, even delivering it to the doorstep. The giver of aid, by principle, neither asks for nor expects thanks. However, as a practical matter it would be unthinkable to deliver a spaghetti dinner to a neighbor who shoots-up our children as they play. Hungry or not, when a society, government, or culture seeks your destruction, the last thing you want to do is enable that effort. It seems completely irrational to us, but a rationale exists in the minds of devout Muslims that it is proper to teach their youth to hate and seek the destruction of America. The foundation of those attitudes as are instilled into young people by mothers and fathers, religious leaders, school teachers, the media, and by civic organizations and national governments in hostile lands. The root of all prejudice, including the hatred felt by those who hijacked the four aircraft on Sept 11, is first taught in the home. Egyptian Mohamed el-Amir, whose son Mohamed Atta hijacked the first plane that crashed into the World Trade Centre, initially declared that he did not understand how his son could have acted in such a way, claiming he had raised his son to be a good Muslim. More recently his true colors were revealed as he praised his sons actions and declared his intent to support more terrorism. Though it may seem cruel, we need to re-evaluate if we should be providing support to any people pursuing a murderous agenda destructive to democracy.

Yasin Hassan Omar, the Somali asylum-seeker, is the London Warren Street bomber caught on tape on 7/7/05. Omar shared a flat with the No 26 bus bomber, Ibrahim, who moved in with him 2 years ago. Omar had been getting a £88/week housing benefit to pay for a council property flat since 1999, and also received substantial income support, immigration officials say. So for six years British taxpayers have financed Omar's preparations to kill to the tune of £27,456 ($47,789) in rent, plus even more in other support. As it turns out all 4 bombers had been the ungrateful recipients of significant 'welfare' payments. Apparently violently inclined Muslim immigrants are quite savvy at exploiting such programs.

The question of personal/foreign aid to hostile peoples/nations needs to be re-addressed within the context of the newly redefined "War on Hateful (Islamic) Ideology". The popular idea promoted by leftists that poverty causes terrorism has been shown in numerous terrorist profiles to be false, yet still the UN repeatedly asks wealthy nations to re-double foreign aid, naming poverty as a cause of terrorism. Former Secretary of State Colin Powell has also weighed in saying: "We have to put hope back in the hearts of people. We have to show people who might move in the direction of terrorism that there is a better way". Businessmen like Ted Turner concur, saying: "The reason that the World Trade Center got hit is because there are a lot of people living in abject poverty out there who don't have any hope for a better life". Bush policy has responded by increasing aid to impoverished Muslim peoples worldwide. The vast majority of Palestinians, because of the focus on its people and leadership on terror, live hand to mouth on the 'charity' of European, American, and Muslim states. Some argue the entire pseudo-nation are paid mercenaries serving in the cause of Islam. For our support and subsidy of the people, Americans diplomats were targeted and murdered in the West Bank trying to deliver scholarships to needy Palestinians, and then locals stoned their would-be rescuers. We give nearly $2 billion a year in aid to Egypt, second only to Israel, while its media openly spews anti-American hatred, and which is in fact the Arab epicenter of such pollution. For our investment we have purchased not gratitude, but disrespect. The US and other countries have expended billions trying to rebuild Iraq, while devote Muslim 'insurgents' blow up the work as fast as possible killing as many workers as possible. Even before Sept 11th the US had been the largest contributor of humanitarian aid in Afghanistan and other parts of the Islamic world. The Taliban were all-to-willing to accept Western aid to further their efforts, just as the Palestinian Authority is all-too-willing to accept foreign funds in support of its aims. Gullible US/European governments struggle to comply with extortion requests as Palestinians clamor for ever more money, equipment, training, and infrastructure. On Feb 11, 2003, The United Nations Relief Works Agency (UNRWA), asked donating countries for more money to continue its assistance to Palestinians. Its representative, Hansen, said UNRWA exceeded its $400 million budget distributing food parcels, rebuilding houses destroyed by the Israeli military and maintaining emergency clinics for the sick and wounded. It was recently learned than even significant amounts of financial aid provided to Islamic countries affected by the Dec 26 2004 deadly Tsunami have been diverted to terrorist causes.

Paying subsidies to Islamic states to suspend global Jihad terrorism is tantamount to paying ransom, in effect temporarily buying one's own peace and security as a ransomed privilege. But according to Osama and his ilk that 'privilege' expired long ago and cannot be bought back, which leaves even promoters of such subsidies wondering exactly what it is we are paying for today? With enough money thrown at Islam, is it even possible to put the Jihad Genie back in the bottle? Any who still think so know nothing of Islam and its long love affair with Jihad. Payers continue to live in delusion thinking they can control Jihadists with generosity, whereas in fact extortionists always dictate the terms of such arrangements, with the extorted continuing to have little or no influence. History has demonstrated convincingly that societies who pay such tribute are destined to eventually disappear. Those who pay ransom for peace and security will always find themselves subservient to their new masters. It can never work, because Islamic terrorists hate us because of their ideology, and filling up the coffers of Third World governments and the pockets of their despots and cronies will do nothing to change that central, governing fact.

Bill Clinton promised and delivered huge sums in economic and humanitarian support to North Korea, including oil shipments, food, and even a light-water nuclear reactor. The American people received in return a piece of paper promising to suspend development of nuclear weapons. That agreement, never honored, has no value except as proof that providing blanket appeasement and aid to hateful regimes is a very unwise thing to do. The policy may yet prove fatal to millions of South Koreans, if not millions of Americans if/when the rogue state delivers one or more device to proxies lusting to set them off in the USA. Today technicians in North Korea still chow down on food provided by free peoples, as they build bombs designed to kill huge numbers of their benefactors. Aid to North Korea still has not, and will not, result in removing the North Korean threat. Instead it will only serve to prop-up the very government responsible for the food shortages.

Policies of bribery and appeasement are a slippery slope that strengthens an enemy and weakens the giver. In light of current realities, all aid should probably now be qualified to insure none of it will be used, directly or indirectly, to destroy us, or to strengthen in any way militant Islamic societies committed to our destruction. It's time to collectively confess that governments that either cannot or will not stop promoting or allowing such hatred are not our allies, are not even neutral, but are in fact belligerents whose enmity should be accepted rather than ignored. State department coddling and financial/humanitarian-aid notwithstanding, nothing we can ever do will make Islamic terrorists love us, we can only make them fear and respect us. We must ask ourselves, does aid given to these people enable the luxury of spending their time planning Jihad, or would the militants and extremists be less anxious to destroy us if circumstances required them to be more actively engaged in their own support? Would the absence of aid force these able bodied individuals to instead concentrate on legitimate efforts to meet basic needs of food, shelter, and clothing? We must be pragmatic and realize that the first order of business of any society is self-preservation. We must without paranoia see our enemy, Islamic Hatred, clearly with all its roots and support structures, even if part of that structure comes from our own government and other charitable sources of aid.

To help in raising the standard of living and self sufficiency of others is a noble cause worthy of pursuit, but common sense and self preservation now cry out for re-focusing those efforts toward more worthy recipients less inclined to kill us. Certainly there is no shortage of needy peoples in North, Central, and South American countries, or in Russian and European societies as they struggle to transition to democratic governments and free economies. So how to respond … do we bury Islamic peoples in charity, sympathy, goodwill, and understanding? At issue is whether we should be providing logistical support to any nation where majorities of extreme Muslim people express hatred towards free democratic nations, and wherein organizations exist, drawn from a core anti-American culture, with designs to harm us.

When the British retook the Falkland Islands, the fact that Argentina had failed miserably to provide for the support of their own forces was an important factor in the decision making process for those beleaguered foot-soldiers to give up the fight, and which ultimately resulted in reducing friendly causalities and expediting the campaign. This is the nature of war. A military siege, by definition, is to force an enemy into submission and capitulation by extreme methods, which outside of war are considered inhumane. Historically, the 'civilian' population suffers all kinds of shortages when a government struggles for conquest or its survival by force of arms. Although collateral damage and innocent blood are regrettable and should be avoided, an enemy cannot be allowed to cower behind the protection offered by its own innocent victims. It is incumbent on the peoples who suffer at the hands of repressive and dictatorial leaders who bring nothing but war, despair, and hunger to their own lands, to rise up and depose of the scoundrels. The people who suffer must understand that the solution to the problem is for Muslims to rise up against terrorists in their neighborhoods, including violent Imams preaching hate, and bring real reform to their religion and culture. Humanitarian aid and rebuilding activity is normally considered appropriate after capitulation, because logistical support to an enemy is unthinkable. Yes, it is cruel and brutal, but war is impossible to sanitize to a form palatable to liberal western sensibilities.

The Red Cross and other international aid organizations did not make humanitarian deliveries to Japan in the period between Pearl Harbor and Japans unconditional surrender, nor to Germany and Hitler. Anyone suggesting that food and monetary aid be sent to Hitler in hopes to influence the reform of Nazism would have been mocked and then sent to the insane asylum. Equivalent outrageous suggestion get a pass today. On Dec 7th 1941 a beleaguered West realized that pacifism meant suicide, and the Sermon on the Mount was temporarily suspended in pursuit of War. During the Cold-War no aid was provided to prop-up communist regimes, which led directly to the downfall of the failed system. On Sept 11th enemies we neither provoked nor sought bring death to us, eating the bread we gave them.

As we struggle to make sense of September 11 and decide how best to fight Jihadists, it would be instructive to remember the 1801-1805 war that first brought the United States into conflict with Muslim terrorists from countries in the Middle East. The example of the fledgling US government dealings with Muslim terrorist pirates in the late 1700's operating in North Africa's Barbary Coast (and protected by Muslim nations) demonstrated clearly that paying tribute never works anyway, rather it simply emboldens them to take further action.

In the late 1700's it seemed impossible for Muslim states along the Barbary Coast to ignore awkward American merchant vessels, no match for the speedy Muslim corsairs, traveling through the Mediterranean. After the War of Independence, the Royal Navy no longer protected shipping from the rebellious American colonies, and piracy became intolerable. After seizing their cargo and scuttling the vessels, the pirates would ransom the ill-fated seamen, or sell them into slavery. It was a lucrative for the pirates, and the Muslim states also dependant on the plunder. The US responded and sent missions to the Barbary states of Tripoli, Algiers, Morocco and Tunis proposing to pay an annual sum to each of the local

Muslim warlords for American vessels protection. The amounts paid were equivalent to the billions paid to Muslim states today.

By 1801 it became clear that the policy of appeasement had failed. The Pasha of Tripoli along with other Barbary States demanded larger sums, and when they were not offered piracy resumed. America learned its policy of accommodation only encouraged the Barbary brigands to seize more ships and take more captives. Things were to change with the election of Thomas Jefferson, principal architect of the Declaration of Independence, and an outspoken opponent of the practice of tribute. He argued that any policy of appeasement would fail because, "in conveying weakness, it encouraged further treachery". Jefferson's response to the renewed piracy was to dispatch naval forces. Tripoli responded by declaring war on the United States. For the next two years the U.S. Navy conducted running operations against the Barbary pirates. The American battle cry was "millions for defense, but not one cent for tribute". The fighting during those days saw many acts of heroism that established the U.S. Navy as a force to be reckoned with. In an 1805 action (*now immortalized in the Marine Corps hymn*) the USS Constitution supported the landing of Marines on "the shores of Tripoli". The Americans and their allies destroyed the harbor citadel serving as the headquarters for the pirates. For much of the next decade, American merchant shipping passed unmolested through the Mediterranean. Good policy supported by firm action replaced the foolishness of appeasement, and brought success in America's first war with Middle Eastern terrorism. Let's not forget that in the end nations paying tribute are neither respected nor left unmolested.

Chapter 20
Spin ...The Art of Ignoring the Obvious

As in all wars, this one is also fought with words. Waged for minds and hearts, propaganda is employed by all sides. It is the age-old struggle for converts to adopt a cause. The stakes are very high, as it the rhetoric and passion of the opposing ideals.

In any debate, to confuse an opponent, the classical approach is by and through obfuscation, tangential diatribes, and/or classic political spin. The desired effect is to create confusion, to weaken an opponent's resolve and momentum through diversionary tactics. It is an age-old approach employed when ones own arguments have weak moral or logical foundations. The tactic is often the only option when tasked with presenting an inferior argument, which cannot otherwise be promoted through persuasiveness based on reason, logic, or moral clarity. This method becomes the only viable option because a more progressive concept cannot be beaten by an inferior philosophy without those arguing in behalf of the lower standard first concealing obvious truths in layers of fog. On hearing such rhetoric, a reasonable layperson may detect that there is something wrong with either the message or the delivery, but sufficient time for careful analysis and appropriate response is seldom available, as expediency quickly sweeps both the obvious facts with the muck into the past.

Once the audience has been so prepared, one can then make suggestions and offer premises that would have otherwise been easily recognized as irrational or unconscionable. When carefully prepared and delivered under the axiom "the bigger the lie, the easier it is for people to swallow", otherwise outlandish suggestions can result in a mental shock effect, which over time can break down resistance. To the masses for which the spin was constructed, the net effect is confusion and the blunting of reasonable responses and actions, as well as more of an inclination to accept the unacceptable, or at least to tolerate the intolerable. Indeed, when not properly recognized and challenged, there is the potential that otherwise good people might eventually accept that good is evil, or that evil means can be sanctified if associated with a seemingly good cause.

Take the Israeli-Palestinian conflict, for example. Claiming that Israel is the sole instigator and villain in this passionate and tragic play is a tactic designed to hide many truths in plain sight. The weak-minded demonstrate personal failure when they bury their heads in the sand, and are akin to the Germans who "closed their drapes" as the Jews were rounded up. We all see and hear about the things going on in the Middle East every day, yet many continue to hide behind silly libels against the US and Israel to either justify continued support for the Palestinian cause and methods, or to remain silent.

In a population of 6.3 million, Israel has endured over a hundred suicide bombings. If the same proportion of attacks had occurred in the USA (288 Million people), there would have been 4571 suicide bombings with over 40,000 killed and hundreds of thousands wounded (often maimed for life). The number killed would be the equivalent of twelve 'Sept-11/Pear-Harbor' type mega-attacks! Almost everyone would know more than one victim. Pause ...and think about it. The reaction of this nation would likely be more severe and violent than the Palestinians have faced to date from all Israeli actions. Without second thoughts or significant dissention, our armies would be given marching orders to destroy everyone suspected of supporting the attacks in any way. Political correctness would yield to the logic of survival and nearly every American would support any and all means necessary to completely ruin individuals, organizations, and governments deemed remotely culpable, with collateral damage of *-much-* less concern.

Truth is truth, to the end of reckoning. Spin may distract, but does not diminish her. When "Old Europe" and our own schizophrenic State Department say, "create a Palestinian state, coddle the Saudis, don't offend anyone", it only serves to embolden despots and their terrorist foot soldiers. When we respond to left-leaning media, our Arab "allies", and the Europeans, we lose moral authority and giving sanctuary and encouragement to despots and terrorists alike. As with the Israelis, our survival and democracy depends on us living with both eyes wide open, willing to do the hard things necessary to protect our children's future. Islamic extremists, and Palestinians in particular, continually debase themselves as they bask in their hatreds, blood lust, and thirst for revenge. Ongoing anxiety and suffering cries out for intelligent deliberation, judgment, and then effective action. State department coddling and financial / humanitarian-aid notwithstanding, nothing we can ever do will make fascist fanatics love us. We can only make them fear and respect us.

The world should with unison loudly reject when terrorists weave pure spin claiming violent murderous tactics are a legitimate option in pursuit of freedom and self-determination. In fact they have had, and do have, complete control of their future and far superior options to choose from, but have chosen to surrender that future by engaging in illegal and immoral activities. They have spent their entire allowance pursuing these doomed options, and now claim to be victims when facing the unavoidable consequences of their poor choices. Obfuscation aside, no people have the right to exercise their right to self-determination, if the path they choose in pursuit of the same involves bombing café's, night-clubs, busses, targeting women, children, students, simple commuters and pedestrians, and families in their homes. It is the opinion of this author that engaging and supporting such activities disqualifies an individual, culture, even a whole people from normal inherent rights to freedom of movement, association, assembly, self-determination, and self-rule. Palestinian extremists, who appear to enjoy support by the majority of locals, are simply not advanced, mature, or grown-up enough to be trusted with certain freedoms. Current events and past history has proven they will only exercise those freedoms to terrorize, kill and maim. To propose otherwise is to essentially argue to immediately empty all prisons worldwide and to abolish all laws and punishments based on concepts of personal responsibility. And it follows that opposing the rule of law is in fact a proposal for wholesale regression to principals akin to middle-age tribal conquest and rule. While it is heart wrenching to see and hear of the suffering of innocent Palestinian children in the current conflict, yet we must not forget the culpability lies squarely on the shoulders of the parents and leaders who have failed them. The only thing we can do to help them take that necessary first step of real change (accepting personal responsibility for their mistakes and failures), is to expose and resolutely reject the spin they spew to deceive themselves and others.

Conveniently ignoring the vast majority of official violent passages and verse, promoters acting in the cause of Islam will continue to quote the same oft-repeated minuscule 'goodies' from the Qur'an to tell us the 9-11 episode is not 'real Islam'. From President George Bush to brother Yusuf Islam (Cat Stevens) every 'lover' of Islam is using a huge loudspeaker to announce to the world that *'Islam is a religion of peace and tolerance. Islam does not preach violence, terrorism, murder, killing, raping, burning, and looting... etc. The terrorists have hijacked peaceful Islam.* How very nice those words are. ...Islam is the light of the world. The world would surely plunge into a new dark age without the light of Islam... One can't help wondering why they feel inclined to praise Islam and its works quite so often. Self-praise is no recommendation, and the barrage seems aimed to both reassure themselves and to deceive the uneducated.

The world asks, why does Islam feel compelled to constantly remind the billions of 'ignorant Kafirs' that it is a virtuous religion. 'Islam is peaceful' ad infinitum, as if repeating it often enough can alter reality, or perhaps even create truth out of thin air. No other religious organization needs such a huge advertising campaign to deflect criticism. Could it be there is something fundamental amiss with the religion and her followers? Of course not, everything is perfect and glorious with Islam. That great cry form the dust of tens of millions of dead and persecuted is simply the wind. If anything seems amiss with Islam, it is not the fault of the 'best religion' of Allah, but is by sinister design from the evil Jews, the satanic West (Christians), the vile Indians (Hindus) and the repugnant secularists/ freethinkers. In the classical strategy of transference, when challenged they parlay and deflect criticism by accusing the accusers of being guilty of what Islam is itself most guilty of; persecution, misinformation, intolerance, prejudice, and bigotry. Violence and spin, the chief exports of Islam, grows louder daily, yet somewhere in the fog, truth still stands silently and solidly in opposition to the din.

Chapter 21
The Gathering Storm

To quote Edmund Burke – *"All that is necessary for the triumph of evil is that good men do nothing."* Germany proved this true in 1942 when hundreds of thousands of intelligent, educated, and basically good men said and did nothing, thus failing to slow down or stop the Nazi juggernaught. Today in Islam, hundreds of millions stand silent, allowing men with irrational prejudices and violent inclinations to dominate their cultures, peoples, and children. History repeats itself. Leaders and lay alike seem sympathetic to anti-American Jihad. Before the tide turned in WWII, Germans were also united in their support of "Total War" against non-Germanic peoples. The negative consequences of adopting this philosophy against an adversary capable of waging war were demonstrated to Germans when the Allies struck Hamburg. Casualties reached 42,000, exceeding all British civilian losses. The lesson to the people and culture were painful, but effective. Japanese Imperialists learned the same lesson about the same time. For 60 years, as a people, they have refused to create an offensive military, least some politician is tempted and history repeats itself. To their credit, love for their own children and aspirations for prosperity and happiness were strong enough for them to both recognize the fallacy of earlier actions and beliefs, and to repent. Terrorist/expansionist Islam grossly underestimates the intelligence and survival instincts of its declared enemies (i.e. the non-Muslim world). It assumes that, through strategic use of patience and violence, the toad will not notice nor react in time to the rising temperature of the water. In doing so it insults the intelligence and foolishly ignores the destructive capacity of a peaceful freedom-loving people. Someday it will find that the toad did indeed jump out in time, and further will find that the toad is not a toad at all, but rather a scorpion with a deadly sting.

Westerners are taught from birth to respect variety in religious beliefs, racial backgrounds, and cultural differences. These same tolerant principals, having led to peace and prosperity for us, are viewed with contempt by many Arab and Asian Islamic tribal cultures. They are viewed as conclusive evidence of Western corruption and weakness. Replacing these concepts are core values where people are taught from birth that blind, fanatical obedience to whatever their local clerics demand is required for their eternal salvation, indeed for their temporal well being as well.

Islam, by virtue of current popular interpretations of its tenants (and lack of a controlling governing body) renders many average worshipers susceptible to abhorrent suggestions, making it all too easy for common Muslims to become transformed into "terrorists". Justifications for prejudices/intolerance, and demands for fanatical obedience, up to and including the murder of non-Muslims by any means possible, are common. Unless you have been intimately exposed to their culture, one has absolutely no idea of the total and irreversible dedication of the faithful. The ferocity and the depths of their hatreds are insurmountable. My family spent ten years living in Saudi Arabia and traveling to most Arab countries in the region. Most of the younger Muslims we came in contact with seemed irrationally resentful of the West, repeating emotions impressed on them by religious and media figures. Young men are all too anxious to believe any religious leader calling for Jihad over any perceived insult to Islam.

Understanding fanatical Muslim reasoning requires thinking 'outside of the box'. One must be prepared to first accept the inconceivable. To many devout Muslims tolerance means something quite different than to the rest of us. Unfortunately, tolerance usually means accepting different degrees of hatred and extremism within their own neighborhoods and amongst their Imams and Clerics. True tolerance toward non-Muslims or 'Infidels' is unthinkable, except as required by political necessity, then temporarily employed for appearance sake only (usually as part of a strategy of eventual conquest). This judgment of Muslim culture and thinking seems harsh, but before you call it bigoted to point out Islamic bigotry, examine the facts. Ask yourself, aside from rare carefully crafted rebukes spoken only in English to Western news organizations, where are the 'peace marches' in Palestine and protesters against homicide bombers, and other terrorists the non-Muslim world has to contend with? Is there no opposing political party, no differing opinion, or 'other side' within Islamic countries in any current or past Arab/Muslim conflicts with any other culture or people on the planet? Surly there must be opposition to Islamic fanaticism, terrorism, and 'holy war' solutions proffered in so many conflicts. Pro-Palestinian and anti-Jew protests are present in Tel Aviv, New York, Washington, London, and everywhere. But where are the anti-terrorism / pro-peace protests or the smallest protest against Hamas, Islamic Jihad, or the al-Aqsa Martyrs Brigades by moderate or left-wing Arabs in Lebanon, Syria, Egypt, Iran, Libya, Turkey, Jordan, Indonesia, or Saudi Arabia? The answer is simple; we do not see them, because they do not exist! They do not exist, because their core religious values do not allow opposition. Even most American Muslims have not shown any real revulsion at what is done in Islam's name, instead they seem unnaturally quiet. Surely this vast quiet is the silence of fear, guilt, or …reverence.

The problem is certainly not for lack of sensitivity, passion, or the inability to identify injustice, as history has clearly demonstrated the willingness of all Muslims to rally around many causes they see as relevant. Neither are they blind, uneducated, nor unaware of the basic facts relating to current and past terrorist events. The silence and inaction of 'Moderate Islam' is due to an overall irreversible and intractable culture prejudiced against non-brothers, and Westerners and Jews in particular. The root of the problem is based in the fact that most do not interpret the violent acts of their extremist 'brothers' as too terribly serious of a problem since the victims are, after all, only *infidels*.

The superiority many Muslims feel over non-brothers is enshrined in the Qur'an, embedded in Islamic Law, and unquestionably enforced by principalities and governments. It should be emphasized that virtually all Islamic institutions of training propagate this kind of thinking and prejudice. It is either forcefully taught or passively tolerated (with a wink) by the vast majority of religious leaders, pounded in hour after hour, day after day, year after year. As such the religious leaders (and therefore the religion) are the impetus for the hatreds and its destructive results. It would be wrong to say that Islamic militants have lost their way, as what we witness today *-is -* their way. Further, the nature of Islam does not nurture men like Gandhi, Lincoln, or Martin Luther King …they kill them.

Societies based on Islamic law can and do discipline, up to death, anyone perceived violating their strict unbending tenants. Your government, where Qur'anic Law is codified into law, will also prosecute and pursue anyone who is perceived to gently or aggressively speak out against Islamic rule, policy, or law. Justifications for prejudices/intolerance, and demands for fanatical obedience are simply a part of common every-day life. Blind acceptance, devout and passionate adherence to every doctrine sanctioned by the local leaders is required. Punishments for expressing or following any more tolerant doctrine are extreme. The consequences are often severe, up to death. Conversion to any other religious doctrine is also punishable by death. This extreme, intolerant social code of right and wrong is also enforced within the home of simple Muslim families. Dissent is simply not an option within families or neighborhoods. Opposition, critical thought, debate of any kind is simply not allowed. It is very much like Gang mentality in that once you're in …you can't get out. Today and in recent and distant history, other examples of this type of culture exist. What we are talking about is pure political totalitarianism, unique only in the fact that today it hides behind the guise of, and seeks the protection of, a religion.

Violence has a mind all its own, and the effect of an individual or people embracing its seductive venom is guaranteed to cause sickening internal malformations and gross external manifestations. Islam amplifies (instead of attenuating) its follower's feelings of violence towards others. For decades now, Yasser Arafat brainwashed his people with primitive hatred glorifying all its lethal consequences. Revenge and savagery has become bread and butter to them. Palestinian TV, newspapers and books (all PA controlled) have prepared the Palestinian people for nothing but murder, revenge and graphic violence. Arab Media and leaders have stoked Palestinians religious fervor and hatred (Jihad) to such a degree, that it has now reached an extreme fervent level sufficient to override normal reasonable human reaction, reason, and feeling. The enemy fighting the US today is similarly depraved. A spokesman for al Qaeda cheerfully and proudly promises the murder of millions, as quoted in the Arab Newsletter:

> "America, with the collaboration of the Jews, is the leader of corruption whether moral, ideological, political or economic corruption. We have the right to kill 4 million Americans — 2 million of them children — and to exile twice as many, and wound and cripple hundreds of thousands."

Every religious movement calls their dead '*Martyrs*', but does the God of us all really welcome anyone into paradise who acts to kill in the name of revenge and hatred? Doesn't it occur to anyone that the guarantees of his/her Cleric may -not- be recognized or respected by an omnipotent and omniscience

God, the creator of this earth and all creatures in it (including us lowly kafirs)? From normal human instincts for self-preservation, most reasonable people hope there are no Martyrs in their family, and many for the enemy who seeks our death. Reasonable people are more than willing to postpone inclinations to prematurely leave this earth, completely content to wait as long as possible to find out who is a Martyr, and who is just some stupid dead guy. The fact that Palestinians find it easy to convince their impressionable young to seek Death without question is certainly no indication of a superior religion or philosophy, but rather it is evidence of extreme error in both logic and reason. It speaks volumes that the world has yet to see Arafat, other militant leaders, or the local fire breathing Clerics, strap on an explosive belt, and trod the path they so easily encourage the sons and daughters of their neighbors to tread. The leaders of Islamic Jihad, Hamas, and the al-Aqsa Martyrs Brigades sent their sons overseas at the start of the Infada, some to study in America and England.

To all those who have apparently lost the ability to think for themselves, here is a clue… If someone tells your son or daughter to murder themselves and other innocent men, women and children … they are neither your friend, nor particularly religious or 'holy' …find better friends! To mothers who encourage their children to murder themselves and others, wake-up! Do not disgrace the sacred institution and role of motherhood and defile the human family. Shame! Neighbors, friends, and governments who encourage and reward such sick degeneracy are not fit to call themselves human, let alone religious. Such people should be sanctioned, not rewarded. The whole-civilized world groans, turning away from the utter depravity of any culture and/or religion engaging in innocent murder and violence for the sake of terror. Islamic militants continually debase themselves as they bask in their hatreds, blood lust, and thirst for revenge. The time for fence sitting is over, and it is indeed by their fruits that they should be judged. Is not the chief export of Palestine terrorism? Are not the fruits of Islam violence, prejudice, ignorance, poverty, misery, and death? When they weave pure spin to the world claiming violent murderous tactics are the only option in their pursuit of freedom and prosperity is it not, on its face, a lie?

The actions and inaction of Islam are making it increasingly difficult to support unconditional religious tolerance. A thinking man must replace passive tolerance with active opposition when the net result of tolerance results in making a people more susceptible to murder, terror, sorrow, and poverty. Religious tolerance should still be the rule of thumb, unless the religion turns out, in the classical sense, not to be an actual real religion after all. If Islam has otherworldly political aspirations that in reality disqualify it as a peaceful religious organization (i.e. dedicated to improving her followers and harmless to others), then Islam is not simply another religion. Islamic theology prejudices and corrupts the minds and spirits of her victims, and the dangerous doctrine has infected almost the whole body of Islam. The patient is in a very bad state, and there is hardly any reason to hope for any degree of recovery. The prognosis …sadly … is eventual pain and passing, as the world continues to refine her ability to identify the malady and apply the necessary medicine to insure self-preservation, security, and prosperity.

Against the unthinkable the world is loath to admit, and understanding is digested at a glacial pace. The problem of political Islam is a huge human tragedy currently in the making. The final solution may be larger in scale than any global social/political upheaval experienced to date. Islam, as it is known today, will not disband nor experience some sort of spontaneous intellectual, spiritual, or democratic renaissance. The seeds of conflict and war were planted a long time ago, have been maturing for centuries, and are now fully ripe. To date effective corrective activity has been postponed as the weed deliberately deceives the world saying, "*I am not a weed, I am a beautiful peaceful branch of humanity, the victim of every conflict and persecuted in all places*". The facts of history show that Islam always acts in this way, until it achieves a demographic proportion necessary to accomplish a military and/or political conquest of her tenders, afterwards subjugating non-believers to pay tribute and remain second-class citizens, if allowed to survive at all. But eventually the world will learn that Islam has no intention of living peaceably with either Israel, nor the rest of the world. All contract and treaties signed with Infidels will continue to be broken, as they have in the past. Islam's size, her successes of the past, and her current efforts, will eventually be the key to her demise, just as Hitler's overt ambitions finally woke the world up to the dangers of Nazism. Hopefully, the prospects for Islam continuing her propaganda, deceit, and conquests in the information age, where truths are broadcast from rooftops, are near zero. Time and truth are both arrayed against radical, political Islam, but only if free peoples make wise use of those valuable commodities.

Though the future looks strewn with trial and sacrifice, and until the day the struggle begins on a large scale, opportunities abound to put our arms around clear-thinking good-hearted Muslims to bring them out from the frenzy. There are many very intelligent families in the Arab/Asian world with good values that can recognize and reject political Islam and racism when presented with the facts and given alternate opportunities to escape and exist peacefully. Education is the key. Not Islamic revisionist history, but clear, real, accurate presentations on the origins, nature, history, and consequences of Islamic fascism all the way back to Muhammad.

There will always be pockets of extremists, just as today there are still 'skin-heads' who still worship Nazi philosophy, but they will eventually be isolated, marginalized, sanctioned, and censured, ... finally recognized by all for who and what they really are. Those who should be targeted for enlightenment, are those who will actually flinch when reading the following publication:

The Importance of Jihad as a Means of Destroying 'Infidel Countries' August 24, 2002, www.jehad.net. Article in issue #16 of the online magazine Al-Ansar (affiliated with Al-Qa'ida), a columnist identified as Seif Al-Din Al-Ansari discussed the Qur'anic verse "Allah Will Torture Them [the Infidels] At Your Hands":

The Annihilation of the Infidels is a Divine Decree "Regardless of the norms of 'humanist' belief, which sees destroying the infidel countries as a tragedy requiring us to show some conscientious empathy and... an atmosphere of sadness for the loss that is to be caused to human civilization – an approach that does not distinguish between believer and infidel... - I would like to stress that annihilating the infidels is an inarguable fact, as this is the [divine] decree of fate..."

"When the Qur'an places these tortures [to be inflicted on the infidels] in the solid framework of reward and punishment... it seeks to root this predestined fact in the consciousness of the Muslim group, asserting that the infidels will be annihilated, so as to open a window of hope to the Muslim group..."

"Nevertheless, [this divine decree] has become, for some, a tranquilizing pill... When the enemy launches operations of colonialism and destruction, we find that a few [of the Muslims] refrain from entering the battlefield claiming that the elements of the collapse of Western civilization are proliferating [in any event]."

"Their conclusion is indeed true, but the way in which it is presented is misleading, and it is aimed at removing responsibility [to fight the infidels] from the Muslim, with the claim that Allah has already promised to take care of the infidels' annihilation."

Muslims Must Not Wait Passively for the Divine Decree to Just Happen "...I would like to point out the danger of this analysis, because it... [may] make the Muslims passive and turn [them] into one who does not act to carry out [the commandments] of the religion or to dispel falsehood, but lives always in an atmosphere of passive waiting, that is cloaked – always – by a call to trust in the ability of Allah!!"

"When Allah told us of the certainty of the annihilation of the infidels, He did not do so using ambiguous concepts. He clarified that this would be achieved in one of two ways: by means of a direct act of Allah... or by means of the Muslim group, which would, in accordance with the Islamic commandment, serve as an implement for carrying out [the divine decree], as it is said: '...Allah will torture them [the infidels] Himself or at our hands (Qur'an 9:52).' "

"Yes, perhaps it is predetermined that the infidel country will be annihilated. But [if the believers do not act] this kind of annihilation will never be in favor of the Islamic state. The infidel country will be annihilated in favor of an infidel country like it or even worse than it..."

"Therefore, the belief in 'annihilating the country of heresy' [only] opens up for us a window of hope, and sets for us a goal that is in the realm of the possible – but it does not annihilate the infidel country for us, nor does it even affect it!!"

"This is merely a belief, which, if unaccompanied by the words 'at your hands' that appear in the Qur'anic verse [9:14, 'Fight them and Allah will torture them at your hands'] – it will remain in the wonderful realm of ideas that float in the theoretical universe, and is like beautiful dreams that arouse conscientious emotions – yet, when we awake, we find that the infidel country still exists, falsehood is not destroyed [by itself] in favor of the truth, [except when] the truth goes into action..."

"The importance of the human effort to annihilate the infidels... is what Allah sought to teach the Muslims at the Battle of Uhud [625]. Then, there were [Muslims] who thought that because they were right they would most certainly defeat the enemy. The [Muslims] paid a high price for this..."

"By Means of Jihad – Allah Tortures [the Infidels] with Killing" "The question now on the agenda is, how is the torture Allah wants done at our hands to be carried out?... This torture will not, in any way, be carried out by means of preaching [Da'wa], because preaching is activity of exposure, aimed at clarifying the truth in a way that makes it more easily acceptable. Preaching has nothing to do with torture; Jihad is the way of torturing [the infidels] at our hands." "By means of Jihad, Allah tortures them with killing; by means of Jihad, Allah tortures them with injury; by means of Jihad, Allah tortures them with loss of property; by means of Jihad, Allah tortures them with loss of ruling. Allah tortures them by means of Jihad – that is, with heated war that draws its fire from the military front..."

"The Tortures Will Bring the Infidels to the Path of Righteousness" "Material power is [to be] confronted with material power, and ideological power is [to be] confronted with ideological power... It would be idiocy to rely on the power of the truth in the face of F-16s. Allah is capable of destroying His enemy without anyone's mediation and without anyone's help, as His capability is absolute and unsurpassed. In spite of all the characteristics of power at their command, these infidel states are no more than a handful of creatures on the speck of dust called Planet Earth... [But] Jihad serves as a trial by suffering for the Muslims by means of the infidels, and for the infidels by means of the Muslims." "The Muslims' trial by suffering is manifested in Jihad's being the instrument by which it is possible to differentiate between the believers and the hypocrites... The infidels' trial by suffering is manifested in Jihad being an exemplary lesson in values, delivered by a group of the pioneers of the Islamic nation, in a practical presentation"

"Many of the infidels will be shocked; their emotional entity will be shaken; and perhaps some of them will repent and learn their lesson. In addition, Jihad is a means of defeating them, and perhaps by means of this victory... the tortures will bring them back to the path of righteousness..."

Chapter 22
Seeds of Armageddon

As events continue to unfold, and despite the political leanings of mainstream media, the heart of terrorists and all their supporters and sympathizers continue to be exposed. Special attention should be given to the plight faced by Israelis today at the hands of Muslims. Many Christians are very concerned about the events occurring in Israel for all the usual humanitarian reasons, but also for reasons not always understood by either Muslims or Jews. Of course the educated understand what Palestinians mean when they repeat the well known saying "Saturday people first, Sunday people next". But additionally, in accordance with prophecies in John's 'Book of Revelations', some fear that what we are witnessing is the groundwork for the prophecies relating to the last days and Armageddon, while others think that Islam may be that 'Great and Terrible Church' referenced therein.

Whatever the future may hold, the present condition on the ground is untenable, as the Muslim leaders do everything they can to encourage terrorist strikes, and nothing to stop them. The root of the problem for Palestinians is they do not see the extremists amongst them acting badly as a great problem as the victims are, after all, only infidels. For the West, it is easy to diagnose such incorrect perceptions and attitudes as thinking errors, and so the solution becomes obvious. It would be prudent at this point to embark on a worldwide education program to teach all Muslims nations and peoples to think independently and critically. Unfortunately, the problem is not quite so easily solved, because within their own culture they do not see thirsting for blood and revenge as a character flaw, but rather they worship and reward the concepts when it is directed toward infidels. Additionally, all institutions of training and schooling are the very religious institutions that led to their current state of self-defeatist thinking. In Pakistani religious schools called the Haqqania madrasa, Osama bin Laden is a hero, Taliban's leaders are famous alumnus, terrorist suicide bombers are worshiped and eulogized as martyrs, and follow-on generations of mujahedeen are being conditioned and militantly groomed. The curriculum centers on the memorization and interpretation of the Qur'an (Koran) and the Hadith. Similar curriculums are taught in Palestine, Saudi Arabia, and elsewhere. It should be emphasized that virtually all Islamic schools propagate this prejudice. The superiority Muslims feel over non-brothers is enshrined in the Qur'an, embedded in Islamic Law, and unquestionably enforced by principalities and governments. Any effort to teach their youth non-Muslim concepts would be violently opposed. Conversion to any other doctrine or religion will remain punishable by death, just like Mafia or Gang mentality. Once you're in you can't get out …your own family is sometimes required hunt you down and apply punishment.

June 23rd, 2003 marked 1000 days of conflict, with over 100 homicide bombings. In the current Infada, Palestinians have also carried out hundreds of other attacks aimed at ordinary civilians, killing over 900 and wounding thousands in a nation of 6.3 million people. Yet it was recently reported again that the Israeli West Bank offensive (and re-occupation), which caused and fueled Arab rage. For some strange reason, Palestinians and their supporters do not seem to be able to associate the incursions with the earlier string of suicide attacks coming from elements within the occupied territories. To the Palestinian media and people, all subsequent Israeli Military and Police actions have been undeserved and completely unprovoked. This is the literal state of mind to these people. A clearer picture of what is happening inside the mind of Palestinians goes something like this; *'The terrorist bombings and killings have no bearing on the matter, because after all, they are only Jews, and any act against them is warranted by divine decree. As such they really don't matter, any more than the daily killings of cows and chickens at the slaughterhouse matter. On the other hand there is no such thing as justifiable acts against brothers by Jews and Infidels.'* The UN International Court seems to agree with this premise, and has further discredited itself in the July 2004 ruling that the protective wall being built to keep terrorists from slaughtering Israelis is 'illegal'.

Meanwhile, back in reality, the unwritten commentaries and absence of rage toward those carrying out the suicide murder missions -prior- to the offensive, or for that matter toward Bin-laden or Sept 11, confuse Westerners. The image of jubilant celebration after 9/11 by so many Palestinian revelers in the West Bank and Gaza are forever burned into the minds of cognizant Americans. So before we judge the responses of Israel to repeated gross attacks against her people, we should consider they have seen these sorts of celebrations after every terrorist act for decades, which are also engraved in the memories of the people and policy makers in Israel.

Lynch mob mentality has now completely taken over the hearts and minds of these poorly led people. There is also the correct perception amongst themselves that dissent is even less tolerated, evidenced by the murder of dozens of their own perceived to have collaborated with the enemy (about five dozen known as of this writing). So it is that on the Palestinian side, hatred, thirst for revenge, or outright fear of vigilantes is what is driving the conflict. What is not spoken of in our supposedly balanced media, is the fact that the evidence of collaboration of their own citizens could be as harmless as a personal phone call or communiqué with a previous non-Arab friend or associate, or any expression of sympathy toward Israelis or opposition to violent groups, the same groups who in the end murdered them for being different. The extremists ensure the lessons are not being lost on average Palestinian families, as they execute the 'collaborator' in the most public way possible for maximum effect. Do not expect to see anyone with a 'Martin Luther King' type message of permanent peace stumping anytime soon, as even a suggestion of non-support of the policies and practices of their leaders can be in itself a death sentence. Internally, debate is confined as to where and how to strike Israeli interests next, if a temporary truce would be helpful, and whether, when, and where to attack American interests.

So how should Israel respond to the scourge of terrorist bombers? Empirical evidence abounds that all responses to date have been ineffective in stopping the threat and deployment of terrorist bombing strategies On Oct 5th, 2003 a female homicide bomber detonated a bomb in a popular Haifa Café killing 19, including several children, and wounded over 60. Israel responded by sending in warplanes to attack an empty Syrian camp used to train the Hezbollah. Syria's immediate response was to complain that the action was an escalation and act of war, which 'broke the rules of the game'. In case you missed it, these are the rules of the game, which Syria and other terrorist sponsors want Israel to play by:

- Israel can employ all the security measures it wants and play cat and mouse to try to catch the minions we send against you, have fun!
- Israel may try to catch the terrorists and factories in military incursions and raids into the west bank or Gaza, but if you do we have the right to deploy Rule #3.
- If Israelis respond by going into Arab territories, we may shoot at you from behind women and children, from simple homes, mosques and schools, and you may not respond. We also have the right to lay claim to such actions as full justification, providing blanket political coverage for both our initial and all subsequent terrorist envoys we send against you.
- Israel is not allowed to strike at the 'elected' 'democratic' popular individuals or governments who hide, support, fund, supply, train, outfit, or transport terrorists.
- Since Israel (like nearly every nation) is demographically at a huge disadvantage in a war of attrition, Israel must continue the debate of 'how to respond' forever, thus allowing causalities at approximately current or better ratios. The principal of 'proportionate response' must be strictly adhered to.

First, we need to demystify suicide terrorism and see it for what it is. It's not about the beliefs or personality of the fanatic carrying the bomb, rather it's all about the people behind him, the *true* terrorists. Therefore suicide terrorists are not some other breed of men, unsusceptible to the usual tools of war and statecraft. Those responsible are still alive, reachable, and perhaps even teachable. The first thing that needs to change is that all democracies, including Israel, need to strictly institute policies to deny the handlers their hoped for political prizes and concessions. If we make sure that suicide terrorism does not pay, it will surely begin to lose much of its luster. Offering autonomy or eventual statehood in response to terrorism is a huge mistake and feeds grass roots support of terrorist methods. But to simply deny the true terrorists, the handlers and supporters their spoils, does not go nearly far enough. Indeed it would require withstanding a number of years of attacks without the previous rewards to educate the instigators and convince them to choose another path. That is not a politically survivable option for endangered democracies (i.e. to only change our response to terrorist acts by hanging tough and waiting long enough for these people to get a clue). Political prize or no, handlers and their leaders would love to be allowed to continue their practices unmolested, thereby weakening and attriting their enemies peoples, economies, cultures and governments.

In any contest, the first rule of victory is to fight on your own terms and not your opponents. Israel has too long been fighting a serious political and military conflict constrained by an international thought police more adept at narcissistic judgment than rational thinking. Israel has been fighting the battle on the terms directed and dictated by the propaganda machines of many Islamic and even some Christian countries that have, to put it mildly, an agenda unfriendly towards Israel. At this moment in history, the notion to reward the Palestinian Authority with a 'State' is catastrophically stupid. It would prove that it works to blow up bus riders and Bat Mitzvah girls, and would place all peace loving peoples and democratic cultures hostage to such tactics. Christians everywhere should become familiar with this slogan known to all Palestinians: 'Saturday people first and Sunday people next'. What it means is if Israel and the Jewish people were ever defeated, Christians in Palestine will be next. From recent events, that should be obvious. By lending moral and political support to Palestinian leaders, Christian leaders abet their own people's demise in 'Palestine'.

The normal reaction by victims after experiencing death and destruction from a terrorist suicide/homicide bomber is rage toward the individual(s) perpetrating the attack. Those feelings are mixed with frustration upon realization that immediate justice and closure is not attainable because the vile person who carried out the evil act is already dead! Then to add to that frustration and anxiety, we are told by that deterrence is impossible against the kind of religious wackos intent on suicide attacks. How inexplicable are their behaviors and astonishing their commitment! That is true when speaking of brainwashed carriers and detonators of bombs aimed at innocents, but one must remember that those carrying out the acts have neither the smarts nor the means to conceive and carry out their acts alone. These are not the brightest and best from the world of Islam; they are simple pawns in a much larger game. They are murderous, inhumane, and despicable for sure ... but the ideas, suggestions, tactics, goals, and plans originate from someone else. As such, the vast majority of suicide attacks are not really primarily the work of psychos, nor are they the random and unpredictable acts of fanatics.

It's an absolute fact that free societies, if they are to remain free and open, will never be able to stop all deranged zealots loaded with explosives or other weapons from carrying out their heinous crimes against innocents. On the other hand it seems likely we may find success deterring the handlers, financers, and supporters of the maniacs, because they are people who do *-not-* intend to die for their cause. The handlers and state sponsors are not interested in sacrificing their own children nor themselves to advance their agenda, they are only interested in exploiting other people's sons and daughters to serve the specific political/religious cause they ascribe to. It is certainly an act of wanton cruelty, but carried out for reasons known and understood more by the handlers than the hapless bombers themselves. Those sending the young bombers have so far been successful in hiding behind them to escape responsibility and consequences, but we must remember that all suicide bombers are simply the brainwashed witless tools of the individuals sending them. The silly deceptive argument offered by bleeding heart liberals who claim that they are individual acts of desperation by the dispossessed is patently false, if not deliberately deceptive. Having handed over the last measure of individuality and sane judgment to a handler, the psychology of the individual suicide terrorist is indeed incomprehensible, but this is not the case of those who recruit, train, outfit, and send them to their deeds. Suicide terrorist handlers are not so eager to die, and there is reason to hope that effective deterrence is possible if it were consistently and forcefully applied against the true source of the suicide threat.

It is notable that the response most hated by the handlers is the targeted operations against their leadership. The other response by the Israelis, which is producing shrill complaints, is the activity surrounding the security fence construction. Do these actions, combined with a continuation of previously applied consequences and pressures, have potential to convince the Palestinian people to stop their terror culture? By the level of complaining and crying, it seems that to take the war to the leaders of terror organizations may have more effect than all closures, incursions, and home demolitions ever did. But unfortunately both actions are still unlikely to produce a level of pain likely to make the opposition cry 'uncle' and change its tactics. This is because of three reasons: 1) there seems to be an unlimited supply of zealots (a zeal inspired by the pure hate from pure Islam) anxious to push a button killing themselves along with scores of Israelis; 2) It will be too easy for handlers and supporters to hide from effective military targeting, and; 3) The fence can not fully protect Israelis against a determined enemy.

It seems safe to say that amongst Palestinians in power there has been no serious debate concerning abolishing terrorism as a tactic. Before the handlers will even consider terminating their practices, there must be the threat of personal consequences that have hitherto been largely absent. It's time to take off the kid gloves, and start going after *all* those responsible and culpable. Its time we stop allowing the truly evil men and women to continue their murderous ways as they hide behind their own neighbors, their young children, their women, and their religion. As brutal as it may sound, all those used as cover to shield them or hide them also need to be held accountable for not recognizing and eradicating the depravity from amongst them. These policies and practices do not happen in a vacuum, scores are involved. The acts perpetrated against innocents by terrorists are certainly acts of 'total war' by one people against all people, institutions, and governments they target. Its past time that each and every terrorist attack or bombing is recognized and considered for what it is, … an individual act of "total war". As much or more than a barrage of artillery or a bombing run by uniformed hostile forces.

In total war, victory goes to the party most effective in convincing the opposing party that surrender is preferable to a continuation of hostilities. Given their history, it may now be time for Palestinians to be force-fed a diet of sorrow until they come to the same conclusion the German and Japanese did in WWII. Survivalists will only force the end to the terrorist activities springing up from amongst them when made to pay a terrible price.

If allowed to continue, the current war of attrition and international propaganda will eventually culminate in the end of Israel, as she cannot compete with Palestinians demographically. War is terrible, horrible, and evil, but in fact it would not be that much worse than the current standard of fear and living of ordinary Israelis. Only a foolish nation would refuse to recognize and respond to war declared and instigated against them. To avoid war in the first place is preferable. But once started, for any war to actually end, full engagement must start. Both parties must risk all and throw their futures and fortunes into the conflict. To refuse to fight a people and culture who are mobilized and intent on destroying you is to guarantee your own eventual extinction. The Jews of Europe were marched into the ovens unarmed and helpless in the previous century, it remains to be seen if they will, out of aversion to war and fear of international opinion, continue to march into the ovens in this century fully armed.

Personally I would not march peacefully into the ovens, any more than 9/11 United Flight 93 Passenger Todd Beamer and his associates did. As the bombing victims continue to mount, many are left wondering how the people of Israel can possibly continue to live with such neighbors. You have to admire the Israeli people for their patience, faith, hope, and restraint up to a point. But as history continues to repeat it self over and over again, one can't help but think that wisdom has now left their leadership. It is the true mark of national insanity to continue to repeat policies and actions yet expect different results to suddenly, spontaneously appear.

The prospect of sudden enlightenment leading to a spontaneous renaissance resulting in termination of terrorist activities by the Palestinians themselves is at or near zero. Israel still faces a growing terrorist threat, primarily because they ascribe to policies of measured response and increased security measures. The only thing these limited responses have proven to date is that weakness emboldens the handlers and supporters of terrorists. Most Palestinians truly believe that there are no innocents amongst the Jews, and feel little to no sympathy for the women and children killed and maimed to date. The Jews need to realize that (aside from the very young not yet brainwashed) there are few amongst the residents of the West Bank and Gaza who do not have murderous thoughts towards their neighbor. Every terrorist is still worshiped as a martyr and saint, and has been for decades.

This enemy the US faces today has the ***same*** face, heart, mind, and intent as the one Israel faces. Any notion that the U.S. response to the daily suicide/murders in Israel should be to reward the Palestinian Authority with a state … is catastrophically stupid. As a recent poll showed, the majority of Palestinian people are fighting not to establish the state of 'Palestine', but to "eliminate Israel". There may have been a time when most Palestinians truly wanted a separate state and to live in peace with their Israeli neighbors, ... but time has proven that Mr. Arafat never, ever did. While accepting aid, Nobel peace prizes, and red carpets from governments around the world, he has remade the Palestinians in his own terrorist image. The Oslo Accords, crafted by naïve well-meaning State Department officials in 1993, have proven to be a complete failure (18,000 terrorist attacks including 270 suicide bombings since then). The State Department, unable to reconcile fact with Oslo fantasy, continues to churn out variants of the same thinking. But the Palestinians continue to choose conflict and despair over autonomy or statehood as *fatah* (the violent conquest of Israel) continues to be the chosen path, despite mounting evidence of its inherit hopelessness and failure.

It has been a long intellectual and moral path to finally arrive at an inescapable and very distasteful conclusion; that before it can possibly all end, the poorly led Palestinian people with their murderous intents will likely need to be forced at bayonet point to abandon their despicable actions and to kick out or jail the murders from amongst them. The same is true for all Islamic militants everywhere who practice terrorism for political gain. Osama and his ilk (read: sympathetic governments, cultures, societies, friends, financiers, enablers and, yes, even families) will never voluntarily change their tactics; they can only be beaten into submission or swept away. To criticize Israeli responses to attacks on her, is to join Palestinian leaders and their deranged supporters against all that we value the most. Most thinking Americans are disgusted with shortsighted criticism by Arab and some European countries to actions the US has taken against terrorists and their enablers in Afghanistan and Iraq. We should not adopt that same pose against Israel when she does the same thing, for the same reasons, against the same enemy.

Note: In a recent article for The American Political Science Review, *Robert Pape rigorously researched every suicide-terrorist attack in the world from 1980 to 2001 from Lebanon, the West Bank, Sri Lanka, Chechnya, India, Turkey and points between. He shows how suicide terrorism operates, and why it became a growth industry over the last several decades. His work dispels the widespread notion that suicide terrorism is incomprehensible and without possible remedy. One of Pape's most important finding is that suicide terrorism is guided by clearly identifiable strategic goals. Suicide terrorism occurs in clusters, and it is nearly always deployed as part of a larger political-military campaign, carefully calibrated to accomplish the political goals of nationalists groups. Of suicide-terrorist strikes from 1980 to 2001, a whopping 95 percent were undertaken as part of an organized political campaign, and interestingly every suicide attack in the period under study was launched against a democracy. Hezbollah used this weapon to force the United States and France from Lebanon in 1983; Hezbollah and Hamas have used it repeatedly to force concessions from Israel; Tamil terrorists have used it against the Sri Lankan government; the Kurds against Turkey; the Chechen rebels against Russia; the Kashmir rebels against India. This is an extraordinarily important finding. Clearly, the terrorists have reached certain conclusions about democratic regimes. They think we are "soft," and they surmise that democracies in particular are vulnerable to nihilistic coercion. Sadly in this regard terrorists are not entirely wrong, for another pattern Pape unearths is that suicide terrorism against democracies is largely effective. It is also more destructive than regular terrorism –from 1980 to 2001 suicide attacks made up 3 percent of total terrorist attacks but produced 45 percent of all casualties (and that's not counting the carnage of September 11). Moreover, of the eleven separate major suicide campaigns from 1980 to 2001, six produced significant policy changes by the target state toward the terrorists' major political goals. So suicide terrorism more often than not achieves its strategic goals, which bodes ill for the future of democracy and free western societies in general.*

Chapter 23
Roots of Today's Campaign

To fully comprehend the present, we must first know the past in some detail. Nothing makes sense when taken out of context, and the 'War on Terror' is no exception. Following its inception and the conquest of Arabia, the 7th-century "breakout" of Islam led to the rapid conquest of North Africa, the invasion and virtual conquest of Spain, and even a thrust into France that carried the crescent to the gates of Paris. It took half a millennium of re-conquest to expel the Muslims from Western Europe with the Crusades. The Crusades, as it happened, fatally weakened the Greek Orthodox Byzantine Empire, the main barrier to the spread of Islam into southeast and central Europe. As a result of the fall of Constantinople to the ultra-militant Ottoman Sultans, Islam took over the entire Balkans, and was threatening to capture Vienna and move into the heart of Europe as recently as the 1680s.

This multi-millennial struggle continues today in a variety of ways. The recent conflicts in Bosnia and Kosovo were largely a savage reaction by the Orthodox Christians of Serbia to the spread of Islam in their historic heartland, chiefly by virtue of illegal immigration and a higher birthrate. Indeed, in the West, the battle has been largely demographic, though it may at any time take a more militant turn. Muslims from the Balkans and North Africa are surging over established frontiers on a huge scale, rather as the pressure of the eastern tribes brought about the collapse of the Roman Empire of the West in the 4th and 5th centuries A.D. The number of Muslims penetrating and settling in Europe is now beyond computation (because many if not most of them are illegal). They are getting into Spain and Italy in such numbers that, should present trends continue, both these traditionally Catholic countries will become majority Moslem during the 21st century. As they begin to dominate those democracies and control the levers of government, peoples there will at some point be facing the same choices endured by so many ... flight, fight, or convert.

As has been outlined carefully herein, what we call the 'War on Terror' is simply a continuance ...a modern extension of Islamic practices in play since Muhammad began his initial military conquests. But the active targeting of the Americas is a relatively new phenomenon for the people of this country. Today we seem to be ignoring other countries that sponsored and support terrorism as we focus mainly on Iraq. But since the demise of the Taliban and Saddam, Iran has emerged as the main keystone of the terror network. The widespread terrorism and political demonstrations in Iraq since Saddam's capture have less to do with the shattered Baathist regime than terrorist elements from abroad. American officials on the ground in Iraq have seen abundant evidence of Iranian support for terrorist operations. The war against us in Iraq and Afghanistan is now guided, funded, and armed by tyrannical regimes in Iran, Syria, and Saudi Arabia. Our forces in Iraq will remain under attack so long as the tyrannical regimes in Damascus, Riyadh, and Tehran are left free to kill embattled Iraqis, our allies, and us. Prior to the liberation of Iraq, Syrian President Bashar Assad made no secret of his intentions when he publicly called for a "Lebanon strategy to be implemented." In August, Sheikh Hassan Nasrallah (head of Hezbollah) called for the entire Muslim world to join in Jihad against Americans in Iraq. Iranian leaders and Saudi clerics have also denounced the American actions in Iraq and joined the call for Jihad. The terror masters will not limit their Jihad to Iraq. Late last month, the Iranian newspaper Jomhuri-ye Eslami published an open call to the Egyptian people to assassinate President Hosni Mubarak. Pakistan's Musharraf has been repeatedly targeted for assassination. Turkish authorities captured one of the organizers of the suicide bombings in Istanbul last December as he was trying to cross the border into Iran, and it is now generally acknowledged that top al Qaeda figures (including bin Laden, Zawahiri, and Zarkawi) have long stayed in and operated from Iranian territory. While Iraq is the current front-line, the real war extends far beyond its borders. Policy makers and the general public still seem reluctant to connect the dots and face the fact that this war is an existential struggle against worldwide Militant Islam. By becoming overly obsessed with the re-election and Iraq, the 'War on Terror' is being unnecessarily extended and our forces and citizens are needlessly put at risk, whereas our enemies self-impose no such constraints.

For some time now, at least the last century, there has been a worldwide struggle for the soul of Islam between the preachers of hate and the less numerous preachers of peace. Unfortunately, the preachers of hate are currently winning decisively. In fact the war of ideas occurring within Islamic cultures has already been won in the most populous Islamic lands, and cleaning up loose ends like Nobel laureate Shirin Ebadi will take place in due time. State-appointed clerics throughout the Middle East are preaching to the faithful that it is their "duty" to murder Jews, because Jews are "rejected" by God, who turned them into "monkeys and pigs". There is no hope for people like Ebadi re-creating Islam or convincing large numbers to divorce itself from dependencies on violence and Jihad. Their scripture is considered final and immutable, but if it were edited to remove sections supporting or calling for violent or forceful methods of conversion and conquest, there would be little left. In large parts of the world Ebadi represents more a fringe minority than a majority, and she and others so inclined continue to face mortal danger for such heretic views which are indeed in opposition to true Islam and the example of their esteemed prophet.

While perhaps most Muslims here are peace-loving people wanting to *"live together in peace and harmony"* with those of other beliefs, the question that must be answered is: Are these Muslims for peace *because of* Islam or *in spite of* Islam? The fact will remain that Muslims are saddled with a system that has a spiritual force behind it, with violence firmly planted as a systemic root. In the end it is inescapable that to be a Muslim is to be aligned with the same spirit that choked and influenced Muhammad in the cave, that caused Muhammad to wage war and massacre those who rejected him, and that caused Muhammad to teach his followers that it is an unalterable eternal imperative to continue to do the same. To truly reject militant Islam is to reject Muhammad and much of what he taught, and such a choice offers only mortal peril to Muslims so inclined.

Most people think that the 'War on Terror' began Sept 11th, and as far as our active participation in the conflict they are partially right, but in the larger view such thinking is naïve. 1979 is when the shah of Iran fell, and the Saudi royal family, out of greed and fear, capitulated to pressures and started financing the worldwide expansion of militant Wahhabi Islam. These two key events represent the foundation and beginning of the current Jihadic movement launched against the West by militant Islam. Not long afterwards, Islam fired the first volley to initiate a new campaign against the West in Lebanon, which is in reality just the latest in its ongoing multi-millennial campaigns to spread its ideas through the sword of Jihad.

Lebanon was once the most progressive, free, and most democratic state in the Arab world, but quickly thereafter fell into civil war, with conflicts arising out of ideological differences, pushed from behind by newly empowered Islamists inspired by Wahhabi preaching and funding from Syria and Iran. In Syrian-occupied Lebanon, Hezbollah Islamists were battling moderate Arab Muslims, Arab Christians, and internationalists who had once found Lebanon to be a safe and congenial place. Unfortunately, if not predictably, the Hezbollah Shiite terrorist group had no interest in compromise or peace. Hezbollah was determined and eventually successful in seizing control of Lebanon and subjugating all local Arabs who opposed them. When challenged they drove the Americans out in a brutal attack on marines asleep in their barracks, massacring 241 of them. As we collected our dead and went home, none realized how that retreat would embolden the terrorists. But Islamic terrorists everywhere remember it well, and still celebrate it as a great first victory for their side against America and proof that their God is behind them. Our retreat reaffirmed their faith and reassured them that eventual victory is assured even against the better-equipped American military. Their belief that America is a paper tiger was reinforced again and again in subsequent years, most dramatically in Somalia.

Still most Americans did not then connect the dots, failing to grasp the fact that we were already in a low-grade war; until al Qaeda Sunni copycat terrorists mounted its attack on September 11. Afterwards, most of us understood that war was indeed upon us, but many still struggle to connect all the dots, failing to recognize the source of the true threat and the more recent origins of the current Jihad declared against us. Fewer still understand how our own missteps of the past have encouraged and animated terrorists worldwide. We have tended to focus exclusively on the threat from al Qaeda and its offshoots, forgetting Hezbollah altogether or seeing it only as a menace only to Israel. In Afghanistan, we deposed al Qaeda and its Taliban allies, scattering terrorist forces. But meanwhile, the terrorists who ruined Lebanon, murdered our sons, and drove us out still strut about free and unafraid, ruling openly. Hezbollah has big, secure bases in Lebanon and Syria, is hurting our efforts to stabilize Iraq, and is expanding its global reach to places like the tri-border region of Paraguay, Argentina, and Brazil. It is a much larger and more formidable foe than Al-Qaeda, and has been killing Americans for much longer. One hopes that planners in the US military realize that its past time to make Hezbollah and all its admirers understand that there are no exceptions to the new rule stated so eloquently by George Bush: "*If you attack Americans, America will bring you to justice, or bring justice to you.*"

When Osama makes good on his promise to attack 'Red' States (who voted for Bush in the 2004 elections), will the 'Blue' states finally connect the dots …or will they just say; '*too bad they voted for Bush*' and only offer heart-felt condolences. To win, we must become the 'United' States of America, take off the kid gloves, and more persuasively dissuade all Islamic militants from their violent inclinations.

Chapter 24
Liberty Threatened

The appeal of Islam has many roots, some are even noble, but those mandating violence against non-brothers are not, or at least not by the standards of non-Muslims. When Islam is judged against universally accepted standards of morality, this Arabian religion fails to qualify as the friend and guide of humanity it claims to be. Muslims will protest against this point of view, and as usual will produce weak tidbits or far-fetched evidence to prove that Islam advocates the love and brotherhood of mankind, ignoring the larger realities of Jihad and 1400 years of history. This type of sorcery has worked wonders for Islamists and their apologists in the past, but with modern dissemination of knowledge, one hopes it will become more difficult to cloud the truth with the magic of misinterpretation and spin.

America has appreciated and duly noted the official moderate Muslim perspective, but in addition to well thought-out official releases … what action will Islam now take to manage its own? What are Muslims going to do to reign-in and punish clerics inciting hatred, violence, and constantly calling for the most popular interpretation of Jihad? Are moderate Muslims strong and powerful enough to actually do something about the fire-breathing clerics and militants amongst them? Can they wrest power from the militants and take control of defining and administering the central tenants and teachings of Islam? Will effective action ever be taken against the supposedly holy clerics inciting and celebrating hatreds and violence? To have any chance to ultimately win what promises to be a long war against Islamic fanatics, we must, as Sun Tze in "The Art of War" says, "Understand the enemy." To date America has done a very poor job of identifying to its citizenship just exactly who is the enemy and what is the ideology driving them. There is also a constant stream of misinformation spewed by Islamic apologists and propagandists, which has resulted in confusion and lack of focus, with its resulting ambiguity of policy and inadequate responses. Islamic terror continues unabated in Iraq, Indonesia, the Philippines, Sudan, Israel, and elsewhere, with no end in sight. Islam, the so-called "Religion of Peace", continues to be a breeder of hatred and an incubator of willing foot soldiers, having neither boundary nor limits. Nor is there any semblance of humanity in Islamic extremists' brutality. The beating and hanging from a bridge over the Euphrates River of four lifeless, mutilated, charred American civilian bodies, and the brutal beheading of Nick Berg are just more graphic and indelible testimony of their inhumanity.

Responsible members of the human race hope that among the first things Islam would do is to officially condemn the racist use of the word INFIDEL, and to recognize in both its teachings and law the equality of all races, religions, and sexes. It should also apologize for all past prejudicial teachings and practices. Sadly, the only intelligent conclusion which can be drawn by a pragmatic analysis of fundamental Islam, is that hope for reform and modernization is impossible for the majority of Muslims. To admit any flaw whatsoever, or to reform any basic wiring or tenant of Islam is to discredit the whole philosophy to its roots. Another fundamental weakness of Islam is that it does not have a central administration or organized self-regulatory mechanisms. This weakness leaves the door wide open for the hijacking of individuals, families, clans, mosques, sects, regions, or countries, by any despot with a personal agenda. Anyone can claim to represent Islam and rise to be a holy man without any appointment, education, or actual calling. The first and only requirement appears to be a strong aspiration to the position, or in other words, greed for power and influence. Islam needs to correct this mistake, or it will continue to be used as it has in the past, to inspire and express hatred, for violence, and as a lever used to gain personal power.

Some think, and it seems reasonable, that Islam herself was the most injured by the attacks on 9/11. Could it be that those four airliners inflicted a wound on Islam that will result in untold turmoil and sorrow amongst her own? God is not subject to interpretation by mere mortals, nor is He the personal property of any group or individual. Certainly, if there is only one God, then the question begs asking; are these extremist Muslim leaders actually affiliated with Him? Whether they represent the majority or minority in their cultures, angry hateful Muslims could not possibly be acquainted with a kind, benevolent, and loving God of us all. Further, as long as their minds are so clouded with Hate, the probability of spiritual enlightenment or an intellectual epiphany is at absolute zero. However, one might deduce that the most intelligent, talented, logical, peaceful, and reasonable individuals and families within their own societies might well recognize the inherent failings of Islamic culture and seek enlightenment elsewhere, or at least demand change. But we should not hold our breath for any internal evolution, as history demonstrates that humanitarian sympathies have never been a priority for Islamic philosophy nor her people, and indeed opposition in any form is considered betrayal and treason.

History of Terror

The political and economic record of Islam is wretched, with only one of 18 Muslim states (Turkey) democratically governed. Some warn that Turkeys professed secularism is only skin deep. In fact, 'Infidels', a racist term referring to non-believers/non-conformists, are persecuted everywhere in the world where real Muslims are in power, including Turkey. Infidels and Muslims alike suffer when governments attempt to rule using rigid Islamic principals and law. Unlike Christianity, which, since the Reformation and Counter Reformation has continually updated itself and adapted to changed conditions, and unlike Judaism, which has experienced what is called the 18th-century Jewish enlightenment, in many parts of the world Islam remains a religion stuck in the Dark Ages. It contains many sects and tendencies, quite apart from the broad division between the majority Sunni Muslims (comparatively moderate and include most of the ruling families of the Gulf), and Shia Muslims (who dominate Iran). But virtually all these fundamentalist sects are in practice more militant and uncompromising than orthodox conservative Islam, which itself is moderate only by comparison, but by western standards is still extreme. It believes, for instance, in a theocratic state, ruled by religious law, still inflicting (as in Saudi Arabia) grotesquely cruel punishments, which became obsolete in Western Europe in the early Middle Ages. Moreover, Qur'anic teaches that the faith or "submission" can be, and in suitable circumstances must be, imposed by force, and as such the history of Islam has essentially been a history of conquest and re-conquest.

Former (US President) Carter administration official Samuel P. Huntington, now a Harvard professor and founder of *Foreign Affairs* magazine wrote in the 1966 book '*The Clash of Civilizations and the Remaking of World Order*":

"Some Westerners, including President Bill Clinton, have argued that the West does not have problems with Islam but only with violent Islamist extremists ... Fourteen hundred years of history demonstrate otherwise." Indeed, he says, we've been deeply engaged in a quasi war that, as we know now, has become something much larger.

The West is not alone in being under threat from Islamic expansion. While the Ottomans moved into South-East Europe, the Mongul invasion of India destroyed much of Hindu and Buddhist civilization there. The recent destruction by Muslims in Afghanistan of colossal Buddhist statues is a reminder of what happened to temples and shrines, on an enormous scale, when Islam took over large areas of India. The writer V. S. Naipaul has recently pointed out that the destructiveness of the Muslim Conquest is at the root of India's appalling poverty today. Indeed, looked at historically, the record shows that Muslim rule has tended both to promote and to perpetuate poverty. Meanwhile, the religion of "submission" continues to advance, as a rule by force, in Africa, in Nigeria and Sudan, and in Asia, notably in Indonesia, where non-Muslims are given the choice of conversion or death. And in all countries where Islamic law is applied, converts (compulsory or not), who revert to their earlier faith, are often punished by death.

The survival and expansion of militant Islam in the 20th century came as a surprise. After the First World War, many believed that Turkey, where the Kemal Ataturk regime imposed secularization by force, would set the pattern for the future, and that Islam would at last be reformed and modernized. Though secularism has *(so far)* survived in Turkey, in the rest of Islam fundamentalism, or more properly 'orthodoxy', has increased its grip on both the rulers and the masses.

Before the September 11 attacks, and despite Iran where its first victory was won, some argued that Islamist totalitarianism was a movement in decline. For the past quarter-century, radical Islamist fundamentalism has roiled nations in which it arose. But in the decades since the Iranian revolution, formidable Islamist movements have built up around the Islamic world, with inadequate opposition. In Sudan, the Muslim government in Khartoum imposed Islamic law nationwide in 1993, and has killed 2 million Sudanese Christians and animists, and enslaved countless more, in an attempt to Islamize the country. Coptic Christians in Egypt, whose presence in that country predates the arrival of Islam, have been slaughtered by fundamentalist Muslims, with authorities doing little or nothing to stop them. In the Philippines and East Timor, Christians are being massacred by Muslims. Churches and Christian homes in Nigeria are being burned, and Christians murdered, by Muslim extremists. The ancient Christian presence in many Arab lands – Syria, Lebanon, Iraq, among others – has been decimated in the last century by Muslim persecution.

Although totalitarian regimes have come to power in Indonesia, the Sudan and formally Taliban Afghanistan, elsewhere some attempts are made to counter the insurgencies (in Algeria, Egypt, Iraq, and Chechnya). Even in Iran, revolutionary fervor seems to be slowly giving way to disillusionment and cynics. When the reformist government of Mohammed Khatami started creeping gingerly toward a more moderate course, the hardliner Imams put the quash on it, leading to more discontent by the Persian people of Iran. It is unclear whether the U.S. military responses since Sept 11 will precipitate new waves of radicalization in the Islamic world toppling existing regimes and bringing Islamic totalitarians to power, or the opposite.

In June 1950, Kim Il Sung posed a large problem for the U.S in Korea. But he was not *the* problem. Stalin was, and Truman never lost sight of that fact. The problem today is not a scattering of global terrorists, but a whole raft of challenges to western culture through the script and sword of Islamist totalitarianism.

The Threat!

Now Islam has reached out to wage a direct, frontal assault on its antithesis – its "Great Satan": the United States, or, to be more accurate, liberty. All the while it attempts to pacify and confuse by claiming to be the victim, and claiming to represent peace, equality, and justice. This movement follows the standard '*modus operandi*' of falsehoods by claiming to be the opposite of what it is, whispering in our ears that evil is actually good, and that good is evil. That evil 'lies' is not surprising, but that anyone of any intelligence and education still believes it is astonishing. Indeed it seems that "the bigger the lie, the easier it is for unenlightened masses to swallow".

At first glance, shadowy Islamist terrorists look very different from any enemy we have ever faced, and indeed, the tactics they employ are novel. But on closer scrutiny, the fundamental nature of our present adversaries, once seen plainly, is all too familiar. What we confront today is repackaged totalitarianism: Osama bin Laden, al Qaeda, their coconspirators and enablers are the modern-day successors of Lenin and Stalin, Mussolini and Hitler, Mao and Pol Pot, as they join the list of the worst found among human beings. If one wants a literary parallel that sheds light on the operation of Osama bin Laden and his lieutenants, one should look to that enormous bestseller, published in two volumes in 1925 and 1926, *Mein Kampf*. Hitler was candid about his ambitions, aversions, and intentions. His virulent hatred of the Jews is patent on every page, as is his narcissistic egotism, his sense of himself as a destiny, his cold-blooded lucidity. *Mein Kampf* is the testament of a man bent on war, conquest, and slaughter. Civilized society in the 20s and 30s did not take him seriously, being widely viewed as the ravings of a lunatic too far out on the fringe to be of any credible threat. It was thought that surely voices of reason in a country and people as enlightened as Germany in central Europe would not allow it. The world was wrong then, and those who do not learn from history…

Osama bin Laden has been similarly candid. In a 1999 interview published in *Esquire*, bin Laden was perfectly clear that his first ambition was to remove the American military from Saudi Arabia. "Every day the Americans delay their departure," he said, "they will receive a new corpse." It does not require much intelligence to understand that sentence. Nor was bin Laden ambiguous about his willingness to attack civilians: "We do not differentiate between those dressed in military uniforms and civilians; they are all targets in this fatwa". Published February 23, 1998 in the Al-Quds al-'Arabi was a statement signed by *Sheikh Usamah Bin-Muhammad Bin-Ladin* and other like-minded leaders;

> " … [To] kill the Americans and their allies—civilians and military—is an individual duty for every Muslim who can do it in any country in which it is possible to do it" … "We – with God's help – call on every Muslim who believes in God and wishes to be rewarded to comply with God's order to kill the Americans and plunder their money wherever and whenever they find it. We also call on Muslim ulema, leaders, youths, and soldiers to

launch the raid on Satan's U.S. troops and the devil's supporters allying with them, and to displace those who are behind them so that they may learn a lesson".

When the U.S. Marines landed in Somalia at the end of 1992 as part of a U.N. humanitarian effort, Bin-Laden's troops were there, shooting down our helicopters and dragging the bodies of our murdered sons through the streets. No action ever taken by Bill Clinton, who assumed office in the immediate aftermath of the Somalian debacle, ever did anything to dissuade bin Laden of his convictions or slow his minions. What lessons should we learn from this? The same lessons the world ought to have learned in the late 1930s when Hitler occupied the Rhineland, remilitarized, and set about gobbling up his neighbors in an attempt to make his Third Reich the –only- 'Reich'. The first lesson is that weakness is provocative to those who would conquer us.

Whatever is or is not authentic transcription of Islamic dogma, we do know that the people who ran the airliners into the World Trade Center believed that a Qur'anic voice was telling them to do what they did. We have the four-page document that told them not only what to do, but what to think. "Kill them, as God said; No Prophet can have prisoners of war ... God has prepared for believers in endless happiness for martyrs ... Be steadfast and remember [that in] God you will be triumphant."

Can we continue to refer to large parts of angry Islam as simply another religion when it clearly seeks the destruction of western civilization? Carefully selected, there are Qur'anic preachments that are consistent with civilized life, but we would be blind indeed to exclude the dominant Jihadist text and the political and cultural realities of the remainder of widely taught dogma that incite issue after issue of violent edicts (Fatwas) from its local leadership. On September 11th we were looked in the face by a deed done by Muslims who understood they were acting out Muslim ideals. It is all very well for individual Muslim spokesmen to assert the misjudgment of the terrorist, but we must recognize that the Islamic world is substantially made up of countries that ignore, countenance, if not support terrorist activity.

In December 1994, Bassam Alamoush, a prominent Jordanian fundamentalist, began talk before the Muslim Arab Youth Association in Chicago with an anecdote: "Somebody approached me at the mosque [in Amman] and asked me, 'If I see a Jew in the street, should I kill him?'" From a videotape in his possession, Steven Emerson, the well-known authority on international terrorism, describes what happened next: After pausing a moment with a dumbfounded face, Alamoush answered the question to a laughing crowd: "Don't ask me. After you kill him, come and tell me. What do you want from me, a fatwa [legal ruling]? Really, a good deed does not require one." Later in the speech, Alamoush was interrupted by an aide with a note "Good news there has been a suicide operation in Jerusalem" killing three people. Thunderous applause followed his statement.

A little more than two weeks after the 9/11 attack, an *Associated Press* reporter in Hamburg, Germany was with some 200 worshippers who listened raptly as the imam at al-Quds mosque delivered a fiery 45-minute sermon on the sins of the infidels and the arrogance of the West. "God, we implore You to destroy the United States of America," shouted the imam. Not a soul flinched. The congregation recited in unison, "Amen.". Mustafa Kamal Uddin, a 32-year-old body-and-fender man in Karachi, explained it to a *New York Times* reporter. You see, he said, holy wars come about only when Allah has no other way to maintain justice, times like now. "That is why Allah took out his sword".

We demand to know: Who taught Mustafa Kamal Uddin to reason in that way, and the crowds in Karachi to support such thinking? Can the answer be other than Islam and many or most of its clerics? Pending an answer to the question, and the unmistakable responsibility by reputable Muslims to extirpate such mis-teaching, it is incumbent on all civilized peoples to renounce modern acrimonious Islam. Responsible and thoughtful Muslims themselves need to recognize the fatal flaws within Islam's society, teachings, and structure, which are responsible for so many sorrows. Honest introspection will prompt the wise, moral, and the spiritually alive to abandon dark anti-western tenants, and if still inclined to look for purpose and structure from God, to a search for a superior source of inspiration.

The Answer

All Arab/Muslim grievances together could not possibly justify their actions or hatreds towards this people, but rather are only very poor excuses from an errant thought process, otherwise known as "magical thinking". But those errors in thinking and subsequent acts cannot mitigate in the slightest culpability nor consequences. Whatever excuse Muslims offer, whatever cause they claim to champion must now be dismissed out of hand. They damn themselves and their causes with their acts, and care must be taken not to reinforce them by advancing or even giving voice to them. Let us stop allowing their propaganda machines to assign the blame back to the USA for the hatred and failings of these people and their culture. Let us simply hold individuals, groups, and nations responsible for their actions. There is no excuse for the hateful actions they freely choose, and we would be weak not to respond with great force and determination.

Now is not a time for caution, now is a time for ferocity. Liberty will only be preserved if this generation is willing to stand up and fight to protect their fathers and mothers, brothers, sisters, and children. After Pearl Harbor, the persecuted, often interned, immigrant Japanese-Americans were eager to send their sons to join the war effort. They wanted, in large measure, to prove their bona fides as Americans. Those 33,000 sons served honorably as true patriots in Europe. What a contrast with the young Muslim people interviewed by the *New York Times* in Brooklyn and elsewhere since 9/11 who largely pledge to go fight for "Osama".

We can either sit around making diversity quilts and thinking happy thoughts, or we can seek clarity and knowledge, purge from thought the contradictions suggested by enemies, intent on killing us, and fully commit ourselves to soberly assessing the historical and present-day reality of radical "peaceful" Islam and its relations and intentions with non-Muslims and Muslims alike.

There has been a lot of talk about terrorist "sleeper cells" in countries worldwide: followers of bin Laden and his ilk that have integrated themselves into society and are waiting for marching orders. That is a possibility very much worth worrying about. Yet at the moment even more worrisome, because more certain, are the forces of capitulation: those who induce slumber in us through expressions of politically correct sentimentality, cowardliness, and moral ineptitude. Any victory less than total conquest and eradication of existing groups of extremists, as well as control of the radical religious elements that inspire it, will be interpreted in history books of the future as nothing more than a marker to Islam's conquering march.

So how to respond, throw bags of wheat at them? Do we bury them in charity, sympathy, and understanding? Is there any other answer other than to put our sons and daughters at risk in a sustained effort to destroy them and their infrastructure? It is vitally important that we execute the campaign relentlessly and thoroughly. Although assistance should be welcomed, it is better in the long run for us to act without many allies, or even alone, than to engage in a messy compromise dictated by nervousness and cowardice. Now is the ideal moment for the United States to use all its physical capacity to eliminate large-scale international terrorism. Every civilized member of humanity hopes for the interment of Islamist totalitarianism in what President Bush so stirringly referred to as "history's unmarked grave of discarded lies". The cause is overwhelmingly just. We must not allow our focus to be blurred when the weasel words of caution, proportionate, and restraint are pronounced. Religious and personal freedoms are at stake and under attack. We must clearly see them for who they are, and then without mercy or hesitation, pull-the-trigger. Not just once in Afghanistan, or twice in Iraq, but again and again until the cancer is eradicated. Anything short of a total and complete whipping will only embolden them to plan and execute even more heinous actions against this country and all her people.

President Bush on Oct. 7th 2001 spoke from the White House Treaty room on *Duty* and *Sacrifice*. He told us of a very special communiqué he had received from an important diplomat;

> "I recently received a touching letter that says a lot about the state of America in these difficult times – a letter from a 4th-grade girl, with a father in the military: "As much as I don't want my Dad to fight", she wrote, "I am willing to give him to you." ... This is a precious gift, the greatest she could give."

This young hero and her father are the finest and most noble liberty has ever produced. When joined by others like them, they represent the greatest hope for this nation, if not humanity itself. They stand united with noble veterans, visionary forefathers, great heroes from the creation of democracy to this day, as one nation under God. You can feel and almost see their strong presence, pride, and support. My hope and prayer is that we are worthy of that support; we are going to need it.

Chapter 25
Hard Options in Israel

So much emphasis is being placed on finding Peace in Israel, so much unwarranted blame for the world's Islamic problem laid at the feet of the Israeli people for their failure to sufficiently accommodate and pacify Palestinian demands. The whole conflict, couched as it is in terms of a disenfranchised persecuted people, is not the force that guides Islam's hand against Israel and the West. Arabs and Muslims living in Israel as citizens are treated infinitely better than Palestinians living in Jordan, Kuwait, and other Arab lands. For orthodox Muslims, it's all just a convenient pretext to practice Jihad on the world stage while hiding behind the cloak of more widely accepted nationalistic goals. We go back to this topic for study because the struggles facing Israel and the stark options she faces against a world sympathetic to the Palestinian cause may be similar to the options the US faces in its "War" on terror.

In a misguided attempt to be even-handed, liberal editorialists suggest Palestinian terrorist activities against Israel should be viewed as legitimate wartime action against a more powerful adversary, but all such suggestions are nothing more than immoral attempts to manipulate public opinion to accept suicide bombers and terrorists as legitimate. Without saying as much, these arguments presumably extend from the 'total war' philosophy adopted to justify attacks against a nation's infrastructure and civilians as necessary for defense and victory. However, absent from these suggestions is the implication that any nation or people adopting a 'total war' fighting philosophy, must also accept the same approach from their declared enemies without complaint. As such, Israeli incursions are as legitimate as the bombers, and anyone who laments Israelis response, while at the same time justifying the bombers and those who send them as legitimate wartime activities, are nothing more than hypocrites. In fact, by extending the logic, carpet bombings, or indiscriminately targeting the *entire* Palestinian population by any means is as legitimate as the homicide bombing activity of the Palestinians.

Lets not beat around the bush, if a people or culture declare total war against another people or nation, and employ total-war methods against that nation, that nation has the legitimate right of self defense and **_must_** respond with even greater destructiveness and effect to avoid becoming the vanquished. Those who support Islamic militant actions have absolutely no right to whine and complain about fences being built or Israeli incursions. A people as a whole deserve any resulting hardship or loss as natural consequences of their gross thinking errors and the acts that come from them. They and their children will undoubtedly continue to point fingers at Israel, the US, the West et. al., but they lie to themselves. They are individually and collectively responsible for all natural consequences arising from the actions of terrorist leaders, sons, daughters, and neighbors springing from amongst them. On July 11th 2002 even Amnesty International, the London-based human rights organization normally against Israel, condemned Palestinian suicide bombings and other attacks on Israeli civilians as "crimes against humanity" and unjustified by Palestinian political grievances.

The range of effective measures Israel could apply to protect itself against an autonomous neighbor is limited. It would seem to be an impossible situation with no easy answers. Indeed there is nothing currently on the table, which the warring parties can agree upon. The hard answers are rarely spoken. If the current 'cessation of hostilities' declared by Sharon and Abbas do not hold, the possible Israeli approaches to improve the safety of its citizens are guaranteed to be impalpable to all, and include the following:

1. The do nothing approach, simply hope that international pressures and good conscience result in the Palestinians abandoning their violent methods, so that Oslo or other 'road map' negotiations will later become possible.

> History has taught Jews more than any other people that weakness is not respected, but ruthlessly exploited. Empirical data shows, and survival now dictates, that the passive, patient, and measured approach now be rejected. Few live under illusions that any accords bearing similarity to Oslo offer any real hope. Most would agree that Israel is correct in believing that pacifism means suicide. The mindset is very instinctive, fight or flight. With each passing day, Israeli pacifists are becoming harder to find.

2.   The April 2002 approach. Send in military units to find, arrest, disassemble, and/or destroy terrorists groups and their physical infrastructure. Temporarily occupy the areas as necessary to undermine terrorist planning, and arrest those responsible for past terrorist acts, surging as needed to dissuade terrorists.

> The hope is that it will serve to persuade Hamas, Fatah, and Islamic Jihad to abandon violence, or at least weaken, delay, and/or prevent the number and frequency of suicide attacks. The political reality is that it is a weak approach and not respected by the Palestinians. It actually serves to further radicalize moderate Arabs and generate more extremists to plan and carry out terrorist events, along with more foreign support for terrorists. Imbedded in this approach lies two opposing goals, the goal of the Israelis to punish the attackers and alter Palestinian policy thus preventing attacks, …and the goal of the Palestinians to demonstrate that the attacks will continue or increase until Israel changes its policies or capitulates. Both the Palestinian and Israelis are mistaken in hopes for a change in the other sides policies and tactics. The extremists will not change, and their lot will grow, their deepest religious convictions require it. The Israelis will not yield to terrorist's tactics as further concessions could compromise security and endanger the nations existence.

3.   Capitulate to the terrorists terms, hand over all pre-1967 areas to Palestine, capitulate to the 'right-to-return', (plus whatever else they demand), and hope and pray the people currently trying to kill you will suddenly become kind, considerate, tolerant, and forever respect the rights of the new Jewish minority, and never harm them or their children again.

> To the Palestinians, it seems this is their minimum hope for the outcome of all the current infada and, however strange it may seem to us, is actually what they expect the rest of the world to support. The inherit problem in this approach is two fold. **First** is that the extremists in the area have well known aspirations that would likely drive them to continued violence despite any concessions. **Second** (and related), is that the Israelis have a healthy and normal desire to *breath*. Consider the promises just made preceding the Israeli withdrawal from Lebanon. The Hezbollah have already proven they cannot be taken at their word except, perhaps, their word articulated in the goal to drive the Jews into the Mediterranean. Arafat had proven on numerous occasions that he is a dishonest and untrustworthy broker, Abbas has also demonstrated duplicity.

4.   Physically separate the two groups where they stand and live today. Under the premise 'Good fences make good neighbors', allow the Palestinians to have their de-facto state behind the fences. [*This has become a big part of Sharon's disengagement plan*]

> The hope is that both countries will eventually find it in their best interest to avoid costly war and cooperate in mutually beneficial ways. Thus far the fence is proving to result in further hardships to the Palestinians, many who depend on access to the Israeli economy, and hardship to the Israeli economy, which depends on Palestinian labor. Upon completion the Palestinian population is totally and permanently dependent on foreign aid from the EU, the US, and Arab nations. Building a fence to separate combatants (who have demonstrated that they cannot make peace between themselves in 60+ years of continuing conflicts) is actually a practical approach to a huge national security problem. It is certain, however, that the Palestinians and their supporters will find a way to continue their methods despite any fence, and the main Palestinian export would not change from what it is today, … terror and violence. The other problem is that state to state relationships from nearby hostile regimes would quickly result in the formation of a much more lethal and dangerous Palestinian national army not likely to behave themselves behind new fences and walls they loath, so such an approach seems certain to end up resulting in a nasty war, followed by another occupation (back to square-one). It is all but certain that improved Quasam rockets and artillery, along with successful efforts to breach the structure, will force Israelis to re-enter the walled territories.

5.   An extension of the June 2002 approach. Revoke permanently autonomy in progressive sections of the occupied territories from which terrorist activities originate, controlling and limiting the scope, power, and limits of Palestinian lives within the newly drawn borders. Were talking true occupation, …a police state, …annexation. Occupy the areas and control resident's lives as necessary to undermine and prevent all armed resistance and all terrorist activity. The logical extension to this policy is to outlaw violent political opposition and deport anyone who refuses to live under Israeli law.

> This did not work from 1967 to the mid 1990's in its various forms, and so returning to it would surely fail to stop extremists today. There is obviously no future in this for anyone, but has been implemented temporarily in the past presumably as a potentially less dangerous and costly option to allowing things to continue as they were. The problem with this approach is that for the common Palestinian, it is not in reality very much different than the existing political climate, and so there will be little or no perception of loss or cost by continuing

violent opposition to Jewish police or military attempting to put down violence. This approach will always be deemed weak, and despite the fact that such attempts are always in response to violence, will always be used as an excuse (pretext) for continued murderous acts by Islamic terrorists worldwide.

6. A combination of methods, including more effectively and ruthlessly attacking and dismantling the groups using more heavy handed methods similar to Egyptian approaches to terrorists. Increasing boarder security and travel restrictions between Israel/territories and Egypt, Syria, Jordan, Lebanon, and by sea. Decreasing access from the Palestine areas by stricter internal border controls (less freedom of movement for foreign and perhaps even Israeli Arabs). Fences and walls and/or other high tech monitoring systems that make practical and economic sense. More manned checkpoints with a forgery proof national personal and vehicle ID/tracking system that makes it easier/faster to identify legitimate individuals cross-referenced with the vehicles they occupy and any legitimate need/rights to be at a given location. Occupying or annexing for long periods areas or regions from which the worst terrorist activities originate. Immediate, irrevocable deportation of anyone involved in illegal groups or tainted by terror. Relocation and/or massive demolition for areas tainted by terror groups. Targeting leaders for assassination.

> The problems related to a combination of responses are the cumulative problems related to each individual reaction, and the prohibitive costs associated with implementing a comprehensive Orwellian police state. Targeting terrorist leadership and recruiters has proven helpful in reducing attacks, but have not stopped them.

7. The Sharon unilateral disengagement plan. Many hope Israel's just completed unilateral withdrawl from Gaza and part of the West Bank will appease militants and finally result in real peace. In Germany during the Second World War, unarmed Jews walked helplessly into the ovens and gas chambers. Jews say *"Never Again"* often enough, but the big question of this century is: Will fully armed Jews continue to paint themselves into a smaller and smaller box, walking carefully but deliberately towards slaughter? The Israeli government's removal of its own citizens from Gaza will go down in history as either a suicidal error of huge proportions, or a tactical political/military move serving the survival of the country, depending on how Israel now responds to the coming provocations of its new defacto neighbor-state, Palestine. The retreat under fire from Gaza cannot but encourage more terrorism, because the Israeli retreat has sent an unambiguous signal: Terrorism works. Terrorist groups like Hizbollah, Hamas and Islamic Jihad have made it clear their campaign to destroy Israel will continue unabated. Even PLO leaders have declared their intent to continue tried and true methods of violence to rid Jerusalem and the entire West Bank of Jews. The military retreat is seen by passionate Palestinian Islamists as a signal that Israel is weak and ready to be pursued and destroyed. The withdrawal from Gaza and parts of the West Bank will soon enough be followed by a terrorist push to cause even greater harm. Considering Sharon's earlier statements and policies, surely one assumes he must understand this.

> In 2003 Sharon defeated Labor party candidate Amram Mitzna. At the time Sharon ridiculed Amram for advocating unilateral withdrawal from Gaza, declaring then: "*A unilateral withdrawal is not a recipe for peace. It is a recipe for war.*" Later that year he did an apparent Kerry flip-flop articulating a nonnegotiable policy of abandoning Gaza. To many, this represents betrayal of core principals of Zionism. Whether this is in fact a betrayal, or Sharon simply accepting the inevitability of war and positioning Israel to fight an unavoidable battle with the Palestinian militants, is anybody's guess at this point. Sharon has promised to respond to any violence with greater force after the withdrawal, which is the only encouraging sign that the man has not lost it. Unfortunately, there are even more signs that Sharon does not always act in militarily cognizant ways. In a clear tactical error, Sharon exchanged 429 living terrorists and 59 dead ones for one captured Israeli civilian and the remains of three soldiers in Feb 2004. Not to mention the unilateral withdrawal from Lebanon five years ago. The results of these actions were: a) more Israeli deaths as many of the release criminals returned to their terrorist ways, and b) Hizbollah committed unspeakable atrocities on Israel's former Lebanese Christian allies and deployed huge numbers of rockets aimed at northern and central cities. Does Sharon know what he is doing? It is hard to guess.

The only way Sharon's evacuation could possibly work to stop Muslim terrorists is if Israel backs up the Gaza giveaway by loading up the Israeli side of the security barrier with missiles and artillery, and to fire multiple warheads into population centers for every rocket coming over the other way, and lob even more shells for every terrorist act inside Israel, …until all Palestinian barrages stop. But somehow that seems out of character for Israel. Currently only Palestinians are employing brutal but effective methods of *'Total War'*, while Jews are employing 'measured responses' (*which is why the Muslims have no motivation to stop*). As such, the current equation of war is solidly against the long term survival of Israeli Jews. It is not altogether clear that Sharon understands this, so one cannot be sure if he is a fool or not. If he is positioning for all out war, then the man is no fool, as all out war may well be the only practical solution remaining considering the increasing number and range of Hezbollah rockets in Lebanon, future Palestinian armaments, and Iranian missiles (*Palestine will soon enough get a major sea port in Gaza with unfettered access to support by sea, to go along with virtual free land access via Egypt*). Creating a Lebanon type buffer zone will not suffice, as any new buffer zone would have to go from the sea to Afghanistan to guarantee security.

8. All out war, including the expulsion of the entire Palestinian population into Syria, Jordan and/or Lebanon. Attacking the Hezbollah in Lebanon and the Syrian forces protecting and supporting them, followed by creating wide unpopulated buffer zones and effective borders as necessary (along the lines of the effective Korean demarcation line).

> This is dangerous and costly, but actually the most practical and reasonable solution if one was to accept the premise that the probability of the two peoples ever living as peaceful neighbors is at (or near) zero. If that premise is true, then the only answer is for one group or the other to truly be victorious and the other become the vanquished. Although tragic and unnecessary, this approach may eventually become the only realistic option left on the table in order to guarantee one of the groups remains viable to survive intact. Pessimists wait for such a final solution to be eventually adopted by the parties, optimists hope to avoid the calamity. However, for many civilized, intelligent, and educated peoples in the world, if forced to choose as neighbors either; a) the existence of Israel, and end of Palestine, or b) the existence of Palestine, and end of Israel, the choice would be uncomfortable, but easy. The world should not be surprised if this 'final solution' is adopted by Israel should Palestinians start killing Israelis in the thousands in Mega attacks.

All familiar with Middle East history realize that there are trained killers claiming to represent both Islam and the Palestinian people determined to prevent any form of a real, lasting, negotiated peace. Their path is set in concrete; they will not be converted to accept another way, and so the fact is that the only way to stop them ... is to eliminate them. This is a hard thing to think about. As peaceful options evaporate with ever increasing Palestinian militancy, and as Israel continues to be maneuvered into a corner, no one should be surprised at Israelis responses, which must become increasingly severe and violent. The options to insure survival and prosperity are hard and distasteful, but are probably preferable to a continuation or escalation of the existing situation.

The (latest) declared cease-fire will not hold forever, as it can only be considered temporary (hudna) by Islamic terrorists while they re-group and re-arm. Sadly the obvious eventual logical course of action, and possibly the only approach with any hope permanently ending hostilities, is also guaranteed to be the most painful and distasteful. Perhaps when thousands upon thousands have died, the people of Israel will be prepared to take such a drastic decision. What ever that point is, when the pain and anguish has reached a tragic crescendo of intolerable proportions, some ugly scenario will likely be played out.

Many in Israel and even America are beginning to understand that the problem was not Arafat, or is not Mahmoud Abbas, or Abu Mazen or Abu whoever; it is the existence of the Palestinian Authority itself, which is little more than a hothouse for terror, corruption and bloodshed. Installing a new Godfather does not make the Mafia less of a criminal organization. Palestinian leaders have made their true aspirations plain all along, in Arabic: There are no Palestinian leaders who want peace, and there never were. Oslo was a sucker's game from the beginning, nothing more than a diversionary war tactic. The Palestinian Authority is what it has always been: A terrorist organization at war with Israel and the West, willing to settle for nothing less than total victory, starting with Israel's total destruction. Thus, it's not just Hamas, Islamic Jihad, Hezbollah, and al Qaeda that must be destroyed for Israel to survive and for America to win the broader war on terror: It's the PA itself. The idea that a Palestinian state under the PA would ever be anything other than a terror state also needs to be retired. In fact, a survey released March 19th, 2003 showed that 60 percent of Palestinians believe that Hamas and Palestinian Islamic Jihad should continue their armed struggle against Israel even if Israel leaves all of the West Bank and Gaza, including East Jerusalem, and a Palestinian state is created, and also 80 percent say that the Palestinians should never give up the 'right of return'. (*The poll of Palestinians, Israeli Jews, and Israeli Arabs was released in Washington by Itamar Marcus, founder of Palestinian Media Watch and written by pollster Frank Luntz. It was conducted by two polling firms, the Public Opinion Research of Israel and The Palestinian Center for Public Opinion.)*

Chapter 26
Islamic Contradictions and Hypocrisies

America is hated in large parts of the Middle East and Asia, but the more educated and affluent Muslims usually wear Levi jeans while shouting 'death to America '. When the cameras are gone and the frenzy is over, they can often be found cueing up at Western embassies, hoping for a visa to immigrate in search of a 'better life'. This hate/love relationship many Muslims have with western democracy, freedoms, culture, and technology is despised by their more aged Imams, who then respond by ratcheting-up the hate-America sermons. They paint illusions of Western conspiracies into young minds in the region, desperately trying to hold back the forces of enlightenment and change.

Muslim spokespersons claim moral purity in their fight against 'decadent' Westerners. Indeed, Muslims told an infidel forced himself sexually on a nine years old girl would quickly condemn such a man for being a pedophile, and then he would be lynched. But mention the Prophet Mohammed slept with a girl of the same age, and watch Muslims overact with all kinds of rationalizations such as *'girls in those days matured fast*' or *'it was normal and acceptable in that culture'*, etc. Apparently it was also normal in those days to rape a widow the same night you slaughtered her beloved husband in an unprovoked raid. To normal thinking feeling human beings, the phrase *'most merciful'* would not seem to apply to either of these divinely sanctioned acts by Muhammad, yet somehow such contradictions are lost on Muslims.

We hear that Muslims believe the Black Stone circled in Mecca is conscious and will testify for and against them on Judgment Day *(though they will deny it, the stone and ritual is based on a pagan deity)*. Meanwhile Muslims all over the world gleefully bring down 'un-Islamic' idols, statues, and figures representing deities in other religions. The physical manifestation of Allah, in the form of a conscience stone, is an important core of Muslims' connection with deity. A pillar of Islam states that every individual must make a pilgrimage to the stone and pay homage. Having done so, a good Muslims can then return to his/her home and with greater piety plot violence against pagan idol worshipers of all sorts.

The world continues to find disappointment as it waits for the majority of 'moderate' Muslims to bring the extremists into line. The problem is that even moderate Muslims have enormous capacity to absorb great hypocrisies. It appears the vast majority of people from Islamic lands develop early a capacity to accept extreme contradictions without question. Remaining completely unfazed, they continue to call monsters who target innocents 'mujahedeen' (holy warriors). With nary a blink, moderates and extremists alike call fiends who target Jewish children in Israel 'mujahedeen'. Arab Muslim societies, instead of developing any empathy for the victims of Muslim terrorists, race backward into ever deeper superstition, bigotry, and a culture of blame which renders reformation impossible. Huge parts of the Muslim world are afflicted with what can only be called world-wide denial, if not a deep psychosis characterized by a false sense of superiority and irrational hatred of all others, particularly those capable of defending themselves. If a small group of Muslim terrorists are humiliated in Abu-Graib prison, and all Muslims take it personally, gathering in great numbers to demand revenge. But the treatment of Iraqi western 'collaborators' by the prisoners 'peers' evokes little concern. If any American (non-Muslim) soldier were to be captured, is there any doubt as to his fate? Muslims around the world appear largely indifferent to the most in-humane treatment of infidels in Iraq. Many even relish videos and reports of atrocities as if it is some sort of Islamic national sport *("An American is killed with a road-side bomb …score one for Muhammad!")*

But then, even the term "holy war" (Jihad) is an oxymoron. There is nothing 'holy' about War, even when necessary to preserve a society, and there is certainly nothing warlike in any pure religion based on a kind benevolent God. The last 1400 years of history warn us that the typical Muslim variant of War usually involves targeting innocents, raping, and pillaging. Thinking, feeling human beings consider such acts much less than 'Holy', despite the usual chants of "*Allah Akbar*" by vile marauders. Muslims, however, seem largely oblivious to the self-evident truth that the greatest blasphemers in any religion are those who kill in God's name. Numerous videos exist showing chanting Islamists sawing off the head of some poor victim. Such videos are in high demand in Islamic lands, in what can only be described as some form of sick Islamic rapture. What are in reality the worst examples of hypocrisy and human depravity, is to many Muslims wonderful examples of pure spirituality. If a spirit is involved with such human depravity, it can only be an evil spirit, and could not be a spirit based on kindness, love, mercy, and forgiveness. Those who take pleasure from someone else's pain are correctly called *Sadists*, and are mentally and emotionally maladjusted (ill). In Iraq, nary a peep is heard as devout brothers kill while using a white flag as a cover, civilians are exploited as shields, or passers-by are blown apart with or without damaging the declared enemy. Add to this the deafening silence connected to hundreds of kidnapping of civilians, UN and NGO workers, and the decapitation of all such "prisoners." In Muslim minds, condemnation remains unthinkable for reasons of a faith and a theology which dehumanizes all non-Muslims.

Acts by sadistic terrorists produce by design extreme human suffering and pain to innocent and unsuspecting victims. Instead of an act of wanton brutality and murder producing shame for the family of the perpetrator, it is common for a festive ceremony known as "the wedding of the martyr" ('irs al-shahid) to be held in honor of the murderer. The celebration is held to symbolize the murders wedding in paradise with 72 virgins. At these events, the family receives guests who offer more congratulations than condolences for their son's martyrdom. Feb 28, 2005, suicide bomber Raid Mansour al-Banna detonated a car bomb at a busy bazaar in Hilla Iraq, killing 132 Muslims and seriously injuring 120 more. Iraqis were incensed that a *'irs al-shahid* was celebrated by the Jordanian family of the murderer. But would these same angry Iraqi people objected if the victims had been Americans, Jews, Russians, Hindus, Christians, or <your religion here>, or would these same concerned Muslims likely have *attended* that hated celebration. Today, many worldwide take glee witnessing the various beheadings, executions, and other unspeakable images shown repeatedly on Arabic satellite TV to a demanding audience. Tongues click in many 'peaceful' households for what passes as spirituality to these people. In an ongoing blatant example of Islamic hypocrisy, a deafening silence is observed throughout the Arab world while horrendous crimes continue to be committed by Muslim Arabs against their Muslim brothers, sisters, and children in Sudan. Islamic leaders strain and choke on a sand fly, yet it seems an adult camel can easily slide down their throat.

Honor killings are yet another blight tarnishing Islamic claims to be the worlds 'best' religion. The same culture that requires a son to brutally murder a daughter to *'preserve family honor'*, also celebrates wholesale murder of innocents, both considered pious acts justified to defend the demands of family/religious 'honor'. It's a strange thing, this Islamic concept of honor. As George Orwell said; "*There are spectacles before which even satire herself stands mute.*" Duplicity is the ability to articulate and adhere to two completely opposing moral standards at the same time, and is a sign of both intellectual immaturity and moral bankruptcy. Sadly, even reading these words, most Muslims will refuse to see any contradictions whatsoever, the natural result of a lifetime of conformity to Islam and shunning critical thought. Anger is the only reaction allowed to words not gushing with praise and adulation towards Islam. If Islam really were a great and peaceful religion, we might expect peace, prosperity, and enlightenment to break out all over in lands it governs. Instead everywhere Islam goes, all the locals get is poverty, oppression, corruption, murder, rape, and thievery. The facts on the ground confirm this, notwithstanding the vigorous, often threatening denials of Islamists. "*How beautiful the Emperors robe*", they exclaim, while the rest of the world sees the ugly nakedness of a violent people and culture. "*Islamophobic bigot!*" they scream, as they sharpen their blades and plan their next vile act in the name of their hateful God *Allah*. Today's Middle East is a region where even words have been systematically corrupted. Dictatorship is called "*nationalism*", stealing is called "*Jizya*", terrorism is called "*holy war*", murder is called "*martyrdom*", and terrorists have become "*insurgents*".

The intractable problems embedded within Islamic doctrine and culture is often quite obvious, to anyone but Muslims who seem to have their Islamic blinders super-glued on. As in Gene Roddenberry's classical Star Trek '*Borg*' culture, individuality and humanity were the first causalities of Muhammad's Ummah (Muslim collective). Normal human reasoning and feeling were replaced with teachings and practices which serve to blunt conscience, suppress the heart, and cloud the mind. Muhammad's 'religion' supplanted any opportunity for individual virtue and spiritual growth, replacing it instead with required obedience to a culture steeped in misogamy, bigotry, racism, and violence. Whereas most of us see ourselves as humans first and consider other humans as sanctioned beings, Muslims see themselves as

Muslims first and non-Muslims as something much less than human. Muslim militants are constantly reinforced with the idea they are the 'best' of people and reminded non-believers are worthless to their Allah. With this bigoted/racist theology placed firmly in their hearts, they can easily view the pain and death of all non-brothers as a good thing, by whatever method. In this way horrible acts committed by Muslim 'martyrs' become sacred acts to be revered. When firmly in place, this Teflon theological/psychological construct shields victimizers from normal guilt or regret, easily allowing the Muslim collective to escape all culpability in their own minds and hearts. As they pile one misfortune after another upon themselves and their communities they easily escape all culpability. Being neither blind nor stupid, they plainly see the blood on their own hands, yet remain unmoved in sincere belief that Allah is pleased at such a spectacle. Were the millions of victims persecuted by devout Muslims following the enshrined tenants of anti-Semitism, bigotry, and racism, themselves bigots deserving of their fates? Were the 3000+ infidels brutally murdered 9/11 deserving of their fate at the hands of Islam? Were they truly worthless and 'unloved' by Allah? Are Muslims really superior and entitled to the lands, wealth, and lives of non-believers? We should not be so surprised that an entire culture can be deceived by such pure evil, as it has happened on a national level before in recent history. Nazi thugs justified vile acts in the same way, using the same kind of thought processes and methods of psychological manipulation/intimidation.

While making excuses for vile behavior of brothers, defenders of the Qur'an also claim the book promotes scholarly leaning, when in fact it is filled with nonsensical fantasy often in direct contradiction to scientific fact. Muslims present Islam as a religion which encourages learning, reminding others that Muhammad said "s*eek knowledge even if it is China*", while at the same time any book of knowledge perceived as contradicting the Qur'an is considered satanic. The direction remains for such heresy to be destroyed forthwith. The Royal Library of Alexandria in Egypt, founded at the beginning of the 3rd century during the reign of Ptolemy II, was once the largest in the world, at its peak storing up to 700,000 scrolls. In 640 AD Moslem marauders took the city, and upon learning of "a great library containing all the knowledge of the world" the conquering general asked Khalifa Omar for instructions. Omar is quoted as saying of the Library's holdings, *"they will either contradict the Qur'an, in which case they are heresy, or they will agree with it, so they are superfluous"*, whereupon he ordered the library to be destroyed and the books burnt.

For the last 1400 years, millions of victims have been persecuted by devout Muslims following Muhammad's enshrined tenants based on anti-Semitism, bigotry, and racism. To 'real' Muslims, the infidels brutally murdered 9/11 were deserving of their fate, because they were worthless and 'unloved' by Allah. Muslims continue to follow a doctrine to dominate and subjugate others, believing in a man who told them God sanctifies murder, slavery, lying, rape, arson, and thievery against other human beings (albeit non-believers), as acts of great piety which will be rewarded in Islamic heaven. All the while Islamic historians continue to rewrite history to turn Muslim marauders into champions, and blood-thirsty terrorists into Saints. From the distorted Muslim prospective, Muslims are always presented as the poor, picked-on, persecuted lot, such self-pity providing justification for any and all criminal acts. Their culture feeds extremism instead of sanctioning and subduing destabilization. Chaos is a tool of Islamists to weaken and subdue other cultures and societies, and contributors to such anarchy are congratulated instead of jailed. When no provocation exists, one can always be easily created before or after the fact. Conspiracies abound in the mind of Muslim leaders from Muhammad to today, which have served to more than justify 1400 years of very 'real' Muslim conspiracies against her neighbors. For centuries, from the Iberian peninsula to the Indian subcontinent, jihad campaigns waged by Muslim armies against infidel Jews, Pagans, Zoroastrians, Christians, Buddhists, and Hindus were punctuated by massacres, including mass beheadings. Iberia (Spain) was conquered in 710-716 AD. During this period of "enlightened" Muslim rule, the Christians of Toledo (Iberia Spain) first submitted to their Arab Muslim invaders, but then revolted under dhimmi in 713. In the harsh Muslim reprisal that ensued, Toledo was pillaged, and all their Christian leaders had their throats cut. More Toledan revolts followed. In 806, seven hundred inhabitants were executed, and yet again in 811-819 when the Christian 'insurgents' were crucified, as prescribed in the Qur'an. *"For those who do not submit to Allah their punishment is . . . execution or crucifixion, or the cutting off of hands and feet, from the opposite sides, or exile from the land." (Surah 5:33)*

Islamic politicians demand western societies show tolerance toward Islamic laws and customs, while no such accommodation is offered non-Muslims in Islamic lands. CAIR and other Islamic organizations in the US are quick to pull the trigger claiming religious persecution, seeing civil rights violations in every shadow. Meanwhile the same 'sensitive' individuals remain in complete denial to human rights violations perpetrated by Muslims worldwide. The UN and Organization of Islamic States are equally quick to complain of the slightest appearance of bias, but even quicker to ignore gross violations of 'human-rights' perpetrated by Muslims against non-believers. Muslims throughout Europe and the US were enraged when Tariq Ramadan (an Islamic 'intellectual' with radical, anti-Christian, anti-American ideas) was denied a visa and so tenure at the University of Notre Dame in Indiana. Suddenly so many Muslims were terribly worried about stifling intellectual freedom. Of course no one thinks to ask just how many Christian or openly anti-Islamic scholars have jobs at Islamic universities, as such a question is unthinkable. It is amusing to see Muslim folk rise to promote diversity, freedom, moral values, or equality. Sort of like the owners of the sunken Titanic coming out to promote 'Iceberg Awareness Week'.

The 'Red-Crescent' was formed to be an answer to the Western 'Red-Cross', yet it follows strict Islamic doctrine in limiting its services to Muslim Brothers and Sisters. When terrible, brutal things happen to non-believers anywhere, at the hands of Muslims or not, shoulders are shrugged as they say "it is the will of Allah". But such antipathy disappears when Muslims strike a blow maiming any part of a population of non-believers, say …Americans, Indians, Russians, Jews, Australians, Italians, Spanish, Brits, Philippines, etc etc. Each success at such malice, instead of invoking sympathy or regret, serves as proof manifest that their 'most compassionate, most-merciful' Allah is indeed God. Hell, they seem to get the same warm giddy feeling of self-righteousness and superiority when Sunni and Shiite kill each other in large numbers.

It is an Islamic mandate that all Muslims victims must be properly avenged, but apparently there is no such thing as an Infidel victim. When the victim is not Muslim, or insufficiently Muslim, hyper-sensitivity suddenly turns to mind-boggling apathy. With the knowledge that the victims in Beslan were not Muslim but the attackers were, acute empathy and compassion is instantly replaced with casual indifference. Yet if the attackers would have been non-Muslim and the children and their parents Muslim, is there any doubt protests and revenge attacks would have spanned the globe? Indeed, horrendous crimes continue to be committed by Muslim Arabs against (insufficiently Muslim) brothers, sisters, and children in Sudan, while a deafening silence is observed throughout the Arab world. Arabs know all about what is going on in Darfur, even Al-Jazeera and Al-Arabiya have started reporting some aspects of the crisis, but they don't react. Muslim public opinion with regard to the ongoing genocide has remained muted, causing barely an eyebrow to be raised. Yet had the slaughter targeted Arab Muslims perpetrated by Infidels, there would have been an uproar.

In Iraq, nary a peep is heard as devout brothers kill while using a white flag as a cover, civilians are exploited as shields, or passers-by are blown apart with or without damaging the declared enemy. Add to this the deafening silence connected to hundreds of kidnapping of civilians, UN and NGO workers, and the decapitation of all such "prisoners". As Shiite Muslims continue to be slaughtered by their more extremist 'brothers' in Iraq, moderate Muslim nations seem to be able to find very little to criticize. Thousands of innocents Iraqis have been deliberately targeted and died at the hands of merciless terrorists, yet somehow America is to blame for the carnage.

Muslim spokesmen claim to oppose intolerance, and then in the same breath attack anyone who exposes the criminality of any Muslim brother. When U.S. Marine in Iraq killed a wounded terrorist, in a place where wounded terrorists are a fatal threat, Muslims demand justice and revenge. But when vile Muslim murderers kill a helpless woman serving needy Iraqi Muslims for decades, Muslims can only shrug their shoulders, and the perpetrators are protected instead of being brought to justice. If a Palestinian is killed in Israel, even if he has been involved in hundreds of attacks against Jews, Muslims worldwide chant and demand revenge. Yet if hundreds or thousands of Spaniards in Madrid, or Americans in New York, are massacred, their stone-cold hearts feel nothing. When Dutchman filmmaker

Theo Van Gogh was silenced by an Islamic assassin, Muslim leaders so concerned with accommodation and tolerance suggest he brought such misfortune upon himself by insulting the Qur'an. These sensitive, socially concerned Muslims tell us no one is allowed to criticize the Qur'an or Islam. Apparently free speech refers only the right of Muslims to preach bigotry and hatred, but any right to free speech must remain subservient to Islamic hyper-sensitivity to criticism. Pious Muslims tell us that critics of the teachings or person of Muhammad are blasphemers who have lost their right to live. Obviously the word 'tolerant' does not mean the same thing to both Muslims and Westerners. As Dorothy said in the <u>Wizard of Oz</u>; *"I don't think were in Kansas anymore, Toto"*.

Chapter 27
Never-Ending Islamic Conspiracies

Pragmatism and candor are prerequisites enabling an individual or culture to grow and progress. If an individual consciousness is unaware of its own short-comings, then he/she is unlikely to choose a path different from the one repeated as a matter of habit or tradition. Healthy human beings are thinking entities inherently capable of both knowledge acquisition and cognitive development. However pride and/or apathy are known to be personal attitudes which can interfere with normal cognitive growth. On a social, cultural, or national level, there are other 'group think' errors that can and do prevent normal growth and development. Clever local or regional propagandists, to serve their own interests, can cause or propagate certain attitudes or feelings to stymie rational thought, which might otherwise result in good judgment contributing to social advancement. Our attitudes and emotional state either prepare us for learning and growth, or preclude advancement.

The capacity to feel fear is an inherent human emotion deep within the psyche of all of us. This primal instinct is normally dormant, but relatively easy to evoke and quickly bring to the surface. This basic emotion has served our species well to insure behavior that guaranties survival, but this powerful instinct also renders us all susceptible to emotional manipulation. Unreasonable fear is called paranoia. Unjustified paranoia usually results in poor choices in behavior, sometimes with egregious harmful or hurtful effects. While the correct perception of a true threat is critical to survival, the perception of a threat which does not exist wastes energy and effort and also prevents any focus on personal, economic, or cultural development. On the other hand, having no perception of a threat, when an actual threat is present …is just plain stupid. The world is a dangerous place for mortal man, and diligent attention to it dangers is wise, while excessive focus on distant unlikely threats is not. Then there is the old saying, one of my favorites to mention to those preoccupied with slaying windmills; "Just because you're paranoid, doesn't mean they are not really after you…"

In case you have not yet noticed, Muslim peoples and nations seem very prone to a wide range of illogical and irrational 'conspiracy theories'. By their own words and actions, it seems vast numbers of the Muslim 'Ummah' (community) are preoccupied with various perceived conspiracies, and are thus perpetually locked into a cycle of fear and overreaction. Often, to distract their populace from the realities of their own shortcomings or failures, governments/dictatorships permit or perpetuate misinformation. In the Islamic world, social or cultural fears are also flamed by rumor, by news and editorial content, by TV and radio productions, by internet and satellite broadcasts, and most importantly by their religious leaders. It is no accident that all these arms of communication support this dynamic for deception. To understand the mindset that creates and feeds these endless theories, one needs to look more deeply at the philosophy and doctrine of Islam, and its history in relationship with non-Muslims. Many works are now emerging to assist non-Muslims understand the way Islam emotionally and psychologically affects and limits its adherents. Such books are critical to gaining true perspective on Islamic psychology and culture, as the concepts and dynamics involved are outside typical western patterns of experience. Before enlightenment can occur, one has to study unusual concepts and think 'outside of the box'. This work you are reading now is just one of many accurate evaluations of true Islam available today. www.jihadwatch.org and www.faithfreedom.org remain two of the better internet sites to gain a perspective based on reality vs. propaganda.

A most recent rumor gaining legs in the Islamic world, is that the Dec 26th "Black Sunday" tsunamis, which killed almost a hundred thousand Muslims, was triggered by a combined Indian-American nuclear experiment in the 'belt of fire' region, or possibly by massive American bombing in Afghanistan. A respected Egyptian newspaper has just rendered support to this concept by repeating the claim in a recent article. Whereas most humans can easily recognize a natural disaster based on an act of nature, apparently it is impossible for Muslims to accept that their Allah could permit such barbarity against the worlds 'best people', which is how they have been taught from birth to view themselves. As such any natural catastrophe simply can not be an 'act of God'. Instead, pressure builds to find some other rational to explain the calamity. The easy target these days are the vile Hindus, the evil Christians, and/or the dirty

Jews. This latest in a long string of conspiracy theories is pitiable. One might feel inclined to laugh at and mock such simple mindedness, were it not for the sad implications to us of the many people trapped in this kind of Islamic 'groupthink'.

In another instance, since 9/11 rumors quickly surfaced in the Middle East that thousands of Jews were forewarned and did not go to work at the World Trade Center that morning. Despite the absence of any evidence supporting such outlandish claims, those rumors have now become facts in the minds of vast numbers of Muslims. Notwithstanding we are now 3 ½ years since 9/11, and despite tactic and actual acknowledgment by al-Qaeda of responsibility, vast numbers of Muslims in the Middle East, including the most educated, actually believe that Mossad (Israel's intelligence service) carried out the September 11 attacks on America. This suggestion remains laughable to westerners, and an insult to the intelligence of anyone with a basic grasp of the facts. But while no-one in the West believes such absurdity, Westerners still fail to grasp an important reality; It is not just a handful of wackos who are swallowing such rubbish in other lands. It is possible that hundreds of millions of Muslims around the world largely believe it, convinced that that Mossad was behind the attacks in a design to provoke an American response against Muslims. Their truth manifest, …Islamic lands and Islamic militants have been targeted in response.

For some reason, Muslims seem incapable of facing the reality of their co-brothers culpability. The reason for that denial is both simple and foreboding, and is based firmly in Islamic doctrine and mindsets. The malady is both systemic, and intractable, because it is based on a core Muslim belief that Muslims are Gods 'best people', far superior to non-believers whom the Islamic God 'does not love'. As such, whatever goes wrong, …simply has to be the fault of non-believers. To believe otherwise shakes the very foundation of an individuals Islamic identity. If you take away a Muslims sense of superiority, there is usually very little left (in terms of family, culture, or economic quality of life) to support the poor creature. To a good Muslim completely lost in Islam, there is nothing else to fall back on, because such an individual has already 'broken all ties' in his efforts to win carnal paradise in Islamic heaven with 72 virgins, 'boys like pearls', gluttony, and endless mansions and riches.

African Muslims regularly accusing "Zionists" of spreading AIDS. Last year Imams in Africa issued a fatwa telling the poor African Muslims not to go for polio vaccinations because Western doctors were conspiring to cause them harm thereby. They were told that the 'Jews' were behind the contamination of the vaccine which might cause Aids or infertility, …and they believed it. Of course, the claims were outlandish with no basis in fact, yet they still served to successfully manipulate the behavior of the entire Muslim populace. Only after some small outbreaks of polio threatened to become wider, did the clerics permit vaccinations to resume. Despite all kinds of logical and scientific evidence available to everyone, it was only the very 'real' fear of polio epidemics which could overcome the false fear from their religious leaders. In this case the paranoia proved to be harmful to the paranoid, but unfortunately in most other cases paranoia usually harms others. There are innumerable examples of excessive violent overreaction by Muslims, but point to any subset of historical data showing such harm caused and be prepared for the usual reaction; "Lies, lies!", they will scream, claiming victimization and/or conspiracy. Insecure followers of Islam learn early in life how to react to shield themselves from all blame and humiliation. In a typical display of 'transference', anyone pointing out Islamic paranoia is quickly vilified as 'paranoid' (i.e. Islamophobic).

A book long since exposed as pure fiction, Protocols of the Elders of Zion was initially spread by the intelligence services of the Russian czar in 1895 to provide support and justification for its anti-Jew policies. Leaders and lay alike in the Muslim world actually still believe the work contains actual minutes of conspiratorial meetings among Jewish leaders, who were plotting to take over the world. The Protocols book provides a complete conspiracy theory of history in which satanic Jews relentlessly strive for world domination. It claims that even Communism, Freemasonry, Zionism, and the State of Israel itself are all deemed to be instruments in this diabolical scheme of Jewry. Its attraction to gullible Muslims has grows with each successive Muslim defeat by Israel. The book is gospel truth to these people, and no amount of logic or rational argument can steer those who believe this type of nonsense away from it. There can only be one purpose to continue the otherwise pointless propagation of the lies within the document, …to justify any and all means to defeat and kill all Jewish conspirators.

Monsieur Meysson wrote a bestseller in France that claims that no airplane crashed into the Pentagon, because allegedly no debris from the ill-fated aircraft were recovered at the crash site. To his mind, and readily accepted by Muslims, it was all a plot by the CIA and the U.S. military, who used an U.S. Air Force cruise missile to murder Americans in a conspiracy to justify a new Middle East war. One Islamist site states: "Our analysis indicates that in reality, sophisticated shaped-charge explosive technology was used to create a scene comporting with the appearance of an jetliner crash, while simultaneously a 757 over-flew the area and landed at nearby Reagan National Airport".

Arab countries also regularly host conferences where Holocaust deniers masquerading as historians claim to be able to "prove" there was no massacre of Jews by the Nazis during World War II. Whereas many Muslims worldwide praise Hitler for his services, yet almost in the same breath they deny the Holocaust as "a big illusion of the Jews". Muslim revisionists, normally happy at reports of Jewish defeats and deaths, seem angry about the effect of the Holocaust on world opinion, and would rather the world felt no sympathy for Jewish victims. The claim that Jews control American government, Hollywood, western media, and most global banks have long since been accepted as obvious truths. The oft repeated claim that Israel poisons candy, food and water delivered to the Palestinians has been repeated in all regional Arab news papers and TV. The ridiculous conspiracy theories about Jews and Freemasons advanced by Muslims are on about the same level as believing that Elvis was abducted by aliens.

In Iraq today, conspiracy theories are spreading fast and easy. Many even claim that Al-Zarwaqi is an invention of the American propaganda machine. The prominent Egyptian Islamist Mohamed Selim El-Awwa, Secretary-General of the International Association of Muslim Scholars (IAMS), wrote in the Al-Ahram Egyptian daily Dec 2 2004 that the Iraqi resistance had been infiltrated by "Zionist and international intelligence services". El-Awwa explained that Muslims would not decapitate hostages stating; "It is no coincidence that decapitations or the brutal killing of innocent hostages always occur just after a scandal exposing the violations of the occupation forces." In fact many claim that Mossad have personnel in Iraq to organize terrorist activities to guarantee that Iraq remains unstable so that Americans need to stay. Theories that Israeli forces have joined the Americans serve to incite more volunteers to join the 'resistance', as hatred of Jews is the single common denominator that unites all Muslims of all creeds. Of course, there is always the firmly established theory that the Americans are only in Iraq to steal Arab oil. On Dec 12, columnist George Haddad in Al-Hayat repeated another popular conspiracy noting; "During a few weeks only, a third wave of outrageous bombing of Christian churches occurred in Iraq… If we look at these crimes from a criminal investigation point of view, and ask who is benefiting from these attacks, it would not be difficult to discover that the American occupation, international Zionism, and Israel get the real benefits from such attacks". Thus the CIA and Mossad receives the blame for the carnage, and Muslim fighters retain their Teflon coating. After all, evil cannot possibly come from the worlds best religion and its people. It has also been claimed, and apparently widely accepted, that U.S. soldiers cannibalized Iraqi civilians, and the U.S. was responsible for the car bomb that killed Iraqi Shia leader Muhammad Bakir Al-Hakim.

Some popular theories gain credence no matter how far-fetched they seem, like conspiracy theories in the Arab world that claim Jews were behind the explosion of the space shuttle Columbia, and the U.S. is behind the SARS virus. Columnists in prominent Arab newspapers, including Saudi Arabia and Kuwait, blamed the Madrid Spain bombings on the Jews. Indeed, the deputy editor of the Egyptian government daily Al-Gumhouriyya, wrote a March 18 2004 article accusing the Jews of perpetrating virtually every major terrorist attack throughout the world which westerners blame on Islamic extremists. Some have gone as far as to claim the CIA controls Osama bin Laden.

More recently, a 75 year old aged Palestinian man in ill health died in a French hospital. Never mind that the life expectancy of Palestinians is in the 50's, many believe that Israel conspired to poison and kill Mr. Yasser Arafat. Of course, no one in the world expected anything less than yet another claim of an Israeli conspiracy, along with more calls for vengeance, …and so no one was disappointed. Even if the man was 100 years old, its quite probable that a scenario does not exist which would have saved Israelis from responsibility for Arafat's death.

Meanwhile, back in the real world, the only 'real' global conspiracy worthy of attention is the one being acted out by Islamic extremists to force the whole world into Islam, or destroy any part of it which refuses to cooperate. As opposed to all examples previously cited, that is not paranoia, that is a reasonable fear based on 1400+ years of history, up to and including today. Studying the Quran and Hadith, one can read of the conspiracies which Muhammad saw all around himself, and which he used to justify several offensive campaigns to kill, plunder, or subjugate those he perceived as a threat. What we see today is the natural extension of that example. No doubt all those earliest victims of Islamic conspiracy theories also thought the unjustified concerns would be settled by means other than Jihad. They were probably concerned, but undoubtedly all hoped for reason and logic to prevail. They all probably thought pretty much like we do today, counting on mans better nature to prevail. As they faced their last moments of life, undoubtedly they all regretted not taking the threat more seriously. It's too late for them, but what lesson should we be taking from them?

Islamophobia is defined as; "an unreasonable fear of the people and philosophy Islam and all it represents". But that definition contains a huge contradiction, as all concerns and fears relating to the behavior of Islamic adherents toward non-believers have a firm foundation in historical fact. Today and in all ages, when a individual, society, or culture finds itself in proximity to Islam, then it also finds itself in opposition to the expansion and goals of that philosophy. The act of not 'believing', or opposing sharia, constitutes behavior worthy of Islamic reprisals. So being concerned or fearful of the designs of Islamic followers is both a reasonable and rational state of mind. It's just silly, if not stupid, to criticize a practical mindset which is likely essential for continued survival. What is more important, to appear politically correct, or to survive as individuals, societies and cultures? Do we want to appear 'cool', 'PC', and 'sophisticated', or are we willing to shed that image and act to preserve ourselves, our families, our neighborhoods, our towns, and our country. For the sake of both Muslims and non-Muslims alike, we all hope that the 'Ummah' can overcome its own grandiose sense of superiority, which is at the root of a dangerous psychosis evident in rampant denial and the ever growing body of perceived conspiracies. We hope for this because when a madman sees ghosts and lashes out at the creature, it is the physical world which suffers from the blows.

Chapter 28
The Final Analysis on Real Islam

Instead of trying to comprehend and facing the true roots of militant Islam, we have preferred to hope that Islamic violence is just the pernicious work of a few twisted individuals in small radical groups. We hope that by pounding the al-Qaida network the threat of Islamic terrorism will cease. We can then put it out of our minds and hope that it will no longer affect us, returning to more pleasant pursuits centered around sports, Harry Potter, the Lord of the Rings, and popular rock stars. We are happy that the DOW is back up and interest rates have lowered, and hope the recession is finally over. Yet, those planning our destruction are still living among us saying that *their* Islam is a religion of peace. All the while, just as Maslama deceived his good friend Kab in order to murder him, militant Muslims are prudently, patiently planning their next acts of terrorism, with tactic support from 'faithful' Muslims world wide, including here in the US. There is a reason why all those Madrassah educated Taliban, the Mullahs and Maulanas of Pakistan, India, Bangladesh and other Muslim countries unanimously support Bin-Laden, ...Osama bin Laden and his followers are pure Muslims per the Qur'an and Sunnah.

Now the inescapable inferences must be stated. Near the beginning of this work we asked the reader to keep three questions in mind during this course of study. Reading, visualizing, and digesting the facts outlined herein has undoubtedly been distasteful. It tears at the natural human heart to contemplate and visualize what so many suffered at the hands of early and modern Islam. Though intelligent clear thinking individuals have undoubtedly drawn their own conclusions, the questions are repeated here, along with some of the obvious inferences drawn now with full support from the material covered.

1) What are the teachings of real Islam found in the Qur'an, Hadith, and Sira with respect to the use of violence, call it Jihad if you like, to aggressively spread its power over non-Muslims, and are these teachings valid and applicable today?

ANSWER: It should be obvious that real Islam still calls for the use of Jihad, force and violence, when able, to spread Islam's power over non-Muslim people. The Jihad may take the form of passing out literature for Islam, or it may take the form of assassination, or a bombing of a building, or a massacre, or worse. These teachings are valid, applicable, and still required for Muslims today.

2) Is real Islam behind and does it condone the murder of 3000 Americans and the destruction of the WTC, or are these Muslim terrorists doing something well outside Muhammad's religion?

ANSWER: Yes. Real Islam is behind the murder of thousands of Americans and it condones the destruction of the WTC. Official Islamic theology taught in most parts of the world justify violent acts to further the cause of converting all to Islam, especially acts designed to weaken the "Great Satan", deemed the biggest threat to that cause.

3) What does the future hold for Islam and America, and in time for the rest of the non-Muslim world?

ANSWER: Continued Islamic violence. Would that it could be said otherwise, but it appears likely that Muslims will yet perform many large and small acts of murderous violence against us. If given the chance they may one day detonate a nuclear warhead, or warheads, in large American cities, as many in the movement see it as their only viable option. In order to advance Muslim theology as they see it, these militants know that America must be brought low, regardless of the cost. They are dedicated and may eventually succeed in obtaining the bombs or bomb material from Iran, Pakistan, Korea, or perhaps from a former Soviet Country. Muslim militants are cognizant of how to go about this, their goal is our incapacitation, and they believe the best way to accomplish this is through the use of WMD's.

Remove all the religious trappings surrounding that great religion/nation of Islam, take down all the tapestries and linens, remove the robes of honor and power, strip away the false claims of accomplishment and achievement, unwind all the spin and guile, and you are left with the simple naked truth, Islam undressed, ...and it is not a pretty sight. Terror and violence continues to twist and distort the soul and body of Islam into ever more unrecognizable shapes, so that it hardly seems human. The image of Islam undressed is as frightening as the image of its never ending Jihadic crusades, bathed as they are in carnage, blood, pain, and sorrow of millions of men and women, young and old. Unlike Christianity that teaches one should love their enemy, Islam offers no quarter for any unbeliever unless they convert.

There are 149 overt and easily found verses of the Qur'an alone that invoke Muslims to fight against non-believers, with scores more of supporting and more subtle references. Justifications and encouragement in Muslim's other sacred works are even more abundant. Despite the constant repetition of the view that Islam is a religion of peace, only the most naïve and foolish could possibly look at events around the world and conclude there is any truth to this. Time and again, the many biographies of Muhammad and the Caliphs that followed him reveal that he employed murder and war repeatedly to advance Islam. He was particularly obsessed with killing Jews.

A few brave souls struggle against its core teachings to move Islam toward civility, but Islam's response to terrorism is largely rhetoric, platitudes and disingenuous 'lip-service', in continuing contrast to her actions. Actions like running training camps of hatred and war in Islamic schools where the chief teaching tool is the Qur'an, a book that reads like a terrorist manifesto. It is wise to be wary of a people that embrace a religion based on texts filled with bigotry, hatred, and graphic violence. Islam proclaims peace as it engages in Jihad, tolerance as it persecutes, and freedom as it enslaves the rest of humanity. The truth is that Islam's religious tenants and philosophy are not benign but full of vile hatred, which is continuing to drive terrorist acts. Yet this cult continues to deceive others at an astonishing pace to accept the philosophy as a legitimate religion, and then later moves them to join in Jihad, a Jihad directed towards each of us individually, our families, our neighbors, our friends, our Constitution, our government, our nation, and our religious beliefs (or lack thereof).

So, why is it that so many Muslims want to see America broken or destroyed? The answer is simple, America is a powerful superpower; indeed some say the last superpower. Its military strength and pervasive cultural power represents the best hope against the violent spread of Islam. Obviously, if America is weakened or incapacitated, then Muslim terrorists can begin to act with much more impunity throughout the world. The attack against the WTC was not simply an effort to kill large numbers of American people, had they wanted to do that they could have found better targets. Rather, the attempted attack against the Whitehouse, and attacks against the WTC and Pentagon were strikes at America's financial strength, government, and military command and control center, conveniently coupled with the murder and destruction of ordinary Americans. Muslims believe that if they can hurt us badly, we might capitulate and not reply to the threat from the extremists, or at least hope to weaken us and make it much more difficult to deal with or pursue them elsewhere in the world. Just as Muhammad destroyed the financial strength and morale of the date-palm groves of the Banu Nadir, and had key leaders assassinated, so to, these Muslims have struck at our financial strength and leadership.

Consider the current war in Afghanistan and Iraq costing hundreds of billions, no country can long sustain such expenses. Eventually, our capacity to counter Islamic violence will diminish as it is spread thin. Calculate the results of 9/11/01 with its billions of dollars lost and tens of thousands of Americans out of work. The stock market crashed, taking over two years to recover, and its recovery may still be somewhat tenuous. The economy fell deeper into recession. Looking further down the road, the militants probably hope that once America is broken or destroyed, then the rest of Europe, Australia, or other regions can next be targeted with impunity.

If Muslims in Algeria can slit the throats of small Algerian children and throw them down wells, then zealots cut from the same violent cloth will not care one iota about any American life. These murdered children were fellow Algerians and sometimes fellow Muslims. Perhaps they weren't Muslim enough to the Muslim terrorists. In either case, the devoted Muslims we are dealing with are of the same spirit that murdered these children, who slaughtered the children of Beslan, Russia, and the same spirit that had the Jews of the Banu Qurayza tribe massacred. This is a spiritual war, where militant Muslim extremists are pawns in the hands of a force with a truly evil agenda …the utter domination and complete control of the entire human race! My claim is that the spiritual power behind terrorism is bigger, and more perverse, than all failed political theologies propagated to date, because it does not know human bounds. Militant Muslims serving their terror masters will not care about millions of American deaths, they will cherish it. Just as devout Muslims in Chicago and on American campuses rejoiced at the destruction of the WTC, so too large numbers of Muslims here and abroad still look forward to the day that America can be brought low.

Frequently we hear that these terrorists are very, very few, and that the Islamic community is universally peace loving. Now should we blindly accept those assurances and really believe that this type of Islamic terrorism is the work of just a few individuals? Everyone should be asking himself or herself; did the 19 Muslim hijackers operate in a vacuum? Should we believe that no other Muslims currently living in America knew about their plans? The thinking man would have to conclude that these Muslims were known about and aided by many other Muslims living here. These abettors and many other Muslims have been coming here over an extended period as men on a mission. Both the hijackers and their handlers were known and supported by Muslims throughout America and the world. If need be, Muslim accomplices will proclaim that "Islam is a religion of peace", fly an American flag, cry crocodile tears, and proclaim, "we feel your pain". But just as Muhammad's followers betrayed fellow citizens at an opportune time, these Muslim handlers (terrorists) and their Muslim accomplices betrayed America. "Islam has broken the former ties", just as the early Muslims betrayed those who were once their friends. They eat with us, drink with us, even share part of their lives with us, but the call of Islam is stronger then American citizenship, personal friendship, or simple values of integrity and trust. Make no mistake about it, when the time is ripe, many more Muslims living here in the states may support or commit the same type of violent actions that were committed on 9/11/01. They aren't done, and in their hearts they know it isn't over yet, not by a long shot.

In truth the world is chock-full of Islamic violence, committed by Muslim terrorists found in all nations. The 19 Muslim hijackers came from several Muslim countries. The Taliban are filled with Arabs, Chechens, Indonesians, Chinese, Afghans, Pakistanis, and so on. Even some British and American Muslims had gone to Afghanistan to fight fellow British and American soldiers. This type of Islamic terrorism is a worldwide movement; it is not the work of a few hot head radicals. It is the work of dedicated, devout, determined Muslims. American Muslims will continue to betray American citizens as they have done in Guantanamo and Afghanistan. The next batch of Muslim terrorists need not be Arab, or dark skinned. They may be white, blue-eyed, and, blonde. Their dedication to Islam will override any commitment to America and its people.

Below is the text of fatwa urging Jihad against Americans which was published in Al-Quds al-'Arabi on February 23, 1998.

> On that basis, and in compliance with God's order, we issue the following fatwa to all Muslims the ruling to kill the Americans and their allies--civilians and military--is an individual duty for every Muslim who can do it in any country in which it is possible to do it, in order to liberate the al-Aqsa Mosque and the holy mosque from their grip, and in order for their armies to move out of all the lands of Islam, defeated and unable to threaten any Muslim.

> This is in accordance with the words of Almighty God, "and fight the pagans all together as they fight you all together," and "fight them until there is no more tumult or oppression, and there prevail justice and faith in God."

By their own words and works, we can conclude that Islam is apparently a violent religion after all, and large parts of it continue to condone and allow the use of aggressive violence to spread its dominion over non-Muslims. The war that Muhammad launched long ago continues today, but the stakes are getting higher. America, European and Asian nations will continue to be adversely affected by the actions of real Muslims – those that are obeying their god and prophet – as they have been in the past. America (and other countries) previously insulated by distance and oceans are no longer safe and have become the relatively new targets of expansionist Islam. For all the cries against Zionism by Muslims, it is Islam which has the most aggressive ambitions and designs on other peoples and lands.

> "Will you listen to me O Meccans? By him who holds my life in His hand I bring you slaughter." (Muhammad, some of the earliest words spoken in Mecca, shortly after his first visit by "Gabriel", to people who rejected his claim to prophethood). "The Life of Muhammad", by A. Guillaume, page 131. Make war upon such of those to whom the Scriptures have been given as believe not in God, or in the last day, and who forbid not that which God and His Apostle (Muhammad) have forbidden, and who profess not the profession of the truth, until they pay tribute out of hand, and they be humbled."

We see that Muhammad had many people murdered. By request, by command, by implication, Muhammad had many killed, some while they slept. There were no trials, no judgments, no dialog. If you insulted Muhammad, if you doubted his credibility, or if you spoke out, you were killed. Men and women, young and old, all were killed because of Muhammad's intolerance, anger, hatred, and disdain toward those who spoke out against him. Today, fatwas continue to be issued demanding the faithful kill any perceived to insult the prophet or discredit his divinity. One wonders if the thin skin and short temper of Islam is due to insecurity stemming from the inherit weaknesses of its doctrine. The fact remains that challenging the doctrine of Islam or hearsay against the prophet carries the penalty of death to this day. Jihad still forms an integral part of the Islamic morality, an open behest of Allah to murder, pillage, rape and create widows and orphans for imposing Allah's will on enemies guilty of the "sin" of unbelief. Indeed, whereas war is the least desirable state of affairs for most men, vile/violent Jihad is considered holy by Muslims, and Allah guarantees paradise for all who embrace it.

The intellectually insincere individual full of hatred will certainly not benefit from this book; rather he will undoubtedly be greatly offended by the facts outlined herein. As the saying goes ... "A man convinced against his will, is of the same opinion still". A closed mind will forever be unable to draw correct inferences from a set of facts plainly laid out before him. There are too many people stuck with fixed views, which don't permit them to see the writing on the wall. The fact that the writing was written in blood on Sept 11th in New York, March 11th in Madrid, and now Sept 3rd in Beslan, still there is hesitation, if not fear, about looking at the matter of religiously based terrorism in the 21st century squarely in the face. Sadly, some choose to remain in denial forever. Some take it a step further and actively obstruct self-protective policies and actions. While fighting for causes that place both themselves and the rest of us in peril, they at the same time arrogantly claim some kind of clairvoyant moral clarity. Haughty and condescending, they are ignorant of history and outright dismissive of all facts conflicting with their superior wisdom. Their arguments are without factual foundation or substance, which is why the rhetoric is rife with criticisms and insults. Though claiming to be American patriots (and often lacking any French ancestry whatsoever) they offer no suggestions but appeasement, or in other words, peace through surrender.

Make no mistake about it: By any standard of any age Muhammad deployed murderous tactics that can only be described as terrorist in nature. Muhammad indeed taught his followers to oppress and kill non-Muslims. Today's Muslim terrorists are following his actions literally ... like prophet, like followers. They commit their acts will full understanding and belief that they are based upon what Muhammad said and did, and what he expects of them. So, soundly based in pure Islamic doctrine, large parts of Islam continue to practice, justify, support, finance, or tolerate terrorism against non-Muslims today. It appears the life of Muhammad will continue to be used by militants as justification to attack and murder those who differ from them. Muhammad taught his followers that Islam is the final and universal religion. Where Islamic law has been instituted, no other religion is tolerated unless it agrees to submit to Islamic rule. Today, more than forty nations have a majority population of Muslims, and Muslim leaders have spoken of their goal to spread Islam in the West until Islam becomes a dominant, global power. That global agenda is in keeping with Muhammad's final clear orders: convert... pay with submission ... or die.

In 1861 Sir William Muir Esq. studied Islam in great depth and detail and in his work 'The Life of Mahomet' issued the following warning, still applicable today:

... chief radical evils flow from the faith, in all ages and in every country, and must continue to flow so long as the Koran in the standard of belief.

FIRST: Polygamy, Divorce, and Slavery, are maintained and perpetuated; - striking as they do at the root of public morals, poisoning domestic life, and disorganizing society.

SECOND: freedom of judgment in religion is crushed and annihilated. The sword is the inevitable penalty for the denial of Islam. Toleration is unknown. ...Many a flourishing land in Africa and in Asia, which once rejoiced in the light and liberty of Christianity, is now overspread by gross darkness and a stubborn barbarism. ... The swords of Mahomet, and the Koran, are the most fatal enemies of Civilization, Liberty, and Truth, which the world has yet known.

Islam's nature will always prevent it from accepting criticism or suggestions from outsiders, reform will only occur from within, ...but then you have the problem that in Islamic societies men of Gandhi, Lincoln, Martin Luther's stature are killed as soon as they open their mouths. And as for non-Muslims in the West, the moment anyone mentions anything remotely critical of Islam, the first response you get hit with is "you are a racist", which is silly, of course, as Islam is not a race but an ideology. Muslims include large numbers of people from all races, so a more accurate word describing ideological intolerance would be a bigot, defined as "a prejudiced person who is intolerant of any opinions differing from his own", but Islamists have correctly surmised that the 'race card' carries much more weight in our super-sensitive society. The 'bigot' term is also problematic because it describes, in a nutshell, Muslim attitudes to non-believers. In fact it is perfectly legitimate to criticize the social and political errors and consequences of Islamism, communism, liberalism, feminism, socialism, or any other 'ism' without regard to race. Thin-skinned Muslims worldwide regard every criticism of Islamic culture or practice as Islamophobic and sacrilegious. Instead of invoking thoughtful reflection or introspection of any kind, any question or critique results in even more vitriolic anti-western invectives. Intelligent debate or discussion is impossible, as in the end all debates are resolved as they are in the 4th grade play-yard, through tantrums and name-calling. It appears critical self-analysis of any kind is impossible for the worlds 'best' religion. The inability of the religion to engage in critical self-scrutiny continues to prevent any possibility of meaningful discussion with outsiders, which otherwise might assist in Islam's peaceful co-existence with other peoples and religions.

The real issue, then, is what can the West do to inspire and help Muslims choose moderation over extremism. Since the West is locked out of the internal debate, and suggestions or criticisms from inferior infidels cannot be permitted, the only role the West can play is one it is playing now. The West can only provide an example of the advantages of democracy, freedom, and respect for human rights, and it can (and must) demonstrate to Muslims the futility and error of choosing expansionist Islam by soundly defeating every attack. But that's the conundrum isn't it, respecting freedom of speech, religion, and human rights, while at the same time killing large numbers of militants, taking down governments supporting them, and discrediting Mullahs advocating Jihad. Ultimately, it is not enough to shut down terrorist training camps and kill today's marauding Jihadists. We must also stop the "jihad factories", …the mosques and educational institutions that are turning out tens of thousands of tomorrow's aspiring terrorists, suicide bombers, and the next generation of radical leadership. The requisite initiations on speech, assembly, and political freedom needed to protect democracy from a militant religious credo are not easy to define and enforce. There is some precedent in limiting and restricting activities and speech designed to overthrow legitimate government, enslave, kill, riot, ect. Incitement to harm society at large, including hate speech against a particular group (in this case all non-Muslims) can be monitored and regulated. But such regulation is repugnant to many Americans, who overall desire no state involvement in religion. But then Islam is not benign like other religions, and to ignore this fact may be politically correct, but stupid. How long can someone not purporting to be a comic ignore a very large, deadly pink elephant in the same room? This difficult thorny problem must be successfully dealt with in within all affected institutions in this country first, so that the model may serve as an example and template for other regions faced with the same threat.

While the information and propaganda war is rethought and engaged at home, the issue of existing Jihadists must not be ignored. Jihadic terrorism is the greatest single threat to the existing world order and the advance of humankind. Active groups like Hamas, Hezbollah, Lasker-E-Tobia, Al Bader, Taliban, Al Qaeda, Tehreek-E-Jihad, Hizbul Mujahidden, and a host of others seem to have no trouble recruiting new foot soldiers to replace or augment existing fanatics. A study recently revealed that despite the *'war on terror'*, terrorist acts are increasing worldwide, proving that Jihadic terrorism is being insufficiently fought. In the Feb 24, 2004 annual assessment of global threats to the Senate Intelligence Committee, CIA Director George Tenet and FBI Director Robert Mueller testified that the al-Qaeda terror group is seriously damaged but has spread its radical anti-American agenda to other Islamic extremist groups that now pose the greatest threat to the United States. "The steady growth of Osama bin Laden's anti-U.S. sentiment through the wider Sunni (Islamic) extremist movement, and the broad dissemination of al Qaeda's destructive expertise, ensure that a serious threat will remain for the foreseeable future - with or without al-Qaeda in the picture ... And what we've learned continues to validate my deepest concern - that this enemy remains intent on obtaining and using catastrophic weapons." As recent destructive attacks in the U.S, Israel, India, Turkey, Kenya, Spain, and Indonesia have proven, Jihadists will remain a threat to all within their ever-increasing range of operations for some time to come. Jihadist terrorism is unabated in Israel and India, continuing to claim thousands of innocent lives each year. All over the world, Islamic terrorism remains a serious threat and impediment to peace, security, liberty and democracy. Today's murderous fanatics are so deeply brainwashed, so devoted to their prejudices and hatreds, that any hope of reform is completely unrealistic. The only possible successful combat strategy must focus on the entire Jihadic organization including all internal structures, the theologians setting the goals, and all social and religious values giving comfort and moral support and sanctuary. The act of terrorism by a specific community following a specific theology should be viewed for what it is, a collective criminal act. We, therefore, need to address both the psyche and all social defects of the whole Islamic Jihadi community. But we also must face the uncomfortable fact that sometimes one simply has to admit that sometimes you cannot tame a wild animal lost in primal lusts long forgotten by civilized human beings, you can only kill such a wrenched creature. Feel sorry for it, but kill it none-the-less, for if you don't it will surely kill you and your children. The cunning creature is already at the door and perhaps even in the kitchen. Take your eyes off it and it will strike, sleep and it will take advantage to kill your neighbors and children, feed it and it will thank you with a poison bite. It is both a hydra with many heads, and a swarming nest requiring repeated blows to make our lives secure and our homes safe. A weak blow that does not put the creature into the next world will not drive it away, but will only result in a more cunning attack the next time. Negotiations and truce will only delay its ambitions and methods. Weak Tit-for-tat responses only embolden it to harsher measures and further depravity. The same choice faced by so many since the 7th century is now upon every citizen of the US, convert ...or fight.

It is not just Americans and some Europeans who are becoming "Islamophobic" (a made up term to fit a void for Islamists and their apologists in the ideological war of ideas). Australians, Koreans, Japanese and other nations that have almost no previous history with Muslims are also starting to fear Islam as it proves to continue to be consistent in its dealings with its ever expanding borders. This is not a phobia, or an unreasonable fear based on an unreasonable thought process, but a fear that is very real, justifiable, and firmly based on the simple fact that Muhammad's Islam is a religion of terror. In the Qur'an (8:12) Muhammad promised to "*instill terror in the hearts of the unbelievers*", and he and his devoted followers continue to succeed at doing exactly that. And so now much of the world is learning to fear Islam. As it turns out being Islamophobic is not such a bad thing after all. All who faced the personal terror of their own demise on Sept 11th did not fear Islamists or their agenda prior to their own victimization. That lack of knowledge and fear did not serve or protect them, just as many millions throughout history have been surprised at the murderous behavior of Jihadists. Lack of awareness and appropriate fear makes individuals and nations more vulnerable to attack. Initially, surely most victims throughout history never imagined that their Muslim neighbors, and sometimes even partners and friends, might someday seek to enslave or destroy them. Being both aware and fearful of Jihadists intentions does far more to ensure safety and survival than not, so being in such a state is both desirable and laudable. If the past 1400 years of history have proven one thing, it is that the lack of knowledge, respect, and fear for Islamists and their intentions has proven fatal for many individuals and even entire cultures. In fact any non-Muslim who is not 'Islamophobic' is either an ignorant fool, or guilty of hubris. Although the term is meant to be derogatory, being accused of having a fear of Islamimanics is in fact a compliment. To be Islamophobic is to be educated, to be aware, to have a firm grip on reality and healthy grasp of a very real threat to peace, prosperity, country, and family. On the other hand to be aware of the threat and to choose to ignore it, is to capitulate to slavery over freedom, and servitude over prosperity. Whether this country is still the land of the free and home of the brave, or simply (as are the Europeans) a land of aspiring dhimmis, will be answered by a generation of Americans who have heretofore never been tested, and who still remain largely ignorant of the theology and peoples seeking their destruction. When called, will they put down their X-Box controllers and pick up a weapon to defend their families, friends, and country, or will they continue to join the ranks of Michael Moore's anti-government conspiracy legions? As with the Roman Empire, will this fledging nation fall victim to its own prosperity and resulting moral weakness? When it becomes more apparent that the future of our democracy is at stake, will more answer the call than the relative handful of strong, brave, and faithful in the armed services today? Did they even notice Sept 11th, or Madrid, the thousand plus US soldiers killed by marauding religious fanatics lusting to kill Americans in Iraq? Will they defer self-indulgent pursuits for the greater good, or continue to escape responsibility using the usual relativistic rational. Will the current 18-26 year olds continue to vote in a block to surrender everything to left-wing concepts of 'peace at all costs' (as if anything, including full surrender, could stop Jihadists from killing our culture turning every citizen into either obedient Muslims, slaves, or dead infidels). Will the black community continue to vote in a block to support policies and politicians that are guaranteed to eventually return them to slavery to their new Muslim masters? No one knows, but time will tell, and then history will record it. What will be placed in the historical record will depend on whether the historians are Muslim, or not.

Islamic Culpability

It is way past time to give it up people. We have tried to target various vile terrorists, while at the same time pumping up Islam, but its just not working. As we fight terrorists, we have been unable to face the stark reality that Islam, and the example of their revered prophet, are the chief motivation behind various terrorist foot-soldiers. It's not a 'culture', it's not a few deviants, it's not a government or nation, it's the religion. As we look first one way, and then the other, in-you-face Muslim leaders and lay continue their Jihad against us, pushing their young men to commit acts of inhumane brutality in the name of their hateful god Allah. Previously unthinkable news and images invades our living rooms on a daily basis. Only the dead and dumb can continue to hide from the facts surrounding a philosophy calling itself a religion, hell-bent on murdering or enslaving the rest of humanity. For those able to think, here is a news flash: The 9/11 hijackers, the London Bombers, the Beslan child-killers, the Chechen terrorists, the Palestinian terrorists, the Madrid terrorists, the Darfur killers, the Iraqi murderers, The Bali bombers, and innumerable acts of murder and carnage, are all linked. The common linkage is that the victimizers are all devout Muslims! Yes, that wonderful *'religion of peace'* we have been so careful to respect. And while the foot-soldiers act to weaken Western influence and institutions, 'moderate Islam' continues to do what it does best, hide militants living amongst them and silently cheer from the sidelines. The common denominator in this equation of violence is ISLAM. The common script for all these violent plays is the Qur'an, the Sira, and the Hadith collection. The identical characters for all these ugly occurrences are devout Muslims well steeped in Islamic verse and prose.

In our need to believe all religion is good, we continue to place blame everywhere else, anywhere else, even ourselves, except where it is due. Naïve to the methods and history of Islam, most of us transfer our own religious experience onto undeserving Muslims, incorrectly assuming that going to the Mosque and more prayer will dissuade Muslims from acts of evil, when it works exactly the opposite. Whereas most religionists leave their places of worship more docile, reflective, and less likely to do harm to others, in Islam worshipers leave the Mosques on Friday and go on murderous riots to avenge some perceived slight. Never, NEVER, encourage a disturbed Muslim to read the Qur'an, or go to a mosque and pray. It is only when nominal Muslims actually learn the facts of just who Muhammad actually was and what he expects, that they are at risk to become terrorists. Thank heaven most Muslims don't know too much of their own history and teachings, and it is best to keep it that way. Unfamiliarity and lack of dedication to the Torah and Bible prevents good Jews and Christians from becoming better men and women, but unfamiliarity and lack of dedication to the Qur'an prevents good Muslims from becoming terrorists.

For non-Muslims, self-preservations dictate that it is essential to become familiar with the actual teachings and example of Muhammad. Even if you don't know your own religion very well, or if you have no religion at all, each of us had better become knowledgeable of the philosophy and people bent on killing, converting, or enslaving us all. Without that armor of truth, our societies, cultures, and nations will eventually fall to Islam's methods and tactics. NO ONE should listen to the taqiyya (misinformation) constantly issued by Islamic apologists and propagandists. Each of us needs to take personal responsibility to know and understand the enemy seeking our demise. I suggest you continue after reading this work to other sites like www.faithfreedom.org and www.jihadwatch.org. To gain insight into the reality of Islam's culpability, consider also the following article recently released:

> CNN - Jul 20 2005 - Father of 9/11 hijacker Mohammed Atta warns of 50-year war. The father of one of the September 11 hijackers said today he had no sorrow for what had happened in London and claimed more terrorist attacks would follow. Egyptian Mohamed el-Amir, whose son Mohamed Atta commandeered the first plane that crashed into the World Trade Centre in New York, said there was a double standard in the way the world viewed the victims in London and victims in the Islamic world. El-Amir said the attacks in the US and the July 7 attacks in Britain were the beginning of what would be a 50-year religious war, in which there would

be many more fighters like his son. Speaking to a CNN producer in his apartment in the upper-middle-class Cairo suburb of Giza, he declared that terror cells around the world were a "nuclear bomb that has now been activated and is ticking". Cursing in Arabic, el-Amir also denounced Arab leaders and Muslims who condemned the London attacks as being traitors and non-Muslims. He passionately vowed that he would do anything within his power to encourage more attacks.

So after reading this, who is responsible for Mohammed Atta's acts on 9/11, does this revelation implicate his father? Certainly it makes it clear there was a family/culture component supporting his malicious choices, but from where in turn did his father derive the value system which he obviously instilled in his son, Mmmmm? Well, get a grip, and stop looking the other way, …the manifest truth is that both the father and son have a clear grasp of real Islam, and they practice it! Stare it right in the face, and do not blink. They learned it from sacred Islamic scripture and from a lifetime at the mosque listening to pious Imams. The father fears no backlash to his comments from his friends, neighbors, and Muslim countrymen because ….there is nothing to fear. The man receives more congratulations than condemnations. This from Egypt, a supposedly friendly nation who receives as much US aid as Israel. From the growing Muslim Brotherhood group in Egypt we get men like this, and the original terrorists who first attempted to bring down the NY Twin Towers. To travel into the minds of Muslims is like going to the land of OZ, everything is different, and much is manifestly evil. Be sure you have your ruby slippers on before going there, you will often feel the urge to click your heals three times and say; "there's no place like home…". When you get back, you will be wanting a shower. If you are not Islamophobic yet, then you are either already dead, or stupid. Becoming Islamophobic is the graduation certificate you get upon moving from delusion and ignorance, to full-awareness. When you have arrived, wear it with pride.

Chapter 29
The Path Ahead

"If there must be trouble, let it be in my day, so that my children may have peace." - Thomas Paine, American patriot

Because of its asymmetrical nature, most people don't appreciate that the War on Terrorism is actually a World War. In this conflict Nation states are pitted against a myriad of terrorist organizations without borders and the Islamic theology pushing them, and not against other states like in previous World Wars and the Cold War. Although the theoretical battle is similar in the fight between Democratic freedom and Islamic subjugation, the contest is much less familiar, yet still physical in nature, and fatal. This is also unlike the Cold War where the free world fought repressive communists who wanted to live and could be deterred by nuclear Mutually Assured Destruction (MAD). But the similarity with earlier World Wars is that it has an ideological component, with both sides thinking that they are the good guys. On the one side are the people who believe that democracy with all its accompanying civil liberties is the best way for human beings to organize their societies, whereas the other side spits at democracy and fights for the world to be ruled in accordance with the medieval laws of Allah, the *"oft-forgiving, most merciful"* Muslim God who, unfortunately, does not love non-believers. In many ways, this asymmetrical warfare is more dangerous because the enemy (men eager to die so as to be rewarded with carnal Paradise) could be living amongst us, and most probably are.

The war on the ideological front, which should be so clear in its boundaries, unfortunately is not going very well at all. Western concepts of civil rights, along with legal, political, and cultural constraints currently preclude government intervention of organized religions, and make it difficult to prohibit or punish inflammatory sermons of imams in mosques, or to punish clerics for issuing fatwas justifying terrorism. Myopic organizations like the ACLU, with support from activist judges, claim no boundary or limits can be placed on speech. Even without such opposition, within politics it is problematic to differentiate where free speech ends and incitement begins. As long as it so restricts itself the West remains at a severe disadvantage in the War of Ideas. Guilt related to colonial legacy also deters some Western governments from taking steps that may be construed as either anti-Muslim, or as signs of lingering colonialist ideology. Although statues are in force in many European countries to cope with destructive and dangerous political and racial crimes (anti-Nazi and anti-racism laws), in democratic countries no statute has ever been considered to date against religious ideologies deemed a threat to existing governments and citizens. Most of the new terrorism prevention legislation enacted in some counties depends on surveillance and subpoena powers but does not empower agencies to deal with religion-based "ideological crimes". This mindset and approach needs to be reconsidered if the West hopes to counter the unquestioned fatwas being issued calling to Muslims to take up the sword and kill infidels. As long as we are only dealing with the brainwashed Islamic soldier, and not the teacher who sent him, we will never stop the flow of terrorists planning and carrying out more attacks against us.

The conflict and struggle between competing ideologies had always been a component of total war, but in this war the US has somewhat abandoned ideological warfare, restricting its criticism to terrorists who 'got their religion wrong'. Even Bush tells us that Islam means peace, recognizing that most Muslims are not terrorists and some even disapprove (quietly) of the terrorist tactics pursued by militants. But the teachings of Islam make it quite difficult, if not impossible, for more moderate Muslims to openly wage war against the terrorists. It should be clear to any casual observer that the vast majority of Muslims instinctively rally to support fellow Muslims when they come under attack. It seems that no matter how unworthy or how violent and repressive a regime is, Muslims always prefer a bad Muslim to a good Infidel. Thus when the US attacked Afghanistan (ruled by the brutal Taliban), or Iraq (ruled by a murderous regime) Muslims all over the world protested. Saddam Hussein killed many more fellow Muslims than arch-enemy Israel ever did, yet many Muslims from all over the world volunteered to fight for him against the Coalition forces entering to liberate Muslims from the despot. What this means for America is that the war will not be effectively enjoined by any Muslim state, as even moderates cannot be counted on to support the forces of democracy against other Muslims. All we can reasonably hope for is a little bit of lip service and, hopefully, non-interference. The UN is not likely to suddenly improve its vision or develop a backbone either; it is left to us to protect ourselves.

In its affluence, peace, and untouched by the violence of 'total war' for over a half century, Americans look back with revulsion at the horror of Hiroshima, but hardly any of today's self appointed moral elitists know anything about Okinawa. Whereas the exploits of George S. Patton and Douglas MacArthur, as well as campaigns in Iwo Jima and Normandy are heralded in books and films, almost none commemorate the far greater struggle on Okinawa in three months in 1945. Few appreciate what impact the suicidal fanaticism exhibited there had on our policymakers. American forces suffered 35 percent casualties in and around Okinawa, with over 12,000 American dead, 35,000 wounded, and over 300 ships damaged or sunk. The Japanese suffered 100,000 killed (many in hand-to-hand fighting) plus an additional 100,000 civilian casualties. Okinawa is a large island but minuscule in comparison with the far better defended Japanese mainland, which facts weighed heavy on the mind of our president who faced stark predictions of over a half million expected losses likely to be incurred in a Normandy type invasion. The Enola Gay and her crew, vilified by anti-war and anti-nuclear groups worldwide, killed tens of thousands to save hundreds of thousands (if not millions) of Japanese and American lives. Ten to hundreds of lives were saved for every life taken.

In all wars emotions run high and there is danger in extremism, but in this case there is also mortal peril in naïveté. It is crystal-clear that militant Islam is at war with the US as has declared as much by writ, word, and deed, so we should cease the intellectual dishonesty and accept that by default we are at war with them. The danger is very real, and we as individuals and as a nation must choose our method of coping. The decision is a simple one …fight …or flight. The elite and peaceniks seem content to bury their heads in the sand and hope it will all go away, the rest are left with the hard task of accessing the situation and deciding how best to preserve both them and the rest of us. Both Hitler's SS troops and radical Islamic Jihadists are cut of the same totalitarian cloth. You simply cannot talk to or negotiate with a rabid dog; this sort of animal must be eradicated to insure the safety and survival of the human race.

What form will the next attack take? There is a high probability of near-term attacks on airliners using shoulder-fired anti-air missiles, probably simultaneously at several major US airports. In the first documented action against a commercial airliner outside of a war zone, a missile attack against an Israeli charter plane off the coast of Kenya in November 2002 missed its target. The incident is likely a "precursor" for anti-U.S. attacks in the future. There are hundreds of thousands of shoulder-fired missiles [MANPADs] throughout the world. In August 2003 the FBI (with assistance from Russian and British authorities) thwarted an attempt by a man with links to Al Qaeda to purchase a MANPAD in Russia and smuggle it into the United States.

The likeliest scenario would include multiple attacks against high-value/ high-casualty potential targets using the terrorist 'go-to' weapon, the truck/car/suicide bomb. If planned carefully and executed simultaneously, terrorists hope that the shock and horror would demoralize this country and result in political/military capitulation. Another scenario is an attack at a fuel terminal or depot, where a massive explosion or series of explosions could be ignited. The Valdez oil terminal in Alaska is under special protection because of intelligence suggesting that possibility. The model would be the May 23, 2002 attempt at the Pi Gilot fuel depot in Tel Aviv, Israel's largest facility, and located near heavily populated areas. Hamas terrorists strapped a bomb on a tanker truck that was detonated inside the depot. Luckily, the terrorists had chosen the wrong target — they bombed a diesel fuel truck that burned rather than exploding. Had they planned the attack better the terrorists might have killed an estimated 20-40,000 people. A strike at similar facilities in the United States, such as at the Port of Houston, would have huge human and economic costs.

Another possibility is the commandeering at sea of large tankers and rigging them with explosives, and using them to instigate a Muslim terrorist signature suicide attack at a major US port. Other possibilities include a poison attack of a major water supply center, and/or the destruction of several major dams. Attacks against large public gatherings (sports, other celebrations, or transportation hubs as happened in Madrid) are also possible. The possibility of biological or nuclear attack also grows larger daily. There are large stockpiles of nerve and biological agents in the hands of Syria, including probable recent additions from Iraq. Syria is a country that has repeatedly used Hamas as a proxy in its war against Israel and the West.

The worst possibility is, of course, the nuclear threat. The following news release highlights only the tip of the iceberg of extremist activity and the market availability of WMD's. Much more activity lies beneath the surface well hidden, and therein lies the greatest mortal danger civilization has ever faced.

(*UPI*) Nov 15 2003 - Brno, Czech Republic - Czech uranium smugglers arrested. Two Slovaks were arrested in the Czech Republic for trying to sell what appeared to be low-grade uranium, police revealed Saturday. The men were arrested Friday during a sting operation at a hotel in Brno, police told the BBC.

The men were tricked into selling the material to a plainclothes police officer, and then arrested as they counted their money in their hotel room, police said. The head of the Czech Republic's nuclear safety authority said it was most likely low-grade uranium and could not have been used to produce nuclear weapons, the BBC said. Testing on the material, however, continued Saturday. It was the largest seizure of radioactive material anywhere in the world in the last nine months, the BBC said. Officials speculated the material may have come from Russia or another country in the former Soviet Union.

Rumors persist that Al Qaeda has already obtained several nuclear weapons and is just waiting for the right moment to set them off in US cities. Front page magazine published this article of warning.

In the Feb 24, 2004 annual assessment of global threats to the Senate Intelligence Committee, CIA Director George Tenet and FBI Director Robert Mueller testified that al-Qaeda is seriously damaged but has spread its radical anti-American agenda to other Islamic extremist groups that now pose the greatest threat to the United States. *"The steady growth of Osama bin Laden's anti-U.S. sentiment through the wider Sunni (Islamic) extremist movement, and the broad dissemination of al Qaeda's destructive expertise, ensure that a serious threat will remain for the foreseeable future - with or without al Qaeda in the picture ... And what we've learned continues to validate my deepest concern - that this enemy remains intent on obtaining and using catastrophic weapons."*

Once the fanatics finally obtain one or more nuclear devices from whatever source, they must quickly use them because they cannot be held indefinitely. The fissionable material in a nuclear weapon decays rapidly, and must be replenished with freshly enriched material about every six years. Terrorists will have a weapon long before they have the ability to indefinitely maintain it, so the clock will be ticking from the moment it is in their hands. The device(s) will probably already have some time on it, and the prospect of obtaining additional weapons may be doubtful. Once obtained, it will be 'use it or lose it' for the terrorists, and no one should doubt their eagerness to set it off in a major city like Washington DC.

The timing and mechanisms are unknown, but the one thing that is certain is that by whatever method, another strike is coming. It is inevitable that terrorists will continue their efforts to attack us. The next attack is out there. It may not succeed; it may be detected and broken up, it may fail because of poor planning, poor execution, or maybe we will just get lucky, but do not doubt that it is nearing. The science of terrorism and destruction is not difficult to grasp or execute. Anyone with half a brain can find innumerable ways to destroy, kill, or maim. The victims will include Democrats and Republicans, liberals and conservatives, young and old, men and women. The sequel to that horror film "Sept 11th" is currently in production and coming soon to a theatre near you!

On September 11, 2001 we were sucker-punched and are still struggling to regain our bearing and composure. The chief task at hand since then has been in identifying and targeting enemies previously protected under the often-misguided umbrella of 'tolerance'. The 'politically correct' media remains convinced that every religion is 'right' and none are 'wrong'. Indeed it is taboo to even speak in a way that may be offensive to someone's religious sensibilities, as if laws separating church and state also apply to church and media-speech. Though many with weak moral foundations remain uncertain, continuing to wrestle with what is right and wrong, truth does indeed 'stand clear' of spin and excessive relativism. It is time to wake up from the 'ignorance-is-bliss' mentality, recognize and acknowledge the root of the problem and get into the heads of these hateful people to decide out how best to destroy their will to harm us, even if that means killing large numbers of them to convince them of the errors in their thinking and goals. The only possible successful combat strategy must focus on the entire Jihadi organization including all internal structures, the theologians setting the goals, and all social and religious values giving comfort, moral-support, and sanctuary to terrorist foot soldiers. Each act of Islamic terrorism should be viewed for what it is, a collective criminal act.

Both the executive and judicial branches of the U.S. government are essentially declaring itself to be the ultimate authority of what is truly Islamic and what is not, inadvertently providing cover to the very theology acting to destroy its protectors. With little intimate knowledge of Islamic doctrine and teachings, and almost completely ignoring recent and distant history, our government continuously attempts to sever the association between Islam and terrorism. Officials do not deny that self-proclaimed Muslims are constantly trying to kill Americans, but it stridently denies any connection between violent aggression and genuine Islam. Despite the fact that those proclaiming it are politicians, bureaucrats, judges, and other members of U.S. officialdom, such proclamations are patently false. Not everyone making such claims are being deliberately deceitful, most are simply making certain assumptions about one of the worlds largest religions, having no particular competence to decide what is or is not Islamic, and so are under-qualified to make such judgments. Officials should contain themselves and not issue opinions on what constitutes the Islamic faith and which are its true representatives. Any individual who has struggled to review the material presented herein knows much more about terrorism and Islam than all of them, and indeed probably more than most Muslims know about their own religion as well.

Hubris, defined as "outrageous arrogance", has brought down many powerful and great civilizations before. Just like the Roman Emperors and its citizenry who never imagined their most advanced society would become part of 'ancient history', Western elites display exactly the same stupid arrogance. Today there is hubris in the Senate and House of Representatives where a few, sworn to preserve and protect, visited the enemy in Iraq offering themselves as unwitting propaganda tools for dictators and despots. Recently the potential Democratic presidential candidates exacerbated the difficulties of a nation at war, all willing to weaken national resolve in hope of gaining sufficient votes from 'the convenient masses' to secure the position of 'Commander in Chief of the Armed Forces', which forces they essentially denigrate. The party suffers from myopia, seeing all kinds of far-right conspiracies, but unable (or not allowed by the 'politically correct' blinders it designed and advocates) to see the enemy poised to strike us again and again. The Democratic Party seems only equipped to protect its advantage on 'progressive' judges, the environment, abortion rights, privacy rights of terrorists, and the entitlements and delicate sensibilities of special interest groups, but otherwise seem wholly ill equipped to protect us from anything more dangerous than vague unintended insults from the 'insensitive' Republican Party. Possibly the greatest Democratic president of all time, Kennedy, understood well the perils facing the US by communist totalitarianism and was willing to risk all to stand up to it, but sadly there are no Democrats of his caliber in our day.

All the while Islam, by its very nature, remains in permanent competition with other civilizations. This theory was expounded by the Harvard political scientist Samuel Huntington, who coined the term "Islam's bloody borders" -- a reference to the fact that wherever Islam rubs up against other civilizations -- Jewish, Christian, Hindu -- wars seem to break out. His work 'Clash of Civilizations' should be required reading at high schools, colleges, and universities. Amir Tahiri, the editor of *'Politique International of Paris'* noted October 2001 that of the 30 wars going on at that time, 28 involve Muslim people fighting either non-Muslims or other Muslims. The true Islamic concept of peace goes something like this: "Peace comes through submission to Muhammad and his concept of Allah" (i.e. Islam). As such the Islamic concept of peace, meaning making the whole world Muslim, is actually a mandate for war. It was inevitable and unavoidable that the conflict would eventually reach our borders, and so it has.

Sura 9:122-123 "Believers, make war on the infidels who dwell around you. Deal firmly with them. Know that God is with the righteous".

So far we have gone to great lengths to reassure the Muslim world that we are not in a war with Islam, but only terrorists. However much of Islam understands better than our leaders do, that to fight the orthodox extremists in Islam is to fight against all that Islam holds sacred, and so in their minds we are indeed fighting Islam . But in reality we are not fighting all Muslims, just those who send, support, train, supply, fund, handle, protect, sympathize, admire, or hide Jihadic warriors worldwide. What percentage of Islam is that? A conservative estimate might be 25% of Muslims, which is still a number in the hundreds of millions. This is a huge problem any way you look at it, not likely to be solved by bombing a few camels and decrepit tanks in Afghanistan even when followed by a spectacular armored column run strait into the heart of Baghdad. In fact tens of thousands of fundamentalists, particularly their 'religious' leaders, will need to be helped into paradise to convince the rest it is in their best interest to reform their schools and abandon their terrorist ways. The most dangerous potent extremists in the world currently reside in Iran, Pakistan, Syria, and Saudi Arabia. All these nations need to be rendered impotent economically, militarily, and politically in order to cut off the head of the venomous snake poised to strike us.

If we are willing to accept our lot and protect our present and future nation, major changes will be needed in all aspects of our lives. Change is not easy, but as Thomas Jefferson once said; "*A little revolution every now and then is a good thing, it clears the atmosphere*". Jihad is not going away on its own, it needs to be helped. An awakening and 'Cultural Revolution' must first take place here before we can successfully commit to the task at hand. The set of changes and actions that could define victory are the responsibility of our military and political leaders, but require the full support and participation of every citizen who must now trust that judgment.

Much more needs to be done to dissuade Muslims from their lust to destroy the West and kill non-believers. Our current measures of providing blanket legitimacy to Muslims through the failed principals of multiculturalism and diversity will bring us more Jihad not less. Such suicidal policies will not protect us in any wit, rather they give Islamists cover to continue recruiting and planning for the demise of the very institutions currently protecting them. Unfortunately, to discuss what could be done to protect us from the next terrorist mega-attack is an exercise in futility with current political realities. Whereas no one would have thought of providing Nazi prisoners of war a personal copy of *Mein Kampf,* today we provide respect and copies of the Qur'an to interned terrorists. Then to add insult to injury, we allow our idiotic overtures to be used to discredit our own military. Almost four years since 9/11, and a multitude of Muslim terrorist activity since, still the theology that creates them remains largely immune from challenge because it calls itself a religion. In previous conflicts against totalitarianism, success meant we did not support or excuse 'moderate' Nazis, Fascists, Imperialists, or Communists ...all followers *and* supporters of the dangerous philosophies were brought low in total war. Both Hitler and his vile Nazi credos were criticized in order to defeat it. From 1933 onward, anyone wearing a swastika and reciting from *Mein Kampf* would be immediately recognized as a dangerous enemy and dealt with. Today Qur'an carriers wearing beards are given wide berth to carry on their anti-Western Jihadic crusades. When the other shoe drops, and tens of thousands to millions of Americans are dead and maimed, perhaps effective measures might yet be adopted. Until then we can present only watered down wish-lists which are bound to be defeated by CAIR, the ACLU, and all their suicidal leftist apologists.

While there are things we can do within the scope of what is currently politically feasible, there are many more things which we should, but cannot do because of suicidal leftist opposition. Some things in the latter category will likely move into the former, after the next mega-attack on American soil. But for now, I will group them all together in this synopsis, leaving it to the reader to decide what is feasible, and what is fantasy.

#1 Educate. A crystal clear grasp on reality would provide a tremendous boost to assist beleaguered Western civilizations. To achieve that, University and High-School student text material needs to be purged of anti-American, anti-democratic, and pro-Islamic propaganda. Real history relating to communist, socialist, and Islamic histories should be taught in a dispassionate, accurate manner. Americans need to be taught how to recognize all totalitarian theologies and identify their various means of brainwashing the general public. The true history of Muhammad caravan raiding tactics, his political achievements, and his methods of assassination and Jihad need to be comprehensively and fearlessly exposed. This also provided the added benefit of preventing immature young people from becoming the unwitting tools of today's Islamists.

#2 Prosecute. Under Rico and other laws designed to protect this country from the promotion of seditious acts designed to overthrow civil society, arrest and imprison anyone advocating Jihad against both Americans and our allies. Relentlessly prosecute treason, sedition, racketeering, inciting to violence, and hate-speech crimes perpetrated by Muslim leaders and lay. Seize property, including mosques, of any individual or group found promoting violence and bigotry. Once their prison term is up, the same individuals need to be exported to their country of origin. The first phase of this 'extremist' round-up would include all Wahhabi assets and leaders.

#3 Respond. The claim that violence begets violence is not always true. In fact well executed, professional violence works quite well when the other party has been sufficiently subdued, especially if they are dead. Just witness the behavior of dhimmi in Islamic lands. Hands must be untied to be able to strike with the kind of lethality required to finish the ugly task and put it behind us. Those not willing to live as slaves must be willing to execute greater violence than those trying to enslave them. Islamists are executing methods of 'total war' while we worry incessantly about 'Arab opinion', and 'collateral damage'. Our current 'hands-off' policy towards the government and forces of Syria and Iran, while they provide considerable support to Jihadists worldwide, is reminiscent of the failed Korean and Viet Nam military policies. The enemies of freedom anxiously seek to enter the next world to receive their reward for their hatred and efforts to kill non-believers, and we must as quickly as possible expedite that journey for them. That may sound like warmongering, but it is simply a practical reality of survival to kill creatures threatening your family with cold calculation. The dogs of war must be unleashed to convince not only Jihadists, but all social/religions institutions supporting them, that terrorist policies will bring unacceptable consequences. They are going to hate Americans and Jews no matter what we do, so we might as well follow policies that will actually destroy our enemies and their supporters, instead of vainly trying to win some sort of popularity contest.

I also proffer the following suggestions. They may seem extreme now, but hearts will change if and when enough pain and death has been visited upon this people, so they are offered here in advance of that consensus:

1. The President should clearly and unequivocally identify the Islamic threat and Congress officially declare war on all groups and governments promoting Islamic Jihad against America or her allies, or who in any way support, justify, or enable terrorist threats and acts. Habeas Corpus should be suspended for all matters related to national security (as Lincoln did in the Civil War). We must not allow liberal weasels from the ACLU, whacked-out tree huggers or an activist interfering Judiciary to obstruct the execution of the war.

2. Retroactively reclassify Islam from a religious organization to the socio-political organization it is, subject to all the taxes, rules and laws of political organizations. Move to control Muslim schools. Socrates was quite correct when he warned "Ignorance is the mother of all ills". Islamic clergy and texts should be outlawed in our prison systems, including Gitmo. Other works glorifying treason, rape, murder, and thievery are not allowed, Islam should be no different.

3. Extend, strengthen, and enlarge the 'Patriot Act' to allow vetting of all Muslim Americans and all immigrants from Islamic lands, including penalties for municipalities who fail to support it. Profiling is good, monitoring of Muslim mosques and imams is smart. This should not bother any true patriots who have nothing to hide. Japanese and German citizens were not allowed to immigrate during World War II. Its dangerous to allow people from Arab and Moslem nations to immigrate. The borders should be shut down, with broader legal work/immigration policies implemented for friendly (non-Muslim) foreigners.

4. The CIA should recruit and create an army of indigenous operatives to infiltrate all organizations suspected of planning harm to our nation. How hard can it be to memorize parts of the Qur'an, bow 5 times a day, praise Allah, grow a beard, spew anti-Jew/American invectives on cue, and (god willing) shoot an AK47. These recruits should not be Muslims, but very knowledgeable of Muhammad (peace be upon him).

5. Bite the bullet and shut down Iran's oil economy with a blockade. Iranian Oil is a main funding source for Islamic aggression and expansion worldwide. Also fund and support indigenous opposition groups in Iran with weapons and, if necessary, air support.

6. More quickly build up the police and national military forces in Iraq, wish them luck in maintaining a democracy, then leave. Recognize the 'Marshal Plan' will not work in Islamic lands, and stop trying

to buy friends. The people deeply resent help from inferior Infidels and will not develop a sudden case of gratitude and become our best friends like Japan and Germany. Let Iraq rebuild borrowing against future oil sales.

7. Terminate all aid to Iraq, Palestinians, Egypt, Jordan, Somalia, Algeria, Sudan, Pakistan, Kosovo, Afghanistan, Albania, Indonesia, and any other Islamic nation who persecutes non-believers. Pour the Jizya aid we now give them into emergent democracies, and under the still infallible 'Monroe Doctrine', the Americas. Assist the good people of Russia with troops and material in their war in Chechnya. Warn Pakistan, Egypt, and Saudi Arabia that continued friendly relations with the US absolutely depends on an immediate and comprehensive reformation of their schools as well as all new religious leaders abandoning Jihadic concepts. Warn first, and then if they are not serious about reform, seize all assets.

8. Forget the EU, forget the UN, and completely rework NATO cutting out France, Turkey, and Germany. Withdraw all support and funding to the UN and send the inept diplomats packing with their flags in tow. Withdraw all forces from Western Europe, leaving the Bosnian/Serbian/Kosovo problem to the 'morally superior' French. Under a new framework, sign all new military alliances with Great Britain, Russia, Poland, Italy, Australia, India, Japan, the Philippines, and other friendly nations.

9. Assign an all new 75¢/gal tax on gasoline/diesel to drive down demand and fund the following:

    a. Require development of oil reserves in Alaska, offshore, and elsewhere. Support and subsidize new and expanded Coal and Nuclear energy sources. Nuclear power plants are much less polluting anyway.

    b. Invest in fusion research with the goal of harnessing the power of the helium3 (via lunar mining) or the hydrogen molecule to generate electrical power. $D + 3He \rightarrow p(14.7 \text{ MeV}) + 4He (3.7 \text{ MeV}) + 18.4 \text{ MeV}$

    c. Create more incentives for oil/gas conservation like car pooling, higher efficiency engines, braking regeneration/conservation, lighter/stronger vehicles employing smaller engines, more efficient methods of mass transit, capturing solar/wind/water potential, etc ect.

10. Open another front against the other tool Islam uses to both weaken us and finance its efforts. Open a front against drug use and drug pushers. Educate citizens on how proceeds are used to fund terrorist activity, and call for volunteers to fight the war on terror and drugs. Stiffen penalties for those who profit in despair, and provide more help getting young people off their dependencies.

11. Rework START to allow the US, Russia, and other friendly allies to both dominate space and rework their nuclear arsenals, including spares for replenishing weapons expended in wartime. If it proves that the Islamic threat becomes unmanageable by other methods, a huge stealth armada of hydrogen and neutron bombs should be developed and deployed in orbit, while at the same time preemptively shooting down any space asset launched from unfriendly countries who will not guarantee verifiable non-nuclear ambitions. Mechanisms can be built into the weapons to physically prevent their use against friendly countries.

12. It should be made clear to all nations that the US will respond to nuclear or biological attacks, not in kind, but with such force to destroy all nations and peoples deemed remotely culpable or even sympathetic to acts of terror and genocide against us. It should be denoted the new YAD doctrine (as opposed to MAD), which stands for 'Your Assured Destruction'.

These proposals require courage, vision, sacrifice, and a complete changing of the 'politically correct' guard. The voice of pacifists will sound shrill as ever, but as Islamic violence continues to expand, patience for ignorance and fools will grow short with increasing knowledge of the goals of terrorist foot soldiers, and awareness of the hoards of Muslims cheering them on from the sidelines. The sleeping giant stirred briefly after Sept 11th, but slumbers still. That giant may soon be forced to awaken …for if not he will surely die in his sleep.

In taking measures to protect ourselves and dissuade governments supporting Muslim militants, we should not be so arrogant as to think such actions will end the huge problem of Jihad for all peoples and places, especially for the billions trapped by the cult in majority Islamic countries. When Muslims see that their philosophy is flawed and their God cannot help them, it will be but the first small step in the long process of Islam's eventual ruin and subsequent reformation. In reality Islam can only be brought down from within, by men such as *Ali Sina* who runs a site to help his fellows see the error of their ways, and who offer the 21st century equivalent of a 'freedom train' to assist those wanting to escape the misery of its spiritual slavery (visit www.faithfreedom.org). After all the death and misery, the end of the danger which Islam brings to the world will come at the hands of good Muslims following conscience over Islam. As we act against militants and their supporters, every effort should be made to support all *legitimate* freedom movements in Islamic lands.

Epilog

Dark Premonitions

(revised from a Feb 6, 2003 NRO article by John Derbyshire, with permission)

Am not sure quite what's going on, or what drives me to pursue this work. Possibly the Sympathetic Fallacy is playing tricks with my soul. Still, I hope at springtime to open a window to hear birds and smell flowers, but know those sweet simple sensory images will likely seem surreal once again this year. The air has been sort of quiet lately, but such serene relief is fleeting as something keeps whispering it is only the calm before the storm. It is not quite visible with the naked eye, but one can sense a force like 'The Nothing', that malevolent entity in the *'Never Ending Story'*, nibbling at the edges and poised at any moment to gobble up our entire world. I fear that, as Myers says, we may be sailing off the edge of the world, into the realm of chaos. Don't get me wrong, I have no specific cause to be obsessed with apprehension. As a single father of several young children I am much too busy to waste thought and energy chasing ghosts or slaying windmills. Perhaps it is too much reading J. R. Tolken and C. S. Lewis that put me in this frame of mind, or pushed me deeper into it, or perhaps it is the endless string of news releases filled with violent manifestations cascading down my consciousness and sucking hope dry. Masked terrorists on TV resemble too much the dreaded 'Uruk Hais' of Saruman the White in *'Lord of the Rings'*. All these crazed, mindless groups acting in lock-step waging Jihad seem exactly like minions of the 'Borg Collective' …intending to assimilate our society. The phrase *'resistance is futile'* disturbs both my dreams and drifts into daytime thoughts.

Anyway, it didn't start like that. In the numbness following Sept 11th my spirit self-comforted with the idea that truth, right and the American way would prevail once again, believing every foe would soon repent or be destroyed. Then I read a piece by Paul Johnson in the Spectator reprinted below, its first sentence reading as follows: "The sound of the explosion was so loud, so prolonged, and so unusual that I knew at once I was listening to a historical singularity." There followed a great wind sweeping over his London house, in the library of which he was sitting, and something that felt like an earthquake.

Stepping up to the flat roof of his house, he saw "destruction on an immense scale." He saw London being consumed by a vast swelling ball of fire and smoke. It is all described with terrific fluency and vividness, in just a thousand words, with the skill that comes easily to a man who has written a shelf-full of thick books and innumerable pieces of throwaway journalism. What he is seeing is the detonation of a hydrogen bomb, a megaton-scale nuclear weapon. "As the darkness increased and the compensating fire drew nearer, I grasped that the catastrophe would soon swallow up my house and me, too..." In the last paragraph, of course, he wakes up. Johnson's nightmare was the more striking because he normally doesn't write like that at all. A levelheaded, practical sort of fellow, worldly and very knowledgeable about politics, he usually has his feet firmly on the ground. Johnson's dream still lingers, buried in the nether portions of my consciousness, ready to reappear like a sudden thunderstorm to ruin any bright sunny feelings.

Then there is the stuff about wacko North Korea having nukes, and reports of Iranian Mullahs receiving streams of prominent representatives from the Muslim world like a wedding reception, all paying honor and seeking favor for some achievement of nuclear proportions. Libya also, had mature programs previously well hidden until recently revealed, and Syria may have inherited the bulk of forbidden Iraqi arsenals and programs. Thinking about that, it dawned on me, as it has on many others, that there has been some qualitative change in world affairs. In the past, scary as it was, all nuclear nations had long histories, and ancient imperial or grand-republican political traditions - traditions, that is, of responsible governance. None of them was fundamentally nihilistic, with a desire to do mischief in the world just for its own sake. That state of affairs went on for decades, and lulled us into thinking it was permanent.

It wasn't. The genie is now out of the bottle. Now nutcase nations or pseudo-nations like North Korea and Pakistan have nukes, and the base principle upon which deterrence is based, which served us so well since 1949, has broken down. Deterrence only works with responsible people, people who give a damn, and who, if they plan conquest, plan it the old fashioned way - armies, battlefields. It is useless against Mohammed Atta, or any nation that cares to use his sort as proxies.

Well, those were the lines I was thinking along. Then I started to notice how many other people were thinking the same way. "Thinking" is actually the wrong word. This isn't something thought so much as something felt, something in the air. And what I really didn't like a bit was that the people who are thinking it are people I have found to be pretty reliable guides to what is going on in the world. The things people say in conversation nowadays! - things like: "It'll take another 9/11...". And then there is the image of the guy living on Long Island, waving his arm at the busy suburban landscape beyond the window of a diner, and saying: "When New York City's been taken out, all this real estate will be worth zip." Nobody talked like that ten, five years ago. Nobody even *thought* those things.

Is something unspeakably horrible going to happen? I don't know for certain. I'm only saying that there is something in the air - a grimness, a *bracing*. Perhaps I'm just scaring myself over nothing. As in all times, the future casts its shadow over the past helping us to forget it, but the past ever projects its image into the future to form it. I can't shake off the feeling that we are living, right now, in that chill shadow cast from recent and distant Islamic history. Surly we have come to the end of a golden age of relative peace and security, and there are nasty things lurking in the not too distant future. Is chaos the only option left for our great Western society obsessed as we are with consumption and self-absorption?

Look at us! Look at the gross vulgar overflowing fat wealth we live amongst! Look at the great cars that 20-year-old kids drive 300 yards to the mall, to buy things they don't need, gadgets to pack into houses already overflowing with gadgets, clothes to cram into closets stuffed with clothes. Look at the work we do, sitting in humming cubicles scrolling through screens full of words and numbers as our wealth grows. Look at the bright, airy schools our kids attend, to be taught that their ancestors were moral criminals, their parents are liars, and their culture is a sham. Look at our popular heroes, all self-absorbed rock stars, sports icons, or made for movie fantasy personalities. Look at our "reality TV" programs, where people with empty heads wallow in infantile hedonism. Look at our fool politicians and diplomats, pouring over their poll numbers and UN resolutions, playing tug-of-war with pork while young men with burning eyes slip silently into our cities with boxes, canisters, cargoes, vials, and suitcases curiously heavy.

As they arrive at our unprotected borders, while entertainment Icons live in a make-believe world continue using their popular influence to undermine national values. Hollywood weenies like Martin Sheen and Sean Penn rake in millions playing soldiers in films like "Apocalypse Now" and "Casualties of War" and then, in real life, give the finger to those who really wear the uniform and risk all to defend us. Violent rappers get rich issuing songs like "Cop Killer", and "Die, die, die, pig, die! Fuck the police!". Michael Moore denigrates all of us in his hate America propaganda film "Fahrenheit 9/11". The elite from among us (Actor, Artist, Intellectual, Union leader, Tenured Faculty, Judge, Lawyer, ACLU, and powerful advocacy groups including left-leaning media) arrogantly live their lives demanding the full measure of entitlements and freedoms paid for by the blood of the kind of men they disparage. Young people at universities regurgitate excessive relativism leaving campus with no core, no love of country, and no willingness to sacrifice for it.

For decades now we have selfishly chased vanity, postponing and/or limiting our offspring, thus limiting the available pool of young men and women we wish to call upon now for our protection. Is there enough, are they strong enough? One wonders why Osama bothered to create such a fracas to kill 3000, and why he did not simply sit back and watch with satisfaction as we continue to do it to ourselves, on a scale orders of magnitude higher, using the arbitrary tool of abortion. From the surviving young who do walk amongst us, premonition often prompts me to look hard into their eyes and hearts searching for strength, but probing the windows into their souls has revealed a vast cavernous emptiness bringing little comfort. Look at this proud tower! And feel its foundations tremble.

There Arose out of the Pit of Smoke a Great Furnace

by Paul Johnson (7 Dec 2002)

The sound of the explosion was so loud, so prolonged and so unusual that I knew at once I was listening to a historic singularity. Indeed, it may not have been an explosion: more a catastrophic global event. Was it the end of the world? As the initial noise fell in volume, though it did not cease, a pentecostal wind swept over my house in Notting Hill. It faces north into the street, and the air current came from the south, as I could see from the trees bending over in our south-facing garden. I was sitting in my library, in my habitual chair near the French windows, and was astonished to see fallen leaves plastered on to them and held there by the fierce wind. Then I felt movement. It was not like an earthquake, which I had experienced in South America. In such tremors parts of the earth's crust crack and move in relation to each other, to produce disorientation and dizziness. It was, rather, as if the entire earth moved, as a unit, but out of its regular axis.

Despite the feeling of movement, I went to the bottom of the stairs and began to climb them, up to the top floor, where a glass door in my bathroom leads out to a flat roof. It was midday, but I became uneasily conscious that I was ascending not into light but into darkness. There was no disturbance inside the house and the roof door opened easily. But once I stepped outside I knew I was in a different world, and that the constants of the old, familiar one had changed utterly. The noise continued but spasmodically, ranging in its decibels and nature in an erratic and unpredictable fashion. It was now, audibly, the noise of destruction on an immense scale. The wind, too, came in gusts. I feared the wind. I was beginning to fear everything. The light, or rather the comparative absence of light, was sinister. To the north, the sky was blue, yet there was no daylight. The light was thickening. When I glanced south, into central London, I saw why, and I began to get, for the first time, an inkling of what was taking place.

The whole of the southern view was occupied by a dense, swirling, expanding and ascending column of smoke. It was many miles wide and already tens of thousands of feet high. Though five miles distant at its nearest (I guessed), it was moving with great speed, not so much horizontally as vertically. It was punching a colossal hole in the sky, filling it, then finding fresh energy to punch another, so that at intervals the column was encircled by giant haloes, stretching out vast distances into the stratosphere. I could not see the top of the central column. It was covered by one of these haloes, which was now stretching into the northern portion of the sky, so producing that progressive light reduction I had already noticed. I call the column smoke, and some of it was smoke — the result of a giant conflagration — but most of it was dense, throbbing, twisting cloud, white and grey vapour, of the kind emitted by the steam-engines of my childhood but on an unimaginable scale. How had so much water — or whatever it once was — been turned so swiftly into trillions of square yards of foggy miasma, still piling itself up at high speed into the stratosphere and beyond? What incalculable force had done this monstrous thing?

As my eye fell to the bottom of the column, I began to grasp the source of its power. A white incandescence, low by comparison with the column but still perhaps a mile high and 20 or more broad, filled the skyline of the south horizon. Its fiery heat mitigated the gloom caused by the towering cloud above obscuring the sun. As my eyes grew accustomed to looking at this radiant epicenter, I saw that it was composed not only of white-hot elements, but also of fiery red particles, orange and blue flames, shooting heavenwards like the gigantic tongues which leap out of sunspots thousands of miles into space. There were also sporadic flashes of white, caused, I assumed, by continuing detonations on a stupendous scale. The epicenter was spreading steadily; or rather not entirely steadily, for it moved in spurts and formidable leaps, as well as munching and digesting its periphery. It was alive, this prodigious sore or cancer in London's heart, expanding its frontiers all the time. It had swallowed and vaporized all Westminster, and sucked out the entire contents of the Thames and turned them into thick clouds. It had gone down the river at thousands of miles an hour, engulfed the City and its tall towers, vaporizing steel, concrete, glass and water as it punched and thrashed and pounded the streets of massive buildings into nothingness — or, rather, minute particles of its flaming column, surging high into space. Now it was crumpling and atomizing St James's.

The glittering, searing edge of the immense fire, with its bottomless black crater beneath, advanced before my eyes, having snuffed out Buckingham Palace and the Mall in an instant, snapped at Mayfair with cavernous jaws, swallowing it in three rapidly succeeding mouthfuls, while simultaneously devouring all Belgravia in one tremendous gulp. Appetite unappeased and seemingly unappeasable, it was now guzzling up Hyde Park, its trees whooshing into brief candles of flame, the Serpentine quaffed and vaporized in an instant, the Round Pond licked away in one fiery rub of its tongue.

As the darkness increased and the compensating fire drew nearer, I grasped that the catastrophe would soon swallow up my house and me, too. This was not an episode, like an earthquake, leaving a giant print on the earth in a minute of time, but more like a volcano, spreading its lava with all deliberate speed over a vast area. How many billions of tons of high-explosive equivalent had gone into what I assumed to be the detonator, at ground level, of an enormous hydrogen device, I could not guess. Yet, surely, even the largest blast conceivable must be of limited duration, and its immediate physical consequences reckoned in minutes, not hours or days. But there was no sign yet of an end, or even a diminuendo.

I suddenly noticed that I was not alone. At my feet, or very near them, was a curious congregation of creatures. First, there was a fat wood-pigeon, who usually gives me the widest of berths for he knows he is not a favorite. He was motionless, cowering, his feathers dank and bedraggled as though he was in a cold sweat. There was a crow I had never seen before, more composed than the pigeon and looking about him with alert eyes. There was the hen-thrush, who nested in the tree a few feet from my study window this year and produced a brood: no sign of them — flown off, perhaps, already — and she was clearly frightened, too. Above all — and I was strangely comforted to see him — was Randolf, or Randy, my audacious squirrel, not bold now, however, but sitting stock-still in terror, waiting for a doom which he could not evade by flight. It suddenly struck me that these varied creatures, enemies or competitors as a rule, were crowding together for comfort, and looked to me for salvation. But how was I, or anyone, to render help in this Armageddon, or apocalypse?

At that point I became aware that my eyes were open, and focused on family photos near the foot of my bed, all steady and correct. Behind my head, my beautiful crucifix, carved by a holy monk in the hardest of woods, hung motionless, not a millimeter out of place. The sun was wintry, but it shone nevertheless.

References

[1]. Mir, Mustansir, "Dictionary of Qur'anic Terms and Concepts", Garland, New York, NY, 1987.
[2]. Jeffery, Arthur, "Islam: Muhammad and His Religion", Bobs Merril
[3]. "Encyclopedia of Islam", published by Brill, Leiden, The Netherlands.
[4]. Warraq, Ibn. What The Koran Really Says, Amherst, N.Y., 2002, pp. 67-69.
[5]. Muslim, Abu'l-Husain, "Sahih Muslim", translated by A. Siddiqi, International Islamic Publishing House, Riyadh, Saudi Arabia, 1971 [Internet version available at: www.usc.edu/dept/MSA/fundamentals/hadithsunnah/muslim]
[6]. al-Tabari, "Ta'rikh al-rusul wa'l-muluk", (The History of al-Tabari), volume 8, State University of New York Press, 1997.
[7]. Ibn Ishaq, (d.782), "Sirat Rasulallah", compiled by A. Guillaume as "The Life of Muhammad", Oxford, London, 1955
[8]. Sell, Canon, "The Historical Development of the Qur'an", published by People International.
[9]. Bukhari, Muhammad, "Sahih Bukhari", Kitab Bhavan, New Delhi, India, 1987, translated by M. Khan [Internet version available at: www.usc.edu/dept/MSA/fundamentals/hadithsunnah/muslim/]
[10]. Kassis, Hanna, "Concordance of the Qur'an", University of California Press, Los Angeles, CA, 1983.
[11]. "Shorter Encyclopedia of Islam", edited by H.A.R. Gibb, published by Brill, Leiden, The Netherlands.
[12]. Ibn Kathir, "Tafsir of Ibn Kathir" published by Al-Firdous, New York, NY, 2000.
[13]. "Reliance of the Traveler", (A Classic Manual of Islamic Sacred Law), by Ahmad al-Misri, translated by Nuh Ha Mim Keller, published by Amana publications, Beltsville, Maryland, USA 1991, 1997
[14]. Ibn Abi Zayd al-Qayrawani, La Risala (Epitre sur les elements du dogme et de la loi de l'Islam selon le rite malikite.) Translated from Arabic by Leon Bercher. 5th ed. Algiers, 1960, p. 165. [English translation, in Bat Ye'or, The Decline of Eastern Christianity Under Islam, Cranston, NJ, 1996, p. 295]
[15]. Ibn Taymiyyah, in Rudolph Peters, Jihad in Classical and Modern Islam, (Princeton, NJ. : Markus Wiener, 1996, p. 49)
[16]. From the Hidayah, vol. Ii. P. 140, in Thomas P. Hughes, "A Dictionary of Islam," "Jihad" Pp. 243-248. (London, United Kingdom.: W.H. Allem, 1895).
[17]. Al- Mawardi, The Laws of Islamic Governance [al-Ahkam as-Sultaniyyah, (London, United Kingdom.: Ta-Ha, 1996, p. 60).
[18]. Ibn Khaldun, "The Muqudimmah. An Introduction to History," Translated by Franz Rosenthal. (New York, NY.: Pantheon, 1958, vol. 1, p. 473).
[19]. Khadduri, Majid. War and Peace in the Law of Islam, 1955, Richmond, VA and London, England, pp. 63-64.
[20]. Tibi, Bassam. "War and Peace in Islam" in The Ethics of War and Peace: Religious and Secular Perspectives, edited by Terry Nardin, 1996, Princeton, N.J., pp. 129-131.
[21]. Ibn Sa'd, (d. 852 A.D.), "Kitab al-Tabaqat al-Kabir", (Book of the Major Classes), translated by S. Moinul Haq, Pakistan Historical Society
[22]. Dashti, Ali, "23 Years: A Study in the Prophetic Career of Mohammad", Mazda, Costa Mesa, CA, 1994. Translated by F.R.C. Bagley
[23] Wensinck, A., "Muhammad and the Jews of Medina", pub. by K. S. V.
[24]. WILLIAM MUIR, ESQ. "THE LIFE OF MAHOMET. VOLUME III" [Smith, Elder, & Co., London, 1861], Chapter 13 (http://www.answering-islam.org/Books/Muir/Life3/chap13.htm)
[25]. Abu Dawud, Suliman, "Sunan", al-Madina, New Delhi, 1985, translated by A. Hasan [Internet version available at: www.usc.edu/dept/MSA/fundamentals/hadithsunnah/abudawud]
[26]. Ayoub, Mahmoud, "The Qur'an and Its Interpreters" vol. II - The House of Imran, Albany, N.Y.; State University of New York Press, 1992
[27]. Payne, Robert, "The History of Islam", Dorset Press, New York, 1990
[28]. Fregosi, Paul, "Jihad", Prometheus Books, Amherst, New York, 1998
[29]. Amir Taheri: "Holy Terror", Sphere Books, London, 1987
[30]. Ayako Sono "Arabu-no Kakugen" (Arabic maxims) published by Shinchosha, 2001
[31]. Stephen Schwartz, "Terrorism: Growing Wahhabi Influence in the United States," testimony before the U.S. Senate Committee on the Judiciary, June 26, 2003, www.globalsecurity.org/security/library/congress/2003_h/030626-schwartz.htm
[32]. Report in the San Ramon Valley Herald; quoted by Daniel Pipes in CAIR: Moderate Friends of Terror, New York Post, April 22, 2002.
[33]. Gairdner, W.H.T. "Mohammed Without Camouflage", Moslem World, 1919, Vol. 9, pp. 51-52.
[34]. Ibn Hudayl (French translation by Louis Mercier), L'ornement des âmes, Paris, 1939, p. 195.
[35]. Dufourcq, A.D. La Vie Quotidienne dans l'Europe Medievale sous Domination Arabe, Paris, 1978, p. 20.
[36]. Al-Mawardi, The Laws of Islamic Governance, trans. by Dr. Asadullah Yate, London, 1996, p. 192.
[37]. Abu Yusuf Ya'qub Le Livre de l'impot foncier, Translated from Arabic and annotated by Edmond Fagnan, Paris, Paul Geuthner, 1921, pp. 301-302.
[38]. Ibn Abi Zayd Al_Qayrawani, La Risala ou Epitre sur les elements du dogme et de la loi de l'Islam selon le rite malikite, Translated from Arabic by Leon Bercher. Algiers, 1980, p. 163.
[39]. Ibn Taymiyya, in Rudolph Peters, Jihad in Classical and Modern Islam, Princeton, NJ, 1996, p. 50.
[40]. Ibn Khaldun, History of the Berbers and the Moslem Dynasties of Northern Africa, translated from Arabic [into French] by Baron De Slane, Paris, 1925, p. 316.
[41]. Al Kufi, from The Chachnama, in Elliott and Dowson, A History of India As Told by Its Own Historians, Vol. 1, 1867-1877, (reissued 2001) p. 181.
[42]. from, the translation of Malfuzat-i-Timuri of Timur, A History of India As Told by Its Own Historians, Vol. 3, pp. 435-436.
[43]. from, The Baburnama -Memoirs of Babur, Prince and Emperor, translated and edited by Wheeler M. Thacktson, Oxford University Press,1996, p. 188.
[44]. Averroes, in Rudolph Peters, Jihad in Classical and Modern Islam, Princeton, NJ, 1996, p. 36.
[45]. Al-Ghazali (d. 1111). Kitab al-Wagiz fi fiqh madhab al-imam al-Safi'i, Beirut, 1979, pp. 186, 190-91, [English translation by Dr. Michael Schub.]

[46]. Ibn Taymiyya, in Jihad in Classical and Modern Islam, 1996, p.49.
[47]. Chronique de Jean, Eveque de Nikiou, translated from the Ethiopian with notes by Hermann Zotenberg, Paris, 1879, pp. 228-229; 243-244.
[48]. From O. Tafrali, O. Thessalonique – Des Origines au XVI Siecle, Chapter VI "The Capture and Pillage of Thessalonika by the Saracens (in the year 904)", pp. 151-154.
[49]. Segal, J.B. "Edessa- The Blessed City", Oxford University Press, 1970, pp. 252-254
[50]. Chronique de Michel Le Syrien, Edited and translated from the Syriac by Jean-Baptiste Chabot, Paris, 1899-1905, Vol. 3, pp. 261-262; 270-271.
[51]. Hirschberg, H.Z., The Jews of North Africa, Leiden, Vol. 1, 1974, pp. 127-128.
[52]. Kanhadade Prabandha, translated, introduced and annotated by V.S. Bhatnagar, New Delhi, 1991, xii.
[53]. Kanhadade Prabandha, p. 49.
[54]. Ibn Battuta, in Foreign Notices of South India, Collected and Edited by K.A. Nilakanta Sastri (2001, University of Madras), pp. 278-279
[55]. Vryonis, S. Jr., A Critical Analysis of Stanford J. Shaw's, "History of the Ottoman Empire and Modern Turkey. Volume 1. Empire of the Gazis: The Rise and Decline of the Ottoman Empire, 1280-1808", off print from Balkan Studies, Vol. 24, 1983, pp. 57-60,62,68.
[56]. Vryonis, S. Jr., A Critical Analysis, pp. 58-59.
[57]. Vryonis, S. Jr., A Critical Analysis, p. 59.
[58]. Vryonis, S. Jr., A Critical Analysis, pp. 60, 62.
[59]. Vryonis, S. Jr., A Critical Analysis, p.68.
[ref]. "The Nobel Qur'an", translated by Dr. Muhammad Taqi-ud-Din Al-Hilali and Dr. Muhammad Muhsin Khan, published by Maktaba Dar-us-Salam, PO Box 21441, Riyadh 11475, Saudi Arabia, 1994. [Internet version available at: www.witness-pioneer.org/vil]
[ref]. Dawood, N. J., "The Koran", Penguin, London, England, 1995
[ref]. Gatje, Helmut, "The Qur'an and its Exegesis", Oneworld, Oxford, England, 1997
[ref]. Rodwell, J. M., "The Koran", by, published by Everyman, London, England
[ref]. Ali, Yusef, "The Holy Qur'an", published by Amana, Beltsville, Maryland, USA, 1989 [Internet version available at: www.usc.edu/dept/MSA/quran]
[ref]. Asad, Muhammad , "The Message of the Qur'an", Dar Al-Andaulus, Gibraltar, 1980

About the Author

Many years ago, performing a multi-year service mission in a foreign country, I had the occasion to discuss religious concepts with many practicing Muslims. Not long afterwards I had a university study partner who was a devout Muslim from Lebanon, and we had several discussions concerning the Qur'an (a.k.a. Koran) and Islam. Our relationship was typical and warm, but later became strained following a bombing in Israel. In a discussion I learned he would be happy to use his degree in electrical engineering (acquired at tax-payer expense) to facilitate killing Jews upon his return home. Prior to that, my family enjoyed the company of three Muslim University students from Jordan we call friends today, some staying at our home, none of whom seemed capable of such thinking. My father, stepmother, and their siblings spent 10 years living and working in Dhahran, Saudi Arabia. While living there, my father visited Afghanistan several times, traveled to Yemen, Iran, Abu Dhabi, Bahrain, Quatar, Kuwait, Oman, Srinagar, India, Beirut, Damascus, Indonesia, Sri Lanka, all over Saudi Arabia and have had many discussions with Muslims about their perception of the US and the West. In all cases the young men (young women are unapproachable by edict and mandate), although not expressing animosity toward any particular Westerner personally, had problems with Western nations, peoples, and cultures in general, and all had a deep irrational hatred of all Jews. My father tells me that he learned there are many decent Muslims in the world, including many he now calls personal friends.

An engineer by trade, I have also been a student of history and have studied in some depth various religious philosophies throughout my life. I have also visited Israel four times, and have taken the time to learn from both the Israeli and Arab points of view religious concepts and perspectives relating to the ongoing conflicts in the region. I have tried to be open-minded and to make friends with both Muslims and Jews. My contacts include merchants, some religious leaders, and even Israeli military officers from whom I have attempted to understand their perspectives and passions. I was especially impressed attending a huge celebration of 'Purim' in Tel Aviv on my own where numerous young people and whole families danced and socialized. As an obvious outsider I remember feeling very safe amongst the many young people at that event, the same way feel attending church-sponsored youth social events at home. I did not observe the usual trappings of gothic, gang, punk, or other threatening paraphernalia that accompany public events in the US. For whatever reason, generations of Israelis seem more cohesive than Americans. My overall impressions were that Israelis are a competent, family oriented, a hard working and industrious people generally disposed to treat others well. My dealings with Palestinians also showed me they are generally intelligent, hard working, and family oriented. To me it seemed that both groups of common people would prefer to avoid war, however the distrust and paranoia of each toward the other is great, based as it is on the long litany of conflicts with no end in sight. Aside from these and some other limited contacts, the author admits that his experience with Muslims is otherwise limited.

As mentioned earlier I am an engineer by training and trade, and as with many of that discipline comes a certain inclination and aptitude to disassemble every problem to its most basic root-form components as the first step in the problem solving process. After Sept 11th, 2001, it became apparent that few were searching for the root cause of the war declared on us, and my natural curiosity and a certain passion has driven me to explore in some detail the true source driving the varied violent acts of Islamic zealots. My studies have revealed unexpected data, which it appears is not widely known, or is often very much misunderstood. The initial curiosity and effort was to identify for myself just exactly where and how Muslim militants erred in deviating from peaceful Islam by choosing a violent path. Much to my chagrin, I could not discover any error, only support. As it turns out, it's not the wrong interpretation of the Qur'an (Koran) that produces terrorists; it is the *exact* interpretation of it which creates them. These findings, and the inescapable inferences that must be drawn thereby, served to inspire this effort to share this vital knowledge with my fellow citizens. This book, considered in its entirety, could and *should* alter convictions and politics for the sincere searcher of truth and knowledge of all political persuasions.

At the risk of alienating some, I must now delve into personal opinion, and even politics. It has been difficult to present this material factually, avoiding (or trying to avoid) personal opinion. I admit that separating my personal emotion from the passion, pain, and sorrow connected with all I have learned has been difficult, surely my feelings have leaked out all over. But now I must reveal my whole heart, the stakes being as high as they are. The issue, survival, should not be not politicized, but it is. Although I am a conservative Democrat at heart, I can no longer support the current direction of a National Democratic party that is largely ignorant of the nature and scope of the Islamic threat. It seems more a coalition of fringe myopic special interest groups than a truly National Party, none of whom seem to grasp the threat of militant Islam. My once great Party fell ill at the time of Jimmy Carter, our fierce peanut farmer appeaser, became morally and mortally ill with Clinton at the helm, and lost its heartbeat completely following the Gore Campaign. Great men like Zell Miller notwithstanding, nothing has come from the once great representative party since but the awful stench of moral death. Suffering from Hubris, it slips noisily into irrelevance, the entire country forced to endure shrill hateful screams of frustration from the likes of Al Gore, Ted Kennedy, Michael Moore, Howard Dean, and John Kerry. My hope is that reasonable people will seize the party back from the fringe of lunacy and make it great again.

A personal note to any truly pious Muslims who feel their faith is compromised by the truths and logic outlined herein. The truth, from the mouths of your leaders yesterday and today, is surly a bitter pill to swallow, but please accept the reality staring you in the face and balance it against what your heart tells you is good, true, just, and right. Truth can be hard to contemplate, but when humbly accepted it will always be redeeming and cleansing. For those inclined to believe in deity, God is still God, and surely is not threatened. His existence and plans do not depend on the man Muhammad. To all believers of a caring creator, there is no God, but God, …and God is indeed greatest! But such a Creator must also embody all-knowledge and all-power, and so He must also be a God of Truth, above any inclination or need to deceive or lie. It follows that any who truly know and represent Him would be similarly disposed. By that standard Muhammad, a man of deceit who created a cult of deceit and manipulation, could not have known such a deity, despite all his self-aggrandizing proclamations otherwise. If he was inspired by supernatural visits and direction, which considering what he accomplished may be entirely possible, then that 'angel' who directed him could be best described as the 'father of lies', 'the author of slavery', 'the king of contentions', 'the purveyor of greed', 'the source of false pride'. In other words, Muhammad's extraordinary exploits and achievements were helped by that old false angel of light, the devil himself. If God lives, so does His counterpart, and that very Lucifer must be laughing that so many have accepted his philosophy based on fear, forced compliance, and worship of him and all his evil methods so hurtful to victims, and in spirit to the victimizers. Would that I could be a bug on the wall as all Islamic terrorists arrive at that way-station between life and their spiritual holding place, to watch as shock and disappointment covers their countenances and to witness their anguish and panic grow as they realize they spent their last wage of agency on Earth serving the enemy of love and free-agency, …the enemy of God.

Despite the fear and difficulties faced by those seeking to separate themselves from the 'faith', the difficult question must be posed to any and all true peace loving Muslims, "Why follow Muhammad? Why follow Muhammad in every respect – including his commands to do violence against those who reject him as a prophet? If you truly disapprove of Muslim terrorist actions, why continue to tie yourself and your families' eternal future to the man?" If you truly believe that Muslim terrorists are and were wrong, then find a way to separate yourself from it. A person who chooses to follow Muhammad and trust his eternal future to Muhammad's word, by extension approves of Muhammad's brutal teachings …including all his brutal acts. The same will surely reap the same reward, but it will not be the 72 virgins, thrones, and mansions so often spoken of and hoped for. There are already millions of 'martyred' Muslims on the other side of the veil separating life from death, who lament that fact today from their spirit prison, …but the dead cannot change anything.

Because one is the embodiment of the other, the religion can and should be judged by the behavior of the people who practice it; you cannot in fact separate the two. Isa (Jesus) identified this simple fact when he said: "By their fruits ye shall know them", or in other words it is the acts of a religion or following that define the value of the theology, …not the beauty of words, the magnificence of buildings, robes, etc etc. By this standard, (the fruits of his totalitarian religion created to promote his vision of Arabic Imperialism), we know that Islam in fact has no connection with God whatsoever. Such bitter fruits as have been described herein, along with all the branches of humanity which made them, have no intrinsic value. The many who claim it as their religion notwithstanding, an incorrect opinion based on a false premise is still wrong, even if repeated by a billion people. As such, Islam cannot serve as any kind of guide to humankind, except as an example of the utter failure of all totalitarian systems of control.

The Muslim God is a god of deception, self-gratification, and war, whereas the Christian God is one of truth, self-sacrifice, and peace. Muhammad was a man of violence who bore arms, was wounded in battle, and preached holy war against non-believers. Christ, on the other hand, healed the wounded soldier's ear who came to arrest him. If you openly disagree with a Christian on religious doctrine, he'll probably pray for you. If you openly disagree with a Muslim on a matter of faith, he is likely to try and kill you. In Muhammad's day, converts were gained to Christian Faith by witnessing the constancy with which its confessors cared for others and suffered martyrdom; whereas they were gained to Islam by the spectacle of the readiness of its adherents to inflict death on others. Indeed, for devout Muslims, there seems to be no limitation to act in vile and inhumane ways towards non-believers, jihadists being allowed to enslave, rape, rob, pillage, and kill to advance Islam. In Christianity, by contrast, the direction is to 'do unto others as you would have them do unto you'. These two groups truly worship very different beings, and represent polar opposites in both belief and practice. Muslims claim to honor all prophets prior to Muhammad, including Jesus, yet conveniently dismiss all previous revelations regarding proper behavior in human relations. Muslims accept without thought that their great 'seal' of the prophets, 'abrogated' (canceled out) all previous revelation by all earlier prophets. Knowing almost nothing of earlier teachings, Arabs now and then swallow easily all the self-serving ideas the man Muhammad presented, whereas Christians and Jews, with some knowledge of those earlier revelations, were and are unable to accept a philosophy which effectively wipes out all previous understandings of the nature of God and directions on good behavior. Consider the radical change in religious philosophy born by Muhammad, whereas previously God loved all inhabitants of the Earth, then suddenly afterwards only Muslims. How terribly discontenting for the non-believers, for whom the newly reformed Muslim God unexpectedly had no more patience nor love. It completely escapes Muslim theologians how a perfect and fully developed and mature being (God) could suddenly decide that his previous feelings for His children, as revealed to his prophets, were in error and needed abrupt adjustment. Is the universe really that fragile, and can mans faith in God be based on that kind of uncertainty associated with a God whose feelings for his own children are in such flux? Obviously not, the concept fails all logical standards of reason. Muslim terrorists claim to kill people in the name of the one God, while vast numbers tolerate such actions, which surely is the greatest sacrilege and affront to God possible.

Can deeply indoctrinated, yet intelligent Muslims ever see the fraud Muhammad for what he is and what he has done to them, their ancestors, and to faith in the God of this universe and creator/father of us all? Certainly not if the full array of Islamic controls are in place preventing critical thought, personal development, and so personal virtue. For those hopelessly brainwashed, the only two remaining distasteful solutions left for the rest of the peace-loving world are; to either destroy them utterly, or; to completely defang, marginalize, segregate, encapsulate, and contain them.

When an entire culture embraces the vile butchery of innocents, its whole civilization is in trouble, as are all others within striking distance of a people out of control. We must all stop trying to compare Islam to other benign forms of religion, as there is really very little in common to compare outside of the term 'religion'. Comparing Islam's ethics, or its followers 'fruits' to other religions, Islam does not have recognizable spiritual standards that can be called lofty. Such a statement is easily understood by all peoples everywhere, except poor Muslims who have been brainwashed since birth to believe violent Jihad is the highest expression of personal spirituality. Indeed, any preview of its ethical precepts in relation to conduct toward non-Muslims are deplorable by any standard of human and civil behavior, ...except Muhammad's. As such, with neither spiritual nor ethical precepts of a genuinely religious nature, and because it aims to conquer the world, it's much more realistic to call it a political system. Politically correct or not..., sensitive or not..., the philosophy and methods of group control, otherwise known as Islam, is simply not a religion. We must stop trying to protect them from the truth, and hide from it ourselves. And why, exactly, should anyone really care about the 'feelings' of people following a cult seeking to kill us, our families, and dedicated to the destruction of everything we value. When they show a little empathy, sensitivity, and remorse for current and past atrocities, then perhaps we can approach our relationship with a little more delicacy. Until then, why tip toe about carefully worrying about their tender feelings? I mean, they aim to brutally kill us all anyway and take our young women as sex slaves, who cares if their feelings are a little hurt. Should not we all become much more concerned with our own tender feelings of survival, or the feelings of the tens to hundreds of millions of victims who in the past 1400 years suffered extreme horror, pain, humiliation, and death, at the hands of Muslims? Shouldn't their precious religion be mocked by all of humanity, instead of respecting, thereby reinforcing, their own silly grandiose feelings of accomplishment and superiority, which is at the root of their dangerous psychosis? This corset of political correctness is way too tight and must be loosed …before it kills us.

There will always be a large pool of feel-good, do-nothing appeasers who ignorantly continue to claim that Islam is a peaceful and tolerant religion. Because some effort is required to move from a state of ignorance and oblivion to a state of knowledge and awareness, sadly there will ever be many such nitwits amongst us. In addition, there are always some who can not draw a correct inference no matter how plainly the facts are laid out before them. You can walk that horse carefully and gingerly to water, but you can not make the animal drink, even to preserve its own life.